THE DECI

C000135530

MERIDIAN

Crossing Aesthetics

Werner Hamacher
& David E. Wellbery
Editors

Edited by Albert Dichy

Translated by Jeff Fort

*Stanford
University
Press*

*Stanford
California
2004*

THE DECLARED ENEMY

Texts and Interviews

Jean Genet

Stanford University Press
Stanford, California

This work, published as part of a program of aid for
publication, received support from the French Ministry of
Foreign Affairs and the Cultural Services of the French
Embassy in the United States.

Printed in the United States of America
on acid-free, archival-quality paper

Library of Congress Cataloging-in-Publication Data

Genet, Jean, 1910–1986
    [L'Ennemi déclaré. English]
    The declared enemy : texts and interviews / Jean Genet.
        p.   cm. — (Meridian, crossing aesthetics)
    Includes bibliographical references.
    ISBN 0-8047-2944-1 (alk. paper) —
    ISBN 0-8047-2946-8 (pbk. : alk. paper)
    1. Genet, Jean, 1910–1986—Interviews.   2. Authors,
French—20th century—Interviews.   I. Title. II. Series:
Meridian (Stanford, Calif.)
PQ2613.E53 Z46513 2004
840.9'0091—DC22

                                                  2003022583

Original Printing 2004

Last figure below indicates year of this printing:
13   12   11   10   09   08   07   06   05   04

Typeset by Tim Roberts in 10.9/13 Adobe Garamond

Contents

Preface

Jean Genet had outlined a plan for a collection of his articles and interviews when, in 1984, he entrusted the editing and publication of the work to Claude Gallimard. It would be left up Genet, however, to determine the order of presentation, which was also to be used for an English edition.

Once the majority of these writings or spoken interventions, published over a period of twenty years, were collected and retyped, his intention was to organize them and in a sense to recast them, without regard to their chronology, in order to highlight the reflections and convictions that had informed his positions. Rather than rallying to an ideology based on a political morality, he was more interested in evoking chance and curiosity.

Jean Genet never gave a definitive form to this project. But in reflecting on it, he was no doubt prompted to search for the original composition of a work that would incorporate the many notes taken during his travels and his long periods of solitude, notes inspired by his observations, his encounters, and his lucid perception of a world in motion; hence his last work, *Prisoner of Love*, which plays on memory and writing to recreate a universe reflecting his personal sensibility, just as *The Thief's Journal* had done, although in a very different way.

The second volume would most likely have included, in one form or another, the majority of texts collected here, which remain a valuable and relevant testimony; the originality of their procedures, together with the writer's tone, make them very clearly a part of Genet's larger corpus.[1] The order of this collection follows the exact chronology of the pieces; each of them are marked with the date of their composition or, when this is unknown, the date of their first public presentation (whether as an address, an intervention, or an interview); two texts whose original versions are lost, have been placed in an appendix.

M. Albert Dichy was able to edit the texts in most cases on the basis of manuscripts, typescripts reviewed by the author, or recordings, and has provided detailed introductions and notes.

This volume thus retraces the final phase of Jean Genet's trajectory, from 1964 to 1986; we have added the unpublished text that he had decided to place at the beginning of the book and whose last words, "the declared enemy," have provided the title.

THE DECLARED ENEMY

"J.G. Seeks . . ."

J.G. seeks, or goes in search of, or would like to find—or never to find—the delicious disarmed enemy whose balance is off, whose profile is vague, whose face is unacceptable, the enemy knocked down by the slightest puff of air, the already humiliated slave, throwing himself out of a window when the sign is given, the enemy who has been beaten: blind, deaf, mute. No arms, no legs, no belly, no heart, no sex, no head: in sum, a complete enemy, already bearing the marks of my bestiality, which—being too lazy—would no longer have to make any effort. I want the total enemy, one who would hate me beyond all bounds and in all his spontaneity, but the subjected enemy, beaten by me before ever laying eyes on me. And irreconcilable with me in any case. No friends. Especially no friends: an enemy declared but not divided. Clean edges, no cracks. What colors? A very tender green like a cherry with effervescent purple. His stature? Between the two of us, let him present himself to me man to man. No friends. I seek a faltering enemy, on the verge of giving up. I'll give him all I've got: blows, slaps, kicks, I'll have him gnawed by starving foxes, I'll make him eat English food, attend the House of Lords, be received at Buckingham Palace, fuck Prince Philip, get fucked by him, live for a month in London, dress like me, sleep where I sleep, live in my stead: I seek the declared enemy.[1]

§ 1   Interview with Madeleine Gobeil

Madeleine Gobeil.—Jean Genet, today you are a famous writer, translated and performed in many languages. Your play *The Blacks* has been running for three years in New York.[1] A film based on *The Balcony* has stirred up a good deal of controversy.[2] The American and English critical reception of *Our Lady of the Flowers* has been excellent.[3] The publication of your book was preceded by that of an important six-hundred-page essay by the great French philosopher Jean-Paul Sartre.[4] But what people associate most with your work, your trademark, if I can put it that way, are the words "thief, traitor, coward, and homosexual."[5] It almost sounds like a "jingle" in an advertisement. What do you think about that?

Genet.—Advertising is very adept at discovering deep motives and exploiting them. If I'd wanted to use this slogan as an advertising campaign, it probably would have worked.

At the time when my books appeared (almost twenty years ago now), it's undeniably true that I emphasized all the things you just mentioned and that I did it for reasons that were not always so pure, I mean not always of a poetic order. So publicity did play its part. Without being completely aware of it, I was engaged in self-promotion, but at the same time, I chose means that were not always easy and that put me in danger. Publicly calling myself a homosexual, a thief, a traitor, and a coward exposed me and put me in a situation where I could not sleep peacefully or create work that was easily assimilated by society. In short, by making all this noise, which was bound to get the attention of the media, I put myself from the very beginning in a position that made it difficult for society to know what to do with me.

M.G.—Why did you decide to be a thief, a traitor, and a homosexual?

G.—I didn't decide, I didn't make any decision. But there are certain facts. If I started stealing, it's because I was hungry. Later it became necessary for me to justify my act, to absorb it in a sense. As for homosexuality, I have no idea. What do we know about it anyway? Do we know why a man chooses this or that position for making love? Homosexuality was imposed on me like the color of my eyes, the number of my feet. When I was a little kid I became aware of the attraction I felt for other boys; I never experienced an attraction for women. It's only after becoming aware of this attraction that I "decided," that I freely "chose" my homosexuality, in the Sartrian sense. Put another way and more simply, I had to get used to it, while I knew that society disapproved.

M.G.—When did you leave prison for the last time?

G.—In 1945, I think.[6]

M.G.—How much of your life did you spend in prison?

G.—All together, if I include the time in reform school, it was about seven years.[7]

M.G.—Was it in prison that your work took shape? Nehru said that his time in prison was the best period of reflection in his life.

G.—Then let him go back!

M.G.—Do you still steal today?

G.—And you, mademoiselle?

M.G.— . . .

G.—You don't steal? You've never stolen?

M.G.— . . .

G.—Okay, I don't steal in the same way as I did before. I receive large royalties for my books—they seem large to me, at least. Well these royalties are actually the result of my first thefts. So I do continue to steal. What I mean is that I continue to be dishonest with regard to a society that itself pretends to believe I'm not.

M.G.—Until the age of thirty, you wandered across Europe, from prison to prison. You describe this period in your book *The Thief's Journal*. Do you consider yourself a good thief?

G.—A "good thief" . . . It's funny to hear the two words put together. A good thief, a thief who's good . . . You no doubt mean to ask me if I was a skillful thief. I wasn't awkward. But there is something in the operation that consists in concealing a share of hypocrisy (but I'm distracted, the microphone makes it hard for me to think; I can see the tape in the recorder and I start to take on a kind of politeness, not for your sake, since with you I can always manage to get out of trouble, but for the sake of the tape that is rolling in silence without my intervention). So . . . in the act of stealing there is an obligation to hide. If you hide, you conceal a part of your action and you don't own up to it. And to confess it to a judge is dangerous. You have to deny it before the judges, you have to deny it by hiding. When you do something by hiding it you always do it clumsily, I mean that you don't make use of all your qualities. There will necessarily be some that are directed toward the negation of the act you're carrying out. For me, the act of stealing came to be pervaded by a concern for making my thefts public, "publishing" them out of vanity, pride, or sincerity. In every thief there is some Hamlet who questions himself and his actions, but who must question himself in public. So the thefts he commits are awkward.

M.G.—Doesn't this awkwardness come from you? From your very cerebral way of formulating the question? The newspapers glorify great thieves, they tell of prestigious crimes. . . . For example, look at the more or less open admiration expressed in the press for the famous English train robbery that put Scotland Yard in a panic. The thieves got away with millions of dollars . . .

G.—Millions of dollars? But the police were in on it! There's no doubt in my mind! Either some officers, former captains or captains still in the service, or else people who work in the civil service. But a thief who accepts being a thief, who wants to be and to live as a thief, and who works alone, he must fail.

M.G.—Like the abject characters in your novels who commit miserable thefts against other homosexuals, for example, or from church collection boxes? The press and the cinema have hardly accustomed us to these kinds of gangsters.

G.—I don't have much direct familiarity with America, but after what I've seen in their films I think that in order to protect themselves, to keep themselves intact, Americans have invented a sort of gangster who is an almost total incarnation of Evil. Of course these gangsters are only imaginary. America has erected an imaginary gangster in such a way that no one can identify it, America, with evil. On the hand there is America the Good, the America of the Constitution, the America everyone is familiar with, in France, in the West, everywhere, and on the other hand there is Evil, an absolute gangster—who, by the way, is usually Italian. America invented a type of gangster that doesn't exist, except perhaps among its union bosses. From what I know of American civilization, it's very boring. One can judge a country by its outlaws. The ones they package for us in their films and books are so brutal that you would never have any desire to meet them. They're completely tiresome. And yet there must be some bandits who are very fine and sensitive . . .

M.G.—Sartre explains that you decided to live evil unto death. What did you mean by that?

G.—It means living Evil in such a way that you are not recuperated by the social forces that symbolize Good. I didn't mean living Evil unto my own death, but rather in such a way that I would be driven to find refuge, if I need to take refuge anywhere, only in Evil and nowhere else, never in Good.

M.G.—And yet your status as a famous writer gives you citizen's rights in the realm of the "good," in society. Are you welcomed by society? Do you go out to social events?

G.—Never. Society doesn't deceive itself in this regard. I'll say first of all that I don't like to go out. It's not from any virtue on my part. People don't invite me because they sense soon enough that I don't belong.

M.G.—Do you have a sense of solidarity with criminals, the downtrodden?

G.—None at all. No solidarity because, my God, if there were solidarity then there would be the beginnings of morality and therefore a return to Good. For example, if there were loyalty between two or three criminals, it would be the beginning of a moral convention, the beginning of Good.

M.G.—When you read the account of a crime such as [Lee Harvey] Oswald's, how do you feel about it?[8]

G.—Oh! If that's what you meant . . . Yes, I feel a solidarity. Not that I have a particular hatred for President Kennedy: he didn't interest me at all. But this lone man who decides to oppose a society so rigidly organized as American society, or even Western society, or even any society in the world that disapproves of Evil, oh yes! I'm rather on his side. I sympathize with him in the same way that I would sympathize with a very great artist who is alone against an entire society, neither more nor less than that. I am for every man who is alone. But no matter how much I am—how shall I put it?—morally in favor of every man who is alone, such men remain alone. No matter how much I am for Oswald, when he committed his crime he was alone. No matter how much I am for Rembrandt, when he painted his canvases he was completely alone.

M.G.—Are you still in contact with your old cellmates?

G.—Not at all. Look at the situation. I receive royalties from all over the world, you've come to interview me for *Playboy*, but they're still in prison. What kind of contact could we have? For them I'm a man who has betrayed them, nothing more.

M.G.—Did you betray them?

G.—I certainly betrayed something. But I had to do it for something that I felt was more precious. I had to betray theft, which is a singular act, for the sake of the more universal operation of poetry. I was obliged to do that. I had to betray the thief that I was in order to become the poet I hope to have become. But this "legitimacy" hasn't made me any happier for all that.

M.G.—You have betrayed criminals and are held in contempt by honest people. Do you like living with universal disapproval?

G.—It doesn't displease me, but it's a question of temperament. It's out of pride, which is not the best side of my character. I enjoy disapproval just as—keeping in mind the proper proportions, of course—Lucifer enjoyed the disapproval of God. But it's out of pride, which is a little stupid. I can't settle for that. It's a naive attitude, a romantic attitude.

M.G.—What, then, have criminals contributed to your life?

G.—Ask me rather what judges have contributed. To be a judge you have to take courses in law. You begin these studies around eighteen or nineteen years old, during the most generous period of adolescence. There are people in the world who are eighteen years old and who know that they're going to make a living judging other people and that when they judge them they will not put themselves in any danger. This is what criminals have taught me: they made me reflect on the morality of judges. But don't put any trust in this; in most any criminal there is a judge, unfortunately—but the contrary isn't true.

M.G.—Isn't your goal to liquidate all morality?

G.—I would indeed like to free myself from all conventional morals, those that have hardened and crystallized and that impede growth, that impede life. But an artist is never completely destructive. The very concern with creating a harmonious sentence supposes a morality, that is, a relation between the author and a possible reader. I write in order to be read. No one writes for nothing. In every aesthetics there is a morality. I have the impression that your idea of me has been formed from a body of work that was written twenty years ago. I am not out to create an image of myself as disgusting or fascinating or acceptable. I'm hard at work.

M.G.—We'll speak in a moment about your conception of morality as an artist, and especially as the author of *The Maids* and *The Blacks*. Let's continue for now with your opposition to conventional morality. In your personal life, do you use narcotics, for example?

G.—I have an almost visceral horror of drug addicts. The drug addict refuses consciousness. Drugs provoke a larval state: I'm a leaf among leaves, a caterpillar among caterpillars, and not a differentiated being.

M.G.—Have you tried to take any drugs?

G.—Yes, and it did nothing for me—except a dull feeling of capitulation.

M.G.—People say that you never drink. Why is that?

G.—Because I'm not an American writer. The other evening I was having dinner with Sartre and Simone de Beauvoir, and they were drinking double whiskeys. Beauvoir said to me: "Our way of losing ourselves a little every evening in alcohol doesn't interest you, because you're already completely lost." Little alcoholic spells don't do much for me. I have lived in a state of lost consciousness for a long time now.

M.G.—But you do eat at least?

G.—I like to eat when I come back from England. It's only through two things that I belong to the French nation: the language and the food.

M.G.—Your book *Our Lady of the Flowers*, which some call your masterpiece, is the poetic account of a long masturbation in a prison cell. It was at that time that you claimed that poetry is "the art of using shit and making people eat it."[9] You spare the reader no description. You use every word in the erotic vocabulary. You even evoke religious ceremonies that end in copulation. . . . Have you ever had any problems with censorship?

G.—Censorship of words considered "obscene" doesn't exist in France. If my most recent play, *The Screens*, isn't being performed in France (although it was in Germany and will be in America), it's because the French apparently find something in it that isn't there but that they think they see: the problem of the Algerian War.[10] It's still too painful for them. I would have needed police protection, and the police are certainly not going to protect Jean Genet. As for words considered "obscene," I can say this much: these words exist. If they exist, they must be used, otherwise they shouldn't have been invented. Without me, these words would have a sort of embryonic existence. The role of a great artist is to be able to valorize any word whatever. You reminded me of the definition I once gave of poetry. Today I would not define it that way. If you want to understand something, not a great deal, but a little something about the world, you have to get rid of your resentment. I still have some resentment toward society, but less and less now, and I hope that in time I won't have any at all. When it comes down to it, I really don't give a damn. But when I wrote that sentence I was full of resentment, and poetry consisted in transforming subjects taken to be vile into subjects accepted as noble, and this with the help of language. Today the problem is completely different. You don't interest me as an enemy. Ten or fifteen years ago, I was against you. Now I am neither for you nor against you, I am here at the same time as you are and my problem is not to oppose myself to you but to make something in which we are caught up together, you as well as me. Today I think that if readers are sexually moved by my books, it's because they were badly written, since poetic emotion should have such a force that no reader can be moved in a sexual way. To the extent that my books are pornography, I don't disavow them, but I say that I was lacking in style.

M.G.—Do you know the work of Nabokov and D. H. Lawrence?

G.—I've never read anything by those authors.

M.G.—Have you been interested in Henry Miller, whose books were considered "obscene" and banned for a long time in America?

G.—I don't know Miller very well. What I know of him doesn't interest me very much. It's a lot of chatter. He's a man who won't stop talking.

M.G.—In your opinion, why was Henry Miller banned for so long in America?

G.—I'm incapable of entering the into the mind of an American censor.

M.G.—If you don't mind, let's talk about this book that has been translated in America, *Our Lady of the Flowers.* You wrote it in prison?

G.—Yes, and it was even a pleasure to write it in prison. My dream would have been to give it to an editor, or to work together with one, who would bring it out with a completely bland cover in a very small printing, say three or four hundred copies. The book would have made its way into unsuspecting minds. Unfortunately, that wasn't possible. We ended up simply having to sell it to a publisher who sold it to homosexuals or to writers, which amounts to the same thing: they were people who knew what they were getting.[11] But I would have liked for my book to have fallen into the hands of Catholic bankers or into the homes of ordinary people, policemen or concierges, people like that . . .

M.G.—What did you use to write on in prison?

G.—They gave us paper we were supposed to use to make one or two hundred paper bags. I wrote the beginning of *Our Lady of the Flowers* on this paper. It was during the war, and I thought I would never get out of prison. I won't say I wrote the truth; I wrote sincerely, with fire and rage, a rage that I held back all the less in that I was certain the book would never be read. One day we went from the prison—La Santé—to the Paris law court. When I got back to my cell, the manuscript was gone. I was called in to see the director of the prison who gave me three days of solitary and dry bread for using paper "that wasn't meant for literary masterpieces." I felt belittled by this theft the director had committed. I ordered some blank notebooks from the supply room, crawled under my covers, and tried to remember word for word what I had written. I think I succeeded.[12]

M.G.—Was it long?

G.—About fifty pages.

M.G.—Does your project have anything in common with Caryl Chessman's?[13]

G.—Not at all. Chessman has always defended himself, he has always refused to acknowledge the acts that could marginalize him and separate him from society. Out of prudence, he denied the essential. He doesn't interest me. The fact that the Americans have been able to use Chessman's case both to give themselves a clear conscience and to put some distance between a thief and a presumed assassin doesn't surprise me at all, that's how they operate. He denied a gesture he should have vindicated. He gained the right to live because he was familiar with American law, and he found a way to live ten or twelve more years. Well, that's a success, but it's not a literary success.

M.G.—Did you start writing to escape from solitude?

G.—No, because I wrote things that made me even more solitary. No, I don't know why I started writing. What the deeper reasons are, I don't know. Perhaps this: the first time I became conscious of the power of writing was when I sent a postcard to a German friend who was in America at the time.[14] I didn't really know what to say to her. The side I was supposed to write on had a sort of white, grainy texture, a little like snow, and it was this surface that led me to speak of a snow that was of course absent from prison, to speak of Christmas, and instead of writing just anything, I wrote to her about the quality of that thick paper. That was it, the trigger that allowed me to write. This was no doubt not the real motive, but it's what gave me the first taste of freedom.[15]

M.G.—How did you first begin to be published?

G.—A lawyer named Guillaume Hanoteau, who is now a journalist at *Paris-Match*, gave one of my poems, "The Man Condemned to Death," to Jean Cocteau, who published it at his own expense.[16]

M.G.—That's how you made your way into French literature?

G.—I never tried to become a part of French literature.

M.G.—It's true that many people would prefer to treat you as a "case history." In your work you speak of saintliness "as the most beautiful word in the French language" and of the "eternal couple of the criminal and the saint."[17] "Saintliness"—your detractors deny you the right to make use of this word.

G.—My detractors are horrified to see me use any words at all, even a comma; Mauriac even wrote an article demanding that I stop writing.[18] The Christians, and my detractors in particular, think they own the word saintliness, and they won't authorize me to use it.

M.G.—What does it mean to you?

G.—And you, what does it mean to you?

M.G.—The search for perfection in the spiritual realm.

G.—My detractors would never rise up against a Saint Camus. Why do they protest against Saint Genet? Listen . . . as a child it was difficult for me—unless I made a certain effort in my daydreams—to imagine that I was or could become the president, or a general, or anybody like that. I was a bastard child, I had no right to the social order. What was left to me if I wanted an exceptional destiny? If I wanted to make the most of my freedom, my possibilities or, as you say, my gifts, since I wasn't yet aware of having any gift as a writer, assuming I do? What was left for me was nothing other than wanting to be a saint, that is, a negation of man.

M.G.—What relation do you see between the saint and the criminal?

G.—Solitude. And you, don't you think that the greatest saints are a lot like criminals, if you look at them closely? Saintliness is frightening. There is no visible agreement between society and the saint.

M.G.—In listening to you, just as in reading you, one is a little surprised. It's quite strange that a man such as you (a bastard child who came out of the public welfare) did not become an intuitive writer. But you make elaborate arguments, you construct. It would be difficult to associate you with American writers such as Faulkner or Hemingway.

G.—I wonder—and I don't see myself as a nationalist—I wonder whether I'm not like that because of French culture, which enveloped me at a very young age. When I was fifteen years old there was a culture spread across all of France, perhaps all of Europe. We French knew that we were masters of the world, not only of the material world but of culture as well.

M.G.—Even a bastard child was taken in hand by an entire culture?

G.—It was difficult to escape it, and my books are perhaps the fruit of a culture that has developed over a very long period and of which I was perhaps more a victim than a beneficiary.

M.G.—More a victim?

G.—Certain more naive qualities of emotion and intuition find no way to manifest themselves because they were continually countered by a cultural mode of expression that pruned them and castrated them, so to speak. Perhaps with my temperament, if I had been born in the United States, I would have been a very fine, very sensitive poet, whereas I am above all a polemicist. I would add that a culture is never a complete whole. European writers, like American writers, more or less clearly choose a mode of expression that responds to a demand. Europe demands an appearance of culture, America sees itself as all roughness and instinct. In both cases, we lie. We lie in relation to a truth that we dimly sense but that we cannot otherwise express. America in general has given itself a form that is brutal and intuitive, Europe has wanted to present itself as culture and reason.

M.G.—Why do you think that the philosopher Jean-Paul Sartre wrote a six-hundred-page essay about you?

G.—Sartre assumes that man is free and that each person has at his disposal the means to take charge of his own becoming. I am the illustration of one of his theories of freedom. He has found a man who, instead of submitting, has vindicated what has been given to him, vindicated it and was resolute in pushing it to its extreme consequences.

M.G.—What do you think of Sartre as a writer and as a friend?

G.—Sartre repeats himself. He's had a few important ideas and has exploited them in various forms. When I read him I am often a step ahead of him. What surprised me is *The Words*, his most recent narrative work. In it he shows such a will to extricate himself from the bourgeoisie. In a world where everyone wants to be the respectable whore, it's very pleasant to meet someone who knows he's a little bit of a whore but does-n't want to be respectable at all. I like Sartre because he is funny, amusing, and because he understands everything. And it's very enjoyable to spend time with a guy who understands everything and laughs rather than judges. He doesn't accept everything about me, but when he disagrees, he has fun with it. He's an extremely sensitive person. Ten or fifteen years ago I saw him blush a few times. And a blushing Sartre is adorable.

M.G.—What kind of impression did it make on you to read the book he wrote about you?

G.—A kind of disgust—because I saw myself naked and stripped bare by someone other than myself. In all my books I lay myself bare and at the same time I disguise and travesty myself with words, choices, atti-tudes, with enchantment. I make sure not to come out looking too dam-aged. But Sartre stripped me bear without mercy. He speaks of me in the present tense. My first reaction was to want to burn the book. Sartre had let me read the manuscript. I finally allowed him to publish it because my concern has always been to take responsibility for what I give rise to. But it took me a while to recover. I was almost unable to continue writing. I could have continued to develop novels mechanically. I could have tried to write pornographic novels in a kind of automatism. Sartre's book cre-ated a void that allowed a sort of psychological deterioration to set in. This deterioration allowed for the meditation that led to my plays.

M.G.—How long did you stay lost in this void?

G.—For six years I lived in this miserable state, in this imbecility that lies at the shallow bottom of life: opening a door, lighting a ciga-rette. . . . There are only a few shimmering moments in a man's life; all the rest is a dull gray.

M.G.—But your play *The Maids* dates from 1947, and Sartre's book wasn't published until 1952 . . .

G.—That's true. Sartre's book made it possible to exploit something familiar; it didn't create it.

M.G.—Your plays have been very successful, especially in the United States, where *The Blacks* has been running for almost four years. How has this success affected you?

G.—I can't get over it. I'm completely astonished. Perhaps the United States is not as I imagined it. Anything can happen in the United States, even a semblance of humanity can appear there.

M.G.—You've written four plays, three of which are known to the public, *The Maids*, *The Blacks*, and *The Balcony*. These plays are perplexing. One wonders whether, in *The Maids*, for example, you are for the domestics and against the employers, and in *The Blacks*, if you are in cahoots with the blacks against the whites, or the other way around. There is a sense of uneasiness about the questions.

G.—I don't give a damn about that. I wanted to write plays for the theater, to crystallize a theatrical and dramatic emotion. If my plays are useful to blacks, it's not my concern. I don't think they are, in any case. I think that action, the direct struggle against colonialism, does more for blacks than a play does. Likewise, I think that a maids' union does more for domestics than a play. I tried to give voice to something profound that neither blacks nor any other alienated people could make heard. A critic said that maids "don't speak that way." They do speak that way, to me, when I'm alone at midnight.[19] If someone told me that blacks don't speak that way, I would say that if you put your ear to their hearts, you'd hear something more or less like that. You have to know how to hear what is unformulated.

M.G.—But your plays deal with people who are not privileged.

G.—It could be that I wrote these plays against myself. It could be that I'm the whites, the boss, or France in *The Screens*, and that I'm trying to understand what's so imbecilic in these qualities. You asked me if I steal. I don't think it has any importance. I've never stolen from a person, I stole from a social position, and I don't give a damn about position.

M.G.—Sartre says that reading you is like spending a night in a brothel. You've had a lot of clients; you're famous. What do you do with all the money you earn?

G.—None of your business.

M.G.—Do you often give interviews.

G.—Never. It was only because of Simone de Beauvoir's insistence that I agreed to give an interview for a magazine I didn't even know existed. This is the first time in my life that I've given any kind of interview that's gone beyond meeting someone in a bistro. I never did anything to stir up attention for my plays in America, for example. You see, I made a bet that my work would be able to fend for itself without the help of any publicity. It will succeed if it's strong; if it's weak, then too bad for me.

M.G.—But you have succeeded; you've become a personality . . .

G.—If I've become a personality, I'm a pretty odd one. . . . "Personalities"—the word makes me smile—can go wherever they want.

I have a visa to go to America; I have a visa for four years, but I think the consulate gave it to me by mistake. They wouldn't let me use it when they found out who I was . . .

M.G.—Is it because of your criminal record or because of your homosexuality? Can we talk about that?

G.—I'm perfectly willing to talk about homosexuality. It's a subject that pleases me immensely. I know that homosexuality is well regarded these days in pseudo-artistic circles. It is still disapproved of in more bourgeois circles. For my part, I owe a lot to it. If you want to see it as a curse, that's your business; personally I see it as a blessing.

M.G.—How have you benefited from it?

G.—It's what put me on the path of writing and of understanding people. I'm not saying that it was only that, but perhaps if I hadn't made love with Algerians I wouldn't have been on the side of the FLN.[20] Well no, not really; I would have been on their side in any case. But it was homosexuality that made me understand that Algerians were men like any others.

M.G.—Have you ever been interested in women?

G.—Sure I have; there are four women who have interested me: the Holy Virgin, Joan of Arc, Marie Antoinette, and Madame Curie.

M.G.—What kind of meaning does homosexuality have in your life now?

G.—I'd like to tell you about its pedagogical aspect. I have of course made love with all the young men I have taken care of. But I wasn't concerned only with making love. I have tried to re-create with them the adventure that I had, an adventure whose symbol is illegitimacy, betrayal, the refusal of society, and finally, writing, that is, the return to society by other means. Is this attitude peculiar to me? Homosexuality, because it places the homosexual outside the law, obliges him to question social values, so that if he decides to take care of a young man, he won't take care of him in a dull and simplistic way. He will show him the contradictions, both of reason and of the heart, that are imposed by a normal society. Now I'm taking care of a young race-car driver, Jacky Maglia.[21] I can say this about him: he began by stealing cars, then he descended into stealing anything at all. I understood right away that he ought to center his life around racing. I bought him some cars. He's twenty-one years old now. He's a driver, he doesn't steal anymore. He was a deserter, but he isn't one anymore. It's because of theft and desertion, and because of me, that he is a race-car driver and has been recuperated by society. He was reintegrated by becoming accomplished, by realizing what is essential to him.

M.G.—Do you go with Maglia when he races?

G.—I've gone with him everywhere he has raced, in England, Italy, Belgium, and Germany. I clock his time.

M.G.—Are you interested in automobile racing?

G.—It's something that struck me as quite stupid at first, but now it seems very serious and beautiful to me. There is something dramatic and aesthetic in a well-run race. The driver is alone, like Oswald. He risks death. It's beautiful when he comes in first. You have to have great finesse and delicacy, and Maglia is a very good driver. The brutes end up getting killed. Maglia is becoming very well known. He'll be famous.

M.G.—Does he mean a lot to you? Do you love him?

G.—Do I love him? I love the endeavor. I love what he is doing and what I do for him.

M.G.—Do you do a lot for him?

G.—If you take care of someone, you have to do it seriously. Last weekend, coming back from Chartres to Paris, I didn't smoke so that he could drive with great concentration and at a speed of about 170 kilometers per hour.

M.G.—Isn't there something feminine in this way of surrendering to the other?

G.—The femininity that one finds in homosexuality envelops a young man, and perhaps allows for the blossoming of more goodness. At the time of the Council I was watching a television program about the Vatican. They were presenting a few cardinals. Two or three were completely asexual and insignificant. The others who were like women looked dull and greedy. Only one, Cardinal Liénart, had a homosexual air about him, and he seemed good and intelligent.[22]

M.G.—Some reproach modern man with having lost his virility. Doesn't homosexuality encourage this tendency?

G.—Even if there were some crisis of virility, I wouldn't be too upset about it. Virility is always a game, a performance. American actors play at being virile. I'm also thinking of Camus, who would put on virile attitudes. For me, virility would be a faculty for protecting rather than deflowering a young girl or woman. But I'm obviously not in a good position to judge. By denying the usual comedy, the shell is broken open and a man can show a delicacy that otherwise would never come out in the open. It's possible that the emancipation of modern women obliges men to refuse the old attitudes in order to discover an attitude that is more suited to a less submissive woman. You've seen Jacky, he doesn't seem effeminate at all, and yet because of his sensitivity he's the kind of person who interests me most. When I gave him his first race car, I asked him how he felt: "A little ashamed," he said, "because it's more beautiful than I am."

M.G.—How long have you known Maglia?

G.—Since he was very young. In every case, with young people, I have had to invent, to take account of their temperaments, their characters and tastes, each time to do something that resembles a creative act . . . somewhat like what I would ask from judges each time they hand down a judgment: that the judge create, and that he be able to sit in judgment no more than four or five times in his life, since each time it should be a creative act.

M.G.—But when Maglia races in France, it's the very society you so dislike that applauds him . . .

G.—I know. It's a national pride that gets exalted. What safeguards Maglia is the fact that he risks his life. An image of himself can be saved because he knows that every time he races he risks his life. If Maglia got caught up in the game of complacency, he would be endangering his life, his skill. An attitude that's too conceited would put him in danger, just as it would be dangerous for me to take the conceited attitude of the gangster and the writer.

M.G.—When you're not at the races with Maglia, what do you do?

G.—The rest of the time I live in a semistupor like anybody else. From time to time I work on my plays; not every day, but in waves, in cycles. I may do an opera with the great musician Pierre Boulez, who presented a wonderful opera this winter, at the Paris Opera, Alban Berg's *Wozzeck*.[23]

M.G.—Is writing a necessity for you?

G.—Yes, because I feel responsible for the time that has been granted me. I want to make something of it, and that something is writing. Not that I'm responsible in the eyes of men, or in my own eyes, but perhaps in the eyes of God—of whom of course I cannot speak, since I don't know much about him.

M.G.—You believe in God?

G.—I believe that I believe in him. I have no great faith in the mythologies of the catechism. But why is it that I should account for the time allotted for my life by affirming what seems most precious to me? Nothing obliges me to do that. Nothing visible obliges me to do that. Why then do I feel so strongly that I must do it? Before, the question was resolved in an immediate way by the act of writing. The rebellion of my childhood, my rebellion when I was fourteen, was not a rebellion against faith, it was a rebellion against my social situation, against my humiliated condition. That didn't touch my deeper faith—but faith in what?

M.G.—And eternal life, do you believe in that?

G.—That's the question of a Protestant theologian on his deathbed. Are you some kind of conciliar priest at Vatican II? It's a meaningless question.

M.G.—Well, what sense is there in this writer's life of wandering not from prison to prison but, now, from hotel room to hotel room? You're rich, and yet you own nothing. I've counted: you have seven books, an alarm clock, a leather jacket, three shirts, a suit, and a suitcase. Is that it?

G.—Yes. Why should there be anything more?

M.G.—Why this satisfaction in poverty?

G. (laughing).—It's the poverty of the angels. Listen, I don't give a damn. . . . When I go to London, sometimes my agent books me a room in the Ritz. What am I supposed to do with things and luxury? I write, and that's it.

M.G.—Where are you taking your life?

G.—To oblivion. Most of our activities have the vagueness and stupefaction of a bum's life. It's very rare for us to make a conscious effort to go beyond this stupefied state. For myself, I do it by writing.

§ 2   Lenin's Mistresses

When a traveler comes from abroad,[1] from Morocco for example, he may read an article in *L'Humanité* on Cohn-Bendit,[2] calling him an *enragé* and a German anarchist;[3] he leafs through *Minute*: Cohn-Bendit is a dirty Jew;[4] he buys *L'Aurore* and *Le Figaro*: Cohn-Bendit is a provocateur; he speaks with a man in the street about Cohn-Bendit and is informed that the meeting with Sartre in *Le Nouvel Observateur* was completely fake,[5] since neither the philosopher nor the agitator had agreed to meet; a student at Censier tells you that he thinks some things are good about him and some things are bad;[6] this student becomes indignant when you tell him you've learned about what I just mentioned from *L'Humanité* and *Minute*, but, nevertheless, in the end he speaks the way the two newspapers write; a worker from Billancourt is beside himself and thinks that the police should "grab the German by the scruff of the neck and run him across the border"; on television, M. Séguy,[7] in response to a journalist who asks him his opinion of Cohn-Bendit, says with contempt (contempt is easily performed as a facial expression): "Cohn-Bendit—who's that?" Some students are asked if they could endorse not everything, but almost everything that Cohn-Bendit has said and written; many say "yes," but they also say they heard he's getting off on a government minister's daughter who they heard is getting off on him and that he was paid by the big newspapers for his photos and interviews.[8] Finally, if I've understood correctly, the CGT [Confédération générale du travail] claims that he has divided the Left, and some rumors are circulating that he is being remote-controlled by the American CIA.

Around 1920 or 1922, the journalist Stéphane Lauzanne, in a very reactionary newspaper called *Le Matin*, wrote several articles claiming that Lenin was living with Krupskaya, that he had numerous capitalist mistresses in all the capitals of Europe, that he led the life of a satrap, but that, when he was a servant in Paris, his housekeeping was very poor.[9]

From this mess of petty rumors we can at least see that this official's daughter might have good taste; that we should rather be asking whether it isn't Séguy who is dividing the Left; whether Cohn-Bendit isn't the first stage in the emergence of a third force more radical than the two opposing forces: Gaullism and the Communist Party. And finally, if the people in the CIA (they are everywhere) have gotten their claws in here, on the one hand they aren't that stupid since they're putting guys like Cohn-Bendit into action, while on the other hand they're completely idiotic since the ideas expressed by Cohn-Bendit have already gone beyond the man who expressed them and are living their own life, making their way among young workers and students. (Someone just phoned me with the latest statement from Séguy, and I quote: "We are aware that the individual in question belongs to an international organization." Perhaps Séguy isn't aware that the International Confederation of Workers, the Warsaw Pact, and the Common Market are also international organizations.)

I saw Cohn-Bendit on television.[10] I saw him in the large amphitheater at the Sorbonne, and it seemed to me that not only was his analysis correct, but his proposals—his concrete proposals, if we want to insist on this word—were also fitting, and among them were these, which I think are very powerful: "All the restaurants, cafeterias, housing, and so on, at the universities will be open to young workers"; "each week, three days will be given to young workers and apprentices so that they can benefit from the instruction given to students, and this not simply in the evening and in a paternalistic way, but during the work week."

After all, it's not impossible that Czechoslovakia has a truly revolutionary youth movement thanks to the schools and popular universities set up by Masaryk.[11]

I don't want to analyze what makes Cohn-Bendit so attractive to young people or to people who aren't so young, nor whether it is based on seduction or on intelligence—personally, I think that the two are intimately connected, and I don't think there's any need to be upset about that.

It's a natural kind of prudence that makes people protect themselves, as well as they can, against the powerful influence exerted by this kid, who is a brilliant pain in the ass for the bourgeoisie. And yet, must they try to protect themselves in such a lowly and base manner, especially when they know that he is transmitting or retransmitting revolutionary slogans and that he himself is acting on them and applying them? The government has forbidden Cohn-Bendit to enter France: this order, it is said, is legal; it therefore shows that legality is often villainous.[12] During the march of May 13, even if it was so well attended largely thanks to the call of the Communist Party and the CGT, it is no less the case that these two institutions heard, if not heeded, Cohn-Bendit's call, and that for a few hours and a few kilometers they followed him and therefore vouched for him.[13]

Cohn-Bendit is the originator, whether poetically or through calculation, of a movement that is going to destroy, or at least shake up, the bourgeois apparatus, and thanks to him, the traveler who makes his way through Paris knows the sweetness and elegance of a city in revolt. The cars, which are its fat, have disappeared, and Paris is finally becoming a lean city, it's losing a few pounds; and for the first time in his life, the traveler has a sense of exhilaration in returning to France, and he feels the joy of seeing the familiar grim faces now turned joyous and beautiful. If nothing more than this comes of the days of May, well . . .

If Cohn-Bendit was at the cutting edge of the struggles the way that others have been at the cutting edge of scientific research, who is he from that point on? No longer anyone and yet everyone, this Ariel drifts away but then becomes the idea of freedom, and it's this idea of freedom that the Pompidou government is trying to assassinate. However old and dusty they may be, Lenin's mistresses are not dead; and yet if they are dead after all, the Pompidou government will do its best to bring them back to life.

§ 3   *The Shepherds of Disorder*

If we are able to recognize in this film the admirable images of a beauty that is at times offensive, such as that of the shepherd who becomes a thief, thus initiating the upward climb and ascent of the couple—this would already be a great deal, since more and more we watch this film the way one reads a book: by weighing each sentence and separating it from the text. In the same way, we isolate each image of a film—an image that no doubt goes to make up the story, but that we take on its own, knowing that that is how the director wanted it. In Papatakis's film, some of the most beautiful images, or shots, contain all the elements that move the modern audience: a well-balanced disorder, the violence of certain gestures (or their excessive extravagance), a ridiculous sort of eroticism (always a little comic), and a truth that comes from disorder. It is a truth that makes one "rediscover" in oneself this image that was already there, and that makes one discover the Greece one has known. The image is not only visual, it is sonorous, and sound and noise add to its beauty: the loose rocks don't fall just any way, they don't make just any noise; it is the noise of the Mediterranean disaster.

They are singular images in both senses of the word: singular in that they are alone, isolated in the story, and singular in that each one lives its own beauty. But each image, moved on by the one before, pushes against yet another, and gradually these images form into a story that reveals not a secret life, but one that is tellable according to those taking part in it: a life of Greek peasants, procurers, Orthodox priests, shepherds, goats, and trees. The plot hardly exists, so astonishing are the details of everyday life.

The first part of the film, which shows the life of the peasants, only appears to be treated like an anthropological report; the story is too violent for that. It is too violent for the spectator to have any time to analyze the relations constantly maintained by sexual prohibitions, the sequestration of women, the cult of female virginity, the attachment at once friendly and cruel to the animals one keeps, to the land that is all the more loved the more sterile it is—the relations, I mean, between man and the world. This first part of the film does not give an account of a way of life; it brings back a drama that continues to unfold hour by hour, gesture by gesture, one vociferation after another: everyone accepts a sort of madness, sometimes grandiose, sometimes miserable.

Papatakis shows, as I have said, the details of a life at once monstrous and exalted, but only to the extent that these details are freely acknowledged and even shown with a certain pride, although one glimpses beneath them a sly and underhanded life, made up of inanity and stupidity.

I will speak ill of Greek history, as it is taught, but it seems to me that it begins in a dazzling brilliance: its mythology bursts forth, exalts its Venuses and its Ganymedes, even when they come down among humans, showing themselves above all in their skyward assumptions, and it is when the gods can no longer continue parading around in a kind of mental asylum, in which every madness is permitted when they can no longer inspire enchantment, that men come together without them and try to live the misfortune of being on earth, abandoned by Zeus and the rest.

What happens in *The Shepherds of Disorder*? The very opposite of this. Papatakis first grasps men in their boastful misery, and then, through the strength of a single man, the shepherd who breaks out of his abjection not by lashing out but by the force of a stubborn determination to live, a couple will be caught up for a few hours in the mythological adventure of a great love. Everything begins when Olga takes the hand of the shepherd who is assaulted with blows and insults, and leads him to his apotheosis in the death of the couple aspiring to freedom.

Beyond autobiography, if the director wanted to show the pestilential life of the Greek people, like that of every people who refuses reason and seeks refuge in reassuring practices, preferring incantation to the open gaze, he also sought through the astonishing inversion I mentioned above to show that the refusal of an admissible life can lead, in life, to freedom, and in the work of art, to poetry—and in this case also to a splendid entertainment; the ascent through the stones, the assault of the police, the game played in the bushes, the voices that deceive us, the couple's final leap into death, according to mythological conventions in which a rebirth is always possible and where emotion is accompanied by a secret smile. These few reflections fall far short of this magnificent film.

That's not all. From newspapers, radio, and television, we know that a very real coup has taken place in this very real country: the army has taken power.[1] It's quite certain that this army, issuing perhaps from the people, even while trying to throw a Noah's blanket over the poverty of this people, has attempted to prevent too many acts of freedom in Greece. The army and the police, born from a stupefied people, instead of being an arm of liberation are crushing the people and thereby participating in the prohibitions, mostly sexual, which they will defend and oppose to the free and poetic acts depicted at the end of the film.

This film had to be conceived with great intellectual rigor so that the final evocation of a real coup, by colonels and a petty king, could provide it with a crown that is both solemn and dubious (which means, I hope, temporary), but one that is also natural.

The spectators will therefore be surprised to see a film whose first part reflects an unexpected image, somewhat as if a monster stuck in the mud before a mirror were to give back the reflection of a beautiful girl floating up into space. One can thus wrench oneself away from the moth-eaten myths, the lingering residues of very old manias; perhaps they were born under Theodora, but they have become what the memory of that self-aggrandizing whore has become in us.[2] Which is to say that the Greece shown here will disappoint the landscape painters in love with the Attic light, but they will see another wonder: a goitrous midget covered with signs of the cross who is transformed before their eyes into a beautiful white horse flying off into the blue.

Olga Karlatos[3]

A Greek tale. She is twenty-two years old, has a husband and one child: this is what she wanted. In a single film, she has been consecrated as a great actress: this is what she dreamed of. All this with the assent of her parents: she had never dared to hope for it. Olga Karlatos is a young Athenian woman with brown hair and blue eyes, large eyes at once devouring and amazed, which prevent one from noticing her delicate form and her serene and feline gait. She is Greek through and through, speaks English and French without an accent, sings and dances, is discovering politics thanks to her husband. Intense and secret, she suddenly becomes excited and wildly curious. No trace of a cover girl or a starlet about her. She is "possessed," like Maria Casarès at the beginning of her career. Like Bette Davis. As soon as one speaks to her of her private life, she becomes evasive. If one speaks to her of her career, she is impassioned. She is happy to be beautiful, "because it might be useful for my fate as a tragedienne." In short, with *The Shepherds of Disorder*, Nikos Papatakis has not only made a remarkable return to the cinema, he is introducing a true artist into the world of film and drama. As in the classic fairy tales of the cinema, he discovered her by chance. In Athens, he had begun to lose hope of discovering the ideal actress for his role. Then he met Olga. She offered him her talent, her heart, and her hand: he accepted them all.

§ 4 Yet Another Effort, Frenchman!

As if the organization of French employers were aiming with precision, and yet as if, being harassed itself, it were also blindly defending itself and shooting into the crowd.[1] The impression we're left with, after the death of so many immigrant workers, is that this winter the French employers killed them coldly. For several months now, wherever you look there is at least one death every day, either in Paris or in the pleasant French countryside, and it is usually an African who dies. And no doubt French employers have no need to worry, French-speaking Africa is a practically inexhaustible reservoir of manual labor for Citroën, Simca, the mines, and the factories. The African governments sell muscle power to the French government, while in Africa there remains a large number of unemployed. And on January 6, four workers from Mali and one from Mauritania died in the cold in Aubervilliers: a perfect occasion for the ambassadors of both countries to pop open a bottle of champagne and to speak, quite lightly, of Fatality.[2]

Nothing more is needed for the death of a black worker—black or white, for that matter—to be passed over in silence. More and more, those who kill them, after using them up, will say that we are really people with bad taste. They will say this, but we, we will continue to speak of the dead.

To Roland Castro and His Comrades[3]

Since a judge, solemn but buffoonish, tough but muddled, stodgy but vain, determined but wavering, imperious but vulnerable—you see, Roland, I have to clarify things again—pretended to believe that a description (which, by the way, was highly stylized and seemed to be based on the techniques of the *nouveau roman*) of your gambols on the lawn could either send you to prison for eternity or give you your freedom: we found ourselves suddenly facing something that was no longer visible, something that was receding far out of sight, and I had to stand fast in the witness stand, I had to bend over almost to the point of falling, squint my eyes, stretch my mind in order to be quite sure of seeing the whole courtroom in its immobility—a courtroom in which only the table and the lamps stood out—and these three figures who were leaving not because they wanted to bolt at full speed, but who were vertiginously carried into oblivion on their own lines of flight. We, however, we stayed on the side, though I wonder on the side of what, unless it's simply "on the other side."

These . . . men and women? By what gender will we designate these three dull figures dressed in black folds? He, she . . . they were even further away. I am familiar with the Paris law courts: the building is hollow, the formulas are outworn, the caryatids are all screwed up, and I thought of Sade's phrase: "Yet another effort, Frenchman!"[4]

You didn't expect from me the usual words able to restore you intact to a society that was already reaching toward you. I said nothing because it is impossible to say anything true about an agitator in a courtroom—and I can hardly imagine you otherwise, your comrades and you, than as very calm agitators who look on with a touch of irony as the gold loses its luster, as hair turns white, as contours are worn flat, as this world goes up in smoke, disappearing into an immemorial distance.

"He has an ideal," said the central figure.
"He's honest," said the same one.
"He has never been convicted."
"He's going to be a father."
"He's such a good son."

But I heard the gay and thunderous voice of your comrades: "And we couldn't give a damn!"

But if the emblems are scratched away, if the figureheads are knocked off, when their words have no meaning for an incredulous youth, what will be there to defend the carcass that thinks of nothing but cash? Its cops will be there.

They were there yesterday, more scrunched down than seated, more heaped together than in their places, there in the audience, beside themselves because they didn't have a grenade handy, in shock because they had just heard, carried by a wind from the east, gently wavering, very gently, almost tenderly, and then in a shout, the Internationale. How sensitive they are, our French police!

We will have to fight again, and I couldn't say to the court that you're necessary because you're a fighter or that in the end victory will belong to you, to your comrades and to you. It will take more than a few gunshots to come to the end of it, but the fact that you have forcefully thought out the disappearance of these ancient paralytics is already something.

"Five African workers died in Aubervilliers." Yesterday we saw this Justice receding, receding, and receding still more—it is perhaps even farther away today—because you and your comrades are all the more present. And you all know that Africa is not only a continent, it is a people who are fighting like you, next to you, a people as strong as you. On the left-hand side of the courtroom there was another figure: the deputy. After the witnesses—all of whom were able to present only a shred of testimony, since the satisfied judge kept threatening us—the deputy was allowed to speak at length without anyone interrupting him. And what did he say? That the French government (which he represents) is taking care of them, the immigrant workers, and that speaking of their deaths and their shantytowns is just digging up dirt. Listen to that: digging up dirt for the shantytowns and for the dead at Thiais![5] That one is running a few risks, too, with his metaphors and their involuntary confessions.

"In a single winter night, January 6, five African workers died, killed by their French employers."

You know that you are the strongest, and already, right next to you, a living Africa, an intent and agile Africa is moving forward.

§ 5 "It Seems Indecent for Me to Speak of Myself . . . "

It seems indecent for me to speak of myself when such a serious trial is being prepared against Bobby Seale and the Black Panther Party.[1] But since I am here for them, I owe you a brief explanation of what I'm doing.

For an inattentive reader, it might seem that what I have written is a kind of confession, not a complacent one with regard to myself, I hope, but indeed a solitary one. The five books I wrote were written in prison, and you can understand that, given my solitude at the time, this situation made it necessary for me to turn toward myself and to the realm of the prison cell.

After that came five or six years of silence, then suddenly I wrote five plays, and the last one, *The Screens*, was nothing but a long meditation on the Algerian War.[2]

That was twelve years ago. In May '68, I realized that I was completely and effortlessly on the side of the protesting students and workers. In May, the France that I so hated no longer existed; rather, for one month, there was a world suddenly liberated from nationalism, a smiling world, an extremely elegant world, you could say.

And May was wrecked by the dramatic return of Gaullism and reaction.

So I can tell you that in June 1968, my sadness and anger made me understand that from now on I would not rest until the spirit of that May in Paris returned, in France or elsewhere.

But if I'm telling you about my own very subjective disposition, it's because I want you to understand just how close I find myself now to the Black Panthers.

In terms of the United States, and perhaps on an even larger scale, it is this party, this revolutionary movement that is most capable, when it succeeds, of provoking an explosion of joy and liberation, an explosion already prefigured in some ways by the events of May in France.

Therefore, wherever I am, I will always feel connected to any movement that will provoke the liberation of men. Here and now, it is the Black Panther Party, and I am here by their side because I am on their side.

Since I have known them, I have not ceased discovering in them this freedom and this exchange of fraternal tenderness.

Now that I've said this to you, do you understand why I am anxious when a man like Bobby Seale is about to be extradited, when, along with fourteen of his comrades, he is in danger of an extremely harsh sentence? When he may be facing death?[3]

It is not the entire United States, but the business and finance concerns in power who will do anything to destroy the Black Panther Party, to prevent the liberation of men who live entirely under the domination of the dollar and the dollar's machinery.

It would be dismaying, after experiencing the powerful emotions of May, if I refused to offer my help in the struggle being waged by the Black Panthers and in the struggle that Bobby Seale and his comrades are still waging in prison.

It is therefore very clear that in struggling with them I will bring the same tenacity and rigor that I drew on when I wrote alone in prison.

I am with the Black Panthers. The way Richard Wright was with me when, for the last time, I left prison.[4]

§ 6   Letter to American Intellectuals

For the white man, History, past and to come, is very long, and its system of references is very imposing. For a black man, Time is short. He cannot trace his history beyond the period of slavery. And in the United States, we're still busy setting limits on black people's Time and Space. Not only is each one of them forced to withdraw more and more into himself, but we put them in prison as well. And when we have to, we assassinate them.

Because of Bobby Seale's exceptional political stature, the trial just begun against him is in fact a political trial of the Black Panther Party, and more generally, a race trial held against all of America's blacks.[1]

The reality of the black colony in the United States is very complex. Disseminated throughout a nation full of pride that sees itself as master of the world, black people, outnumbered among the white population, oppressed by the racism and indifference of whites, threatened by an oppressive police and judicial system, have been forced to work out a very new form of struggle within this unique situation. That is why the Black Panther Party was formed, first to defend the rights of the colonized blacks within the United States, and then also to initiate an original political reflection.

Faced with the vigor of their action, and with the rigor of their political thinking, the whites, and particularly the police, who are an extension of the dominant caste in the United States, had an almost immediate racial reflex: since blacks showed themselves capable of organizing, the simplest thing was to discredit their organization.

Thus the police were able to hide the true meaning of their interventions behind outrageous pretexts: trials involving drugs, murder, or morals. In fact, what they were trying to do was massacre the leaders of the Black Panther Party.

And what about us—what are we doing? When the bombs fell on Hanoi, we had a few epidermal reactions.[2] During the Korean War too. The killing was happening far away. Here and now, we can see that our colonized people, who perhaps still appear to us like shadows in our midst, are about to become our adversaries in our own country.

The majority of blacks live in poverty and deprivation. It's not the police who put an end to drugs in the black ghettos, it's the Black Panther Party itself.[3]

But we close our eyes and stop up our ears, so as not to be too troubled by the poverty and misery of black people. If we looked directly at the reality of America, we would soon understand that blacks are more and more capable of taking care of their own affairs. So the simplest and most prudent thing is to leave them in a state of physical and moral poverty, in total solitude.

Let's not be afraid of words: this poverty makes our comfort possible. Moaning about distant bombings was our luxury. Our cowardice will prevent us from opening our eyes here. In order to complete the scenario, we have perfected an imposture in the grand style: to a few carefully chosen blacks we have granted celebrity status, and we have multiplied their image, but only so that they will remain what we ask them to be: actors and comedians.

Bobby Seale and his comrades have disregarded our instructions; they speak and act as political leaders. And this is intolerable to us. We prefer the misery of blacks, and the racism it implies, rather than recognize the political value of the Black Panther Party.

But we have to understand that Mitchell, in prosecuting Bobby Seale, is prosecuting us as well.[4] More and more, our freedoms are threatened. Perhaps we will do nothing, but our sons and daughters, who have made Bobby Seale a hero in prison, will move more quickly than we do.

We will do nothing, and our children already despise us for doing nothing.

Stony Brook University should be an example to us: when Bobby Seale was transferred to Connecticut, it responded by offering him a position as professor in the university, and by creating, the very day of the transfer, a Committee for the Support and Defense of Bobby Seale and the Black Panther Party.[5]

We have entered a period comparable to the McCarthyism of the 1950s. The same terrorism is being used against the intellectuals who sympathize with the Black Panthers. Must we accept the police state, or fight against it? Must we continue to fear the Black Panther Party as a mythology, at once terrifying and puerile, whose image paralyzes us?

Must we accept the idea that black people, colonized within a white empire, are attempting to liberate themselves?

Because of the very fact that the Black Panther Party and we ourselves, white people, have the same enemy, meaning the police, and beyond the police the White House Administration, and beyond the White House Administration, High Finance, we know that our struggle is a class struggle.

We should not let ourselves be distracted by the sexual myths which are said to be the origins of racism. The origins of racism are socioeconomic. We need to be very precisely aware of this, for it is the point of departure for our solidarity with blacks and the Black Panther Party.

As for the political thought of the Black Panthers, I am convinced that it originates in the poetic vision of black Americans.

We are realizing more and more that a poetic emotion lies at the origin of revolutionary thought. This is why we have to understand that it is on the basis of singular poetic emotions that Mao Tse-Tung was led to revolutionary consciousness, later on to the Long March, then to the revolution called the "Hundred Flowers" campaign, and, finally, to the Cultural Revolution.[6] And it was the same for Ho Chi Minh.

And the same is true for the Black Panther Party, which from the poetic resources of their oppressed people draws the will to elaborate a rigorous revolutionary thought.

Whites, and particularly young whites, must understand that their relations with their own revolutionary organizations must be renewed and that it is important right now to organize *tactical* revolutionary alliances.

I also believe the time has come also to use a new vocabulary and syntax capable of making everyone more aware of the double struggle, both poetic and revolutionary, of the white movements that are comparable to the Black Panthers.

Where I am concerned, for example, I refuse to use the term "brother," which is too laden with evangelic sentimentality; when I speak of blacks, I want to speak of comrades-in-arms fighting against the same enemy.

When the Black Panther Party contacted me in France, I came immediately to the United States to put myself at their disposal. Your youth, your intellectual and physical abilities, your moral imperatives will enable you to act more quickly than I can, and much more effectively. That's why I'm counting on you to help the Black Panther Party and to prevent Bobby Seale's trial.

One has to think that this cultural current, brutally interrupted by the white slave drivers, is being reborn not only in black music but also in a revolutionary consciousness. It is therefore a very simple but very obvious paradox that today makes black people, here in the United States, the bearers of revolutionary thought and action.

§ 7   May Day Speech

I must begin with a few words about my presence in the United States.

My situation with regard to the administration of this country contains an element of unreality that I have to take into account. Indeed, for two months I have traveled around without being disturbed; my entry into the country took place in unusual circumstances;[1] here and elsewhere, I live like a vagabond, not like a revolutionary; my habits and behavior are themselves unusual, so that I must be very careful when I speak in the name of the Black Panther Party, which, for its part, is attached to this country and whose habits are not nomadic, who have to defend themselves with what are called legal means, and with real weapons. What I mean to say is that no unreality should slip into my interventions, for that would be detrimental to the Black Panther Party, and to Bobby Seale, who is in a very real prison, made of stone and cement and steel.

My freedom to speak and to move around must not become a game dictated by whim: and this is one of the reasons why I submit to the necessities of the Panthers.

The second point I want to make is related to the first: racism here is widespread and growing fast. I noticed this as soon as I arrived in the United States. It leaped out at me, but gradually, while staying here, I believe I have also seen some very healthy behavior, I mean in which racism had no part. And then there were the events in the New Haven court.[2] From the moment I entered the courtroom, American racism, which is to say antiblack racism, became apparent to me in all its violence. When I arrived in the courtroom with my black comrades of the Black Panther Party, a cop, without asking me, led me up to the first row of the audience, in the section where there were only whites. It's only thanks to the insistence of my black comrades that I was allowed to go sit with them. To you this may seem like an insignificant sign, but to me, having been there as its pseudobeneficiary, I translated this sign immediately. And when Hilliard and Emory were arrested for disrupting the court by reading out a statement, I myself who had also read a statement before the court—I was simply expelled from the courtroom, but left free.

A few days later another event occurred that confirmed this observation: a black friend of mine whom I cannot name, a few whites, and I were boarding a TWA airplane.[3] In the walkway leading to the plane, a policeman ordered the black man to open his suitcase. Since there was nothing in it but three shirts and three pairs of pants, he was allowed to board the plane; but the policeman changed his mind and, with an escort of five other cops, came onto the plane, showed his badge, and asked our friend to get back off the plane. None of the three whites, including myself, was treated so rudely. (Fortunately, there are other airlines besides TWA.)

My interpretation is this: they didn't bother me because I'm white and as such I present no danger to American society. The blacks, of course, are black, and therefore guilty of being black, and the Black Panther Party is a threat to the bourgeois order of the United States. Now I'm coming to the point that seems very important to me: the kind of relations that exist between leftist organizations and the Black Panther Party. Here I believe that whites need to bring a new dimension into politics: a delicacy of heart. But be careful: it's not a question of sentimentalism, but of a delicacy in relations with people who do not have the same rights as we do. Even if their rights are recognized in the laws of the country, black people are far from fully possessing these rights (as I showed in speaking of New Haven), and the Black Panther Party even less so. De facto discrimination exists, as you know; you see it every day. It is visible everywhere, even and especially in unions, even among workers, even in universities. So it is very clear that white radicals owe it to themselves to behave in ways that would tend to erase their privileges. As for other whites, it should be obvious that if they are so attached to their whiteness, it's really in death that they will find it. The whitest of whites is, for a moment, a dead white.

If the pride of the blacks and the Black Panther Party, and sometimes their arrogance (but what can be said of the arrogance of the whites, and of their brutality against not only blacks but the entire world!), if this pride is the result of a new political awareness, this awareness is still too new for them not to get very upset when they and their positions are challenged. They have a tendency—and they're right to be mistrustful—to see in such challenges a desire on the part of whites, a more or less conscious desire, to dominate them yet again. Everything happens as if whites added to the correctness of their ideas (when they are correct) an authoritarianism in the expression of these ideas, to the point that blacks can already see a budding imperialism in it. This habit of domination is communicated in the ideas of whites, and this is perhaps what they mean when they speak of American dynamism.

It is very important, then, for white radicals to act with candor, certainly, but also with delicacy, when it comes to their relations with blacks, for, once again, blacks run the risk of going to prison for an insignificant gesture, whereas for a white man who makes the same gesture, something like complicity already exists between him and the authorities. This complicity of the white man—it too unconscious—is something that the black man cannot help feeling. To refuse to admit this as a given fact is merely a sign of arrogance, brutality, a lazy mind, or sheer stupidity.

It is quite true that blacks and whites have a gulf to bridge, a gulf opened by four hundred years of contempt and falsified history. There was an alleged superiority on the side of the whites, but the whites didn't suspect that they were being observed—in silence, true, but observed all the better for that. Today, blacks have drawn from this silent observation a profound knowledge of whites, whereas the contrary is not true. Radicals often say that everyone knows this, but since no one really takes it into account, it amounts to saying that everyone acts by lying.

It is therefore up to whites to initiate an understanding of black people, and, I repeat, this can only be done in a delicacy of relations, when whites and blacks decide to undertake a political action in common—as revolutionaries.

Up to now, blacks have found among whites only two modes of expression: brutal domination and a distant and rather contemptuous paternalism. Another way must be found. I have indicated one possible way.

Blacks are asking for nothing other than equality in relations. That's clear. Faced with the disproportion of privileges, whites, if they are resolved to have equal relations, are obliged to act as I have said. Not submissively, but with a discerning attention to what still continues to hurt blacks after these four hundred terrible years.

It may be necessary to have done with symbols and symbolic gestures. I'm not talking about the emblems whose real content is without great significance, but the symbols themselves, as a substitute for revolutionary action. (A provisional definition of this term: every act capable of abruptly breaking down the bourgeois order with the aim of creating a socialist order.)

The American Left, and particularly that part of the American Left that calls itself radical, has the possibility of carrying out effective actions rather than empty gestures. In a sense it has a field of action: its struggle for the liberation of Bobby Seale and its support for the Black Panther Party.

Symbols refer to an action that has taken place, not to one that will take place, since every action that is accomplished (I'm speaking of revolutionary actions) cannot make any serious use of already known examples. That is why all revolutionary acts have about them a freshness that is like the beginning of the world.

But a symbolic gesture or set of gestures is idealistic in the sense that it satisfies those who make it or who adopt the symbol and prevents them from carrying out real acts that have an irreversible power.

I think we can say that a symbolic attitude is both the good conscience of the liberal and a situation that makes it possible to believe that every effort has been made for the revolution. It is much better to carry out real acts on a seemingly small scale than to indulge in vain and theatrical manifestations. We should never forget this when we know that the Black Panther Party seeks to be armed, and armed with real weapons.

To speak to its members of pacifism and nonviolence would be criminal. It would be preaching to them an evangelical virtue that no white person is capable of applying or living for himself.

I said that the American Left, if it considers itself revolutionary, has the possibility of accomplishing real acts, in relation to Bobby Seale and in collaboration with the Black Panther Party. To refuse this would be to accept, here in the United States, that a sort of Dreyfus affair has been declared. Perhaps even more harmful than the Dreyfus affair in France and Europe. It is time to decide whether intellectuals are silent because Bobby Seale is guilty, or because he is black and the chairman of the Black Panther Party, and whether intellectuals are afraid of Agnew's threats against those who aid and encourage the party.[4] And here everything seems to indicate that there is no interest in Bobby Seale because he is black. In the same way, Dreyfus was guilty because he was Jewish.

It used to be that, in France, the guilty man was the Jew. Here, the guilty man was, and still is, the Negro.

Of course this parallel with the Dreyfus affair cannot be maintained at every point. And I have to admit that in America up to now there has been no Clemenceau, no Jaurès, and especially, among the intellectuals, no Zola to write "J'accuse." A "J'accuse" that would condemn both the courts of your country and the majority of whites who are still racists.[5]

When we speak of the Black Panther Party, we must also realize that within a year and a half police repression against them has increased from one to seven. What I mean is that the number of police actions must be multiplied by seven.

Another thing worries me: fascism. We often hear the Black Panther Party speak of fascism, and whites have difficulty accepting the word. That's because whites have to make a great effort of imagination to understand that blacks live under an oppressive fascist regime. This fascism, for them, is not the doing of the American government alone, but also of the entire white community, which in reality is very privileged.

Here, whites are not directly oppressed, but blacks are, in their minds and sometimes in their bodies.

Black people are right to accuse whites as a whole of this oppression, and they are right to speak of fascism.

As for us, perhaps we live in a liberal democracy, but blacks live, really and truly, under an authoritarian, imperialist regime of domination. It is important that a taste for freedom be spread among you. But whites are afraid of freedom. It's a drink that is too strong for them. They have another fear as well, which never ceases to grow, and that is the fear of discovering the intelligence of blacks.

Yet I have hope for blacks as a people and for the revolution undertaken by the Black Panther Party. First, all the peoples of the Third World are more and more conscious of the revolutionary necessity; and then whites, and even Americans, and even Johnson and all the rest, can be transformed.

Personally, I place a certain trust in the nature of man, even the most limited man. The Black Panther Party's endeavor continues to spread, there are more and more people in the general public who understand them, and white intellectuals will perhaps support them: this is why I am here with you today.

For Bobby Seale, I repeat, there must not be another Dreyfus affair.

Therefore I am counting on you, on all of you, to take the protest everywhere, to talk about Bobby Seale in your families, in your universities, in your courses, and you must challenge and sometimes contradict your professors and the police themselves.

And—I will say this again, since it is very important—it is not a question of symbolic gestures but of real acts. And if it becomes necessary, I mean if the Black Panther Party asks it of you, you ought to desert your universities, desert your classrooms, in order to speak out across America in favor of Bobby Seale and against racism.

Bobby Seale's life, the existence of the Black Panther Party, these come before your diplomas. Now you must—and you have the physical, material, and intellectual means for this—now you must confront life directly and no longer in comfortable aquariums, I mean in American universities, where people raise goldfish capable of nothing more than blowing bubbles.

Bobby Seale's life depends on you. Your real life depends on the Black Panther Party.

~

Appendix[6]

What people call American civilization will disappear. It is already dead because it is founded on contempt. For example, the contempt of the rich for the poor, the contempt of whites for blacks, and so on. Every civilization founded on contempt must necessarily disappear. And I am not speaking of contempt in terms of morality, but in terms of function: I mean that contempt, as an institution, contains its own dissolving agent, and the dissolving agent of what it engenders.

I am meddling, you will say, in the affairs of America: this is because it set an example for me by meddling in my own affairs and in the affairs, pretty much everywhere, of the entire world. After meddling with Korea, it took care of Vietnam, then of Laos, today it's Cambodia—and me, I'm taking care of America.

I denounce, in no particular order, the following institutions: first of all, the *Press*. The news provided to Americans is criminal because it is presented in a rosy hue, or not presented at all. The *New York Times* lies. *Look* magazine lies by omission, out of prudence or cowardice. It too is afraid of the naked truth. The *New Yorker* lies, out of mental debility, television lies too when it refrains from giving the true motives that led three blacks to ambush four white policemen. The Press, which possesses all the means for providing information but which refuses to do so, is responsible for the thunderous stupidity of the Americans.

The *Church*, born from an Eastern fable perverted from its original meaning by Westerners, has become a tool of repression, especially here against blacks, to whom it preaches evangelical gentleness out of respect for the master—the white man—and to whom, with the Old Testament, it promises the fires of hell to those who revolt.

The *"Charitable" Institutions*, controlled by all-powerful firms—the Ford Foundation, the Rockefeller Institute, and so on—which in turn control those they claim to help.

The *Unions*, of which I hardly need to speak to you, since they are your enemies, and what is more pathetic, the workers are enemies of themselves. To console themselves for being, ultimately, the victims of their bosses, they take refuge in an idiotic comfort and an aggressive racism against blacks.

I will not forget the *University*. The Universities. They teach you a false culture, in which the only recognized values are quantitative. The University is not content to turn you into a digit within a larger number—for example when they train five hundred thousand engineers—it cultivates in you the need for security, for tranquility, and, quite naturally, it educates you to serve your bosses and, beyond them, your politicians, although you are well aware of their intellectual mediocrity. So that you, who want to be scientists and scholars, will end up in an armchair, at a table—but at the far end of the table—of a mediocre politician. And you'll be proud of it.

To continue, another institution: *Advertising*. The newspapers are full of idiotic advertisements. As are the television stations. And the advertisers, by threatening to boycott the newspapers and television stations, make their directors tremble. So that here, in the United States, what moves you is an immense trembling. Everyone trembles before everyone else. And the strongest before the weakest, and the least idiotic before the most idiotic. What is still called American dynamism is an endless trembling that shakes the whole country.

I will finish this list with one major institution: the *Police*. They too provoke fear. They threaten, but they tremble. They are not very sure of themselves. Three days ago, old Johnson was saying that the Warren Commission was wrong in naming Oswald as the sole culprit in the murder of Kennedy.[7] And—the height of irony—it's the supreme manager of the Police, Johnson himself, who had backed the Warren Commission. This contradiction—or this reversal—might provoke an immense outburst of laughter. In any case, they must be having a good laugh in Peking. But here, in the end, it's pathetic.

§ 8   Interview with Michèle Manceaux

Michèle Manceaux.—How did you happen to go to the United States to meet up with the Black Panthers?

Genet.—Two members of the Black Panther Party came to see me in Paris and asked me what I could do to help them.[1] I think that what they had in mind was that I would help them in Paris, but I said, "The simplest thing would be to go to America." This answer seemed to surprise them a little. They said, "In that case, come. When do you want to leave?" I said, "Tomorrow." They were even more astonished, but they reacted immediately: "Okay, we'll come by to get you." That's how I ended up going. But I didn't have a visa.

M.M.—You haven't had a visa since you wrote on the Democratic Convention in Chicago?

G.—No, I never had a visa. They refuse to give me one.

M.M.—How do you do it then?

G.—It's very easy to cross the border.[2] French writers and union activists should also go to America to give lectures for the BPP. A committee of solidarity with the BPP has just formed in Paris.[3]

M.M.—Is their cause not somewhat different from that of the Black Panthers? How is it that the Black Panther cause is also yours?

G.—If I'm sincere, I have to say that what touched me at first was not their concern to re-create the world. Of course, that will come and I am not insensitive to it. But what made me feel immediately close to them was their hatred for the white world, their concern to destroy a society, to smash it. A concern that I had when I was very young, but I couldn't change the world all alone. I could only pervert it, corrupt it a little. Which is what I tried to do through a corruption of language, that is, from within the French language, a language that pretends to be so noble, and maybe it is, you never know.

M.M.—Do you think of yourself as a revolutionary?

G.—My situation is that of a vagabond, not a revolutionary. How do you expect me to be able to define myself? Besides, the words that people try to pin on me are of no importance: thief, homosexual . . . and now revolutionary. No, I'm not inclined to say I'm a revolutionary.

M.M.—Why did you decide to help American blacks rather than, say, immigrant workers in France?

G.—Really, if I'm helping the Panthers, it's because they asked me to. The immigrant workers have never asked me for anything. And the Panthers accepted me as I am. With them, there's no rigid moralizing. They are militant, twenty-four hours a day. Every Sunday from five to seven, the militants hold classes in political education. I was also present a few times at the training sessions that take place, rifles in hand, in the middle of the night. Women do the same work as men. All the Panthers' houses are well within black neighborhoods and are guarded day and night by armed patrols. The police still find ways of conducting raids, often murderous, using various excuses, the most common of which is drugs. Did you know that the members of the BPP never get behind the wheel of a car? Traffic violations, whether real or invented, are a trap they do not want to fall into.

The Panthers have houses with armored shutters, doors backed by sandbags, mirrors in the stairways to see who's coming, and wire netting to protect themselves from tear-gas bombs. They live surrounded by hatred.

M.M.—Are they also full of hatred?

G.—I can say: yes, they have a hatred for the repressive form of white society.

M.M.—How is it that they agree to collaborate with whites?

G.—They don't do so unconditionally. They make agreements for certain limited operations. Likewise, white organizations have made some agreements with them—for the demonstrations in New Haven and Washington, for example.[4]

M.M.—Do they support "Black Studies" programs and the cultivation of "blackness"?

G.—They're sensitive to the dangers that Black Studies programs may bring with them. By resituating themselves in an African context, they were cutting themselves off from the technology they need more than ever. Since all the political regimes have failed to give them real equality with whites, they understood that their only recourse lay in socialism. It's in this sense that their struggle is not only antiracist; it is a global struggle that people on the Left throughout the world ought to see as their own.

The American Left now has the possibility of carrying out effective actions rather then empty gestures. In a sense, it has a field of action. For example, the struggle for the liberation of Bobby Seale and support for the BPP. Symbols refer to an action that has taken place, not to one that will take place, since every action that is accomplished (I'm speaking of revolutionary actions) cannot make any serious use of already known examples. That is why all revolutionary acts have about them a freshness that is like the beginning of the world. But a symbolic gesture or set of gestures is idealistic in that it satisfies the men who make it or who adopt the symbol and prevents them from carrying out real acts that have an irreversible power. I think that a symbolic attitude is both the good conscience of the liberal and a situation that makes it possible to believe that every effort has been made for the revolution. It is much better to carry out real acts on a seemingly small scale than to indulge in vain and theatrical manifestations.

M.M.—What real acts did you carry out in the United States?

G.—I went from city to city, university to university, working for the BPP, talking about Bobby Seale and about the importance of helping the BPP. These lectures had two goals: to popularize the movement and to collect money. I went to the Massachusetts Institute of Technology, Yale, Columbia, Los Angeles, and so on. In this way, the most important universities opened their doors to the BPP.

M.M.—What did you say to the students?

G.—That they were idiots and that they had to help Bobby Seale. The Panthers also spoke, as much as I did.

M.M.—What did you say about Bobby Seale?

G.—In the Bobby Seale affair at the Chicago conspiracy trial, there were eight accused.[5] Among the eight, seven were released on bail in the end. But not for the exorbitant and absolutely unpayable bails of a hundred and fifty thousand dollars that are set for blacks. Only one of the accused remains in prison, and for a while the American Left lost interest in him; and this man, it just so happens, is black, and the chairman of the Black Panther Party: Bobby Seale. I know very well that he was accused of a murder in Connecticut, but I also know that he was not in Connecticut when the murder was committed; and I also know that the president of Yale, Kingman Brewster, stated that there was little chance that Bobby Seale would receive a fair trial in Connecticut.[6] To remain silent about this situation is to accept that a man is guilty because he is black. Just as in the Dreyfus affair the guilty man was the Jew. Today, in the United States, it's the Negro. The parallel with the Dreyfus affair ends there, for I have to say that in the United States there is not yet any Clemenceau, nor any Jaurès, and especially, among the intellectuals, no Zola to write "J'accuse"—a "J'accuse" that would condemn both the courts of this country and the majority of whites who are still racists.[7]

M.M.—Did you yourself see direct evidence of this racism?

G.—Living there as a white man among blacks, I witnessed it every day. Even in the smallest details. For example, I'm boarding an airplane. The black man in front of me is ordered to open his suitcase. Inside the suitcase are three shirts and two pairs of pants. They let him get on the airplane. No one asks me to do anything. In the New Haven courtroom, they tried to make me sit with the whites, without asking for my opinion.

You can see this racism for yourself. Look at how people talked about the four students killed at Kent State.[8] Huge headlines in the press. An outpouring of concern. A few days later, two students were killed in Jackson, Mississippi. The newspapers buried the story somewhere on the last page. Why? Those two students were black.

M.M.—Does a black racism also exist?

G.—No. It can exist. But if racism means the contempt one bears one's fellow men the better to exploit them, then we have to admit that the definition cannot be applied to blacks in relation to whites.

M.M.—David Hilliard says that the Panthers who are in prison ought to be considered prisoners of war. What do you think about that?

G.—I hesitate to say anything definitive, but it does seem to me that if we think of the situation of blacks in relation to whites as one in which a people is colonized within the borders of a larger nation, then we are obliged to admit that this nation has taken a few prisoners. The struggle of the BPP in the United States must be thought of as a war against the means of repression.

M.M.—Does this struggle include violence?

G.—A war cannot take place without violence. When whites preach nonviolence to blacks, are they aware that a situation of violence has always existed, ever since the time of the slave traders? This massive contempt that has accumulated over three or four hundred years, is that not violence? Is it not also violence when a white man has to pay ten thousand dollars to be released on bail, while, for the same crime, they ask anywhere from a hundred thousand to a hundred and fifty thousand dollars. I've seen many bails set at a hundred thousand dollars for blacks. In this case, preaching nonviolence to blacks is to deny them the means of defending themselves. A nonviolent attitude on the part of whites is nothing more than moral dilettantism. That said, violence and nonviolence must, in my opinion, be used in a tactical manner.

M.M.—What is the ideology of the BPP?

G.—They see their struggle as a class struggle. Their goal is a Marxist-style revolution. This explains why such vigorous measures have been taken to repress them. The administration knows that to look at the Black Panthers is to see red. The Panthers could have a larger audience, perhaps, among the black and even the white community, if they were content to be some kind of slightly politicized Salvation Army, but this would go against their deliberately revolutionary objectives. For me, this is a reason to support them: they are waging a struggle against imperialism right there on American soil.

M.M.—How does this repression occur?

G.—In a very significant way. I have collected and counted all the repressive actions taken against the Panthers since May 2, 1967. The figures are eloquent: from May 2, 1967, to September 28, 1968, there were 55 trials, 130 questionings, 5 Panthers killed. That was over a period of ten months. From October 1968 to December 1969, a fifteen-month period, I counted 373 trials, 735 questionings, and 24 Panthers killed. What happened between these two periods? The Nixon administration replaced the Johnson administration, and if you count, you can see that the numbers increased by about seven.

I'd like to say something about what happened in Baltimore, because it's very important. On April 30, 1970, the FBI raided the Panther headquarters in Baltimore.[9] They arrested ten people, and, according to police, eight people escaped. The pretext? In October 1969 the body of a black man was found; it was claimed that he had been tortured and killed in July 1969. The cops also claim that it was an informer killed by the Panthers. The fact is, they don't know anything about Anderson, the deceased, but they wanted to use his death as a pretext and a semblance of justification for their arrests. The search for the eight fugitives gives them an excuse to do whatever they want . . . and they can blame the crime on whoever they want.

M.M.—So the police do at least feel the need to provide justifications for what they do?

G.—Yes, because the Panthers—and this is where they're smart—don't remain underground. You see pictures of them. They take airplanes. They often appear in public. They've become familiar figures. They do all this as a precaution because, after all, this spotlight protects them more than remaining underground; it's easier to arrest an unknown "troublemaker" than a prominent and well-known figure with a quasi-official title.

M.M.—They have titles?

G.—Yes, there are ministers, leaders with specific functions. Local governments. I was working for the minister of education, Massai Hewitt. But I traveled most of the time with David Hilliard, who is replacing Bobby Seale as chairman. Now the police want to arrest David Hilliard and another Panther named D.C., who is in hiding. They carried out the raid in Baltimore and sent out arrest warrants on April 30, the day before David Hilliard was supposed to speak in New Haven. They tried to intimidate the black population into not showing up in New Haven, but we spoke outdoors to twenty thousand people. New Haven is where Bobby Seale is incarcerated. I mention this because the Panthers asked me to publicize it as much as possible. They see it as a very serious threat.

M.M.—Do the Panthers think of themselves as guerrillas?

G.—What are guerrillas? I can't use words that have been used by others. I can say: this is how they are, this is what they do.

M.M.—How do they get their money?

G.—The money comes first of all from a weekly newspaper they sell for twenty-five cents; it has a circulation of a hundred and fifty thousand.[10] Young blacks sell it everywhere. Part of the black population contributes to the BPP. Almost all the jazz groups give benefit concerts for them on a monthly basis. There are also some donations.

M.M.—Do these come from blacks or whites?

G.—Both. For example, I went to one meeting at a writer's house in Hollywood. Jane Fonda was there. They collected a lot of money in a very short time.[11]

M.M.—In New York the Panthers have a headquarters in Saint Mark's

Church. Benefit plays are put on for them. They're very clever at getting people to talk about them . . .

G.—It's the press, television and radio, that turn them into stars. They don't seek it out. They enter the limelight when they're arrested. . . . The news media willfully distort them anyway, insofar as they portray the BPP as a folkloristic group or else as a band of criminals. Never, of course, as a coherent revolutionary group.

M.M.—When you were traveling with the Panthers, were you aware of your "whiteness"?

G.—No, in fact, it's odd, but it didn't matter.

M.M.—But there was a language barrier; you don't speak English, do you?

G.—No, and that was the biggest problem. All the more so because almost all the blacks were from the ghettos and they speak a slang that's difficult to understand, sometimes even for white interpreters. With David Hilliard I managed to make myself understood; we would write back and forth. He would use words that weren't too complicated and I was able to read what he wrote and to write back.

M.M.—Would you have written *The Blacks* in the same way after living through what you just experienced?

G.—If you don't mind, let's not talk about my plays.

M.M.—You don't want to write anymore?

G.—I don't think that Brecht did anything for communism, and the revolution was not set off by Beaumarchais's *The Marriage of Figaro*. I also think that the closer a work of art is to perfection, the more it is enclosed within itself. Worse than that—it inspires nostalgia!

§ 9   Introduction to *Soledad Brother*[1]

Every authentic writer discovers not only a new style, but a narrative form that is his alone and that he tends to exhaust, drawing out all its effects for his own purposes. Many people would be astonished to hear that the epistolary narrative was still capable of providing us with a resolutely modern mode of expression, but it is enough to juxtapose (and place one after another) a certain number of Jackson's letters, and we obtain a gripping poem of love and combat.[2]

But what is most surprising when we read these letters by a young black man locked away in Soledad Prison, is that they perfectly reflect the path traveled by their author—first the slightly awkward letters to his mother and his brother, then the letters to his lawyer that develop into something extraordinary, part essay and part poem, and finally the last letters with their extreme delicacy, addressed to an unknown recipient.[3] And from the first letter to the last, nothing was willed, written, or composed for the purpose of putting together a book; and yet here is a book, hard and sure, and, I repeat, both a weapon in a struggle for liberation and a love poem. I see no miracle in this, except the miracle of truth itself, the naked truth completely exposed.

So Jackson is a poet, but he may be facing a death sentence. Let's talk about that sentence.

～

A court of justice, a certain number of jurors protected by guards in uniforms, by police in plain clothes, by numerous informers, by all of white American society, will decide whether he and his brothers killed the prison guard. The jurors will answer yes or no.

If they answer yes, a very strange operation will begin. The judges will have to pronounce sentence. Either death, prison for life, or a certain time to be served. So what is this intellectual operation that transforms a simple act (a murder, if it took place) into something completely different: another death, or prison for life, or a period of time to be served?

How these two facts are linked together—the original and hypothetical murder and the sentence pronounced—no one has yet said, since no one knows. The fact is that courts, whether in America or elsewhere, are based on authority, a crude authority that adapts itself quite well to the arbitrary.

And yet this sentence, if it is pronounced, must be lived. And it will be lived by the Soledad Brothers, by Jackson, and lived in this way: either by walking from his cell to the gas chamber, or by living for thirty years or twenty years in another cell.

A guard is discovered, murdered.

A jury answers yes or no to indicate the murderer.

The murderer is murdered in turn, or he lives in a cell for thirty years, to justify a sentence that has been *pronounced.*

To understand the importance of this book as a weapon in a struggle, the reader must not forget that Jackson is in danger of death.

〜

If the same type of complicity binds together works written in prison or in asylums (Sade and Artaud encounter the same necessity of finding within themselves that which, it is thought, will lead them to glory, that is, despite the walls, the moats, the jailers, and the judges, into the light and into minds free from servitude), these works do not meet in what is still called degradation: beginning their search for themselves in that degradation demanded by social repression, they find common ground in the audacity of their undertaking, in the rigor and precision of their ideas and their visions. In the hardest prisons, more than anywhere else, it is absolutely necessary not to simply let oneself go. One cannot endure a penalty so monstrous as the lack of freedom without demanding from one's mind and body a labor that is both delicate and brutal, capable of "warping" the prisoner in a direction that distances him more and more from the social world. But . . .

~

One might think that the site of absolute malediction, the prison, and the cell at its center, would create for those who are confined there, because of its misery, a sort of solidarity required by this very misery, a merciful harmony in which all the social distinctions maintained on the outside would be abolished.

Prison serves no purpose; we might hope that it would at least have the power to tear the prisoners away from their miserable social differences and that, behind its walls and in its shadows, under the surveillance of a cordon of guards—black or white, but armed—new kinds of relations would develop among the prisoners, whoever they may have been during their moments of freedom.

That is an idealistic hope that must be avoided or dropped: Jackson's book makes it brutally clear that in prison, in the cell, the white skin of the prisoners is taken as a sign of complicity with the white skin of the guards; so that while the white guards stand watch over a hell in which white prisoners are confined, the white prisoners stand watch over another hell inside that one in which black prisoners are confined. Now the security of the guards, their independence—since the time they spend on duty is divided by trips into town or by their family life—allows for a certain respite with regard to the white prisoners. But because these prisoners must remain constantly in prison and are never distracted by the outside, all their time and imagination are spent maintaining the hell in which they hold the black prisoners captive.

In general, few prisoners escape from the tendency to form a complicity with certain guards: this comes from a sort of nostalgia for the social world from which they have been cut off (a nostalgia that makes the prisoner cling to what appears, in his prison, to be closest to the social order: the guard. As for the guard, the motives that make him accept the game played out between certain prisoners and himself are so numerous, and so confused!). And this complicity would not have too much importance if its meaning were a temporary dejection or weakness capable of being revoked or abruptly reversed—during a riot, for example. But in the United States it's something different: the complicity of the white prisoners with the guards intensifies, and maintains at its highest pitch, that which forms the basis of relations between whites and blacks: racism.

This racism is scattered, diffused throughout the entire United States;

it is shifty, sullen, arrogant, and hypocritical. There is one place where we might hope that this racism would cease, but on the contrary, this is where it becomes more cruel than anywhere else, where it is aggravated at every moment, where it does its work directly on bodies and souls, where racism becomes a kind of concentrate of racism: American prisons, and, it seems, of all American prisons, Soledad Prison, and at its center, the cells of Soledad.

If, by some oversight, racism were to disappear from the surface of the United States, we could then find it, intact and more condensed, in one of these cells. It is there, secret and not so secret, explainable and mysterious, stupid and more complex than a tiger's eye, an absence of life and a source of pain, an inert mass and a radioactive charge, exposed to all and yet hidden away. We could say that racism is here in its pure state, tautly alert, radiant, and ready to spring.

～

The extravagant adventure of white America, which is the victorious expansion of Victorian England, is no doubt reaching exhaustion; it will dissolve and fade, making it possible to see at last what is cheerfully devouring it, the black nation that was trapped within it, itself traversed by liberating currents and movements, provoking long shouts of misery and joy. What seems new to me in black literature is that now we hear almost no echoes of the great Hebrew prophets. From Richard Wright to Jackson, blacks are stripping themselves of all the Presbyterian and biblical rags: their voices are starker, blacker, more accusing and implacable, tearing out every reference to the cynical conjuring of the religious enterprise and its efforts to take over. They are more singular, and singular too in the way they all seem to engage a movement that converts the old discourses, in order to denounce the curse not of being black, but of being captive.

Is this new?

Incontestably.

Jackson's style is sharp, well tuned, simple, and supple, just like his thought. Anger alone illuminates them, and a sort of joy in anger.

～

A book written in prison—or in any place of confinement—is addressed perhaps above all to readers who are not outcasts, who have never been and will never go to prison, and that is why in some sense such a book proceeds obliquely. Otherwise, I know that the one writing it would only have to take words and fling them onto paper, the forbidden and accursed words, the bloody words, the words spit out in a lather, discharged with sperm, the slandered, reprobate words, the unwritten words—like the ultimate name of God—the dangerous, padlocked words, the words that don't belong in the dictionary, because if they were written there, complete and not maimed by ellipses, they would say too quickly the suffocating misery of a solitude that is not accepted and that is whipped and prodded only by what it is deprived of: sex and freedom.

It is therefore prudent that any writing that reaches us from this infernal place should reach us as though mutilated, pruned of its overly tumultuous adornments.

It is thus behind bars, accepted only by them, that its readers, if they dare, will guess at the infamy of a situation that a forthright vocabulary could never reconstruct: but behind the permitted words, learn to hear the others!

∼

If the prisoner is a black captured by whites, a third motif runs through this difficult pattern, namely hatred. Not the rather confused and diffuse hatred of the social order or of fate, but a very precise hatred of the white man. Here again the prisoner must use the very language, the words and syntax of his enemy, whereas he feels the need for a separate language that would belong only to his people. And there he is once again in an unfortunate and hypocritical situation: haunted by sex, he can only speak of his obsessions politely, according to a syntax that remains legible for others, and his hatred for the white man can be expressed only by means of the language belonging equally to blacks and to whites, but over which the white man extends his grammarian's jurisdiction. It is perhaps a further source of anguish for the black to think that if he writes a masterpiece, it is his enemy's language and treasure that will be enriched by this additional jewel, that he has so hatefully and lovingly carved.

He has then only one recourse: to accept this language but to corrupt it so skillfully that the whites will be caught in his trap. To accept it in its richness, to make it still richer, and to suffuse it with all his obsessions and all his hatred for the white man. An enormous task.

And it is a task which seems to be contradicted by that of the revolutionary. The revolutionary enterprise of the American black, it seems to me, can be born only out of resentment and hatred, that is, by rejecting in disgust and rage, but radically, the values venerated by whites, although this enterprise can continue only on the basis of a common language, at first rejected, finally accepted, whose words will no longer serve the ideas taught by whites, but new ones instead. In a revolutionary work written by a black man in prison, some traces must remain, then, of the orgiastic and hate-filled trajectory pursued in an imposed solitude.

Coming out of his delirium, having arrived at a cold and revolutionary form of thinking, Sade still held on to something of that obsessional delirium that had nonetheless led him to his revolutionary lucidity.

This too becomes clear in the letters that follow.

In prison, Jackson must still be careful to strengthen in himself what sets him against the whites, and to elaborate a thought so incisive that it will be valid for all men.

It was almost predictable that having reached this stage of solitary self-discovery, his revolutionary thought should encounter and find agreement with the Black Panther Party. It is therefore without equivocation and without mystery that in the final letters he names it and is guided by it. For myself, having lived with the Black Panthers, I see Jackson there in his place, fighting alongside them with the same conviction and the same talent as his two brothers accused of murder: Huey Newton and Bobby Seale.

～

If we accept the idea that the revolutionary enterprise of a man or a people has its source in their poetic genius, or more precisely, that this enterprise is the inevitable conclusion of poetic genius, we must reject nothing that makes poetic exaltation possible. Certain details in this work will seem immoral to you; this is because the entire work rejects your morality, because poetry contains both the possibility of a revolutionary morality and what seems to contradict it.

Finally, every young black American who writes is searching for himself and testing himself, and sometimes he recognizes, at his very center, in his own heart, a white man he must annihilate.

～

But let me return to the astonishing coherence of Jackson's life and of this work that was not *willed.* There is after all something quite troubling about it: at the same time as he was living his life (a sort of death or higher life), without realizing it, through letters and through certain notations in his letters, he was also writing his legend, which is to say that he was unintentionally giving us a mythic image of himself and his life—I mean an image that goes beyond his physical person and his ordinary life and is projected into glory, with the help of a combat weapon (his book) and a love poem.

But I have lived too long in prisons not to have recognized, as soon as the first pages were translated for me in San Francisco, the very particular odor and texture of something written in a cell, surrounded by walls and guards, poisoned by hatred, for what I did not yet know with such intensity was the hatred of the white American for the black, a hatred so extreme that I wonder whether every white man in that country, when he plants a tree, doesn't see *niggers* hanging from its branches.[4]

When this book is published, Jackson, who wrote it, will still be in his Soledad cell, with his Soledad brothers. What follows must be read as a manifesto, a tract, a call to rebellion, since that is first of all what it is.

It is all too evident that the legislative and judicial systems in the United States were established to protect a capitalist minority and, with some reluctance, the whole of the white population; but these infernal systems are still erected against blacks. We have known for a long time that the black man is from the start, natively, the guilty man. And we can be sure that if the blacks, with the help of their violence, their intelligence, their poetry, all they have accumulated for centuries while observing their former masters in silence and almost in secret—if the blacks do not themselves undertake their own liberation, the whites will not make a move.

But already Huey Newton, Bobby Seale, the members of the Black Panther Party, George Jackson, and others have stopped lamenting. For them, the time for the blues is past. They are developing, each according to his means, a revolutionary thought. And their eyes are clear.

I did not say blue.[5]

Brazil, July 1970

§ 10 Angela and Her Brothers

Angela Davis is wanted for murder and kidnapping. She allegedly bought, or had someone else buy under her name, the weapons used to kidnap Judge Harold Haley, before he was killed by the police along with his abductors. That is about all the information one can glean from the articles appearing in American or French newspapers. The reason for this laconic treatment is simple: real news doesn't exist in the United States. Of course, in accordance with a certain bourgeois conception of truth, the larger press organs describe the facts in minute detail, or rather certain material facts, in order to create an appearance of objectivity. But it is careful not to explain the why—the *why*, and not the *how*—behind these facts. The press does not say *why* this act was committed. It gives no satisfactory explanation of it whatsoever. Above all, it's a question of rebellious blacks and militants.

Angela Davis is a black woman. A professor of philosophy at the University of Los Angeles, she is a member of the American Communist Party, and she does not hide the fact. She works actively with the Black Panther Party and, since the creation of another group, with the "Soledad Brothers," whose members are fighting for imprisoned blacks.[1] Last June, she was fired from her position at the university.

Between these various elements—black skin, Black Panthers, Soledad Brothers, dismissal from the university, absence of real news—is there not a connection, always the same one in the United States, namely racism?

First, let's look at the information we have. It is obvious that if the press is multiplying the details, the reader ends up being interested in nothing else, because it's the easiest part, he's completely smothered by it, and the facts even end up disappearing beneath this accumulation of details. Satisfied at first by the speed of the press, the reader soon begins to feel oppressed, and, to relieve himself of the oppression, he plays with the details, arranging them in his own way, reconstructing the facts according to his own temperament and ideology. After reading all the articles printed about the abduction of Judge Haley by a group of blacks, about kidnappings committed by blacks, about rapes and assassination attempts, articles in which no detail is overlooked, from the position of a certain car to the contents of some passerby's pockets, the final impression made on the reader is that the press is diligent and honest, and the blacks are brutes. . . .

Angela Davis is twenty-six years old. She was born in Alabama to a middle-class black family. Her mother was a teacher. She was introduced to Marxism at a very young age, before studying French literature at the Sorbonne. Later, she studied for two years in West Germany, then returned to California to write a thesis in philosophy with Marcuse. After that, everything went very quickly. She was appointed professor of philosophy at the University of Los Angeles (UCLA). From 1968 to 1969, she became actively involved with the Black Panther Party; then, without any fundamental disagreement with the latter, she joined a communist group, the Che Lumumba Club.

This young black woman, elegant and beautiful, refuses to be integrated into the black American bourgeoisie. When I first met her in Los Angeles in March 1970, her essential choices had already been made. For the government of California, and especially for the governor, Ronald Reagan, she was a woman who had to be if not struck down, at least taken out of the way, especially when it comes to higher education, since her last course, I think, was on dialectical materialism. Instead of being silent, instead of prudently withdrawing, Angela Davis, in view of the repression weighing on the Panthers in particular and on blacks in general, in view of the invasion of Cambodia, has insisted more and more openly on her opposition to America's threats against certain peoples of the world, against the liberation movements developing both within and outside the United States.

Angela Davis, then, is a member of the Communist Party. It seemed to me that, without being particularly proud of this fact, she sees it as an obvious precondition for any true struggle. There is a question that is hard to answer with any precision: at what moment (if there is one), in what circumstances (if any), does a woman or a man understand that, instead of speaking in vain, they have just come forth to tell the truth? Born into comfort, raised in what is called Western culture, accepted as a teacher, and admired by the American bourgeoisie, when did Angela Davis understand that she had to join ranks with the black ghetto, not only in words but in acts?

The Black Panther Party is now famous throughout the world. It too was born spontaneously, from the almost oracular challenge of Huey Newton, who took the American Constitution literally and applied it to the defense of the black nation: still a very new step to take, but one that is marvelously justified by Malcolm X.[2] The Panthers appeared in full glory in Mexico City, when, during the Olympics, two black medalists stood on the podium with their fists in the air, a black glove on each fist.[3] This is the image that we should keep of them, but it must be completed by that of a daily reality that is extremely dangerous. Day in and day out, the Panthers pursue a difficult undertaking that most often goes unnoticed.

First of all, what do they want? Most urgently, the rigorous application of their civil rights. In the black ghettos, without yet claiming the right to own the slums assigned to them, they are making a few simple demands: to begin with, they demand that only black police, chosen and elected by them, should work in their neighborhoods. Then they want full employment. This is very important. There are more and more unemployed blacks, and the majority of those who work do so only half-time. Black families are often numerous, and the difference in the standard of living between black and white workers is growing. Hence not only a very real poverty, but also a sense of injustice.

By virtue of their origins, and even more because of a system that excludes them from public life, the "black nation" of America sees itself denied any possible means of realizing itself.[4] Black people in America therefore have no reason at all to embrace the belligerent conqueror's causes, so dear to the white American nation in which they find themselves trapped and which disposes of them as it sees fit. They have no reason at all, therefore, to accept being soldiers.[5]

Among other daily activities, the Black Panthers give out free breakfasts to black children. They print and sell newspapers and use the income to pay the enormous bail demanded by judges to release the black militants who have been imprisoned, as well as to provide funds to the widows of black men assassinated by the police or by the Minutemen.[6] The militants also take care of children who have lost their fathers: they organize conferences and jazz concerts, and all the money they raise is used for what we might perhaps dare to call their "good works."

We can already see that beneath the mythological image of the Black Panthers, at once glorious and terrifying, there are the very prosaic activities whose purpose is to keep the party alive. From all of this, something very new is emerging: the fact that for many years now blacks have understood that they were completely capable of running their own affairs, evolving very naturally toward the most complex political vision, elaborating audacious revolutionary ideas, and applying them. And white Americans have understood this too: hence their exasperation and the repression that results. And this exasperation is all the greater in that their children, their heirs, seem to be refusing all or part of their white heritage and showing approval for the Panthers' program. This is indeed the case for an ever larger number of young university radicals and, for a few months now, young factory workers.

I just wrote the word *young*. Angela Davis is young, Huey Newton is young, Bobby Seale, Eldridge Cleaver, David Hilliard—the Panthers are young.[7] One sees the evolution of this people, at first subjugated, driven underground, then suspended in the air and floating—but not at random.

Without denying their African origins (today, far from "straightening" their hair, blacks keep their hair frizzy and make it almost invasive), they have renounced the clothes, ornaments, and illusions that might make them believe they are simply African.

Here too the Black Panthers have known how to think and act forcefully. Informed by the ideas of DuBois,[8] Richard Wright, Fanon,[9] Malcolm X, Cleaver, Newton, and Seale, they have understood that a people long cut off from its true tradition risks losing itself in the one it has tried to retrieve, but which presents itself, in fact, as a form of folklore that is very reassuring to the dominant nation. Over and against this, the Panthers have very deliberately chosen the revolutionary project. This is no doubt the source of their attraction to young whites, but it is also what puts them in ever greater danger, because the white administration sees them as an enemy of American capitalism and, more generally, an enemy of bourgeois society.

The Panthers, like Angela, are young, which means that they are not afraid to carry out audacious plans and that their arrogance is shocking to a naively Victorian American society, which, despite the airs it puts on, is quite constipated, a society from which unionized workers can hardly be differentiated, since they're just as racist as white liberals if not more so. It should be clear that I have no confidence in liberals, all the petition signers who are nonetheless resigned to the Vietnam War, to intervention in Cambodia, to the exploitation of Guatemala, Brazil, and, with the exception of Cuba, all of Latin America.

To accomplish their goal—liberation—which is also Angela Davis's goal, the Black Panthers begin by educating their brothers of color. The Soledad Brothers organization was formed in the spring of 1970 by the parents of blacks who have been imprisoned and tortured in Soledad Prison in California. Angela Davis, Huey Newton's lawyer, Fay Stender, and a few others had launched a campaign to stop the torture and to help the black prisoners' families—who were intimidated at first by the police and by white judges—so that they would no longer be ashamed of their sons or their brothers, so that they could learn more about the means of defense guaranteed to them by the Constitution, and so that they could communicate to each other whatever they manage to learn about the treatments inflicted by the guards and even by white convicts on incarcerated blacks.

Incarcerated—for what? For a simple traffic violation, for selling marijuana (whether in small or large quantities), for the alleged rape of a white woman, or for the murder of a policeman. In all these cases, I believe, the cause of the crimes lies in the situation imposed on black people in America.

Among the members of the Soledad Brothers Defense Committee, Angela Davis was incontestably the most persuasive, the warmest, and one of the most intelligent, and one thing she had going for her—but against her in that country—was having black skin twenty-four hours a day. This is perhaps the source of her combativeness.

Here is what one of the members of the Soledad Brothers Defense Committee (whom I cannot name) wrote to me about them on July 28, 1970: "Three prisoners (a black, a Chicano, and a white) presented a list of demands to the administration of Soledad Prison. So the prisoners have begun to understand their situation and to organize. Many blacks (free blacks, no doubt) are doing a lot to organize the community. Angela Davis and Penny Jackson, George Jackson's sister, are working with us. The press and the radio are paying a lot of attention to what's happening. Groups of independent sociologists, psychiatrists, and journalists have been approached for an investigation of the penal system now in force, at Soledad in particular. . . . Two-thirds of the prisoners in Soledad are black or Chicano. The others are whites who are apolitical and for the most part racist."[10]

After only a few months, the Soledad Brothers Defense Committee, based in Sacramento, has members throughout California and will soon spread all across America. They organize meetings, conferences, picnics, and other events. They have a symbol: two black hands in a handshake.

The name Jackson was just linked with that of Angela Davis. We saw that she was working together with Penny Jackson, whose brother, Jonathan Jackson, threw two pistols from his seat in the San Rafael courtroom to the two blacks who were appearing before the white judge, Herold Haley. Who are Penny Jackson and Jonathan Jackson? George Jackson's sister and brother (the latter was killed by the police at the same time as Judge Haley).

George Jackson—like Huey P. Newton, Eldridge Cleaver, Bobby Seale, David Hilliard, and other Panthers—is a child of the black ghetto. He is now twenty-eight years old. Accused of theft, he was sentenced by an all-white jury to imprisonment for one year to life. This means that every year he has to appear before a court which, according to his behavior, will either free him or sentence him to another year of prison. For ten years his behavior has always been "bad," since he has never hidden the fact that he was struggling, at first, for black civil rights, and now for the liberation of the black nation that is held entirely captive within the larger white nation.

He learned to read and write at school. He began to write in prison, and his letters, which I have now and which will soon be published by prominent European and American publishers, describe for us the evolution that led him to conceive of the revolutionary projects that Newton and the Black Panthers quickly saw as their own and which they encouraged.

Almost all of the white prisoners in Soledad are racists, and this translates into blacks being insulted, having human waste thrown at them, and being directly provoked. Within Soledad Prison there is another prison that the inmates call "the Hole"; the administration calls it the "adjustment center." Last March, in the "adjustment center," there was a row of cells occupied by seven or eight whites, and another (separated from the first by a corridor) with seven or eight blacks and Chicanos.

The white prisoners, all of them racists, continually insulted the blacks and Chicanos, provoking them and throwing human waste at them. The authorities were perfectly aware of the deep hostility between the whites and the "coloreds." Nevertheless, instead of taking them out separately for their daily walk (an hour a day), they took them out together. A fight between the whites and the blacks was inevitable, and one day it happened. From high atop his watchtower, a guard named Miller, a sharpshooter, opened fire and shot into the crowd. Though not exactly "into the crowd," since he killed three blacks and only slightly wounded one white.

As the prison director explained to the journalists who came to investigate the "incident," Miller had simply shot "off to the side" to calm the situation, and the victims had been killed "from the ricochet." When the blacks' lawyers (among them Fay Stender) asked why the guard did not use his tear-gas canisters to disperse the fighting prisoners, the director answered: "*It was too windy.*" After that, the grand jury assembled to judge the case received an order from the attorney general not to charge Miller, who, he said, had acted in "self-defense."

Jackson was not in "the Hole" at the time: he was in "Wing Y" of Soledad Prison. The prisoners learned of the decision over the radio: they knew more than anyone that Miller, in his watchtower, with his tear gas and his machine gun, was untouchable and was in no danger whatsoever from a fight between the prisoners.

Three days after Miller's acquittal, a Soledad inmate finds the body of a guard, John Mills, in a courtyard; he has fallen from a railing on the third floor and died a half an hour later. At first it is believed that he died of a concussion to the head, but after a closer examination, the authorities say that he fell victim to a deadly karate grip. The prison authorities accuse George Jackson of doing the deed, with the help of John Clutchette (twenty-four years old) and Fleeta Drumgo (twenty-three years old). All three are black; one is a Panther. And the same grand jury that acquitted Miller has charged the three blacks with voluntary manslaughter. We see, then, what motivated the actions of Angela Davis, the Panthers, and Jonathan and George Jackson.

It is necessary to describe the climate in America at the time, especially in the black community. The year before, Eldridge Cleaver was forced
into exile, first in Cuba then in Algiers. Bobby Seale, who together with
Newton founded the Panthers, was tried (and gagged, an unprecedented
event) in Chicago, and transferred to the prison in New Haven; he's still
there. His trial has been postponed, but the case has not been dismissed.
Newton has been in prison since 1968 for a murder everyone knows he
did not commit.[11] David Hilliard was sentenced a first time, at the end of
1969, to six months in prison, and then in May 1970 was given six more
months for contempt of court in New Haven.[12] Constantly attacked in
the mainstream press (their only support comes from underground newspapers), attacked by the police who repeatedly raid their headquarters,
singled out by airline companies who arbitrarily deny them access to
flights—I saw this with my own eyes—divided by practical and intellectual disagreements with certain white radicals, the Black Panthers, recognized as a party by Cuba, Algiers, Hanoi, North Korea, and even
Denmark, feel very isolated in the United States, and the entire black
community lives in fear.

An agreement was finally reached between the Panthers (who maintained the leadership of the revolutionary cause) and the most active
white radicals. This made possible the three-day gathering of about thirty thousand young people in New Haven, when we happened to learn of
the American intervention in Cambodia. The news sparked demonstrations on every campus, the murder, by the police, of four white students
at Kent State, and, two days later, the assassination, again by the police,
of eight—that's right, eight—young blacks in the South (an "incident"
about which the press has had very little to say).[13]

More energetically than ever, the Panthers continue their program to
educate both blacks and whites; they know that the threat against them
grows, but they also know that new forces are ready, because in all the
ghettos young men and women are preparing to fight.

Angela Davis has not been put out of action! Thrown out of the university, she teaches young blacks who are completely devoted to her, and
she is more and more involved with the Soledad Brothers. She has finally broken with the bourgeoisie, both black and white, and there is no
going back. She is with the revolutionaries. Not a day goes by without a
young black man being shot down by the police. Huey Newton is out on

parol, which only shows that for two years he was incarcerated for no reason whatsoever.

This is the atmosphere in which a seventeen-year-old Jonathan
Jackson, the brother of George Jackson and a follower of Angela Davis,
attempted, right in the middle of court proceedings, to kidnap a judge in
order to save the two blacks about to be condemned. His plan failed, but
only in part: the white gentleman who was supposed to judge the two
blacks did not pronounce his sentence; he died first, a victim of white
racism. And the only apparent victor in this affair, for the moment, is the
police system.[14]

§ 11 Angela Davis Is in Your Clutches

I'm speaking to Nixon and Agnew; I'm speaking to white liberals and to the white American nation: we know your plan.[1] Ever since you realized the intelligence of black Americans, ever since you figured out that they go far beyond you in their revolutionary thinking, you have decided—I repeat: decided—to annihilate them. Bobby Seale—you're reserving the electric chair for him in Connecticut; George Jackson will be taken to the gas chamber in California; you will try to eliminate Angela Davis, and black people, you hope, will be scared into more and more indirect action, into serving you and keeping quiet. Your plan is ready. Even this television from which I'm speaking to you told us with disgust that Reagan popped a cork on a champagne bottle after Angela was captured.[2]

So everything is in place: your cops—who already shot a judge, the better to kill three black men—your cops, your administration, your judges are training every day, as are your scientists, to massacre more blacks.[3] Blacks, first of all. Every last one. Then the Indians who have survived. Then the Chicanos. Then the radical whites. Then, I hope, the liberal whites. Then all the whites. Then the white administration. Then yourselves. Then the world will be delivered.

What will remain after you pass: the memory, the thought, and the ideas of Angela Davis and the Black Panthers.[4]

§ 12 For George Jackson

To act as if it were a question of just anyone, to speak to you and to leave aside something which, usually, does not seem essential—I considered doing this, considered and reconsidered; but no, it is obvious that the trial of George Jackson can only be carried out in light of one fact that, without exaggerating its importance, must be stated: Jackson is black.

If this word is spoken, then, and if it is spoken in connection with America, suddenly everything becomes clear in a way. That is the heart of the problem. Jackson + Soledad means Blacks + America, wherever it happens to be. This trial has lasted for three hundred years.

∽

Before I have said anything else, you understand that there is a dizzying movement here: a man "like any other" is unable to live like any other, it is impossible for him to have behaved "like any other," he will not be judged "like any other."

We are white, and therefore masters; the black, quite naturally, is a slave.

What, then, is the nature of this vertiginous space that—in America and throughout the Christian West—separates Man (the basis of Humanism!) and the black?

It is still obvious that, as a whole, all the laws of which Man is so proud are not set up for the black. They are even set up against him.

∽

I will ask the question again: what is the nature of this space, vertiginous for one side and reassuring for the other, that—in America and throughout the Christian West—both separates and binds together Man and the black?

I will not answer this right away. Perhaps never and not at all. Black people know the answer. I will try to give a fragment of it: the University of Stony Brook is in the middle of a forest; I was going there to talk to some students. I asked David Hilliard if he wanted to come with me. His answer: there are still too many trees. If, for us, a tree is a celebration of foliage, birds, and fruit, for a black man from Alabama it is first of all the gallows on which generations of blacks have been lynched.[1]

The mental life of black people is marked by fantasms that are not ours.

You are aware of this, aren't you? Besides, you know everything about black people since you are still the masters.

~

We can be sure that Jackson and the Soledad Brothers will not be judged as Men by Men; the distance that separates them from each other is still unbridgeable.

~

You know the facts: the guard, Miller, blond hair and blond eyebrows over blue eyes, in the top of a watchtower overlooking a courtyard of Soledad Prison, shoulders his rifle, aims, shoots, kills three black prisoners and wounds one white prisoner. Miller will not be prosecuted. Like Lieutenant Calley, he is free.[2]

A few days later, a white guard, a different one, is found in a courtyard at the foot of a high wall, in his death throes, and immediately, without any proof, three blacks are charged with the murder: Jackson, Clutchette, and Drumgo.

Everything changed.

A white man kills three black men: he remains innocent.

A white man falls from a wall: three black men will be sentenced.

Without meaning to, I just formulated a sort of equation for black-white relations, in America and throughout the Christian West.

~

We know this and we understand it all: it is according to our white laws that Lieutenant Calley should be freed by the highest authority in the white world, the American executive power, and that for a black, for two, three, or a hundred blacks in pink and blue California, it's the gas chamber.

∼

There are reasons for all this. You have to think of white fright, not at the idea that they would come back colored, but at realizing (and it's very obvious) the intelligence of blacks. Perhaps they know how to read, these whites (too many universities!), and on the blacks' foreheads they have deciphered the inscription: "danger," the same one attached to high-voltage wires.

Black people's intelligence is dangerous because it is political, and Jackson's book is a political book.[3]

Bobby Seale, who has so well understood the white people's shrewdness, is dangerous.

Angela Davis, whose teaching was absorbed by countless young people, black and white, American and otherwise—is dangerous.

∼

Their intelligence, and therefore their doubts that continue to grow before the great parade of the whites: the Temples, the Universities, the Halls of Justice, the Pentagons, the Banks . . . —all these doubts are expressed in Jackson's book even as another order of certainty is affirmed.

∼

Whites, masters of the language? Masters—unhappy in any case—of definitions, when beginning with a point chosen by them and which they call the West, they divide the entire rest of the world into Near East, East, Far East.

Perhaps this was necessary to lend support to the peculiar ideas about geography they came up with in the hope of keeping the West compact.

∼

We're now asking you to speak out for the release of Jackson, of Seale, of Angela Davis, as you did, with the means at your disposal, for the Rosenbergs.[4]

At that time, you didn't have your asses glued to your armchairs. You were sharp and angry. What happened? Have you gotten old? Not really. But the Western regimes seemed like a dawning of democracy; today they are police states: in England, in France, in Spain, in Italy, in Germany, everywhere.

Of course, although they were Jewish, the Rosenbergs were white. The pope railed against Eisenhower's electric chair, the queen (or was it the king?) of England held his hand, as did the president of France, the queen of Holland and her beau, the king and queen of Sweden, too; the intelligentsia and the Jews prayed, inveighed, scolded, threatened; one-half of the Americans, minus one, cried, the other half killed, as we know.

Pope, queen, Princess Margaret, Pompidou, Juliana and her beau, Swedish king, intelligentsia, artists, students, professors, what are you going to do—not for Calley, others will take care of that—what are you going to do for Jackson, Seale, Clutchette, Drumgo, the New York 21?[5] What are you going to do, they're black?

Nothing. You will do nothing. Indeed, very little can be expected of you. Not so much because you're cowards—which you are—but because you have been unable to lessen the vertiginous space that separates Man from the black.

∿

Black people, all black people, want to live. How do you think they'll go about it if you don't do something to correct your European animality? It's simple: the blacks are going to kill you. They will have to kill you if you commit the murder of Jackson, of Seale, of Angela Davis. They will kill, without distinction, all the whites who want to kill them without distinction.

I have come to that part of my speech where, to help save the blacks, I am calling for crime, for the assassination of whites. Other meetings like this one will be held to raise money and to acquire arms to kill whites.

You don't believe me? I'm joking in bad taste? I'm rambling incoherently? I'm just an asinine old fool? But this I declare: black people will be "like you," or you will no longer be.

∿

I'll start again with another tone, a little more Victorian, if you like: no matter what it does, Europe is becoming impoverished. Jackson will explain to you that the loss of the colonies is gradually ruining England and France, which can only mean this: they were rich because they plundered nonwhite land and resources, and nonwhite men. They are plundering still, but less easily than before: you have not succeeded in forever imposing nonviolence on blacks. English imperialism was confused for a long time with the cellulite of your old sovereign lady, French imperialism was hiding behind Foucault's father, and America too has its Billy Grahams—and the blacks have understood.

You loved them very much; they don't give a damn about your love.

~

So what are you going to do, you who are still filled with evangelical love, Sinhalese tea, and whiskey? Nothing. You'll leave it up to Nixon, who will leave it up to a bunch of jackasses on the jury of Soledad, and you'll soon be sighing like that other harlot: "One more minute, Mr. Executioner."[6]

If you don't help save these blacks, they will die, and others will kill you.

§ 13   The Palestinians

[1.] Images, as we know, have a double function: to show and to conceal. These images begin with a gunman and his rifle, but why? And then after that, why so many guns? Why so many photographs showing a Palestine armed and fierce?

Two thousand years of humiliation have allowed us to understand the workings—or the mechanisms—of psychology, and how they are used at a distance. Two thousand years spent in ghettos, or under false civil states, and then the Jews were threatened with extermination. They now know the cunning of those who were their masters. Whether satanic or divine, the Catholic Church gave them some pointers on hypocrisy, evangelical blackmail, and threats. It was to be expected. The counterpart of these vexations is a knowledge of the powerful. Now two thousand years of diaspora are fulfilled and the myth of physical cowardice has been done away with. The Jews want neither to disappear nor to be "assimilated." The Jewish nation will have its territory. Where? Somewhere that can still be colonized perhaps. A search begins. First in Uganda, in Argentina, in Russia, but Herzl holds to his plan, the return to the "Promised Land."[1] And if—according to History as written by an idiot and taught to children—the Jews were driven out by the Romans, the Arabs will have to pay. Palestine, rural and populated, impoverished by the Ottoman administration, will resist the infiltrations of Jews from the world over, and, after finally being duped and dominated by the English, who were in agreement with the growing Zionist movements, it will be invaded.[2] Long before that, but especially between 1880 and 1940, in both secular and Christian Europe, anti-Semitism will go from relatively small-scale pogroms all the way to Dachau and Auschwitz. Europe massacres or threatens the Jews, while at the same time the Jews who have been spared are massacring or threatening the Arabs, with the help of English soldiers who want a secure relay point to the Middle East in order to protect the route to India. Contempt, repression, usurious purchases, confiscation of farmland. The Jews terrorize and kill the Arabs. What European could really be bothered about this? France terrorized and killed the Arabs of North Africa, the Malagasies, the Indo-Chinese, the black Africans. England did the same elsewhere. Belgium too. As did Holland in Indonesia, Germany in Togo, Italy in Ethiopia and Tripolitania, Spain in Morocco, Portugal we know where. The Zionists are guilty, and all of Europe bears the guilt of Zionism. When Europe was forced to replace colonialism, as classic as classic art, Israel managed to ease its way out of British protection and to slip, with great shrewdness, into the folds of American protection.

The Palestinians, driven from their territory, took up arms in an attempt to return. But Palestine now bears the name of Israel. The Palestinians are still alive. They will regain Palestine, but after a long detour that will oblige them to make or to provoke revolution in the entire Arab world. What he doesn't say, the fedayee—the sacrificed—whose image you see, is that he knows that he himself will not see this revolution accomplished, but that his own victory is to have begun it.[3] He may not know that his image, despite the Zionist barriers, will appear to you today. As for Israel, imagined at the end of the nineteenth century as a way perhaps to give security to Jews, it was quickly to become and to remain, in this part of Asia, the most aggressive imperialist threat of the West.

[2.] A spy? It's possible. The image violently refers us back to King Hussein of Jordan as he gives the order to destroy Amman.[4]

"There is only one statesman in history who ordered the destruction of his own capital, and that was Nero."[5]

Too beautiful, too distant, and too grand! Long after Nero, and closer to us, there was Thiers in France, whose stature and dimensions are shared by the Hashemite king. During the bloody week of August 1970 in Amman, between twelve and fifteen thousand Palestinian men and women were burned alive or incinerated.[6] The Americans took advantage of this moment of disarray on the part of the Palestinians to massively arm the Jordanian government, by means of an open airway between Cyprus and Amman. The only restriction placed on this gift was that the Jordanian army could not direct it against Israel. Hussein is a petty bourgeois defending the propertied classes of today, just as Thiers defended those of yesterday.

The State of Israel remains a "bruise," a contusion on the Muslim shoulder.[7] After the discovery and execution of Elie Cohen, every Palestinian, every Arab knows that he is threatened by Israeli espionage.[8] Palestinian information services have been organized. In the month of —— —— 1970, it was possible to find on the bases along the Jordan river a few young men with long hair joking around in Hebrew.[9] Like the other fedayeen, they were waiting for Radio Damascus to announce the end of the Ramadan fast. The only thing one could know about them was that they were *also* soldiers in the Israeli army. They are threatened from both sides of the Jordan River. With such a resemblance to an Israeli archetype, what camp did they belong to? They ate and prayed like any other Arab, and no doubt, when in Tel Aviv, like any other Jew, only to end up being burnt to a cinder?

[3.] This image too is an image of death—as much in the gazes as in the shroud—as are all the images of weapons, whether Russian, Czech, Chinese, or if they've been stolen from the Jordanian army, American, English or French. For we must be clear; the Palestinians' enemy, though it may be merged into one, has two faces: Israeli colonialism and the reactionary regimes of the Arab world. Who was this dead man in a shroud? On the bases, among the fedayeen, between each one of them and the leaders, there circulates a sort of camaraderie-in-arms, not quite socialism, rather a new kind of everyday fraternity. No brutality among the fedayeen. Whether in Golan or along the river in Jordan, a sort of untutored delicacy runs through and suffuses the bases. Between the fighters and the leaders there is an unencumbered courtesy that I have seen nowhere else among groups of men so young, and whose activities—is it the proximity of death that lends many of them a certain gravity?—would tend to make them more boisterous with each other, and more distant from their leaders. They have perhaps acquired the knowledge of a new mode of living, thanks to a more lucid point of view that has unburdened them of the virile need for affection that makes men of forty or fifty seem ridiculous. Or, if you will, they need neither the gazes of an *almah*, nor any fat black mustaches. It is possible that the presence among them of so many firearms so often used fulfills their adolescent needs. In the Middle East a new man will perhaps emerge, and the fedayee, in certain of his aspects, would be for me the prefiguration and outline of this new man.

What happened in the wooded mountains of Jerash resembled in some ways the month of May '68 in Paris, with the important difference that the fedayeen were armed. As in Paris, on certain days, there was on the bases and on the roads or paths connecting the bases an elation bordering on effusion. Freedom was there, as an almost total absence of constraints. Everyone did and said what he wanted to do and say, but with a careful delicacy such that no act and no word could wound. Once the Jordanian border posts were crossed, on the northern road out of Amman, everyone knew he was entering the land of friendship. Whoever could pass through the fedayeen post at the entrance to the forest became "more than a broth-er." In this natural trust and this restraint, there arose a light, festive atmos-phere, almost like a dream. On the bases the sharing of tea, bread, ciga-rettes might have put one in mind of a world tinged with socialism. In fact, those who were there, by a chance reprieve, were young and aware of escaping for a time, there beneath the trees, from the threats of the enemy and the orders of their leaders, but also from the rigors of combat. Talking under the stars, eating, sleeping, and smoking there meant taking part in a malicious feast,[10] malicious with regard to the Jordanian soldiers' rigidi-ty and the Israelis' obstinate activity; it even meant not giving a damn about any of it, and laughing. Today, May 27, 1971, the Jordanian army began to attack the bases.[11] Hussein's government wants to liquidate the revolution. But on the bases a new tactic is ready.

[4.] In the camps and on the military bases, the presence of a camera during a training session can be slightly intimidating to the fedayeen. Their training is real, but here, under the eye of the cameraman, a wrong move will not result in death, even though the instructor is shooting real bullets; but they repeat this crawling under the low-lying barbed wire a hundred, two hundred times, while keeping it clearly in mind that one night very soon they will have to *begin* this same crawling for the first and perhaps the last time, through barbed wire laid down by Israeli soldiers, probably through mud that has been mined: one mistake, one wrong move, will set off fire, flame, metal: death.

The Palestinian women, the ordinary women of the people, are beautiful; their beauty is a sovereign beauty. They are very independent in relation to the men. They know how to cook, sew, fire a rifle, read Mao. After the massacres at Amman, they are the ones who first came out of the ruins and out of the trauma—here as elsewhere the bourgeois women have a liberated air, vain voluble voices and fingers heavy with rings. Consider for example the female presidents of this or that organization, in Amman or in Beirut, lingering in their sitting rooms over a deck of cards they no longer even have the strength to cut. But in the ruins, squatting or standing, the women of the people, prophetic or sibylline, say how things will be—or already are—with Amman, with Hussein and his palace, with the Hashemite family. The women of the people are terrible in the sense that they speak the truth. It was they who, in the Baqa camp in February 1971, stood before the Jordanian tanks.[12] Intimidated and frightened, the royal officers pulled back. That day, the women of the people forced three rows of tanks encircling Baqa to turn back to Amman.

Karameh was a truly Palestinian victory over Israel.[13]

In February, Baqa was the site of another Palestinian victory against the Hashemites.

When one speaks here of socialism, what does this mean? No one knows yet what will become of it. Reference is made at times to China, at times to North Vietnam, and even to the Soviet Union. It will no doubt be something totally new, but in the Islamic world, women have been hidden away too long for their sudden, perhaps brutal appearance not to give them an essential role in this revolution.

[5.] When this patrol has broken out of formation and each fighter is walking out of step, the patrol will sing; that is, each one of them will improvise a melody and words that to be taken up by the others—a sort of canon, if you like—but with words arising from the imagination that plays its role in this war, and with music derived from old Arab melodies, in which the quarter tone and glottal vibrato are preserved.[14] There is humor and irony in the melody, in the words, and in the morning air. The clandestine radio stations, which broadcast military marches composed by the colonialist armies, know nothing of this joy. Already two parallel forms of music are developing among the Palestinians: one traced out according to Western models, and another that is spontaneous and new—and popular—but that has broken with formal tradition.

The complexity of the poetic act, both within and outside of a revolution, forbids me to make or to attempt an analysis of it here. Let us say that a cultural revolution is as difficult to realize as a political revolution. To speak of music again: it is obvious that the performance—before and after the daily news on the radio—of rousing and warlike music best suited to colonial military parades, is no longer relevant to a guerrilla war. The impact it will have on its listeners will be warlike only in relation to a conventional war, with its processions and parades, but not for a more supple, a more agile war. A music for sergeants, expressing not true courage but merely an idiot heroism and bravura, incites empty gestures, not effective actions. Composed by the English, French, and the American colonial armies—the same old drum-and-bugle band!—such music plunges the listener back into chauvinistic habits. Finally, the artistic mediocrity of this music should not be glorified. The drum-and-bugle band will necessarily die when the colonial armies are dead. It would be disastrous to propagate such a dubious art—I'm speaking of things like "Sambre et Meuse"—and to discourage revolutionary musical experiments.[15] It is perhaps by way of a poetic art that each person, in the midst of a project undertaken in solidarity, can safeguard an intimacy and develop a sensibility in which new forms and new values are discovered. It would be mad to think that ideas alone, the exchange of ideas and of actions in common, are enough to change the world. These are certainly necessary, but so is what each person can discover in his or her own singularity. After the reconnaissance patrol, each fedayee who invents his own score, in a traditional but fragmented way, knows this. He is creating a true musical culture—and any true musical culture is essentially popular—by singing songs that skewer, in the same thrust, both Golda Meir and King Hussein.[16]

[6.] Much has been written about guns as substitutes or extensions of the sex organ. It is impossible not to think of this when looking at this image. If you are familiar with the powerful backlash of a rifle, you might be troubled to see it resting directly on the fly of this masked and reclining fighter. But the sparkle in his eyes clues us in. Their irony shows us that it's a game, the staged pose of the warrior at rest. The fedayeen know how to play and amuse themselves. On a base close to Salt, as on the other bases, a Palestinian leader had forbidden card games. One evening some soldiers asked me to come watch a poker game. I watched the two soldiers who were playing cards: the hands spread fanwise, the distrustful gazes, the cheating, the counting off of points, I heard the swearing, the railing, I also saw the spectators absorbed in the game of the two partners, I saw their feints, their anxious worries, I heard encouragements, I saw their amazement when the players drew an ace or a king, and yet: there were no cards, they are forbidden.[17] Something similar is happening with this image. Such an abuse has been made of the masculine sex and the gun, one merging into the other, gun and sex symbolizing each other in turn, that it seems clear to me that this masked fedayee—with his non-chalance (he's smoking) and his irony, with the precision of the rifle's position—dispels any confusion, and that finally this image is very chaste. But the gun is pointed. If it went off, who would be killed? Perhaps the compartment is empty? And the apple—is it hollow?

[7.] What are the fedayeen saying, and how are they saying it? They have renounced the boasting of traditional soldiers and they rarely speak of their armed exploits. Their language has rid itself of top-heavy orna-mentation and complacent volubility. They are clear and precise. They describe facts and comment on them with rigor. With the leaders—but each one knows that he must lead—they speak evenly, as equals, and depending on the mood it may be the leader or the simple fedayee who yells more loudly. They know they are Arabs: they want to be Palestinians. Drowned for a long time in the indistinct sea of the Arab world, they lived in it without too many questions: everything changed when the Zionist threat appeared. Immediately, and only because of this threat, they realize that they are a Palestinian homeland. In 1917, the Balfour Declaration, although ambiguous, sent a shock through a population still reeling from Ottoman colonialism.[18] Once the blow had sunk in, they regained their nerve, but Islam paralyzed them. Zionism was established, with the help of the European nations, by means of terrorism—and today in Israel the terrorism of the Irgun officially bears the name of courage and sacrifice.[19]

The Palestinians, whether crushed or driven out, intended at first only to liberate a territory where their history was made. Through a play of forces that tipped them in this direction, these attempts at liberation would eventually lead them, for a while, beyond the notion of a father-land toward the notion, new to them, of a social revolution. The imme-diate enemy remains Israel, but the absolute enemy is America. And if

America is in Tel Aviv, it is also in Riyadh, Amman, and Kuwait; it is in
Tunis and Rabat; it is in the very heart of ancient Islam, just as it is in
Brazil, Colombia, Thailand, Cambodia, South Vietnam, and Europe.
This is what they are saying to each other over their tea. They speak
frankly about what is happening in Eritrea and in Dhofar. They listen to
the radio. They have learned that too much oil flows through the veins of
the Arab lords. By grasping its own singularity in such a short time, the
Palestinian people had necessarily to create a kind of void around itself,
almost imperceptible, a void between itself and the rest of the Arab world.
Within this nebula, it was a star in the process of formation. It is not difficult to arrive at this comparison of the Palestinian people with a mass of
matter in fusion, nor to see that this movement into itself isolates it, however slightly, from the great cluster of Arab dust. This comparison will
astonish no one who has lived for a while on the Palestinian bases and
camps. We can add that the majority of this people, unable to pursue a
social and political project according to the laws of geometry—since it
has no territory—was constrained, if it wanted to solidify itself, to pursue
another, revolutionary project and to give it this complex form, at once
twofold and unique: the liberation of the Palestinian territory and the
transformation of the Arab world. The official declarations from the
spokesman of the Central Committee affirm that there is no plan to top-
ple the Jordanian regime; but the methods of this regime, on the one
hand, and, on the other, the ever greater rigor of the revolutionary existence of the fighters—among whom there are also some Jordanians—
undermine the existence of the regime supported by the supposed *shu-
rafa*.[20] There are a few doctrinal differences at the higher levels of the various movements that make up the Central Committee of the Palestinian
Revolution, differences—never oppositions—that are good since,
depending on the circumstances, it is necessary to resort either to extremism or to more flexible means.[21] On the bases, there is complete harmony among the fedayeen. Nothing separates the fedayeen. On the bases,
anyone can share in almost everything.

[8.] This refugee camp exists. There are many others like it; about a million Palestinians live in them. What we don't see is the royal army—that
army of Bedouins—and the Jordanian population. Let's lay out some figures. Jordan is composed of about seventy-five million families. The number of men in the royal army, recruited from the Bedouin tribes, is about

eighty-five thousand. Which means that any one of Hussein's soldiers supports some ten people with his pay. The Bedouins know this. And if a soldier is killed, the entire tribe mourns. The royal government pays the soldiers very well. But Jordan is a poor country, with no resources or oil. Who pays the royal government? America. Likewise, America provides significant aid to Israel in the form of money, arms, and military experts. But these two countries, Jordan and Israel, are at war. The Palestinians have set up their camps, here and there, throughout much of northern Jordan. They live from very small jobs; they receive support from the UNRWA; the most educated have accepted positions in the administrations of various Arab countries.[22] Dispersed throughout the world, and especially in Anglo-Saxon countries, some are very wealthy.

The bourgeois press in Europe was very moved by the fact that young Jews the world over went to enlist in the Israeli army in 1967. Not a single paper pointed out that the same, exactly the same, phenomenon occurred within the Palestinian people. There would be no point in giving the names here of all the American university professors or others who left their positions in June 1967 to put themselves in the service of the revolution. And not only them: also doctors, lawyers, businessmen, and of course, students. They now live either in this camp, or in others, or else on military bases along the Jordan River. But if camps like this exist in Jordan, in Amman, in Jebel Amman, or in Jebel Hussein, there are also fine dwellings in cut stone inhabited by the Palestinian bourgeoisie: this is the famous bourgeoisie that calls itself apolitical but that is in fact the Palestinian Right.

[9.] It seems obvious that the liberation of Palestinian women—the women of the people—a liberation that has already taken place, will help a great deal with the liberation of women throughout the Arab world. In the camps, especially at Baqa, young girls are open rivals of the boys in school groups. The camp has about eighty-thousand inhabitants, and except for the very old, everyone can read and write. When the death of a husband or son is discovered, the wife or mother calls on a kind of simple, almost elementary theatricality. The evocation of the dead man brings with it a divine invocation, and a call to vengeance.

[10.] Don't get indignant—or do, if it makes you feel better—if the last image is one of armed Palestinian children. But in our dear old military academies, in our Prytaneums, the ten- or twelve-year-old *enfants de troupe* are trained in the handling of individual arms. An automatic weapon is a gadget that can kill. That's all. The goal of the photos in this magazine is to shed some light on who the Palestinians are—the Palestinians, and especially the fedayeen. But if you really want to understand them, there is only one way: fight with them, and fight like them.

An anti-Arab racism, almost a sickness, is so deeply entrenched in every European that one might well wonder whether the Palestinians can count on our help, however slim it might be. In France we just celebrated the seven hundredth anniversary of the death of Louis IX, called Saint Louis, with such excessive pomp that we might well be seized with a little doubt.[23] First Roland, then Saint Bernard, Godefroy de Bouillon, Guy de Lusignan, Richard the Lion-Hearted, Louis IX, and whoever else, with all their crusades against the Muslims, were so magnified during the period when the Europeans were crushing the Arab peoples—I mean between 1830 and 1962—that one might wonder, but very innocently, whether History—that of France, among others—was not written in the nineteenth century for the purpose of forming men who, in all good and bad faith, would have contempt for the colonized.

The justification of an atheist and bourgeois History that will have used the Catholic Crusades for the miserable ends of a colonialism that remains in place to this day.

This entire history—or History—is nothing but a scam that would turn us into false and distorted men.

§ 14 The Red and the Black

George Jackson's book is a murderous act, beyond all measure, but never demented, even if Jackson's sufferings and fevers drove him to the door of madness, a door he never entered; it is a radical murder, undertaken in the solitude of a cell and with the certainty of belonging to a people still living under slavery, and this murder, which is ongoing, is perpetrated not only against white America, against the American will to power, against what is called the entrepreneurial spirit; it is the systematic and concerted murder of the whole white world greedy to drape itself in the hides of nonwhite peoples; it is the—hopefully definitive—murder of stupidity in action.[1]

The assassination of the guard Mills was a lone, individual act without much revolutionary import: to avenge, no doubt, one assassination with another that was in its own way cruel and fierce.[2]

The two acts might complement each other, but they were not carried out by the same man. In both cases, a psychic energy was required such that a single man could not at one and the same time commit both the murder and this assassination. When the assassination occurred, Jackson was writing his murder (his murderous book). However strong he may be, however much a hero, more legendary than real, and representing the sudden omnipotence of the black world so feared and dreamed of—it is said—by white Americans, Jackson, who was carrying out his murder, could not have bothered with assassinating the guard. Jackson could not have passed from an unsparing analysis of the situation of blacks in America to the physical elimination of a single man. We could say that this sort of digression (assassination) within Jackson's long undertaking (murder by means of the book)—a difficult undertaking, binding body and spirit in great tension—was not possible. It would have required too long a breath—writing this book demanded time, a time that could be called infinite. Once you begin, once you want to write, there is no way to know when you will stop. All time to come is yours. It is not a question of inspiration but of a long aspiration and inhalation. Writing is a discovery that will not let itself be distracted, not even by an assassination. I would say the same of Angela: her entire life and all her teaching were made of an eternal beginning in which little games—buying a gun—have no place. She woke, she slept, in order to tell the truth. If we believe her when she states she is a member of the Communist Party (a dangerous statement in the United States), we must believe her also because her truth begins there. Clutchette and Drumgo existed entirely in revolutionary time. And it is all too clear that Jonathan Jackson, driven by misery and by the pride of being black, lived in a time, a breath, that led to this: preparing himself to become the hero-victim that he would be only through the death inflicted by the pigs of the white world.[3] Let's put it this way: the very conscious logic and reason running through Jackson's entire revolutionary and literary undertaking would be contradicted by this bloody blow (the assassination), which can only be thought of as an individual luxury. Jackson's life and work are devoid of luxury.

It is obvious that if he wrote his book—and he did write it—he was incapable of carrying out the assassination.[4]

As for his two comrades, Clutchette and Drumgo, politicized like Jackson, and perhaps by Jackson—or by the ghetto—they took part in Jackson's revolutionary undertaking. We can see Angela Davis's work and her alleged gun purchase in the same light. Angela's goals—the liberation of the black ghettos, the Marxist education of black people, the transformation of both white and black America—would be annihilated by a purchase of weapons for individual use, capable of inspiring a fleeting terror that would contradict the full scope of the project. Angela did not buy any guns.

Magee got into the van with Jonathan: his crime ends there.[5] The court may judge him, but it will also have to judge, in the very same way, the judge who did the same thing before being shot down by the police. Jonathan Jackson, George's brother, threatened the entire court; but he didn't shoot, and the police killed him.

These men and this woman I am speaking of are black, but that is not their truly inexpiable crime. Black, no doubt, but also red, and the optic nerve of the whites short-circuits, it no longer knows which image or which color to seize upon. Who are these red Negroes, these scarlet blacks? And then there's this: most of them grew up in the black ghettos where Angela joined up with them, and in his book George Jackson also tells us about that, and about his whole long struggle and the struggle of black people. Without using words that are too strong, I will say nonetheless that a rigorous respect for justice would demand that the majority of the jurors be black, whether they still live in the ghetto or not—as long as they have known at least once the insulting look of a white face. Despite the black capitalism we have heard so much about, is it really an accident that the poorest Americans are black, that it is blacks who are turned away and not whites, or that unemployment weighs down on blacks above all? Racism and class struggle are the same thing, but what incisive analysis and what actions will establish this in all its clarity?

George Jackson's name will find a place, now an obvious one, among the slave rebels that preceded him: Nat Turner, Harriet Tubman, Frederick Douglass; not to mention DuBois, E. Williams, Wright, Malcolm X, King, and all the blacks who were hung, lynched, martyred, exiled, and terrorized for the vigor of their revolt against white imbecility.[6] To these we can add Angela Davis, Jonathan Jackson, Clutchette, Drumgo, Magee, and George Jackson.

But to return to the idea of a book as murder: if I am right, given all the evil inflicted on Jackson by white America, he had to exorcise it, let it stagnate within himself, contain it, and liberate it in an act of extreme violence: the book. So much so that, by a sort of inverted reasoning, one wonders whether before being born in America certain blacks did not choose a skin color that would make them naturally enter into revolution. For the "new man" he was able to become, the book alone was important and capable of afflicting white America. And, for this same man, the assassination of a pale guard leaning over a balcony of Soledad Prison meant nothing at all. And this alleged assassination would not have taken place if, a few days earlier, the guard Miller had not committed the very real murder of three black prisoners, which it was necessary to conjure away behind an assassination, real or fictive, in the hope of halting the consequences of Jackson's murder: his book.

Except for Jackson's book, everything I have been speaking of was orchestrated, first, by the guards of Soledad, then taken up by the California police, and the whole thing will perhaps be sealed by the higher judges. Now, the fact that this set of circumstances rests on a coup orchestrated by the guards of Soledad is something the Americans know very well, and they are keeping silent about it: they have not yet found the words necessary to defend a vermilion blackness.

§ 15 After the Assassination

Recently, I mean when it still seemed possible that Jackson would live, I spoke of his book as a murder, and I did not suspect that the murderer would be taken down by the American police.[1] Jackson's assassination at the hands of the American police, from whatever level of authority it was decreed, was an orchestrated coup: whether it emanated from Reagan's meeting rooms or merely from the office of the prison guards, the target remained the same: a black man who thinks and who writes what he thinks and whose book announces and prepares a black revolution.[2]

It is false to speak of a plot in reference to what he, and Angela, and David Hilliard were doing. It was not a plot; it was rather, for Jackson, the preparation of black—and white—consciousness and a first effort to think through a popular insurrection. The whites may laugh at his naiveté; Jackson was indeed naive, or we could say novel, or new—or, dangerous.[3] The whites, awkward as they are, killed him. They did not increase his stature; with his death they have given him his exact proportions, which, however, are incalculable—too vast.

There were never, there are not, and there never will be any victims. If Jackson is responsible for his revolutionary actions, for his book and for his death, the American police are responsible in the same way for the assassination of Jackson. Black Americans are responsible, and not victims, when they agree to go to war in Vietnam, in Santo Domingo, or in Bolivia for what white Americans call the greatness of America. They are responsible when they accept even the smallest parcel of benefits from the imperialism that grows rich off the hides of devastated peoples. Europe too is a part of this vampirism. There is only one way to prove one's freedom for an ever greater freedom: to enter into revolution like the two Jackson brothers, like the Soledad Brothers, the Black Panthers, Angela Davis, all oppressed peoples, like every man and every woman who refuses to enslave and to be enslaved.

To return to Jackson's assassination, and to the imbecilic and transparent fable put forth by the warden of San Quentin, I will say that the only way to refuse the goals of the white administration is to combat it head on, or to betray it.

Jonathan and George Jackson, Angela Davis, the Black Panthers, the revolutionary movements both black and white, have raised to their highest degree either betrayal or unmasked struggle—and therefore the consciousness of being responsible.

The word *struggle* is reassuring, that of *betrayal* causes the mind to recoil; this is because feudal morality condemned it, and this condemnation still weighs on us because we have not yet rid ourselves of this mentality. In order to be what is called chivalrous—still a prestigious word—we end up remaining faithful to people or to institutions who demand from us the worst kinds of abjection. Any black who enters a white administration—police, army, any branch of organized repression—in order to serve it rather than to betray it, has understood nothing of Jackson's teaching. Such a person is, or wants to be, American before all else. He remains black, since his color is indelible, but he wants to be white, and supposedly superior—to nonwhites. He succeeds only in being a zombie, since, as things now stand, for a white man a black man is not really a man. Or not entirely. But George and Jonathan Jackson were.

We do not really know whether the Rosenbergs betrayed or not—if they did, their betrayal was noble, even in the medieval sense of the word.

It is quite obvious that I would not write this if the global revolution had taken place: certain words must now be used again, and others will disappear, making a new language necessary.

One can only agree—even applaud—when men and women refuse to be subservient, in whatever way, to the greater or lesser benefits of the capitalist organizations. It is a somber occasion when a revolutionary is killed; it is a joyous occasion when a revolutionary has scoffed at the power wielded through money, domination, the name on everyone's lips, and, for a few years now, the proliferating portrait.

What is prison? It is immobility. "Free man, you will always cherish the sea!" (Baudelaire). It is becoming more and more obvious that mobility is one of the signs of our times. To restrict a man for eleven years to surveying the same four or five square meters—which in the end become several thousand meters within the same four walls opened up by the imagination—would justify a young man if he wanted to go . . . where, for example? To China perhaps, and perhaps on foot. Jackson was this man and this imagination, and the space he traversed was quite real, a space from which he brought back observations and conclusions that strike a death blow to white America (by "America" I mean Europe too, and the world that strips all the rest, reduces it to the status of a disrespected labor force—yesterday's colonies, today's neocolonies). Jackson said this. He said it several thousand times and throughout the entire world. It still remained for him to say truths unbearable for our consciences. The better to silence him, the California police. . . . But what am I saying? Jackson's book goes far beyond the reach of this police since it is read, praised, commented, and continued by nine-year-old blacks.

It is possible that the white society founded on the dollar, and on the infernal labor of "underdeveloped" countries necessary for this foundation, will be succeeded by another society, modeled on the first, in which forced labor becomes the only virtue. We await yet another society in which free, almost ludic labor becomes the only acceptable reality. Although it may be difficult for me to say here how the world will be changed, you can believe that we are *working toward it*. We will neglect nothing. It may trouble us that we dominate the blacks less and less, but the fact is they don't accept it anymore. They count on their own strength, not to dominate us but to look us straight in the eye. They are also changing the language, which will no longer obey the definitions of the masters. We speak but say nothing. The only question that two men who meet each other can ask is this: "Do you know anything new, or precise, about God? And if so let's see some proof." This question is impossible, since God doesn't exist, and when we speak truly we have one expression, a level phrase on level ground: no one knows any more about it than anyone else. Jackson, with so little room, taught us that all anecdotal knowledge can be reduced to this phrase that is both flat and vain, but also important, marking as it does our limit *in common*. No one surpasses anyone else, nor can he.

What became of Jackson's body in his cell? Neither more nor less than any other in that space. And yet elsewhere two beings have the need and the possibility of joining together. He knew Fay Stender, but in chains.[4] He knew Huey Newton, through written or scribbled messages, through lawyers or other prisoners.[5] He knew Angela, from afar, and from ever farther away. With a light shining on him day and night, spied on by a guard, he knew only his body. It is perhaps from this ten years of abstinence that he wrested his book. Here too a close study would be necessary. But is it true that in order to be punished [*châtié*], a man must be castrated [*châtré*]? Punishment (for what?) is thus no longer merely the absence of freedom.

A few hours after Jackson's death, I had this half-waking dream: nine months apart, or thereabouts, Jonathan and George violently came out of prison, a stony womb, on waves of blood. This expulsion was like the delivery of twins confounded in their identical age. It was not their mother who gave birth to them that night, for she was there, upright, impassive but alert, looking on. If it was a new birth, at once into life and into death, who but History was delivering the two black men covered, as with every birth, in blood.

Why do the name and the image of Mao Tse-Tung suddenly come to me? This name and this image are perhaps the collective gathering of all names, of all thoughts, of all the images that merge together or are absorbed into a single name, a single image: to seek anonymity, even for the man who bears the name of Mao. George and Jonathan, two black Gemini, are not the modern version of the mythology that rose from the abyss or descended from heaven. They simply remind us that we must carry out a human labor directed against the dense and sparkling mythology of the white world.

We must also look closely at David Hilliard (in prison for eight years), at Angela Davis, accused of conspiracy and attempted murder, and at all the imprisoned blacks—whether in jail or in the ghetto—who are in danger at every moment of being assassinated like George and Jonathan Jackson, or of being wasted away by the white world. In fact, we must learn to betray the whites that we are.

§ 16 America Is Afraid

The blacks whom the Americans can neither understand nor buy—these they kill.

It is time now to ask to what extent a man belongs to a country in which, all things considered, he was born by chance. George Jackson was one of ours. If he fell within any jurisdiction, it was that of all young people of every country, and of the men of every country crushed by America: Reagan's police planned an attempt on George Jackson's life, and they shot him down. He is dead, together with two other prisoners whose names the teletype machines are not telling us. A Soledad brother, a revolutionary writer (and what a writer!), Jackson was not afraid of the trial being prepared against him by the San Francisco judges. He had no desire to escape. The American police orchestrated this affair, just as the OAS and the paratroopers used the *corvée de bois* (timber duty) against the Arabs.[1] If you look at them a little more closely, it becomes clear that police tactics are more or less the same everywhere. So the question arises: is there not an international police force tightening itself around the globe like a blue net (or an azure one overseas [*outremer*]—written like "beyond the grave" [*outre-tombe*])?

Whose compatriot, then—to go back to this question—was George Jackson if not ours, we who read, loved, and admired his book, and the people—I mean entire peoples, immense countries of men—for whom, from the depths of Soledad Prison, he wrote his book?

The failure of the Vietnam War, the devaluation of the dollar, the suspicion directed against white America and its moral standing in the world—these are things that can only make the ghettos laugh. Many premonitory signs show that America is afraid; within its borders, it is especially afraid of black people, afraid that they are becoming more and more intelligent. It had Malcolm X killed, it killed Martin Luther King. Last year, the guard Miller, in a kind of game, shot down three black prisoners in the high-security section of Soledad Prison. It killed eight black students in Georgia, it imprisoned and gagged Bobby Seale during a trial in Chicago, it condemned Huey Newton, and it has Angela in its clutches in the San Rafael Prison.[2] But the premeditated assassination of George Jackson is the sign, this time very visible, that America is afraid and that its power is being inexorably extinguished. America is losing its nerve. California does not even have the time to put on a decent face. The death of George Jackson means that blacks, Chicanos, and radicals will raise their voices more than ever.

Jackson was one of ours, like the Black Panthers and the revolutionaries in America. We must take up where his actions left off, and draw inspiration from his book. We must be ready for anything. While I was writing this, the warden of the San Francisco prison repeated his version unaltered: Jackson, armed (but how and by whom?), tried to escape. . . . But he does not say that Jackson had been in prison for eleven years for being an accomplice in a theft of seventy dollars.

During these eleven years, Jackson learned to write and to think—and for that the American police shot him down.

§ 17 Preface to *L'Assassinat de Georges Jackson*

It has become more and more rare in Europe for a man to accept being killed for the ideas he defends. Black people in America do it every day. For them, "liberty or death" is not a clichéd slogan. When they join the Black Panther Party, black people know they will be killed or will die in prison. I shall speak of a man who is now famous, George Jackson; but if the quake his death set off in us has not ceased, we ought also to know that every day young anonymous blacks are struck down in the streets by the police or by whites, while others are tortured in American prisons. Dead, they will survive among us—which isn't much—but they will live among the peoples who have been crushed by the white world, thanks to the resounding voice of George Jackson.

Unlike the Americans who, from of a lack of ideas, victoriously set out to fight in Vietnam only to return broken men, many blacks, already broken, move in the opposite direction, entering into prison or into death only to reemerge victorious. Out of the multiple slaughter of blacks—from Soledad Prison to Attica[1]—George Jackson, assassinated by elite sharpshooters—that is, gunmen for the elite[2]—rises up, shakes himself off, and is now illustrious, that is, luminous, the bearer of a light so intense that it shines on him and on all black Americans.

Who was George Jackson? An eighteen-year-old black man imprisoned for eleven years for being an accomplice in a theft of seventy dollars. A magnificent writer, one of the greatest black writers, the author of widely dispersed letters which, when brought together, make up a revolutionary book. A brother to his brother, Jonathan Jackson, who at seventeen years old entered a courtroom in San Rafael, freeing three blacks and taking one hostage: the presiding judge. Finally, a resolute, that is conscious, martyr, assassinated on August 21 in the courtyard—or in a cell—of San Quentin Prison, on the eve of his trial.

"An eighteen-year-old black man imprisoned for eleven years for being the accomplice in a theft." George was given this strange sentence: one year to life. It's an odd statement. It means that Jackson was sentenced to one year of prison, but that at the end of this year he would have to appear before a parole board which decides whether he will be released or retained. The parole board retained him eleven times in eleven years. It is obvious that the guards of Soledad saw in him, almost every day, and almost at every moment, the force of an independence and a pride intolerable to whites, a pride that they call arrogance because it comes from a black man. Finally, in solitude, with the help of his lawyer, Fay Stender, and with the help of Huey P. Newton, a leader in the Black Panther Party with whom he was in contact, Jackson very quickly became politicized: too quickly and too much so, for the guards of Soledad laid an ambush for him. On January 13, 1970, Miller—another sharpshooter—standing atop a watchtower, shoulders his rifle, aims, fires, nicks a white prisoner but kills three blacks who were fighting. Miller is not prosecuted, neither for murder nor for manslaughter. Three days later, in another section of Soledad, the guard John Mills is found almost dead at the foot of a high wall, having fallen from the third floor. George Jackson—along with two other black prisoners—is charged with murder. All three are transferred to a California state prison in San Francisco.

"The author of a revolutionary book." It is difficult to know whether Jackson and his book would have been possible without the creation of the Black Panther Party, or whether the BPP would have been possible without Malcolm X, or whether Malcolm himself would have been possible without the rebel slaves: Nat Turner, Harriet Tubman, Frederick Douglass. Without going into any detail here, it is necessary to invoke their names and their dedication, their achievements.

As for the style of the letters, Jackson brings a new tone into black literature: he does not refer to the Old Testament. He does not quote from the Prophets or the Apostles. He goes straight into sarcasm:

> "If there were a god or anyone else reading some of my thoughts I would be uncomfortable in the extreme" [152].[3]

"So, if they would reach me now, across my many barricades, it must be with a bullet and it must be final" [153].

"I hope I have trained all of the slave out of me" [154–55].

"Right here in Soledad, a white (nameless and faceless now) stabbed a brother with my surname. . . . In an honest case of mistaken identity, the Mexicans were supposed to be out to get me for it" [162].

"So most of these inmates are sick, my friend, but who created the monster in them?" [163].

"United States prisons are the last refuge of the brainless. If the inmates are failures, at least they were reaching . . . " [163].

"But the restraints come off when they [the guards] walk through the compound gates.[4] Their whole posture goes through a total metamorphosis. Inflict pain, satisfy the power complex, get a check" [164].

"This is one nigger who is positively displeased. I'll never forgive, I'll never forget, and if I'm guilty of anything at all it's of not leaning on them hard enough. War without terms" [165].

"How do you deal with the perverted, disease-bearing, voracious bastard who wants to cast his image over all things, eat from every plate at every table, police the world with racist shibboleths and a dying doctrine of marketplaces peopled by monopolies, top-heavy bureaus, and scum-swilling pigs to gun down any who would object?" [165].

"People's war, class struggle, war of liberation means *armed* struggle. Men like Hoover, Reagan, Hunt, Agnew, Johnson, Helms, Westmoreland, Abrams, Campbell, Carswell, are dangerous men who believe that they are the rightful führers of all the world's people.[5] They must be dealt with now. Can men like these be converted? Will they allow anyone to maneuver them out of their positions of power while they still live? Would Nixon accept a people's government, a people's economy?" [169].

"The thing that fixes me best is how the revolution is gauged to operate on the family plan, children with a role, women in the same roles as men, education standardized" [170].

"The family, the nuns, the pigs, I resisted them all. I know my mother likes to tell everyone that I was a good boy, but that isn't true. I've been a brigand all my life. It was these years in prison with the time and the opportunity available to me for research and thought that motivated a desire to remold my character. I think that if I had been on the street from age eighteen to twenty-four, I would probably be a dope fiend or a small-stakes gambler, or a hump in the ground. ['They' don't know it and certainly didn't foresee it, but they're responsible for my present attitude.]" [172–73].[6]

"Down here we hear relaxed, matter-of-fact conversations centering around how best to kill all the nation's niggers and in what order. It's not the fact that they consider killing me that upsets. They've been 'killing all the niggers' for nearly half a millennium now, but I am still alive. I might be the most resilient dead man in the universe. The upsetting thing is that they never take into consideration the fact that I am going to resist. Do they honestly believe that shit?" [174].

"The fascists, it seems, have a standard M.O. for dealing with the lower classes.[7] Actually, oppressive power throughout history has used it. They turn a man against himself—think of all the innocent things that make us feel good, but that make some of us also feel guilty.[8] Consider the con going through the courts on a capital offense who supports capital punishment. I swear I heard something just like that today.[9] After the Civil War, the form of slavery changed from chattel to economic slavery, and we were thrown onto the labor market to compete at a disadvantage with poor whites. Ever since that time, our principal enemy must be isolated and identified as capitalism. The slaver was and is the factory owner, the businessman of capitalist Amerika, the man responsible for employment, wages, prices, control of the nation's institutions and culture. It was the capitalist infrastructure of Europe and the U.S. which was responsible for the rape of Africa and Asia. Capitalism murdered those thirty million in the Congo. Believe me, the European and Anglo-Amerikan capitalist would never have wasted the ball and powder were it not for the profit principle. The men, all the men who went into Africa and Asia, the fleas who climbed on that elephant's back with rape on their minds, richly deserve all that they are called. Every one of them deserved to die for their crimes. So do the ones who are still in Vietnam, Angola, Union of South Africa (U.S.A.!!). But we must not allow the emotional aspects of these issues, the scum at the surface, to obstruct our view of the big picture, the whole rotten hunk. It was capitalism that armed the ships, free enterprise that launched them, private ownership of property that fed the troops. Imperialism took up where the slave trade left off. It wasn't until after the slave trade ended that Amerika, England, France, and the Netherlands invaded and settled in on Afro-Asian soil in earnest. As the European industrial revolution took hold, new economic attractions replaced the older ones; chattel slavery was replaced by neoslavery. Capitalism, 'free' enterprise, private ownership of public property armed and launched the ships and fed the troops; it should be clear that it was the profit motive that kept them there.

"It was the profit motive that built the tenement house and the city project. Profit and loss prevents repairs and maintenance. Free enterprise brought the monopolistic chain store into the neighborhood. The concept of private ownership of facilities that the people need to exist brought the legions of hip-shooting, brainless pigs down upon our heads, our homes, our streets. They're there to protect the entrepreneur!! His chain store, and his property that you are renting, his bank.

"If the entrepreneur decides that he no longer wants to sell you food, let's say, because the Yankee dollar that we value so dearly has suddenly lost its last thirty cents of purchasing power, private ownership means that the only way many of the people will eat is to break the law.[10]

"Black capitalism, black against itself. The silliest contradiction in a long train of spineless, mindless contradictions. Another painless, ultimate remedy: be a better fascist than the fascist. ["Sylvester Brown is ready to die, or to see our sons die, for the sake of a street sweeper's contract."][11] Bill Cosby, acting out the establishment agent—what message was this soul brother conveying to our children?[12] This running dog in the company of a fascist with a cause, a flunky's flunky, was transmitting the credo of the slave to our youth, the mod version of the old house nigger. We can never learn to trust as long as we have them. They are as much a part of the repression, more even than the real live rat-informer-pig. Aren't they telling our kids that it is romantic to be a running dog? The kids are so hungry to see the black male do some shooting and throw some hands that they can't help themselves from identifying with the quislings.[13] So first they turn us against ourselves, precluding all possibility of trust, then fascism takes any latent divisible forces and develops them into divisions in fact: racism, nationalism, religions" [175–77].

"I was born with terminal cancer, a suppurating, malignant sore that attacked me in the region just behind the eyes and moves outward to destroy my peace.

"It has robbed me of these twenty-eight years. It has robbed us all for nearly half a millennium. The greatest bandit of all time, you'll stop him now" [186].

"Black Mama, you're going to have to stop making cowards: 'Be a good *boy*'; 'You're going to worry me to death, *boy*'; 'Don't trust those niggers'; 'Stop letting those bad niggers lead you around, *boy*'; 'Make you a dollar, *boy*.' Black Mama, your overriding concern with the survival of our sons is mistaken if it is survival at the cost of their manhood" [189].

"A brother to his brother Jonathan." The affection that bound George to Jonathan was, for the former, woven from many long hours of solitude. George had left behind a seven-year-old brother, a child in whom he took a constant interest, but a great distance separated the house where Jonathan lived from George's cell. One may wonder whether George real-

ly knew who his brother was, but he grew close to Jonathan very quickly when he found out that he had become a friend of Angela Davis, and then almost completely melded with him when he learned of the incredible act he had carried out: the truly heroic attempt to rescue three black comrades from a San Rafael courtroom on August 7, 1970.

I think that we must not deny this sort of magnificence of reverie and of action to revolutionaries, when it becomes necessary for them, especially when the action ought to become exemplary, that is, when it serves to reveal with spectacular brilliance the meaning of a life devoted entirely to opposing a false fatality.

"All right, gentlemen, I'm taking over now." These words were spoken by Jonathan in the San Rafael courtroom, and George, while leaving them to Jonathan, seems to make them his own.[14] It was not a question of identifying with Jonathan, on the contrary: if Jonathan's admiration for George pushed him to imitate him, with Jonathan dead, and dying in freedom—in a "revolutionary suicide," to use Newton's expression—George in turn admired Jonathan to the point, it seems, of wanting to imitate him as well. Perhaps then we can see the tightly knit admiration binding Georgia Jackson's two sons, as they helped each other become a defining moment of black consciousness and revolution.

One year apart, history gave birth, covered with the blood of two black Gemini.

"A resolute martyr, assassinated by whites." The penal authorities at San Quentin have not yet allowed anyone to learn the details of the real death—I mean the one that happens when the heart stops and the temperature goes down, that moment when a man becomes a corpse—of Jackson's real death. In his book, in his letters, in conversations, he had announced it, one might almost say he foresaw it, so great was the guards' hatred for him, and so powerful, "born within me from the blows inflicted by this society of haves and have-nots, this flame that will not go out"; when the warden of San Quentin speaks of escape, this does not square with the "logic of life."[15]

It is difficult to believe that, so soon before his trial, resolved to use it for the purposes of a political forum in which he could, in turn, judge America, Jackson would have planned an escape attempt that had so little chance of success—we know, for example, that Clutchette and Drumgo, who were also accused, refused to leave their cells, as did Magee—but his attitude might make sense if, caught in a plot hatched against him—whether in Reagan's consulting rooms or somewhere closer, in the prison warden's offices—Jackson saw that he was surrounded, and, perhaps with a revolver in hand, decided not to bet all or nothing, as the papers wrote, but to rush into the courtyard where he knew he would be shot down by the "sharpshooters" (them again) perched atop two watchtowers. Thus, like Jonathan—but trapped—he freely decided on a death in the light of day, a sacrifice, or better, a "revolutionary suicide."

These few notes fall far short of capturing or depicting Jackson, who continued on for weeks beyond his death, from the uprising in Attica to the one in Baltimore, and yesterday, Tuesday, September 22, another in New Orleans.

The goal of Jackson's book, *Soledad Brother*, and of the one that will soon appear, is not to speak only of Jackson but of all the anonymous blacks trapped in prison and in the ghetto.[16] Let us keep this in mind: the word *criminal*, applied to blacks by whites, has no meaning. For whites, all blacks are criminals because they are black, which amounts to saying: in a white society, no black can be a criminal.

§ 18 Meeting the Guarani

How great an effect will this elegant spectacle have on a disoriented age that refuses internal order and logic, and in one of the most disordered places in the world? While they may not bring anything very ancient into the world, the Guarani Indians teach us once again a lesson too often forgotten: to be effective, that is, to move souls deeply, a performance must be a rite carried out in obedience to a harsh injunction, deriving its laws from its relation to what it claims to express, in this case the grief of a race.[1]

To put it simply: the Guarani sing and dance and tears fill my eyes. Perhaps these tears are brought on by the great sadness of their singing—even their most joyous song is despairing—which tells of slavery, or rather of the origin out of which the misery of a race slowly seeps, and by the desolate mode of their slow dances, in which they curve their heavy spines as though drawn incessantly toward a sterile but consoling earth whose call and terrible attraction is inexorably felt. I have heard sadder songs than these, and have remained as unmoved as a statue. What is happening here? The exceptional quality of the Guarani comes from the fact that they call on us to reflect, not on them but on the exigencies of poetry, whose essential themes are love and death. Our Western actors (we even call them our artists!), even the most talented, succeed in moving us when, by a happy stroke—by chance—they re-create for us an anecdote utilizing one of these themes, or both. Our emotion then has something constricted about it. . . . The song—or dance, or drama—touch on a particular moment in our personal history.

What therefore seems significant to me is that the Guarani do not speak of themselves. Nor of their people; the people—and they believe in their artists!—the people speaks. Not of itself, and not in a confused way; on the contrary, it expresses itself by means of a grave, almost liturgical ensemble. The word I am most inclined to write is the word *mass*. The Guarani neither play nor sing: they recite an office. Any Indian who came down from the Andes, it seems, would be able to move us just as nobly. They show us that any man can dance and sing if he puts himself into the service of a faith and of a rule equally as demanding, without worrying about the beauty of his voice or the purity of his gestures. But if a rule is drawn so dearly from this faith, what faith are we talking about? The Indian transmits to us, alas, the deepest and perhaps the only truth of South America: destitution. They tell us again—and in what tones!—what is essentially poetic: the love and death of a battered, annihilated people, or, if you wish, the variants of love and death: its despair, its suffering, and its tenderness. Their gestures are directed toward the ground, but this people knows the sky because they sing and dance.

Is joy then possible? But this joy, shy as it is, falls away as soon as it is born. Even the play of scarves, rather than bringing a lightness into the spectacle, gives it the desolate air of departure, farewell, and mourning. As if their hands were still too heavy, too earthly, these nostalgic shadows greet each other from a distance with a simple handkerchief. Haughty, sad, ornate, with no overplayed virility, the men are the most visible, and yet their entire procession is in honor of the woman—a light phantom and a pretext for adoration, the almost invisible center of this dark and solemn gravitation of stars. What else to say about what saddens and moves me? Amid the sometimes Andalusian echoes, and through the language of the conquerors and the masters, the disquieted Indians address signs of hidden tenderness to each other, as though out of a discreet sense of shame.[2]

We don't dare applaud for you. We would like to observe in ourselves and for a long time the continuation of your sorrowful tones. You are the Guarani Indians, and you have shown us the ridiculous and insufferable triviality of our bellowing singers, our silly repetitive tunes, our melodramatic hams.

§ 19 On Two or Three Books
No One Has Ever Talked About

Tahar Ben Jelloun, Ahmed, Nabile Farès, Khaïr-Eddine are being forgotten.[1] Everything remains quiet after these voices, and others, have spoken. One of them has no body,[2] it is a naked voice speaking only of its misery in order to tell the misery of its brothers, the immigrant workers, and to speak of the causes of immigration into Europe and into France especially, of the hope they would find in Europe perhaps, and in France especially.

These voices burn with phrases almost torn to shreds: if the intellectuals refuse to hear them, I ask the workers to listen. Ahmed and Tahar Ben Jelloun shout to us the great misery of the poor, from here and elsewhere; their physical misery as workers, the misery of all workers; their material misery as men who are used and who are thrown away when they're used up; their intellectual misery as men who are disoriented by the ferocity of a French language still designed to transmit the hardness of the masters and *their* misery; and, for the first time, their sexual misery as men devoured from within by themselves—and their lacerating voices have been drowned in a heavy wave of silence.

No one says to them, "You will not speak," but no resonance carries these voices, no echo brings them back. What these voices say is that it is perhaps possible to steal a little pleasure in a brief embrace, flaring quickly and soon extinguished, in the most narrow space, but they also say this: that luxury, money, time, space, all that the rich possess in abundance, and which in fact they resell for abundant profits, the impoverished also have a right to all this. These voices also say that everything happens here as if the formerly colonized were still a part of the exotic scenery: the Arab woman hard at work or the black man walking along the path take their place within the restful scenery upon which the rich man gazes from his window. For the rich man is never the scenery itself, or in the scenery. He may present himself as a spectacle to be seen, but he refuses to suffer the suspicious gazes of the oppressed. In fact, as these voices tell us, speaking to us of none other than ourselves, the exploited observe the master ever more closely, ever more attentively.

These voices also say things that a certain press refuses to readers who don't want to be overly disturbed. The Third World, whether here or there, is annoying. For Europe, whatever happens there takes the form of a serial novel; the Third World, in a sterilized form, will therefore remain good company for this press. At best it will be pinned and displayed like a strange butterfly, a rather gray one. But no one except the immigrants who speak and write about it, like Tahar Ben Jelloun and Ahmed, will say this:

"Why not shake up the spaces of the rich, and their time, their leisure time?"

"I want," says an Arab mason, "to build myself a beautiful bourgeois house with an unobstructed view of myself. I'll watch myself work, get sick, rest from exhaustion. But where will the rich man be? What kind of scenery will he become? For now, while I wait, I'm a poorly dressed Arab, I'm with a black man whose attitude is a little too casual, and if we go to a nice neighborhood the police are already there waiting for us."

I must therefore speak, and I will speak again of these voices, more lucid than plaintive, since our intellectuals, those whom we still stupidly call our master thinkers, are nowhere to be seen, those we thought were the best are silent; one of the most generous, Jean-Paul Sartre, seems to have gone bankrupt and to be complacent in his bankruptcy. He does not dare to pronounce a word or name that might help these voices of Tahar Ben Jelloun and Ahmed. And yet he commented so admirably on Frantz Fanon's book.[3] He seems to refuse to say words that are not merely appeasing but that bring real help. He refuses to speak of them, as if he were afraid—for heaven's sake!—of having dirty hands![4] But Sartre is no longer the master thinker of anyone except a very picturesque band that has already disbanded.[5]

Obviously, the intellectuals also have a role in such a situation, but by refusing to shout with the oppressed they are howling with the wolves. But since no echo, no resonance comes from them that would carry these voices and make them heard by those who have almost the same life, the same miseries, one must speak directly to the public: Sartre doesn't matter anymore. Let him and the other aesthetes of silence keep quiet: we'll do without them. The books I am speaking of—and this time I will mention them by name: *Harrounda* by Tahar Ben Jelloun, *Une Vie d'Algérien* [Life of an Algerian] by Ahmed, *Le Cheval dans la ville* [The city horse] by Pélégri, *Le Champ des oliviers* [The olive grove] by Nabile Farès—these are books that you will read in order to know the poverty of immigrants, their solitude, and their miseries that are also our own.

Appendix[6]

That was what, having censored myself, I said yesterday on the radio. I will add that, with very few exceptions, the intellectuals show hardly any concern for immigrants. Provoked especially by the looting of natural resources in Third World countries, by the impoverishment of the land and its minerals, by the wastefulness of the colonial and neocolonial system, immigration is now nothing but the recruitment, for France and the rest of Europe, of an underpaid labor force that has almost no hope of surviving.

Only the Left, by carrying out the Common Program can practice a politics that will satisfy immigrant workers.[7] I will cite here a few statements from the Statute on Immigrants, presented by the French Communist Party:

"The constraints imposed on freedoms and the rights of immigrant workers to participate in unions, and the pressures exerted on them by administrators and employers, weaken the possibilities of union and political action for the entire working class. By struggling together, Frenchman and immigrants alike, to ensure the same union and political rights in the workplace and the possibility for everyone to be eligible for union elections, they will create the common means for strengthening all union actions and demands, and for dealing most effectively with employers and the government.

"Low salaries and social discrimination imposed on immigrants are an attack on all the salaries and social advantages of the entire working class. . . .

"Illiteracy and underqualification among immigrants are weapons in the hands of the employers who want to impose accelerated production rates and undermine working conditions" (André Vieuguet, member of the Central Committee).

Despite the intellectuals—including the work of a few "sociologists" or "ethnographers," which is nothing but silence condensed—this silence has finally been broken by the French and European Left. At least on this level, a call to the "WORKERS OF THE WORLD . . . " has been revived in another mode. Here too, only the united Left was able to do this.

How could the Right represent any hope for immigrants, and why would it protect them otherwise than the slave owner who preserves the health and strength of the slave so as to wring from him an ever greater return? The Right believes that it will have inexhaustible reserves of labor power at its disposal for a long time to come; why would it defend the *rights* of immigrants, since the mythologies—whose purpose is to mask the only true ideology of the Right, that of capital—since these mythologies (Maurrassian, Pétainist, Giscardian, and others) are secreted and elaborated by the extreme Right?[8] It is still a daily occurrence to hear a man of the Right speak of a "darky," that is when he doesn't say "dirty nigger." By what trick (for it would have to be a trick) would the old far Right chauvinism bring itself to propose or to grant rights to "darkies"? Why would it even worry about this at all? The proof of these statements is provided by Giscard d'Estaing, whose security service is recruited largely by henchmen of the now defunct Ordre nouveau and Occident groups.[9] This speaks for itself.

It is deplorable that one of the most generous of all French intellectuals did not consider the concerns of immigrants and recommend to them, at the beginning of such a close race, to vote in every round for the only real candidate of the Left: François Mitterrand.[10] This magisterial "oblivion" on the part of Sartre and other intellectuals who blindly follow him will therefore be remedied by the immigrants themselves, and by the French workers as a whole.

§ 20 When "the Worst Is Always Certain"[1]

At the Democratic Convention in Chicago in August 1968, when Hubert H. Humphrey's nomination was announced, the enthusiasm of the American liberals—that sort of misty, Bavarian, psychedelic delirium—was so unbearable that I got up to leave.[2] Allen Ginsberg had on his angelic smile.[3] He asked me why I was leaving. I answered that I couldn't take it any more. He smiled with an even greater finesse, and said to me: "Personally, I'm very happy. It's so hideous that it will all disappear in no time." Since then, the radicals have grown older without making many waves, the campuses have fallen silent, the Black Panthers and Black Power have lost their fire, as have the Young Lords and the Weathermen, and the police patrol the ghettos.[4] The worst is happening: silence and immobility. Watergate is only the most visible part of a struggle between two great rivals.

The far Left in America was wrong to believe that the worst would eventually turn in its favor.

Here, when Giscard is elected, he will be in office for fourteen years.[5] The Right will be in power, but it will be the far Right and its imbecilic mythology, and this time it will be totally in power.

The treacherous claims that, for two weeks now, certain leaders of the Left have launched against Mitterrand before an unsuspecting public watching the usual foolishness on television—this treachery, which gave no warnings, is in danger of creating long-term effects, leaving scars on all the viewers and provoking a fear of socialism however it may be defined. This sort of spontaneism, which resulted in only 3 percent of the vote for the far Left, will have accomplished nothing else.[6] The "new political force," as *Libération* writes, will be even more dispersed when Giscard is elected. It will have shined brightly during one brief election evening. In seven years, in fourteen years, the Right will provoke another force, just as vigorous and naive, and in fourteen years Arlette will have 0.70 percent of the votes.[7] And what will happen to the workers during these seven or rather fourteen years? They will have grown fourteen years older under Giscard, and it will be under him that they will die.

It's obvious that the 44 percent that went in the first round to the only viable candidate of the Left consisted of men and women who are lucid and capable of understanding their choices. The act of casting doubt on this choice and of insulting Mitterrand would call for a harsher, a much harsher word than *irresponsible*.

The political error, if it is not repaired in the second round, would also deserve another word besides *blunder*.

On May 5, the Right was afraid. It will live with this fear for the next two weeks: the Right, when in power, will make us pay dearly for this retrospective fear. There will be new antiriot laws.[8] The coalition of the Right, shaken for a moment during the electoral campaign, will consolidate again. There will be no cracks for the Left to slip through. We saw the whole array of unsavory characters on television: Lecanuet, Fontanet, Poniatowski, Peyrefitte, Sanguinetti, Chirac, I forget the rest.[9] They will break the far Left not because it is violent but because sometimes it has a few ideas. They will be merciless. What sends shivers down my spine is not so much their brutality as their stupidity, which you can cut with a knife. The multinational capital in whose service they work will remain, like last night, invisible.

Let's admit—we can admit this—that we may well refuse to give Mitterrand our absolute trust, but we must refuse absolutely to give even a relative trust to Giscard. The idea that a sort of far Left vigilance should be exercised over Mitterrand is acceptable, and, I believe, is accepted by him. If he is in power any fighting with him will be stimulating and frank. Against Giscard it will not even take place. No breach will be tolerated in the totalitarianism of the "new majority." The far Left, which knew so well how to dismantle the mechanism and the imposture of the employers and the professors in May '68, now has two weeks left to dismantle this hoax: Giscard's "intelligence." They know what these shams from the École

Polytechnique are hiding, and they have to say so, but let them beware: Giscard's deep triviality may allow him to discover ruses that will delight the bourgeoisie and cripple the arguments of the far Left. We must never forget: the Right is trivial. It needs false fronts, starch, gold plating, glossy paint, as Chaban-Delmas has said, and he knows of whom he speaks.[10] All this show has no other purpose than to conceal the vulgarity of the means at their disposal. Never does the Right use a direct and simple word. If one of its great ruses is the dressing up, masking, and weighing of words and thoughts, the far Left has reason to quake. I have contempt for Giscard; but I do not underestimate his means, nor his resources.

Let us also be wary of anyone who proclaims, "Giscard, Chaban, Mitterrand, they're all the same."[11] An election is not contained entirely in one brief action: it is an ongoing and daily process. The man and the woman who cast their ballot with the name of Mitterrand will not be the same as those who cast one with the name of Giscard. When the voters are different, so are the candidates.

But aside from everything I have just written, what is it that concerns me and obliges me to write? What is my interest here? My own interest in this is something that goes far beyond me and is at the same time no one's concern but mine: I need a transformation of the lot of disenfranchised workers, of immigrants, the transformation of the Third World, even its metamorphosis, together with new relations between Europe and the Third World.

The uncertainty is unbearable: what is emerging here, if we want it, is the appearance of a popular power in France and in all of Europe, or it will be the overbearing brutality of the Anonymous Exploiter, exploiting first all the resources of the Third World, geological resources, minerals, labor power—all underpaid labor power—the accumulation and acceleration of the work demanded of it, a human chattel already herded into monstrous safaris. Then France, Europe, the world of white capital will be rich and powerful. This wealth will mean the destruction of the Third World, its impoverishment in every sense: physical, material, cultural, everything destroyed, everything crushed, myself as well.

If Giscard passes through, he will not do so alone: massive Imbecility follows and precedes him.

§ 21 Dying Under Giscard d'Estaing

It is indispensable to point out the tricks used by Giscard d'Estaing on television.[1] Here are some of them: feigned indignation, mendacity, imposture, bold and contradictory confirmations and denials, calumny, and foolishness.

Giscard is no illusionist, neither a great nor a small one. He's not even a cynic. If he lies it's because he feels he is lacking all authority. The entire Left is threatening his privileges. He panics and speaks of things he knows nothing about.

He is being compared—and he compares himself—to Kennedy, because of his fortune and his age. But who was Kennedy? The failed invasion of the Bay of Pigs, the buildup of the CIA, the assassination of Diêm, the first marines sent to Saigon, the nuclear umbrella imposed on MacMillan, the choice of Johnson as vice president, the invention of an inconsistent slogan: "new frontiers," and so on.[2]

A rather odd assassination has perhaps succeeded in creating, outside the United States, a little mini-myth around Kennedy, with his "youth," his "dynamism," his "future," and his "beautiful, distinguished wife," the famous Jackie.

Giscard may have a little of this.

This talk about his "youth and his dynamic movement toward the future" says nothing at all. Hot air can move quickly too.

Kennedy represented "youth."

His wife was the "height of bourgeois elegance."

Today, Jackie is an Onassis.

The "future" is happening today: it's called Watergate.[3]

Giscard d'Estaing possesses the natural guile of the propertied class. The people are saying, "He must be full of himself to promise us everything." He gives us his huckster's routine but has to be his own barker since his barons are mute and awkward. He wants to sell us some toy version of the Constitution, but he knows nothing about either the use or the function of this toy.

"I'm ready to name a prime minister on May 20," he says.[4]

Mitterrand is also ready to name a prime minister on May 20, but a different one.

VOCABULARY

OF A BIG BOSS IN A PANIC

WITH HIS BACK AGAINST THE WALL

Monopoly.

A "monopoly" of the heart.[5] He did indeed say "monopoly."

The "monopoly of the heart" mentioned by Giscard d'Estaing was meant as a bank of the heart, a bank of the eyes, a bank as a bank, and a monopoly as a monopoly. The word *heart* was, in his mouth, a bloody organ ripped from a dead man, which he was spitting back at us.

Love.

"I love the workers too, I love the French," said Giscard d'Estaing. During the time of the OAS, a colonist said to the Algerians, "I love the Arabs too."[6] The answer he got was this: "Well, we Arabs have had it up to here with your love."

Tool.

"We mustn't break the 'tool,'" said Giscard d'Estaing, who has never handled a tool in his life. In fact, he wasn't speaking of a tool, but of an apparatus: the one that three hundred years of a Triumphant Haute Bourgeoisie have perfected as a way to enclose the poor within a circle of pseudomoral and pseudocultural conventions, a vicious circle they perhaps do not know how to break because it is invisible. This circle is sealed by a haughty syntax and by the miserly, patronizing tone of the master.

When he said this to Mitterrand, he did so with the tone, the indignation—since he knew he'd been unmasked, exposed, stripped bare—with the boorishness, too, of a boss reprimanding a worker who was in danger of breaking the "tool." A tool used in the worker's labor, that is, in his fatigue, but also, and especially, one that ensures his exploitation for the benefit of the boss.

Giscard d'Estaing neither described nor showed this tool because it doesn't exist: he would have had to describe and to show the "system" that contains the "tool."

For the tool he speaks of is the System. His System.

Another man of the Right, Pierre Pellissier, who is only slightly less of a fool than Giscard d'Estaing, noticed the slip and struck the word from the edition of the *Figaro* that appeared on May 8. He replaced it with the word "instrument."[7] Another sleight of hand: if Giscard d'Estaing doesn't know what he's talking about, neither does Pellissier: "instrument" comes from a root relating to "destroy," and "instrumental justice" [*la justice instrumentaire*] means torture.

Center.

"With the participation of the Democratic center . . . ," said Giscard d'Estaing. Which center? Giscard d'Estaing is not the Right, but a curious amalgam of far Right and Right.

Far Right in terms of his methods, his complicity with OAS—and therefore anti-Arab—terrorism, and Right in terms of his upbringing as a member of a leading family. His majority, if he gets it, would be a twisted knot combining the far Right with the Right: this is what he calls the Center.

Reconciliation.

The far Right that was defeated after Pétain never spoke of anything else.

Account.

"I count on taking account . . . ," said Giscard d'Estaing.

Here again, the specialist in high finance uses a word—he even uses it twice in a row[8]—and he knows neither what he's trying to say nor how to say it: he's getting mixed up. His "disciplined language" is taking an ugly beating.

Communists.

"Seven Communists in the cabinet, that frightens me," said Giscard d'Estaing. I can understand why. It wouldn't even take that many in power to expose *all* the evidence, visible or still hidden, for everything that has been set up to exploit the workers.

This is the one and only moment during the debate when Giscard d'Estaing said something he understood: Communists in the cabinet . . . and suddenly a light cuts through his fog.

Future.

"I am a man of the future, you are a man of the past," said Giscard d'Estaing to Mitterrand. Either the word "future," as Giscard uses it, is hollow, or else he is only speaking of his own future and that of his caste. But here again it is very clear: Giscard d'Estaing is striking a pose. He knows that he belongs to a desiccated past, the past of the exhausted bourgeoisie. He also knows that Mitterrand represents the future in the very sense he himself intends, and that Mitterrand is acting in the name of a leftist coalition that is in the process of deciding its own future.

"You speak only of the past." Giscard was lying again, for he had to lie quickly and baldly, so obvious was it that he himself is the past personified, whereas Mitterrand is the future, that of the disenfranchised and the young.

Since yesterday evening the theme of "the candidate of the future" is flowing from all the pens and all the mouths of the lackeys of the Right. The slogan has been launched. It will be in full use during the last week of the campaign. Right away we have to ask Giscard d'Estaing how he could be the candidate of the future when the majority of Mitterand's supporters are young people and workers.

These young people whom Giscard d'Estaing evokes would like for us to mistake their ambition for enthusiasm. There probably are young people whose ideas are very old, whose ambitions are dreary, who accept outmoded values, and Giscard d'Estaing is their representative and their leader—this "youth" who would be happy to see a future in which the Élysée Palace becomes once again the private property of the viscountess Anne-Aymone de Giscard d'Estaing.[9]

THE PEOPLE AND THE AUDIENCE

In fact, this televised event was very painful for Monsieur "d'"Estaing, for he was forced to show us all the methods of this polished, gold-plated but trivial Right. He had to make threats, become indignant, apostrophize, implore . . . , "I beg of you, Monsieur Mitterrand . . . " Everything that is bitter, vain, foolish, hateful. . . . "I will not nationalize Monsieur Dassault . . . ," everything that allows the bourgeoisie to dominate, and that it draws out of its triviality—all this collapsed in a heap before our eyes.[10]

We saw something new in France: François Mitterrand addressing the people; whereas what Giscard d'Estaing tried to do was to turn the people into an audience.

One has to be wary of the latest maneuvers of a man who seeks to fascinate ordinary people by the appearance of a high level of technical expertise which he has not mastered—his "pseudocompetence," as cabinet member Pisani put it—and he knows of whom he speaks—is a good reason to vote for Mitterrand.

"He has wind in his sails," people say of Giscard. May no one be duped by this wind, this hot air, these hollow words.

Seven Communists in the cabinet would frighten him. It would not frighten us. But the idea of seven years, or rather fourteen years of Giscard d'Estaing is enough to make our skin crawl.

Dying under Valéry Giscard d'Estaing, crushed by his contempt, his bulimic hunger for power, his rage at having been afraid yesterday evening and at having been seen in such a state?[11]

We will not accept it.

I will pose the question again: where, when, how, in what moment of his life, by what popular motivation, by what feat of imagination would this man with no imagination understand the farmers, the workers, the immigrants, the people as a whole, if not through paternalism?

How, then, would he serve this people?

§ 22 And Why Not a Fool in Suspenders?

When we heard Giscard talking socialism with the workers at Montceau-les-Mines, it was impossible not to perceive in his snob's voice the inflections of Louis Bonaparte's ineffable *Extinction of Pauperism*.[1] Giscard no doubt authorizes himself on the basis of a possible unholy alliance between one of Anne-Aymone's ancestors and Jules Guesde.[2]

Just as Giscard's claim to nobility is dubious, the unholy alliance with the socialist is also uncertain, but the entire history of France makes it possible to exploit it.

I have only my memories of a schoolboy's lessons. They too are uncertain and dubious, no doubt, through the fault of an education intent on making me—and every other child—a complete Frenchman, that is, one who is double.

Let's recall a few pages that made radical socialism possible.

We begin with Descartes. He writes *Discourse on Method*, but places it under an invocation of the Holy Virgin and the Immaculate Conception.

With Louis XIV we have the Grand Siècle, the triumph of classicism: the columns of Versaille, the tragedies of Racine, the ceremonial of the court—from the Chaise-Percée to the king's *grand coucher*—and the music of Lulli, and so on.

By the time of the Regency and Louis XV, it's already an orgy, and, under Louis XV and within him, the seminal apparition that, it is said, will give birth to Giscard.[3]

And then there's the Revolution of 1789–92, and all its consequences.

Let us continue: Bonaparte is a friend of Robespierre the Younger.[4] As a victorious general, he takes the ideas of the revolution beyond France, with the help of his soldiers. Then—and this is what makes his life exemplary—he has himself crowned, or rather simply crowns himself emperor, and with his remarriage to Marie-Louise, niece of Louis XVI, he becomes the nephew of the king who had been decapitated and stripped bare through the intervention of Saint-Just.

After his defeats, exile, and death, we have the restored monarchy, but we also have Les Trois Glorieuses.[5] We have Louis-Philippe, but we also have 1848 and the appearance, in France itself, of Marx, in response to Proudhon. We have Napoleon III, but we also have the Paris commune.

Throughout its modern history France has alternated between classicism and revolutionary explosion. This is what makes it possible for every demagogue who comes along to refer to order—to absolute monarchy—and at the same time to revolution.

Giscard's household divides the labor: he descends from Le Bien-Aimé, and she comes down to us from Jules Guesde.[6] Everyone, he thinks, is for Them. And it's all the easier—so they think—in that the professors have frozen the great moments of revolution into a Fable as reassuring as the label "the Sun King."

Of course I'm speaking of the image fed to me by a school system that was secular when it came to the Church, but religious when it came to the Fable. I was not the only one to whom History made an offer to dig, according to one's opportunism, now on the Right and now on the Left. Giscard does the same thing: for himself he finds some illustrious ancestors on the Right; on the Left, pulling up the carpet a little, he finds illustrious ancestors for his wife.

But he's going to have to run the country, starting today. First he'll make use of a royal power, by having the people, and the elementary schools, participate in the pomp of an empty rite: he is dismissing, or if you prefer, he is giving a vacation to all schoolchildren on Monday.[7] His public relations people also thought up a gesture that is the exact contrary of de Gaulle's trip down the Champs-Élysées in 1945: he will walk triumphantly *up* the avenue to l'Étoile.[8] He wants to appear splendid and simple.

I submit to the reader these last three words: appear, splendid, and simple.

An appearance can also be something that hides reality.

Splendor is always an appearance.

Simplicity in "appearing" is always the concealment of the truth.

What does Giscard want to conceal? Sanguinetti said it very clearly, whether he meant to or not, on the evening of the election:

"I have taken the full measure of Giscard's intelligence."[9]

One wanted to ask him: "In inches or in feet?" If he measured it, then it's not immeasurable. Already during an appearance (once again) on television, I had been struck by this useless face, pathetically reaching for an intelligence that fled from it at full speed. One could see his rage and discomfiture when this intelligence, leaving him in the lurch, was already far away, gone perhaps to settle on the face of a newborn Guinean.

So he too has been digging, with the famous silver spoon, in the French reservoir that offers him the splendid and the simple. To govern in shirtsleeves or without dressing up, that's another of his tactics.[10]

What's the point of all this? And how does it work? What else does this appearance hide? It's so obvious that I almost can't be bothered to write it: the brute force, the organization of powerful gangs, the villainy and venom of Prince Poniatowski,[11] the ruses of the shadowy special services: all this, and the rest—the influence peddling, the game of the multinationals, real estate too, of course, the happy exploitation of workers, immigrant or not—all this will be concealed by the appearance, the appearances, which, like those of Heliogabalus, will no doubt be quite rare, for the sake of "surprise" (" . . . you will be surprised . . . ") and in order to conceal everything I just mentioned.[12]

Everything involved in this appearance, splendid or simple, will be a bluff concealing the reality of power: brutality, underhanded or out in the open, or both at once, serving to exploit the workers in France and the labor power and wealth of the Third World.

Giscard and his cronies will try out the illusion. It is beginning. And I immediately think of the sinking of the *Titanic*, when the first-class passengers were the first to be given seats in the lifeboats, while the crowd of emigrants behind them shouted on their knees, "My God, we were here first!"

There was a trial. The director of the Cunard Line explained: "The first-class passengers are the elite, and in the elite there is also the intellectual elite: they had to be saved."

If there is a cataclysm with Giscard at the helm, we know who will be sacrificed.

We will therefore find the usual portents in the sky, in the positions of the ascending sun. Ascension, the gift of tongues, Nostradamus, all the fading but not entirely powerless spells.

May it spare us Giscard and his handwriting, which tells too clearly what he himself conceals.

Everyone has already understood the real signs that are emerging: the misery of immigrant workers, racism, the increasing pace of work, the gray and dreary world of the poor, the world dazzled by too much light, the workers crushed by too much rage.

§ 23   The Women of Jebel Hussein

The first image was given to me, and the tone was set, by four Palestinian women in the section of Amman overlooked by Jebel Hussein.[1] Four older, wrinkled women were squatting around a hearth with no fire: two or three blackened stones and a battered aluminum tea kettle. They told me to sit.

"We're at home, you see. Do you want some tea?" They smiled.

"At home?"

"Yes." They laughed. "Stones are all we have to make a fire. Our huts were burned down."

"By whom?"

"Hussein. You're from France. People say your country supports the Arabs; does it know the difference between Hussein and the Arabs?"[2]

At this point there was a very high-spirited argument about the fate reserved for Hussein. They themselves were very cheerful, beyond sorrow, but always ready to fight.

"Where are the men?"

"Our sons are fedayeen, they're in the mountains."

"And the others?"

"Right there."

A thin index finger belonging to a very dry and very beautiful hand pointed for me to a small courtyard nearby.

"We buried them there."

She was talking about old men, women, children. It was one of these four women who took me to task, gently but firmly, when I spoke of "refugee camps."[3]

"You mean military camps; now everyone in them is armed and has learned how to fight."

The possibility for revolt was perhaps greater among the women than the men. They seemed to possess surprising reserves of action, and of discretion in the midst of action. One day I said to a Palestinian woman that perhaps the women imagined the possibilities of revolution with greater calm.

"The revolutionaries," she said laughing, "we know them. We brought them into this world. We know their strengths, their weaknesses."

"You mean you love them."

She was about fifty years old. She was smiling.

"I know them because I love them. Do you want tea or coffee?"

Her son was a fedayee in the Fatah, her daughter and her son-in-law were in Al-Saika.[4]

The women, it seemed to me, moved more quickly toward the most decisive solution.

H., twenty-two years old, had introduced me to his mother in Irbid. It was during Ramadan, one day around noon.[5]

"He's French. Not simply French, and not a Christian either; he doesn't believe in God."

She looked at me with a smile. Her eyes grew more and more mischievous.

"Well, since he doesn't believe in God, we'd better give him something to eat."

For her son and for myself she prepared a lunch.

She didn't eat until evening.

§ 24 Interview with Hubert Fichte

Hubert Fichte.—Yesterday[1] you mentioned a demonstration you were going to.

Jean Genet.—No, I wasn't going; there were demonstrations yesterday that brought together members of the CGT, the CFDT, and the CGC and the three opposition parties: the Communist Party, the Socialist Party, and the Left Radicals.[2] The official purpose of the demonstration was to protest the economic policies of the government. But in reality, the protest was sparked by the arrest of several union activists and even a few soldiers who were accused of undermining army morale and are in danger of being brought before the state security court, where the sentences can be anywhere from five to twenty years in prison.

H.F.—So it was a demonstration against Giscard d'Estaing?

J.G.—It was directed especially against the minister of defense and the minister of the interior.

H.F.—You're not a member of any of the parties that gathered there?

J.G.—No, absolutely not. I don't belong to any party!

H.F.—People say: Jean Genet has no address, he lives in little hotels ...

J.G.—By chance I happen to have my passport on me. Here's my address, you can read it right there.

H.F.—It's the address at Gallimard: 5 rue Sébastien-Bottin.

J.G.—I don't have any other; see, that's my official address.

H.F.—Does living without an address, without an apartment, make it difficult to maintain friendships? You can't invite anyone over, you can't cook ...

J.G.—I don't like to cook.

H.F.—You're always the one who's invited.

J.G.—So what? Obviously it creates some problems, and therefore some solutions; at the same time, it allows for a certain irresponsibility. I have no social responsibilities, and this allows me a sort of immediate engagement, I can join up on the spot. When Bobby Seale was arrested—he was the head of the Black Panthers—two of the Panthers[3] came to see me and asked me what I could do for Bobby Seale. It was morning, I answered, "The simplest thing would be to go to the United States to see the situation." They said, "When?"—"How about tomorrow?"—"So soon?" I saw that the Panthers were thrown off by this. They were used to moving quickly, but I was moving more quickly than they were, all because I was living in a hotel. I had one small suitcase. If I had an apartment, would I have been able to do that? If I had friendships, would I be able to move around with the same speed?

H.F.—Are you worried about being surrounded by a certain bourgeois luxury, because of your fame and your resources?

J.G.—Ah! That's obviously really stupid. No, I don't think so, because I have no respect for bourgeois luxury. I'd need to have a Renaissance castle at least. My royalties aren't enough to buy a court like Borgia's, so I'm not much in danger of that.

H.F.—What fascinates you about Borgia's court?

J.G.—I'm not fascinated, I just think that the last manifestations of architectural luxury date from the Renaissance. I don't see much after that. The eighteenth century in France doesn't really do it for me. The same goes for the seventeenth century. The first time I went to the palace of Versailles, I was horrified. The little stone castle is quite lovely, but when you go into the garden and turn around to look at the large façade, it's horrific! I wonder why that guy—who was the architect? Mansart,[4] wasn't it?—in any case, I wonder why Louis XIV didn't multiply the miles of columns? It's heavy, bulky, stupid, and endless. There are palaces in Italy, from the Renaissance, that appear to be very small, but are actually immense, very beautiful and still inhabitable. The Hall of Mirrors, I don't know exactly what the proportions are, but there are better—Brasilia for example.

H.F.—Doesn't Brasilia seem to you endless and repeatable ad infinitum?

J.G.—No, I don't think so; there are several distinct parts that come together into a whole, it's very harmonious. I flew over the city. I saw it in the sun, in the rain, at night, in the daytime, and in the wind, the cold, and the heat, and I know Brasilia from the tenth floor of the Hotel Nacional, and also from the street. And yet it's odd that that guy, who's a communist, I mean Oscar Niemeyer,[5] when he created this city, he was unable to prevent shantytowns full of Indians from springing up nearly all the way around it. It would seem that the only people who can live in the huge buildings of Brasilia are six-foot-four hulks with blond or brown hair, well built, in any case, more like statuary than human beings. But in reality, they're inhabited by little functionaries, ambassadors, ministers, and not by the Indians or the Blacks of Brasilia. Still, I can't think of any other city that, like Brasilia, was planned and created from the ground up and that is apparently harmonious. There were some things Oscar Niemeyer didn't understand, he didn't succeed because he didn't have the vision of an urban planner capable of conceiving that he could, that he had to build human housing for a proletariat and that he had to eliminate everything that would allow class differences to arise. His city pushes out the proletariat and forces it to collect around the periphery. What struck me most was the Palace of Foreign Affairs. The cathedral, the "concrete flower," says nothing at all to me. I went to Matisse's little church in Vence,[6] the one dedicated to a figure I normally can't stand, Saint Dominic. You have to go inside. There is an incredible use of space; you're inside a poem.

H.F.—There's a similar poetic quality in Romanesque architecture.

J.G.—Yes.

H.F.—In Montmajour, or Solignac. Do you know the domed church in Solignac?

J.G.—Romanesque churches always have domes.

H.F.—Some have barrel vaults, etc.

J.G.—They almost always have domes, because the Romanesque arch requires a dome.

H.F.—In comparing Niemeyer's architecture with Matisse's little chapel, would you say that Matisse is a revolutionary artist?

J.G.—No. One must be very careful in using the word "revolutionary." Above all it must be used advisedly. It's a difficult word. I wonder if the concept *revolutionary* can be separated from the concept of violence. We have to use other words, other terms, to name what was accomplished, say, by Cézanne. I think that artists like Cézanne and the painters who followed him, or the musicians who challenged the notion of tonality, I think that they were very daring, but not really that much; not that much because on the one hand the absolute dominance of the notions of perspective in painting or the chromatic scale in music was already being eroded, but through wit and irony, through jokes. Alban Berg wrote music without taking himself too seriously, and then later it was more fully elaborated, so in that sense it was audacious, it had a considerable impact, but I think that for them, as an intellectual adventure it didn't have the importance we attribute to them. This might explain why Cézanne remained a very simple man. He went to Mass, he lived with a woman he wasn't married to. The fact that Zola, a childhood friend, didn't understand him, that must have hurt him, but I'm not sure that Cézanne believed he would have a posterity or such posthumous glory.

H.F.—Yesterday you spoke of Monteverdi. Is this for you an art that brutally breaks with tradition?

J.G.—For me there is nothing more cheerful, more joyous, than the *Beata Virgine Mass.*

H.F.—You claim to be a-religious, to be an atheist; how do you approach a work like the *Vespro della beata Virgine?*

J.G.—Twenty years ago I read the *Iliad* and found it very, very beautiful; do you think I believe in the religion of Zeus?

H.F.—I think that at bottom you're not far from it, to tell the truth.

J.G.—When I was in Japan the last time, seven or eight years ago,[7] I saw a Noh play that I found very moving. You know that women's roles are played by men. At a certain moment, an actor was wearing the mask of an old woman, the last Buddhist woman. She goes into a cave, covers herself with a fan, and then uncovers her face, and it's the face of a young girl, the first Shinto woman. The theme was the passage from the Buddhist religion to the Shinto religion. Do you think I'm Buddhist or Shinto?

H.F.—I think that your work, your whole life, expresses a fascination with ritual.

J.G.—There's no ritual in the *Iliad.*

H.F.—In the *Iliad* there is a ritual of description, there are refrains and topoi, for example: "and all his guts poured out on the ground."[8]

J.G.—No, that's just a manner of speaking, I wonder if those are really Homeric inventions, or if it's not simply a way to move more quickly.

H.F.—With Homer, the mode of composition is itself almost religious.

J.G.—In the *Iliad*, yes, but not in the *Odyssey*.

H.F.—Why do you like Strindberg's *Miss Julie*, and why don't you like the Brecht of *Galileo Galilei*?

J.G.—Because what Brecht says is nothing but garbage; because *Galileo Galilei* cites the obvious; it tells me things I would have discovered without Brecht. Strindberg, or in any case *Miss Julie*, does not present the obvious. It's very new. I wasn't expecting it. I saw *Miss Julie* after *The Dance of Death*, how do you say it in Swedish?

H.F.—*Dödsdansen.*

J.G.—I liked it very much. Nothing Strindberg says could be said in any other way than poetically, and everything Brecht says can be said and in fact has been said prosaically.

H.F.—That was his intention. He called his theater "epic theater," and he introduced or claimed to introduce the distancing that Strindberg indeed had already achieved in his introduction to *Miss Julie*. Strindberg already assumes a cold spectator, the Brechtian spectator holding a cigar.

J.G.—In this choice of a gesture, smoking a cigar, there is a casualness with regard to the work of art that is in fact not permitted. It is not permitted by the work of art. I don't know the Rothschilds, but with the Rothschilds, you can probably talk about art while smoking a cigar. You can't go to the Louvre and look at *The Marquise of Solana*[9] with the same movement as with the Rothschilds who talk about art while smoking a cigar.

H.F.—So you think that Brecht's gesture is the gesture of a bourgeois capitalist?

J.G.—Looks like it to me.

H.F.—At least when looking at a work of art, since you're smoking a cigarillo right now.

J.G.—If I smoke a cigar as a cigar smoker, if I can be defined as a cigar smoker, if I listen to Mozart's *Requiem* and this gesture of smoking a cigar takes precedence over that of listening to the *Requiem*, then it's not simply a question of distancing, but of a lack of sensibility. It's a question of lacking an ear, which means I would prefer my cigarillo to the *Requiem*.

H.F.—You were talking about contemplation of the artwork.

J.G.—I lose more and more the sense of being "myself," the sense of the "I," and become nothing but the perception of the artwork. Confronted with subversive events, my "ego" or my "self," my "social self," is on the contrary more and more filled, it is more and more inflated, and I am less and less capable, when confronted with subversive phenomena, I am less and less free for . . . precisely for that sort of contemplation. One day when he was conducting *Daphnis and Chloe*, I asked Boulez, "I can't tell to what extent your ear registers each instrument," and he said to me . . . Pierre Boulez said to me, "I can control only about twenty-five or thirty percent," and this is one of the subtlest ears in existence. So someone who is conducting an orchestra has to be immensely attentive, of course, but so does anyone who is listening. Now suppose your ear is less subtle than Boulez's, you have to make such a great effort of concentration that, personally at least, in a museum I can only look at two or three paintings, at a concert I can hear one or two pieces, as for the rest . . . I'm too tired.

H.F.—And reading?

J.G.—Oh! It's the same. I can tell you that it took me two months to read *The Brothers Karamazov*.[10] I was in bed. I was in Italy, I would read one page, and then . . . I'd have to think for two hours, then start again, it's enormous, and it's exhausting.

H.F.—Contemplation absorbs your "self" to the point of destruction?

J.G.—Not to the point of destruction, not to the point of losing the "self" completely, because at a certain moment, you notice that your leg is asleep, you come back to "yourself," but you tend toward a loss of "self."

H.F.—Whereas the revolutionary act? ...

J.G.—In my opinion, it's the opposite, since you have to act. Confronted with the artwork, you have to act, as well. The attention you give to the artwork is an act; if I listen to the vespers of the *Beata Virgine* without at the same time composing it with my own modest means, I'm not doing anything, I don't hear anything; and if I'm not writing *The Brothers Karamazov* while I read it, I'm not doing anything.

H.F.—So it's double.

J.G.—Yes. Don't you have the impression that it's kind of like that?

H.F.—Yes, but revolutionary action is also double.

J.G.—But it doesn't use the same means. In revolutionary action, you put your body at risk; in the artwork, and in whatever recognition it receives elsewhere, you put your reputation at risk, perhaps, but your body is not in danger. If you botch a poem, if you botch a concerto, if you botch a piece of architecture, people might make fun of you, or you may not have the reputation you deserve, but you aren't in danger of death. When you're involved in revolution, your body is exactly what's in danger, and the whole revolutionary adventure is in danger at the same time.

H.F.—When you write, is the act of writing closer to that of recreating *The Brothers Karamazov*, is it more like the contemplation of that "thinning out" of the "self," or is it more like the revolutionary act, that concentration of the "self" in physical danger?

J.G.—The first formula is more accurate. With writing, I never put . . . I have never put my person in danger, or never seriously, in any case. Never in a physical sense. I've never written anything that made anyone want to torture me, put me in prison, or kill me.

H.F.—But it's a body of work that made an impact and that raised the stakes for an entire generation. It's an exaggeration, but I would say that there isn't a homosexual anywhere in the world now who hasn't been influenced, directly or indirectly, by your work.

J.G.—First of all, out of simple prudence, I would be wary about what you're saying. It risks giving me an importance that in my opinion I don't have. Second, I think you're mistaken, too; what I wrote did not bring about the liberation you're talking about, it's the other way around: it was liberation that came first and that coincided more or less with Germany's occupation of France and the liberation and peace after the war. It was that kind of liberation and freeing up of minds that allowed me to write my books.

H.F.—Still, I insist: In Germany, up until 1968, there was a law forbidding sexual acts between adult males. The Genet trial in Hamburg[11] was decisive in securing the freedom to print erotic works, etc.

J.G.—Even if my books had certain repercussions, the act of writing, the singular act of writing in a prison, had almost no effect on me, so that there is a disproportion between what you're describing, which would be the result obtained by my books, and the writing of my books; the writing, which was pretty much the same if I had described a boy and a girl sleeping together, for me, it was no more difficult than that. I even wonder if there isn't a phenomenon of magnification created by the processes of mechanical reproduction and transmission. Two hundred years ago, if someone drew my portrait, there would be a portrait. Now, if someone takes a photograph of me—there will be a hundred thousand of them, maybe more; okay, fine, but am I any more important?

H.F.—No, not more important, but more significant.

J.G.—But the significance is a new one, it becomes a different one.

H.F.—When the manuscript of Sade's *120 Days of Sodom* was hidden in a crack in the wall of the Bastille, it didn't even exist, as Sartre would say; but once it's printed in paperback, it influences an entire population.

J.G.—Do you think the Marquis de Sade liberated the end of the eighteenth century through his work and his way of living? Personally, I think that, on the contrary, it was the freedom that had begun and was already luminous in the age of the encyclopedists, in the second half of the eighteenth century, that made Sade's work possible.

H.F.—Reading your work, one discovers a great admiration for a kind of beautiful brutality, an elegant brutality.

J.G.—Yes, but I was thirty years old when I wrote my books, and now I'm sixty-five.

H.F.—And this fascination, which was so bewildering to me, this admiration for assassins, for Hitler, for the concentration camps—all this has drained away?

J.G.—Yes and no. It has drained away, but the space has not been occupied by anything else, it's a void. It's quite strange for someone who lives this void. What did it mean, this fascination for brutes or assassins or Hitler? In more direct and perhaps also simpler terms, I remind you that I was an orphan, I was raised by Public Welfare, I found out very early on that I wasn't French and that I didn't belong to the village—I was raised in the Massif Central. I found this out in a very stupid, silly way: the teacher asked us to write a little essay in which each student would describe his house. I described mine; it happened that the teacher thought my description was the prettiest. He read it out, and everyone made fun of me, saying, "That's not his house, he's a foundling!" and then there was such an emptiness, such a degradation. I immediately became such a stranger . . . oh! the word isn't too strong, to hate France is nothing, you have to do more than hate, more than loathe France, finally I . . . and . . . the fact that the French army, the most prestigious thing in the world thirty years ago, that they surrendered to the troops of an Austrian corporal, well, to me, that was absolutely thrilling. I was avenged. But I'm well aware that it wasn't me who wrought this vengeance, I am not the maker of my vengeance. It was brought about by others, by a whole system, and I'm aware, too, that it was a conflict within the white world that went far beyond me; but when it comes down to it, French society suffered a real blow, and I could only love someone who had dealt such a serious blow to French society. And then, even as I felt more than satisfied with what had happened, with the magnitude of the punishment that had been given to France, that's when, within a few days, the French army and even much of the French population left, beginning around the Maubeuge-Basel line[12] almost to the Spanish border. When a nation is so completely subdued by military force, one has to admit that France was humiliated, and I can only adore someone who had wrought the humiliation of France. On top of all this, I could only place myself among the oppressed people of color and among the oppressed revolting against the Whites. Perhaps I'm a Black whose color is white or pink, but a Black. I don't know my family.

H.F.—Did the Black Panthers accept you, even though your skin is white?

J.G.—Immediately. I wondered about it many times. I was alone, there were no other whites, I was there with them for two months, and then the police sent a summons to the Panthers saying I had to show up at some cop thing.[13] The Panthers said to me, "It's better if you leave, because it might cause some trouble for us." I left. But for two months, I was alone with them. I ate with them. I wondered, "Aren't they tired of seeing this white man with them all the time?" Apparently not. I saw Angela Davis again, three months ago. I said to her, "We were very afraid for you," and she said, "We were afraid for you, too." She talked about the moment during Bobby Seale's pretrial, which I attended,[14] when David Hilliard, who was replacing Bobby Seale at the time, was arrested. He was trying to show me a piece of paper, the cops grabbed him and started taking him away, I saw that he was going to talk and shout, I said in French, "David, David, don't say anything, be quiet!" and I was very afraid. I was surprised that no one intervened; I went to find a lawyer there, and I said to him—he had a beard like yours, and you know American lawyers don't wear robes—and I took him by the shoulders, I said to him, "Hey, look, do something . . . stop them . . . " and he had me arrested. I'd made a mistake, it was the state prosecutor. Since I didn't understand English, I just let them do it; I was arrested, but without any harsh treatment; they made me leave, but it was almost as if they were just asking me to leave. What different treatment! I'll tell you what happened: we entered the courtroom in New Haven. I was with the Panthers, so there were a dozen Blacks and one White, me, a sixty-year-old white man, in a tiny courtroom. There were two or three rows of chairs in the front of the courtroom, then behind those there were some benches, and in the chairs there were Whites and on the benches there were Blacks. There happened to be a free seat in the first row of chairs, a cop took me by the arm and led me, very forcefully, to the free seat, and I went with him, not understanding what was going on; and it was only when I looked up before sitting down that I saw David Hilliard way in the back. I said, "I'll sit with you," and the cop . . . I knocked him on the hand and said, "Let go," and he did, but you see, I felt the difference. There was something else: when David went out, he left behind a little briefcase with some papers in it, and there was a guy there, a Black, who managed to take it out to the hallway, but then we had to leave the courthouse. Well, who did they give the briefcase to? To me, because they knew they would be searched on the way out of the courthouse and that I wouldn't be; and that's exactly what happened.

H.F.—Would you say that the Panthers were carrying out a poetic revolution?

J.G.—Hold on! Before saying something like that, I'd like for us to agree about something, if possible. There seem to be at least two kinds of communication: one is a rational, reflective communication. Is this lighter black?

H.F.—Yes.

J.G.—Yes. And then there is a communication that is less cer -tain, and yet obvious. I'll ask you if you agree that Baudelaire's verse, "Blue-black hair, a den of taut shadows,"[15] do you find that beautiful?

H.F.—Yes.

J.G.—So we're communicating. Okay, there are at least two kinds of communication, then, a mode that is recognizable, controllable, and one that is uncontrollable. The Panthers' action had more to do with the uncontrollable kind of communication. In San Francisco, I was in a taxi driven by a Black man, and I said to him, "Do you like the Panthers?"

and he said, "Like them, no; admire them, yes." He was fifty years old, he said to me, "But my kids like them a lot." In reality, he liked them, too. You can't admire something without liking it, but he couldn't say so because he had violent images of them that he rejected. It was claimed that they had ransacked, that they had killed, and that's true, they had killed a few cops, a few Whites. Much less violence, in any case, than the Americans caused in Vietnam and Korea and elsewhere. It was a revolution of an affective and emotional order; and that has no relation . . . well, it may have some very discreet relation to revolutions attempted elsewhere and by others means.

H.F.—Your conception of revolution would be analogous to that of the Panthers?

J.G.—No, no, the Panthers put into play an entire affectivity that we lack, and this affectivity did not come from the fact that they were of African descent, that they're black; it's simply that they're banished, they've been banished and outlawed for four centuries, and they found each other again in the expression "brothers." This fraternity is not possible if you're thinking of a global revolution, or so it seems to me. You can't talk about that if don't you have a very long stretch of time out ahead of you.

H.F.—So we're saying that there is a gap between poetic and artistic revolutions and social revolutions.

J.G.—What are referred to as poetic or artistic revolutions are not exactly revolutions. I don't believe they change the order of the world. Nor do they change the vision we have of the world. They refine vision, they complete it, they make it more complex, but they don't entirely transform it, the way a social or political revolution does. If during the interview we're going to speak of "artistic revolution," let it be understood between us that we're using an expression that's a little tired, a little lazy. As I said, political revolutions rarely, I might say never, correspond to artistic revolutions. When revolutionaries succeed in completely changing a society, they find themselves faced with a problem: how to give expression, how to express their revolution as adequately as possible. It seems to me that revolutionaries make use of the most academic means they can find within the society they have just overturned or plan to overturn. Everything happens as if the revolutionaries said to themselves, "We're going to prove to the regime we just overturned that we can do as well as they did." And then they imitate the academic styles, they imitate official painting, official architecture, official music. It's only much later that they envisage revolution as a cultural revolution, and then they sometimes appeal not to academic styles, but to tradition and to new forms in which tradition can be used.

H.F.—Are there no exceptions to this rule? Danton? Saint-Just?

J.G.—Danton! No. I don't think Danton initiated a revolutionary expression, that is, a new way of feeling and experiencing the world and a new way of expressing it. Saint-Just, perhaps. Not in his proclamations, but in his interventions concerning the death of Louis XVI.[16] The style is still that of the eighteenth century, but with what insolence! The rhythm, the syntax, the grammar, everything belongs to the eighteenth century. But this syntax seems deformed, in any case transformed by the audacity of the positions he takes. You might say that he presented it in a very violent courtly language. But the literature of the time, even Diderot and even sometimes Montesquieu, was quite violent. In his second intervention in favor of the execution of Louis XVI, Saint-Just says: If the king is right and he is the Legitimate Sovereign, then we must kill the people who rose up against him—or else the Legitimate Sovereign is the people, and the king is a usurper, so we must kill the king.[17] That was very new. No one dared to speak so directly.

H.F.—Over the course of the different French revolutions, are there other moments of poetic or artistic revolution?

J.G.—No. You see, there was the Paris Commune. In reality, it was the whole Parisian populace that had taken power. Emotionally, that's very beautiful. But the only artist who put himself in the service of a revolution as an artist and at the same time as a revolutionary was Courbet, who was a great painter, but not one who repudiated the painting of his age. Victor Hugo was very proud that a cannon that bore the name Victor Hugo had been cast by the Parisian Foundries. He tried to understand. He understood, more or less, he was even a little terrified by the magnitude of the Paris Commune. But as a writer, he didn't change. Now the Paris Commune seems so short, it lasted so little time, that it was unable to change much. The revolution of 1848? What do we owe to that? Baudelaire was apparently on the barricades, but he had already written the most beautiful poems of *The Flowers of Evil*. *Sentimental Education* came out of the Revolution of 1848. But *Sentimental Education* was written by Flaubert, and Flaubert was not at all in favor of revolution. A new way of feeling that appeared to correspond with the Soviet revolution, at the end of the war, was Surrealism. But then very soon the Surrealists cut their ties both with the Soviet Union—since that was when Aragon wrote "Moscow the Senile"[18]—and with Freud, who misunderstood them. His meeting with Breton made it clear that he was not at all interested in Surrealism and that he did not see psychoanalysis as something to be used for purely poetic ends.

H.F.—Have you traveled to the Soviet Union?

J.G.—No, never.

H.F.—But you were invited to go there?

J.G.—No. Sartre asked me to go with him;[19] I think he was afraid he'd be bored to death if he went alone; with me there, we would have had a laugh, but I wasn't invited; I probably wouldn't have been able to get a visa.

H.F.—Why didn't you try?

J.G.—I was afraid I'd be bored to death.

H.F.—Do you see in the Cuban experience any chances for a poetic and artistic revolution?

J.G.—No, because when Castro saw the literature and painting of the West, of Europe, he saw them only from Cuba, but they were already recognized forms, they had already become academic, he recognized them. But the truly original forms originating in Cuba, he didn't recognize those.

H.F.—You were supposed to go to Cuba, but you turned that down, too?

J.G.—When I was invited by the Cuban Cultural Affairs, I said, "Yes, I'd like very much to go to Cuba, but on one condition: I'll pay for my own trip, I'll pay for my stay there, and I'll go where I want and stay where I want," and I said, "I'd like very much to go, if it really is the kind of revolution I'd like to see, that is, if there aren't any more flags, because the flag, as a sign of recognition, as an emblem around which a group is formed, has become a castrating and deadly piece of theatricality—and the national anthem? Ask him if there is no longer a Cuban flag and a national anthem." He said, "But you don't understand; our national anthem was written by a Black."

H.F.—In Cuba there is an idea of death, "Patria o muerte";[20] how do you see that?

J.G.—It seems very important to me, because, I won't say an artist, but any person takes on his true dimensions once he is dead. That's the meaning, I think, of Mallarmé's line "Such as into himself eternity finally changes him."[21] Death transforms everything, the perspectives change; as long as a man is alive, as long as he can inflect his thought, as long as, while he lives, he can throw you off track and can try to conceal his true personality by negations or affirmations, you don't really know who you're dealing with. Once he's dead, everything is deflated. The man is fixed, and we see his image differently.

H.F.—So for you, giving a taped interview is dying a little, fixing something?

J.G.—No, it's just the opposite, since while I'm talking to you like this I can present an image of myself that's more acceptable, more presentable, according to my desire of the moment. It's hypocritical in a way. When I speak to you, here in front of the microphone, I'm not completely sincere. I want to give a certain image of myself. And I can't say exactly who I am or what I want, because I'm like anyone else, essentially changing.

H.F.—Do you see in the movement of May '68 the possibility of the kind of revolution you would wish for?

J.G.—No, no. A lot has been written about May '68, and some have spoken of a "mimodrama," which seems accurate to me. One of the most daring student groups occupied the Odéon theater. I went twice to the Odéon theater when it was being occupied,[22] and the first time there was a kind of violence that was often downright incantatory. Look: the theater and the stage are here; the revolutionaries, a crowd of students were here on the stage. They had more or less reproduced the architecture of an ordinary courtroom, that is, a large table with a spokesman for the Idea behind or in front of it, and on either side the different groups who were challenging or accepting the Idea of the spokesman. Facing them there was the audience, in the boxes and in the seats below, who accepted what they heard, more or less, or who rebelled against it or . . . etc. The second time I went to the Odéon in May '68, all this violence had disappeared; that is, the words that were spoken on the stage were received by the audience—and it really has to be called an audience—and these words, often slogans, came back like an echo from the stage to the audience, from the audience to the stage, more and more feebly each time. In the end, the students had occupied a theater. What is a theater? First of all, what is power? It seems to me that power can never do without theatricality. Never. Sometimes the theatricality is simplified, sometimes it's modified, but there is always theatricality. Power covers and protects itself by means of theatricality. In China, in the Soviet Union, in England, in France, everywhere, theatricality is what dominates. Giscard d'Estaing, for his part, claims that he has destroyed all theatricality; in reality, he replaced the theatricality of the Third Republic with a slightly more modern one in the Swedish or even Canadian style: a procession on foot up the Champs-Élysées,[23] things like that. There is one place in the world where theatricality does not hide power, and that's in the theater. When the actor is killed, well, he gets up, takes a bow, and starts all over again the next day with getting killed, taking a bow, etc. There is absolutely no danger. In May '68, the students occupied a theater, that is, a place from which power has been evacuated, where theatricality remains on its own, without danger. If they had occupied the Parisian law courts, first, that would have been much more difficult, since that building has more guards protecting it than the Odéon theater, but above all, they would have been obligated to send people to prison, to pronounce judgments; then you'd have the beginning of a revolution. But they didn't do that.

H.F.—Can you say what your political revolution would be like?

J.G.—No, because I'm not all that eager for there to be a revolution. If I'm really sincere, I have to say that I don't particularly want it. The current situation, the current regimes allow me to revolt, but a revolution would probably not allow me to revolt, that is, to revolt individually. But this regime allows me to revolt individually. I can be against it. But if there were a real revolution, I might not be able to be against it. There would be adherence, and I am not that kind of man; I am not a man of adherence, but a man of revolt. My point of view is very egotistic. I would like for the world—now pay close attention to the way I say this—I would like for the world not to change so that I can be against the world.

H.F.—Well, what kind of revolution would be the most dangerous for you?

J.G.—According to what I know about it, the Chinese revolution.

H.F.—What sort of political revolution is it that you hope for?

J.G.—First . . . can I take some grapes? I was invited by two revolutionary groups, the Black Panthers and the Palestinians. Okay. I said to you in our previous conversations what was admissible, the admissible reasons; now, what is more difficult to admit has to do with the fact that the Panthers are Black Americans, the Palestinians are Arabs. It would be difficult for me to explain why things are like this, but these two groups of people have a very intense erotic charge. I wonder whether I could have adhered to other revolutionary movements that are equally as just— I find these movements very just, the Panthers and the Palestinians—but isn't this adherence, this sympathy, also driven by the erotic charge that the whole Arab world or the Black American world represents for me, for my own sexuality? And there's something else, the problem of the game. Going to America with the Panthers after the American embassy refused three times to give me a visa, that was a game. I enjoyed myself tremendously, and that's part of it, that too. Even though the work I did there was perhaps very conscientious, I can't say that there wasn't a spirit of provocation on my part; I noticed, for example, that the police either didn't dare to arrest me or didn't know I was there, and, well, the FBI is a joke, it's a complete mess, they don't know who's coming and who's going, or if they do,[24] then ...

H.F.—They don't give a damn.

J.G.—They don't give a damn, and, at the same time, there's a very old anti-convict law stating that no person convicted of a crime can be allowed to enter the United States; so they broke their own law.

H.F.—For me, what emerges from what you call "poetic revolution" are the following points: eroticism, enjoyment, insolence, and perhaps: being in the margins. Is that correct?

J.G.—Yes. I don't know if it's in the order of priority you chose, but the elements seem to be there; but at the same time with a will to be against all established power, to be on the side of the weakest; because if, not Nixon, but Wallace[25] had invited me to the United States, obviously I wouldn't have gone.

H.F.—I'm not trying to find contradictions; on the contrary, we understand each other perhaps because we accept contradictions ...

J.G.—Yes.

H.F.—You said, as a joke, that you would go to Rome if the Pope invited you.

J.G.—I said that in a certain situation, in relation to the Cuban invitation; I said that I can't go to venerate Castro like all the European intellectuals have done, but after all, since I don't believe in the Pope, not in the least, the Pope is of no importance at all, and going to Rome would have meant nothing.

H.F.—Why does the Chinese revolution trouble you?

J.G.—Because the Chinese revolutionary leaders found a way, first of all, to liberate the immense territory of China from all external powers: the Japanese, the French, the English, the Germans, who else? the Americans, and that seems to me to be extremely significant: all the whites were thrown out; second, and this too is significant, they have fed eight hundred million people, they made it possible for all the Chinese to learn to read and write.

H.F.—From a very simple point of view: I went to Chile during the time of Allende's government, and it seemed to me that with the political posters, the immense murals that covered entire neighborhoods, in a very different style, every artist could express himself freely, the workers could express themselves freely; they made drawings on the walls, in the streets, in every neighborhood; perhaps it wasn't entirely new, but it created a sense of boisterous energy in an otherwise rather gray Santiago de Chile, and there, for me, was the beginning of a revolutionary pictorial art; how do you see this experiment on the part of Allende's government?[26]

J.G.—Really, I don't know. What you're saying is new to me, I didn't know about it.

H.F.—And the economic endeavors of Allende's government, do they seem viable to you?

J.G.—No, on the contrary, they didn't seem viable to me, if you think of the long series of strikes in the copper mines and by the truck drivers, and the extraordinary inflation, it seemed viable only with great difficulty.

H.F.—Caused by ITT.[27]

J.G.—Well, sure, caused by the United States, by ITT, of course, but the government either foresaw it and didn't find the means to remedy it, or else they didn't foresee it.

H.F.—It seems harsh to hear from you that if the revolutionaries or the students of May '68 had taken over the law courts, they would have had to put other people in prison.

J.G.—Or destroy the prisons—but in any case, pronounce judgments and executions.

H.F.—In the case of Saint-Just, it was a question of calling for a death sentence. Is there not, in that audacious and insolent style, the possibility of doing something more progressive than a death sentence?

J.G.—Oh, of course! The Chinese did it in the case of the former Manchurian emperor; they transformed him into a gardener.

H.F.—That seems more progressive to you than a death sentence against Louis XVI?

J.G.—No, more ironic; but in both cases, it's a question of reducing the idea of a man's sovereignty to nothing. Louis XVI was very good with his hands. He was a locksmith, you know. If the French Revolution had made of him a good or an average locksmith, that would have been as beautiful as cutting off his head; but the forces of the moment, during the Terror of 1791 to 1793, were such that he had either to be condemned to death or exiled; and exiling him was very dangerous.

H.F.—Why is it as beautiful to make someone a gardener or a locksmith as to cut off someone else's head?

J.G.—It's as beautiful because it means not exalting death, in the case of Louis XVI, but rendering derisory the idea of one man's sovereignty over others.

H.F.—Is there not for you a certain beauty in the very fact of cutting off someone's head?

J.G.—In the case of the revolutionaries, I don't know whether one can speak of beauty, because they already had power. And you know, when Pompidou refused to pardon Buffet and Bontemps,[28] the two murderers, it wasn't so beautiful. The murder carried out by Pompidou, the double murder of Buffet and Bontemps, I don't see anything heroic in that, or anything aesthetic, or anything at all. He gave in to public opinion, which clamored for death because the wife of a prison guard was murdered by Buffet. I don't find anything admirable in the fact that he gave in to public opinion.

H.F.—Whereas the fact that a poor person commits murder, you find that admirable?

J.G.—First, we mustn't confuse the different perspectives: there is the literary perspective and the lived perspective. The idea of a murder can be beautiful. Real murder, that's something else. Now I saw, really saw, an Algerian murder a Frenchman, just after the Liberation. They were playing cards. I was right there next to them. The Algerian was twenty-four years old, and he had run out of money; the Frenchman had really taken him for a ride. He asked to borrow some money so he could try his luck one more time. He was refused. He took out his knife and he killed. I saw the guy die.[29] That was very beautiful. But why was it beautiful? Because the murder was the culmination, the final endpoint of a revolt that was haunting the Algerian for a long time. It's the revolt that was beautiful, not so much the murder itself. The danger, too, gave it a force, yes . . . in a sense, it made possible a certain conviction, because of the danger involved. The murderer had to run away, and he wasn't captured. For a policeman to kill someone without any risk, no, I don't find that very admirable.

H.F.—And you, why haven't you ever committed murder?

J.G.—Probably because I wrote my books.[30]

H.F.—Have you been haunted by the idea of committing a murder?

J.G.—Oh, of course! But a murder without a victim. I really do have to make an effort to accept a man's death, even if it's inevitable. So whether it's caused by me, by a normal cessation of the heart, by a car accident, etc., doesn't really matter, it shouldn't really matter, but it does. Now you could ask me the question: have you caused anyone's death?

H.F.—Okay.

J.G.—But I won't answer.

H.F.—Do you mean involuntarily?

J.G.—No, voluntarily.[31] The question is this: have you voluntarily caused anyone's death?

H.F.—Okay.

J.G.—I won't answer.

H.F.—Has this weighed on you?

J.G.—No, it hasn't weighed on me at all.

H.F.—Can you describe the steps in your thinking and the path that led from your life to your written work?

J.G.—If you will accept a crude answer, I would say that the impulse to murder was diverted into poetic impulses.

H.F.—How does it happen that we like so much to read about things that are cruel, about murder and torture, that we like to describe murder and torture, and that, in everyday life, we have an extreme reserve toward others, toward the other's body, the integrity of the other?

J.G.—Can you ask the other corollary question suggested by this one? Why do murderers, when they write, almost always give descriptions of themselves, of their acts, or of their imaginary acts, that sound like First Communion?

H.F.—You ask that question. I would like to go back to our remarks on the *Iliad.* I think there is something I would call magic, ritual. You touched on it a moment ago when you spoke of theatricality.

J.G.—I don't agree with you about ritual. What you said the other day, about the formulaic repetition of the same phrases at certain moments, that's not ritual. It's a literary mode of expression that can be used in ritual. Ritual itself is something else. It is the recognition of a transcendence, and it's the repetitive recognition of this transcendence, day after day, week after week, month after month, like the Panathenaea,[32] like the rituals of . . . no, in fact of any ritual, even the rituals of the Catholic Church or Masonic rituals. Books or stories or songs are used for these rituals, but they themselves aren't rituals. The *Iliad* was one of these. During the Panathenaea, the *Iliad* was recited officially. But the *Iliad* itself is neither a ritual nor a sacrament. It's a poem.

H.F.—But within a world that is very ritualized?

J.G.—But every world is ritualized. There is no world that is not ritualized, except obviously the most modern research, in laboratories, or ...

H.F.—Or revolution.

J.G.—Yes, or revolution, obviously. But only when a revolution is under way, because when it's over, it becomes ritualized almost automatically. Look at everything that happened in China with Mao, all those rituals. Just think, they know, they record every minute and almost every second that Mao Tse Tung grants to his visitors. Isn't that true?

H.F.—I'd like to give you a very particular example of ritualization. In certain initiation rites there is a combination of rituals made up of several elements such as flagellation, betrayal of the tribe, betrayal of the family, murder of members of the family, urine rites, excrement rites, rites with animal hides. . . . They are referred to as a "panther society" or a "crocodile society," etc. Rereading part of your work, *Miracle of the Rose* in particular, I see this combination once again, though not within such a narrow circle. Do you think that through your experiences you touched on an archaic and ritual depth?

J.G.—Yes. Here I don't have any knowledge, I have no knowledge of anthropology. What you just described are rites of passage. The passage from puberty to manhood. There is betrayal of the tribe, but in fact it's in order to reintegrate the tribe. There is drinking of urine, but in fact it's in order not to drink it. With *Miracle of the Rose* in particular, it's possible that I tried to discover some rites of passage on my own, but obviously in an unconscious way. This is an idea that never occurred to me before, but it might explain why I didn't write any more books after I left prison, except *The Thief's Journal.*[33] I didn't have any more to write. The passage was complete.

H.F.—And that's why your *Oeuvres complètes* were published in 1952?[34]

J.G.—That's your interpretation. It seems to me to be close to the truth.

H.F.—What importance does violence have for you?

J.G.—Oh! We'd have to talk about things I don't know about.[35] We'd have to talk about the potlatch[36] and destructive intoxication. Destructive intoxication even among the most conscious and intelligent men. Think of Lenin offering the Soviet people public urinals made of gold. In every revolution there is an intoxicated panic, more or less contained, but also more or less unleashed. This intoxication showed itself in France, for example, in all Europe, by the peasant uprisings before the French Revolution, and also in other ways; in a ritual or ritualized form in the Carnival. At certain moments, the entire people wants to be liberated, wants to indulge in the phenomenon of the potlatch, of complete destruction and total expenditure, it needs violence. I go to England quite often. I have a lot of admiration for the Rolling Stones, musically speaking, not for other pop groups, but for the Rolling Stones, I do. I've been going to England regularly since 1948. And really, almost overnight, at the moment, more or less, when England lost its whole Commonwealth, all its dependencies, its whole colonial empire, England at the same time lost its Victorian morals and it became a kind of bazaar, a party.

H.F.—Violence and the potlatch are also subject to rules, to ritualization?

J.G.—Of course.

H.F.—All the violence in your work, every catastrophe, is nested within a rite. Before he was killed, Pasolini said that proletarian violence has essentially changed, that it tends more toward the society of consumption than toward anything else, that today, Italian proletarians kill for things like motorcycles and bourgeois clothes, and that they need to be punished just like Italian neofascists. I find that conclusion completely false.

J.G.—Yes, completely false.

H.F.—But at the same time, do we not see now certain kinds of gratuitous murder, a derangement of ritual in the fact of killing for a dollar, a disorder that is absolutely different from the violence you describe?

J.G.—But you just said the opposite of what Pasolini said. When Pasolini says, or said: The function of proletarian violence is to exert itself for the purpose of appropriating consumer goods. In fact, I wonder—and you yourself just gave the same answer—if it's not a question above all of expressing oneself violently, of being violent and of finding an opening for this violence. It's supposedly for a dollar or for clothes. In reality, it's for the violence itself.

H.F.—So for you, there's no difference between the violence of Querelle[37] and the violence of the young baker who murdered Pasolini?

J.G.—In the case of the baker, I don't know much about it.[38] I think he may have wanted money, or he was horrified by the idea that Pasolini wanted to screw him or put his hand on his ass. I don't know. With adolescents, anything is possible. They can accept every form of sexuality and the most visible sluttishness, and then suddenly they have to show some sort of heterosexuality. "Hey! I'm a man, I don't want to be touched like that!" I don't know.

H.F.—Do you believe that the presumed basis of a murder changes its psychological value?

J.G.—Probably. Man cannot live without justifying himself, and he always finds in his conscience the means and the ability to justify himself and his actions. It's possible that the little baker is sitting in his cell saying to himself, and being encouraged by his lawyer to say to himself and to repeat, "After all, I killed a millionaire who is losing touch with the people, so my cause is just." I don't know, I'm making it up.

H.F.—Apparently Pasolini had some masochistic tastes.

J.G.—I don't know the details. If he wanted to be hit or whipped or beaten, it's quite possible that, as a game and because he was paid, the kid struck the first blows, and then soon enough it's the kid himself who is taking pleasure. He can't stop, and he pushes it to the point of killing the guy. That's possible. I don't know.

H.F.—How do you find the questions I'm asking?

J.G.—They're good questions, but I can never say the whole truth. I can say the truth only in art.

H.F.—What is the truth for you?

J.G.—Before all else, it's a word. It's a word that's used first of all to make someone else believe in your own sincerity. You say: I'm telling you the truth. I don't think I can use this word in an attempt to define it philosophically. Nor can I define it as scientists or scholars do when they speak of an objective truth. Truth is obviously the result of a general observation or observations. But these observations do not necessarily allow one to discover the truth, or, especially, to discover it immediately. Am I going to spend my life or part of my life checking scientific claims?

H.F.—What scientific claims have you been able to verify?

J.G.—Practically none.

H.F.—And which ones would you want to verify?

J.G.—There is one that intrigues me, namely: Are there races? Does the concept of race mean anything? And are there inferior races and superior races? And if there are superior races, should they have precedence if we don't want humanity to become inferior? But can there even be superior races? That is a truth I would like to know.

H.F.—For you, the Negro-African would be of a superior race?

J.G.—Not superior, but not inferior either. Now that requires a demonstration, but I don't have such a demonstration. I know some professors. . . . Well, even the title of professor at the Collège de France doesn't mean very much; they tell me that there are races and that there are inferior races, just as there are inferior and superior individuals, intellectually, physically, etc.

H.F.—Is there any essential difference between approaching sincerity in a conversation and in art, or is it only a difference of degree?

J.G.—Here I will answer immediately: yes. There is an essential difference. In art, one is solitary, one is alone before oneself. In a conversation, one speaks with someone else.

H.F.—And that's disturbing?

J.G.—Obviously it changes the perspective.

H.F.—When you write, don't you address yourself to an other?

J.G.—Never. I probably did not succeed, but my attitude toward the French language is such that I tried to form something with as beautiful a form as possible; the rest was completely indifferent to me.

H.F.—The language you knew best, or the French language?

J.G.—The language I knew best, yes, of course, but also the French language, because it was in that language that I was condemned. The courts condemned me in French.

H.F.—And you want to answer them on a superior level?

J.G.—Exactly. There are perhaps other, more subterranean motives, but in the end, I think, they don't come into it very much.

H.F.—What would they be?

J.G.—Don't ask me. Ask a psychoanalyst that question, he might be able to answer. Because I think it's very unconscious.

H.F.—When did you begin to take on this poetic task?

J.G.—You're asking me to look back in a way that is very difficult, because I don't have many signposts. I think I was around twenty-nine or thirty years old. I was in prison. So that was in '39, 1939. I was alone, in solitary, or in a cell, at any rate. First I should say that I had written nothing except a few letters to friends, both men and women, and I think that the letters were very conventional, I mean full of ready-made phrases I had heard or read, but never really felt. Well, I was going to send a Christmas card to a German friend, a woman who lived in Czechoslovakia. I had bought it in the prison, and the back side of the card, where you're supposed to write, was rough and grainy. And this grain on the card really struck me. Instead of writing about Christmas, I wrote about the texture of the postcard and the snow it evoked for me. That's when I started to write. I believe that was the trigger. It's the trigger I was aware of and able to register.[39]

H.F.—What were the books and literary works that had impressed you up to that point?

J.G.—Pulp novels.[40] Novels by Paul Féval. The kind of books you find in prisons. I don't know. Except, when I was fifteen, when I was in the Mettray reformatory,[41] somehow I got hold of a copy of Ronsard's poems, and I was amazed.

H.F.—And Marcel Proust?

J.G.—Well, I read the first volume of *Within a Budding Grove* in prison. We were in the prison courtyard and were exchanging books on the sly. It was during the war, and since I wasn't too preoccupied with books, I was one of the last. So somebody said, "Here, you take this one." And I saw the name Marcel Proust. I said to myself, "This must be incredibly boring." And then. . . . But here I have to ask you to believe me: if I'm not always sincere with you, this time I am. I read the first sentence of *Within a Budding Grove*, which speaks of Monsieur de Norpois, who is coming to dinner at the house of Proust's parents, or, well, the parents of the one who's writing the book. The sentence is very long. And when I finished reading that sentence, I closed the book and said to myself, "Now I can rest easy, I know I'll find one marvel after another." The first sentence was so dense, so beautiful, and this adventure was a first great flame announcing a huge inferno. It took me almost the rest of the day to get over it. I didn't open the book again until evening, and indeed I found nothing but one marvel after another.

H.F.—You had already written one of your novels before reading Proust?

J.G.—No, I was still writing *Our Lady of the Flowers*.

H.F.—Are there other literary works that impressed you as much as Proust's did?

J.G.—Oh, of course! Some even more than that. There's *The Brothers Karamazov.*

H.F.—And Balzac?

J.G.—Less so. There's an aspect of Balzac that's somewhat trivial.

H.F.—Stendhal?

J.G.—Oh yes, oh yes. Stendhal, of course. *The Charterhouse of Parma,* and even *The Red and the Black,* but especially *The Charterhouse of Parma.* But for me, nothing equals *The Brothers Karamazov.* There are so many different times involved. There was the time of Sonia and the time of Alyosha, there was the time of Smerdyakov, and then there was my own time of reading. There was the time of deciphering, and then there was the time that came before their appearance in the book. What was Smerdyakov doing before being spoken of? Finally, I had to put all this together and reconstruct it. But it was very exciting, and very beautiful.

H.F.—Do you mind if I open a parenthesis on time?

J.G.—No.

H.F.—How do you experience time?

J.G.—You're asking a question that's difficult for me to answer, because for twenty or twenty-five years now, I've been taking Nembutal,[42] and I feel the effects of the Nembutal the entire morning; it makes me sleep almost instantaneously . . . in about ten minutes . . . fifteen . . . yes. But there are effects, for example it's not enough to drink a cup of coffee in the morning. I really have to wait until the Nembutal has stopped affecting my brain. Okay, so during the time when the Nembutal is affecting me, I don't realize how much time is passing. When I have to carry out specific tasks, things that to speak quickly I'll call profane—getting from here to there, buying things—I do them in a very clear-cut way, in a very determinate time, I don't get sidetracked. That's no problem. When I want to write, I have to have all my time for myself. I was a little irritated the other day at Gallimard, since I had just seen M. Huguenin,[43] and I asked for a very large sum of money. And Claude Gallimard wanted to give me a monthly payment, a comfortable monthly payment. But I said, "No, I want you to give me everything today." I want to be absolutely free. To sleep when I want. To go where I want. Otherwise, I won't do anything. I won't do anything, it's not possible. I have to be able to stay for two or three days in bed, writing day and night, etc. Or else for only one hour, etc. It depends.

H.F.—And he refused?

J.G.—Oh, no, he gave it to me. But then there I was with all these bills that I had to stuff into my pockets.

H.F.—A monthly payment for a writer, how much is that in France?

J.G.—I wouldn't know what writers earn. I never asked for details. Since I'm not ashamed of money, of saying how much I earn . . . I couldn't really call it "earning." . . . When I write, there's both a little pain, very little, and a little pleasure. It's not "work." So earn, if you like—well, last year I earned about two hundred thousand francs. And then there are my plays.

H.F.—Does money itself have any importance for you, the actual bills, etc.?

J.G.—Yes, especially if they're large. Yes, I like that.

H.F.—Is money for you a way to gain time, or a way to gain sensuality?

J.G.—No, not sensuality. Time. I don't earn a lot of money. But I earn enough so that I can dress badly, go without washing, enough to do things like that, to let my hair grow without cutting it, which I don't like to do. Having your hair cut is really a pain in the ass. If my hair isn't cut, it doesn't matter in the least.

H.F.—There were times when you found yourself on one side of the gulf. Now you're on the other side. How do you feel about the young antisocial people you meet?

J.G.—I don't feel anything at all. I don't have any guilty feelings. If someone asks me for money (or if I notice, even without being asked), I give it away very easily, really very easily, it doesn't matter to me. There is injustice in the world, but whatever injustice is in the world isn't there because my royalties are relatively high.

H.F.—You yourself have described scenes in which you robbed pederasts who were looking for sex. Has it ever happened one day that a young man saw you as somebody he might rob?

J.G.—Yes, that's happened very, very often. It happened in Hamburg, for example, and that time, I couldn't do anything but let the two guys—there were two of them—let them take the money I had in my pockets.

H.F.—And doesn't that terrify you?

J.G.—Oh! Not at all, not at all. If it's a lot of money, that bothers me. It makes me angry, because then I have to go back to Gallimard. But you see, I turned fifty-six yesterday . . . fifty-five ...

H.F.—Fifty-five or sixty-five?

J.G.—Sixty-five. So I was fifty-six when I was in Karachi.[44] The plane arrived at one in the morning. I was alone. The airport is twenty-five kilometers from the city. So there was a cop who gave me a stamp for a month, and he called a taxi. And I hadn't noticed that the taxi driver was all wrapped in chiffon, and before I could even say no, another guy got in and sat next to me. He was a money changer. He was very insistent. And it was in the middle of the night. "Where are you staying?" he asked me in English. I said, "The Hotel Intercontinental." It's the largest hotel in Karachi. I said, "Can I exchange ten dollars?" Ten dollars won't get you a room at the Hotel Intercontinental. "I have some friends"—this wasn't true—"I have some friends waiting for me at the Hotel Intercontinental." I didn't want to take the money out. But it was still easy for them to get rid of me after taking everything I had. I stuck to my story. I said, "Listen, that's really all I can give you." He gave me the rupees and then he got out when we got to the Hotel Intercontinental. When we got there, though, the ten dollars weren't enough to pay the young guy. So I asked the porter—the hotel was full, it was nighttime, there were people sleeping everywhere, on chairs, on mats and carpets—I asked him, "Do you have a room? I'd like a room at least for tonight?" "No." What could I do? And my million and a half? It was in a big wad in my pocket all held together with hairpins. To take out one bill I had to take out the whole wad. "Can you exchange some money for me right now?" And I took out all the French money. Suddenly, I had a room. Alright then. But the young guy in the taxi, he didn't know I had all that money, and I gave him a little extra to compensate him. But certainly not as much as he would have gotten if he'd left me stranded fifteen kilometers from Karachi. Now there are also times when I've had good luck: I was in Morocco. I met a young Moroccan,[45] twenty-four or twenty-five, very poor. He came up to my room every day. He stayed in my room. He left my money where it was. He never took anything from me. Do I admire him for that? No. I think it was part of a scheme. But I do admire him for going that far with his scheme.

H.F.—Later, you brought him to France.

J.G.—Of course I did, and he was very good at getting what he wanted; I don't regret bringing him to France. In Arab countries, in Third World countries, when a young guy like that meets a white man who shows him a little attention, all he can see is a possible victim, someone to be fleeced; that's just how it is.

H.F.—What sort of relations could a young man have had . . . a young man who is talented, sensitive, intelligent, who likes men, but is miserable, and who robs an old pederast?

J.G.—I couldn't tell you. The first thing is that he might just be hungry, and an old pederast would be the easiest person to rob.

H.F.—When you wrote about that, were you describing yourself?

J.G.—Yes, of course I did it. I did it in Spain, for example, in Spain, in France. So what?

H.F.—Didn't you have some perspective, this perspective ...

J.G.—My point of view, in any case, was that of theft. When I went with a queer, old or not—though I preferred the weakest—it was to steal.

H.F.—Out of necessity?

J.G.—Of course, of course.

H.F.—Didn't it bother you to betray that kind of sexual necessity?

J.G.—I didn't betray any sexual necessity, I wasn't sexually attracted by the old men I robbed; what attracted me was their money; so it was a matter of taking their money, either by knocking them around or by making them come; the only goal was the cash.

H.F.—Didn't you think that by using an old pederast you were lending a hand to a society that hated you?

J.G.—Oh, come on. You'd be asking me to be very clear sighted, to have a political and revolutionary consciousness fifty years ago. Fifty years ago, that was around the time of the schism at the Congress of Tours, the birth of the French Communist Party; can you imagine how much any of that could have meant to a fifteen-year-old peasant raised in the Massif Central, what could he have thought? That was the great epoch of Rosa Luxemburg;[46] do you really think I could have thought about that? You can think it now.

H.F.—When did you discover that you had inclinations for men?

J.G.—I was very young. Maybe eight years old, nine at the most, in any case, very young, in the country and at the Mettray reformatory, where homosexuality was condemned, of course; but since there weren't any girls, there was no other choice. All the boys were between fifteen and twenty-one years old; there was no recourse except in a fleeting homosexuality, and that's what made it possible for me to say that in the reformatory I was truly happy.

H.F.—And you knew you were happy?

J.G.—Yes, I certainly did. Despite the punishments, despite the insults, despite the blows, despite the poor living and working conditions, despite all that, I was happy.

H.F.—Did you realize that this behavior was different from that of other people?

J.G.—No, I don't think the question ever occurred to me. At the time, it was rare for me to ask myself any questions at all about other people. No, for a very long time my attitude remained narcissistic. It was my happiness, it was my own happiness that concerned me.

H.F.—Did you stand apart?

J.G.—Yes, I stood apart. First of all because—though you may think I'm contradicting myself—despite the very profound and solemn happiness I experienced being in this home and having such warm relations with other boys of my age, or a little older, or a little younger, I don't know, I wasn't aware of any protest against this regime and the penal regime, the social regime. Just imagine, it was only when I left, when they let me out to go join the army, that I found out about Lindbergh crossing the Atlantic.[47] I didn't know about it. I didn't know about things like that. You're isolated, you're completely cut off from the world. It's like a convent. Well, my own protest was much harsher and more ferocious than that of the toughs, for example. I think I understood very quickly how to make everyone see what was derisory in this attempt at reeducation and in the prayer sessions, since we had to pray, the gym sessions, the little flags for good conduct, all that nonsense.

H.F.—Did this consciousness extend to erotic life and sexual encounters? Or did you accept, within the world of the prison, the roles that the system laid out for you?

J.G.—No. But I never experienced sex in its pure state. It was always accompanied by tenderness, perhaps a very quick and fleeting affectivity, but until the end of my sexual life, there was always . . . I never made love in a void. . . . I mean without some affective content. There were individuals, young guys, individuals . . . but no role. I was attracted by a boy my age. . . . Don't get me caught up in definitions. . . . I can't define what love is, of course . . . but I could only make love with boys I liked, otherwise . . . I also made love with some guys to make money.

H.F.—Do you have a revolutionary concept of eroticism?

J.G.—Oh no. Revolutionary! No. Being with Arabs has made me . . . has happily satisfied me in general. In general, young Arabs are not ashamed of an old body, an old face. Growing old is a part . . . I won't say of their religion, but it's part of Islamic civilization. You're old; you're old.

H.F.—Has being older changed your relations with your Arab friends?

J.G.—No. I understand them better. When I was eighteen, I was in Syria,[48] I was in love with a little barber in Damascus. He was sixteen, I was eighteen. . . . And everybody, in the street at least, everybody knew that I was in love with him, and they laughed, well, the men did, the women wore veils and were never to be seen . . . but the other boys, the young people, and older, too, smiled about it and made jokes. They said to me, "Well go ahead, go with him." And he himself was not at all embarrassed. I know he was sixteen. So I was eighteen and a half, more or less. . . . And I felt very comfortable with him. Very comfortable with his family, very comfortable with the city of Damascus. I was in Damascus not long after the bombing that followed the revolt of the Druses, ordered by General Goudot. . . . General Gouraud[49] . . . this guy was missing an arm, and he had transformed Damascus into a pile of ruins. He had fired cannons, and we had strict orders always to move around with a weapon and in groups of three, and we had to keep to the sidewalk. If any Arabs, or anyway any Syrians, women or old men, passed by or came toward us, they were the ones who had to step down off the sidewalk. This rhythm was broken, it was broken by me—and only in my case, naturally. I always stepped aside for women, and I went into the souks, which were wonderful in Damascus. I went into the souks without a weapon, and they found out soon enough, because in Damascus there were maybe two hundred, two hundred fifty thousand people living there, and I was very warmly welcomed.

H.F.—In your life now, is there a sort of fatherliness that comes into play in your relations with younger men?

J.G.—Oh yes! But despite myself. It's their doing, not mine.

H.F.—Would you like to give them a certain security in daily life or open the way to art for them?

J.G.—Of course. This is a very old and complicated problem you're bringing up. Today you're asking me personal questions, but it happens that I've reached a point in my life where my person doesn't count for much. I don't think I want to hide anything, it's simply that it bores me. You're trying to touch on my problem in its singularity, but my singular problem no longer exists.

H.F.—But your obsessions, your feelings and resentments, have been projected out into the world. They have had an influence on the behavior of a whole generation.

J.G.—Maybe. But you're talking about things that happened thirty-five or forty years ago and that have been more or less blotted out by age, by memory, by the drugs I've taken, one of their effects being precisely to blot out from memory everything that might be unpleasant and to leave behind only what's pleasant. And you're reminding me of a world of virgin forest that may still exist, but in which I no longer live in the same way. The virgin forest certainly exists, but I have pruned the largest branches from it. I've made for myself a sort of clearing; I can no longer see the primordial forest very clearly. And when you say to me, "But there where you live, there were ferns, there were creepers"—okay, if you say so, I know it's true, but what they were like I don't know anymore. It doesn't interest me very much. All that has withered away.

H.F.—What is your theory of homosexuality?

J.G.—I don't have one. Or I have several. Several have been worked out. None is satisfactory, whether it's the Oedipal theory of Freud, the genetic theory, or Sartre's theory about me in one of his books. He says that I responded in a certain way, but freely, to the social conditions in which I found myself, but that doesn't satisfy me, either. In the end, I don't know. I don't have a theory of homosexuality. I don't even have a theory of an undifferentiated desire. I say: I'm homosexual. Okay. There's not much to it. Trying to find out why or even how I became homosexual and how I realized it, why I am, is a pointless diversion. . . . It's a little bit like trying to understand why my eyes have green pigmentation.

H.F.—In any case, it's not a neurosis, in your opinion?

J.G.—No. In fact, I wonder if I didn't experience it as the resolution of a neurosis, if there wasn't a neurosis that came before homosexuality. But of course, I can't say for sure.

H.F.—Isn't it striking to you that, in all the revolutionary models that we know, there is no freer theory of sexuality than the petit-bourgeois theory of sexuality?

J.G.—One has the impression in the end that revolutions are carried out by family men.

H.F.—When you were with the Palestinians and the Black Panthers, were you accepted as a homosexual?

J.G.—It's very funny. An American television program came to tape me with David Hilliard, there was a Black who was asking questions, and he said to David, who obviously knew since he was reading all my books—he kept them in his bag—he said to him, "Do you know that Jean Genet is homosexual?" David said, "Yes, what about it?" "It doesn't bother you?" "No; if all the homosexuals would come eight hundred miles to defend the Panthers, that wouldn't be bad."

H.F.—He's being nice; there's no substance behind it. Imagine a good socialist, a real womanizer, Castro, for example ... [50]

J.G.—His brother is homosexual. Raoul Castro. So people say.

H.F.—Let's suppose that a good socialist, handsome, powerful, a womanizer, shows up at the Panthers'. They probably wouldn't go so far as to serve as a procurer for him, but they would casually help him, they might even introduce him to some women. To accept in a revolutionary way the homosexuality of Jean Genet in the midst of the Black Panthers would have made it livable, it would have made it concrete.

J.G.—Well, listen. David liked women. He was married, but he also had women on the side. But I know that a Black, and I don't think he was homosexual, one evening after I had spoken at Yale University—we were always embracing, everyone would embrace me, and he didn't embrace me like the others, but very affectionately, he really squeezed me, and he wasn't . . . and he didn't try to hide it, either. He did it in front of twenty Blacks.

H.F.—You spoke a moment ago about the end of your sexual life; did your fascination, your desire not go any further with the Black Panthers?

J.G.—What they asked of me was really very, very difficult. I was still taking Nembutal, since I had to sleep. These were young guys, from eighteen to twenty-five years old, maybe twenty-eight. David was twenty-eight, he had an extraordinary energy. He would wake me up at two in the morning, I'd have to go give a press conference, at two in the morning, and I had to be awake and ready to respond to the questions. Believe me, I wasn't thinking about making love. And then there was another phenomenon, which is that I didn't make any distinctions between the Panthers, I loved them all, I wasn't attracted by one rather than another. I loved the phenomenon of the Black Panthers. I was in love with that.

H.F.—So you weren't imposing on yourself an erotic abstinence that in a more liberal world you would not have accepted?

J.G.—Not at all. To the point that Bobby Seale had sent me a letter asking me to write an article on homosexuality; and this letter was either badly translated or carelessly written, in any case I answered saying, "If you attack homosexuals, I'll attack the Blacks." The next week I received a copy of the newspaper, Newton himself had written an article in which he said that it was absolutely necessary to be on the side of the homosexuals, that it was necessary to defend them, that they were a minority group, and that it was necessary to accept their help in defending the Panthers and at the same time to accept defending them.[51]

H.F.—Are you sure this defense would really have been put into practice?

J.G.—Obviously I have no proof. No, I'm not sure. Because the Panthers were very young as a movement, I met them in 1970, so the movement was only two years old. They said they didn't believe in God, but they wanted to get married in churches, things like that. So ...

H.F.—I would like to go back to the question of your literary creation. Were there other important readings that went alongside the creation of your novels?

J.G.—Dostoyevsky.

H.F.—Already in prison?

J.G.—Yes, oh yes. Before going to prison. When I was a soldier, I read *The House of the Dead,* I read *Crime and Punishment.* For me, Raskolnikov was a man who was alive, more alive, much more alive than Léon Blum, for example.

H.F.—When you left prison, you found yourself surrounded by the literary world. You became friends with Cocteau; he defended you, I believe?

J.G.—Yes, but that belongs to a little pseudoliterary story of no interest, of no importance at all.[52]

H.F.—Do you respect Cocteau as a poet?

J.G.—No. You know, my poetic apprenticeship is very limited. There's Baudelaire, Nerval, Rimbaud, I think, that's all.

H.F.—Mallarmé?

J.G.—Oh yes! Of course, Mallarmé.

H.F.—Not Ronsard?

J.G.—No, no, no.

H.F.—Rutebeuf?[53]

J.G.—Yes, but it's sporadic with Rutebeuf. There are verses by Mallarmé I know by heart, by Baudelaire, Nerval, Rimbaud, I can recite them by heart, but not Rutebeuf.

H.F.—You're preparing a new work; will it be a work for the theater?

J.G.—I can't talk about that. I don't know what it will be.[54]

H.F.—Did I annoy you today?

J.G.—You didn't really annoy me. The questions you asked were less interesting than the ones you asked yesterday and the day before. Today you wanted me to speak of myself. I'm not all that interested in myself anymore.

H.F.—Still, do you think that the interview gives an idea of what you really think?

J.G.—No.

H.F.—What's missing?

J.G.—The truth. It's possible when I'm alone. Truth has nothing to do with a confession, it has nothing to do with a dialogue; I'm speaking of my truth. I tried to answer your questions as closely as I could. In fact, I was very far away.

H.F.—That's very harsh, what you're saying!

J.G.—But harsh for whom?

H.F.—For anyone who tries to approach you.

J.G.—I can't say anything to anybody. To others, I can't say anything but lies. If I'm all alone, I speak a bit of the truth, perhaps. If I'm with someone else, I lie. I'm somewhere else, off to the side.

H.F.—But lies have a double truth.

J.G.—Yes! Try to discover the truth they contain. Try to discover what I wanted to hide by saying certain things to you.

§ 25   Near Ajloun

To the memory of all the fedayeen.[1]

Bodies and faces are given to those who can read. One might think that they willed this hardness so as to create the cloud that surrounds the Arab world, and to tear apart the mythologies that have been depicted on it. It's a form of revolt. And it's a self-affirming but slightly tremulous shout, as if the fighters, even as they want to disperse the cloud, also wanted to protect themselves in its thickness. In speaking of this cloud, I am evoking nothing other than what remains within everyone after studying or simply reading the Quran, in which all the fedayeen looked for a *nom de guerre*, the better to conceal themselves. From this situation something sharp and delicate results: a hesitation. To conquer? To conquer oneself? To become stronger than fifteen centuries of tradition, all the stronger since the expression "pre-Islamic" exists, after which there was Muhammad and his legend, which covers and conceals his life and casts doubt on it, just as every legend casts doubt on the person who was perhaps its origin, but this Prophet, the seal of all prophets, who could not write, who recited what the angel Gabriel dictated to him, who himself was reading the uncreated Quran resting on the knees of Allah (the story is bizarre, rich, modern)—crouched in the sunny or shady squares of Mecca, before men who wrote his terrifying words on dried bones.[2]

~

If the need to regain for themselves an Arab identity—one which perhaps used to exist—is not lived but mimicked, this need and identity will appear as nothing.

The Arabs give the impression of having been emptied out, like certain hermit-crab shells. They live this emptiness, and in order to forget it, they have a sort of dance, an exaggeration of gestures and words. This is necessary: a therapeutic means that will end when the "colonial wound" has ceased. For a European this bombast is incoherent—but *La Marseillaise!* A lack of adaptation to the modern world, for it is a bombast that would fill a void truly lived, a dispossession, an alienation if you like. Ill, that is, alienated and beside themselves, the Arabs feel the need to swell rather than to harden. No doubt these last words evoke suspect images, and we know what swells and hardens in them. The Palestinians who almost took off from the ground, lifted up by Shukeiri's outrages, are exceptions.[3] After dispelling but not filling their emptiness, a very obvious economy of language leads them back into contact with the real. The healing quickens. With a certain astonishment, they listen and watch the rest of the Arab world as it swells.

Roaring, hyperbolic, convulsive anger is a remedy that can calm, for a moment, the ill of being nothing, or very little, of being no one, or almost no one, and when the anger has passed, the person will appear. The Anglo-Saxon cannot really see what it all means, but for the Arab the void and the nullity are lived.

As a way to fill the emptiness, the bombast is found not only in curses and gestures but in the extravagance of the heroism that is recounted. After the massacres inflicted in Amman by the Jordanian army, a young fedayee could, without bragging, tell the story of a battle that took place in the hospital at Achrafieh.[4] He had taken courses in nursing when he was sixteen, and during the first days of the battle he had the idea of setting up an infirmary in the city, near the hospital. "Surprised by the Bedouins while still in the hospital with his rifle, he lies on a pile of corpses and plays dead. The shooting continues all around. The Bedouins step over him without suspecting that he is still alive. The dead continue to pile up. Finally the shooting stops. He carefully raises his head, sits up, lights a cigarette, looks at his watch: it's almost night and three hours have passed since his feigned death. During this false death, he has had the time to aim at several Bedouins and shoot them down. He stands up and walks out."[5]

∼

Let's approach the question again: what is Arabness? Is it analogous to Latinness in Europe or in South America? Taken from the outside, the word is not lived, therefore not understood. It would impart a lived unity, without worrying that it might risk establishing a difference. There is perhaps a lived Jewishness that has as it were crystallized in the land of Islam. Arab, Latin, Jew: what do these terms mean? Thus a man like Abu Omar, who is a Palestinian Arab—does he place himself under the category of Arabness (he speaks Arabic, was born in Palestine) or of Latinness (he is a Christian)?[6]

~

God is generally rather troublesome for revolutionaries, and the Palestinians are not quite sure how to behave with respect to that ungraspable being who, in the Arab world, is recalled several times a day by means of loudspeakers attached to the tops of minarets. The revolution would disturb only a weak clergy, but the attempt by Kemal Ataturk is an unpleasant memory here.[7] Although he succeeded in secularizing the state, the people and almost all of Turkish society remained or became believers. Turning a few mosques into museums will not be enough to drive out the East and put the West in its place. This failure is worrisome, even if it happens that the leaders of the Resistance see themselves as revolutionaries, whereas Mustafa Kemal imposed himself as a dictator. But God, invisible and all-threatening—what about him? Like the one across the way, he is the God of a people and of a storm, and he seems to be opposed to any rupture among those who have "submitted." The fellah and the brick worker may rebel against their situation—mentally or otherwise—when they know about the situation of the emirs of Kuwait or Muscat. To calm the fellah, the emir has to say only one phrase: "I am a Muslim. Like you." Both find themselves within a common identity. Everything is in order. The emir takes the plane to London or New York and the fellah remains mired in his mess. Invisible, God is immobile. Incapable today of conquering the West, he lets himself be raped by it or rather lets it take his earthly resources while he constrains his people to immobility. Must the divine illusion be destroyed?

Even the most revolutionary fedayee is not constantly preoccupied with overturning or transforming social, moral, and aesthetic values. He also dreams, a waking dream: either that the fedayee takes on the role of a prestigious and acclaimed revolutionary, or that he takes refuge in an imaginary bourgeois world. It is possible, then, that he will become a more passionate destroyer of the values with which, in his dream, he was content. A certain nostalgia, or the longing for a bourgeois world that has not been lived, gives him the strength to leave it behind. There is perhaps another thing, which is the same thing: a knowledge as detailed as possible of this bourgeois world allows him to fight it. Sometimes the fedayee, without himself being aware of it, reveals some of his preoccupations— for example, when he interrogates a European visitor in excessive detail, when according to a bourgeois code or rules of virtue he condemns bourgeois life or certain aspects of it, when his own behavior is such that it becomes difficult to tell if he is in the Resistance out of a revolutionary necessity or only to satisfy his warrior's aspirations and his sense of authority.

All this has already been pointed out, and the complex and contradictory but obscure motivations of the fedayeen are perhaps necessary for them to accomplish revolutionary actions in a direct and unambiguous way; or to see themselves in a daydream as a millionaire oil baron, a traditionalist and a cosmopolitan, the better to destroy the oil, the millions, the traditions, and the cosmopolitan complicities by exposing themselves to gunfire. Impoverished boy that he is, whom would he kill, sacrificing himself, if he had nothing but his poverty? He will kill a more significant enemy if he has had the time, before the sacrifice, to give himself over to a daydream in which he can be sovereign.

The other sort of daydream is the imaginary continuation of his present situation to the point of its success, that is, its glory, that is, domination, even if he arrives at glory by refusing the exercise of domination.

How then is a fedayee different from any other boy his age? It must first be said that the Palestinian fighters are very young. In the mountains near Jerash, Salt, and Ajloun, their activities are limited and are no different from those of any other soldier on a campaign. Deprived of women, it is impossible that this absence wouldn't carry them away, if only for a few minutes, into a consoling daydream. And however fleeting, such a consoling daydream quickly leads the one dreaming it to the evocation of a woman, then a mother, in a happy and pacifying situation, the complete opposite of the situation he is living in.

This brief description may be inaccurate, but no one can claim that the fedayeen do not dream, and that their daydreams do not have a bourgeois content that is opposed to their stated ideology. If one is able to go with them into the mountains and listen to them, it becomes clear that their ideological discourses, their revolutionary plans, are fissured, so to speak, and that these fissures reveal, like a consolation, dreams of repose and a nostalgia for the traditional forms they are going to destroy. The Palestinian fighters are perhaps more precise in their attitudes, in their gestures, more concentrated and concise in their manner of speaking, because they have decided to fight in the light of day, which weighs on them obscurely, and if they entertain these daydreams, it is perhaps in order to sharpen the weapons turned against these dreams.

It must not be forgotten either that they are like the "sons of the wind and the rain." No land belongs to them. "Refugee camps": this expression is clear. If all the fedayeen do not literally come out of camps, each one knows that he depends on them because he is a Palestinian in Jordan, and there are no refugee camps for Jordanians there.

If a space of sovereignty is refused to them, along with all the pacifying habits this brings with it in our world; if in the camps themselves they cannot pursue in reality a search for bourgeois pleasures, which each one, according to his personality, would then have the freedom to destroy, perhaps they must invent for themselves this space and these pleasures.

As for occupied Palestine, everyone knows that it is occupied in such an outrageous way that no heroism will allow it to be opened today, except by a miracle: if God wills it, or if one becomes a demi-god oneself. The revolutionary project must be pursued to the ends of the Arab world, at least, and to make this world yield, it must create within itself a base and point of departure, a logistical base, born in a sort of concupiscence with the traditional bourgeois advantages, which one must destroy all around oneself, destroy all the more after having surveyed them within oneself.

~

Already very beautiful—to the extent that the fedayeen freed themselves from tradition—their beauty grew to the point of becoming luminous among the Arabs who remained outside the struggle. Or rather, the imposing presence of certain Bedouins remained external, based as it was on a virility that was accentuated by the robes and the kaffiyehs.[8] The fedayeen had a beauty that was fresh, naive, that addressed itself to the intelligence. Having rejected the slightly affected ancient nobility, their gestures are simple, effective, ready for action. Their language is concise, indicating a desire not to continue the immemorial attitude, but to shatter the image the Arabs wanted to perpetuate. The old subtleties are on the verge of disappearing. In their place, reflection is coming to light. No, everything is not over. Among the fedayeen there still remains the cunning that may be their undoing. This new beauty comes from revolt. While they look like fighters, they also look like young mechanics. Often they joke with girls who do not lower their eyes and do not blush. Ferraj and Hamza are very beautiful, lively, precise, and their beauty is one that no longer owes anything to the darkness of the times.[9] They do not come to the surface to be enveloped by this darkness, they have already escaped from it. Thus many are married and accept that their wives are equals and that they would take care of young wounded men, whom they will see undressed; but others refuse. They will always refuse.

The dancing is revealing. In the camp at Baqa, in Jordan, I attended a celebration of reconciliation between Palestinian fedayeen and the Bedouin soldiers.[10] Embarrassed by their bodies and by the dance steps, the Palestinians were heavy, clumsy, almost ridiculous, whereas the Bedouins were marvelous. In the two camps the dance was the same, but if the Palestinians saw it as an amusement, for the Bedouins it was a sacred display, reassuring them in their condition as men dancing for themselves, dancing before God, dancing for the women.

Through dancing they were reassuring themselves of being themselves, of being Muslim and manly. Neither side was armed, but the Bedouins' dance became so violent, their beauty became so great, their certainty in dancing—and the fact that their dancing was a challenge to be met—became so evident that, already triumphant, if this severe and simple dance had continued it would have put the Palestinians to rout.

Thus the warrior's bravura displayed by the Bedouins is very great—but it is nothing compared to the moral courage of the Palestinians.

~

1977

I reread these notes, remembering that I wrote them in the calm of a zone about sixty kilometers by forty, at the edge of the Jordan River, near Ajloun.[11]

After the massacres of September 1970 ordered by Hussein of Jordan and the Americans, the fedayeen had withdrawn. We were living in tents and beneath the trees. Silence had settled on us once again, after the terrible din of Amman. The fedayeen were very young. They had already gotten rid of the bombastic rhetoric of the Arab capitals. They spoke soberly, almost dryly. It seemed to me that they were shaking off Arab dust, pulling themselves out of it so as to become Palestinians all the more, and all the better.

The women (mothers, sisters, wives) who came onto the bases brought mail.[12] It is from the Palestinian women that the fedayeen learn silence and calm, I thought.

They dropped off the mail and left without saying a word, without a smile or a glance. They didn't take the time to drink a any water. They had come by shortcuts, often watched over by Jordanian soldiers. I will always have great admiration for them, and for their actions accomplished with simplicity.

This zone I spoke of, flanked by the Jordan River, I did not yet know that with each night it was becoming more sparsely populated: fedayeen of fifteen, sixteen, seventeen, eighteen, nineteen, twenty years old would cross the river, would kneel down to kiss the Palestinian earth, and would go, always at night, to explode an Israeli target.

Many did not come back. Very few knew the happiness of return, the kisses on the cheeks and the great glad slaps on the back.

§ 26 The Tenacity of American Blacks

In 1955, a black housewife named Rosa Parks gets onto a bus divided in two by segregation.[1] All the seats for blacks are taken. Only one is free, reserved for whites. Ms. Parks is very tired, her legs are swollen, and with terror in her heart—but with a weary body—she sits down among the whites. The bus comes to a halt, the driver gets up and tries to eject the guilty party, insults are exchanged . . .

The first peace march would begin a few days later: for blacks, a new day is dawning.

The first phases of the struggle would last until the assassinations of Malcolm X and Martin Luther King.

In 1968, the washed-out pupils of the whites still refuse to register images of black people, except the very novel sight from the Mexico City Olympics when two black runners stood on the podium after accepting their medals and saluted, with raised fists and lowered heads, the American national anthem.[2] A slap in the face of official America, seen live by the entire world.

Whites who traveled in subways and on trains witnessed the growth of an extravagant vegetation: the sparse but insidious beards, the vertical hairdos, combed into Afros with combs made of metal. The black ghetto, and then the community in general, encouraged and watched over by the Black Panthers, refused to straighten their hair. Blacks were finally being seen. And heard. To the American challenge they responded, "Black is beautiful,"[3] but what was there to say beneath the laughter that deformed English words? In the trains, on the sidewalks, the white ladies had to listen in a sort of distraction to the words of an unknown slang, words that were probably as obscene as the electric hairs growing from heads and chins.

For three years it was a black celebration that spread its stripes across America from head to foot.

In 1970, Angela Davis was teaching at UCLA. Driven out of the university, she struggled with and for the Soledad Brothers. For their release, for George Jackson's release. Everyone knows what happened after that: the abduction of a judge by Jonathan Jackson, his assassination by the police, Angela's arrest, the assassination of George Jackson, Angela's trial, her release, her decision to transform the various movements that supported her, both black and white, into a vast alliance that fights, most often head to head, to enforce civil rights for everyone, that is, for the weakest.

Here she is at a meeting at La Mutualité, invited by the French Communist Party. Her beauty lights up the room. Once more I feel certain that revolution would be impossible without the poetry of individual revolt that precedes it. Seeing Angela again at the podium, I recognize what still belongs to the Black Panthers, and this too: whatever the reasons for rebelling—and they are indisputable—whatever their arguments and their methods, it is an explosion of poetry that lifted the black community, gave it a light insolence, an amused smile at itself and at the whites, and—but how to describe this?—thanks to the black revolutionaries, politics was a liberating politics.

During lunch, Angela gives me a glimpse of its source:

"There is growing opposition in the United States to integration in the schools. At UC Berkeley, in 1973 there were fourteen hundred black students; this year there are only seven hundred. They're being turned down for scholarships."

"When you were young, did you play with white children?"

She hesitates. Thinks back. Smiles.

"Yes. With a little boy my age. Until about seven years old. Then he disappeared; I mean, he didn't come to play anymore. I was very surprised . . . "

"He didn't come back. Why not?"

"It's something left over from slavery. On the plantation, the master's children played with the slaves' children up to a certain age. Then they were separated; you can imagine why. The remnants of slavery are painful for us, and for a lot of whites, too."

"There are a lot of things left over from slavery . . . the cooking . . . "

She bursts out laughing and gives some recipes for dishes made with the parts from slaughtered pigs that were left to the blacks.

"It's become very expensive," she said.

"Can the (black) community trust the black police?"

"Not always. Not always. There are some black cops who are more brutal with us than certain white ones. It seems they want to prove themselves or make up for being black. But this isn't a general observation, since some black policemen warned me about certain maneuvers planned against me."

"Eldridge . . . "

"Cleaver?[4] He's selling out. He's exploiting the visions of Christ he had in France, and it's bringing in a lot of cash."

"He didn't see Christ in France, he saw the Virgin in America! In France he was sewing pants . . . "[5]

"I know. His presence in Algiers was catastrophic; he managed to convince people that a liberation army was forming there. I remember the thought expressed by Massai: 'American blacks do not trust their charismatic prophets.'"[6]

Angela is very amused by the idea of Cleaver sewing pants with flies that stick out. She asks me:

"Was that when he had his revelation and his visions?"

We talk about her courses at the University of Los Angeles and the threats from the supporters of LeRoi Jones:[7]

"He has changed a lot. Now he is almost as much of a Marxist as I am."

"Yesterday we saw a film about Ben Chavis in prison,[8] and you must remember also another film made in San Francisco about Bobby Seale, it was shown twice on American television.[9] It's hard to imagine the penal authorities in France allowing such stories to be aired."

"In America it depends on the judge. And judges are elected. They make their decisions according to pressure and opportunism."

"The French press reported that 70 percent of the black vote went to Carter?"

"We know and we knew who Carter was: the governor of Georgia. But we were confronted with this situation: voting for Ford was impossible; not voting at all would have been seen—by us and by whites—as a lack of interest in our own status as American citizens. Carter may not be very intelligent, but Ford isn't intelligent at all. All that remained was to vote

for Carter, with disgust, and without ceasing to criticize him, to criticize
his administration, to harass him, to remind him of all the promises he
made during the election campaign. Finally, Young's positions in the UN
are better than those of his predecessors."[10]

"And yet?"

"Right. And yet . . . we're seeing a resurgence of the Ku Klux Klan.[11]
It's a revitalized Ku Klux Klan, led by a playboy type who is charming and
modern—not in his motives, which are perfectly medieval, but in his
methods. This is the Ku Klux Klan that, with the help of the police, drove
out all the blacks living in the city of Taft (California). In Chicago I spoke
of this with some friends, and I thought they'd be astonished by my story,
but a demonstration of ten thousand whites in hoods and white capes,
with banners and flags, had paraded through the streets of Chicago a
week before, in an attempt to stop blacks from walking in Marquette
Park. In Louisville, Kentucky, there was a demonstration of the Ku Klux
Klan, the first in forty years. You know that 1976 was the bicentennial of
the United States. It was marked by other events like these which the official ceremonies could not completely hide. For example, in Boston there
was an attack on a black lawyer. I'll send you the photo, it was in all the
papers, showing a flagman charging at the lawyer with the pole of the
American flag held sideways like a lance. The sociology professor Harry
Edwards will probably be kicked out of the university because he is black
and a leftist. Tommy Smith, the Olympic champion in Mexico City is
being turned down for a position as chair."

"The return of racism is the return of the repressed?"

Angela smiles. She doesn't like the inappropriateness of terms, the
vagueness of comparisons.

"Yes and no. The racism now returning at full speed had probably
never disappeared from consciousness or the unconscious, but its manifest return, its new harmfulness are not spontaneous. They are deliberate,
maintained by the white bourgeoisie. The crisis, which you're seeing in
Europe as well, obliges the Carter administration to take unpopular measures: curtailing the use of resources and the distribution of available
energy; fighting (unsuccessfully) against unemployment and inflation.
Whites are more and more discontented. The Ku Klux Klan gives them
a scapegoat, the one the USA has always had. They're starting to burn
crosses in black people's yards again, like forty or fifty years ago. But we
have a more and more refined awareness of racism, and we call those

responsible by name. Ordinary conversations prove it. It's no longer a question of pigs or whites, but of capitalists and the bourgeoisie.

"And Ben Chavis?"

"He is the one who was attacked and who was put in prison with his nine comrades. The Alliance is committed to doing everything possible to free them.[12] Nor should we deny the seriousness of what is happening. Really, you have to take literally what David said to you. Lynching could come back, and soon."

Here is what David Hilliard, leader of the Black Panthers from 1970 to 1971, said to me. When I asked him to come with me to the University of Stony Brook, in the middle of the forest, he imitated a terrified shiver and answered smiling, "There are still too many trees."[13]

Victims of the triangular slave trade that deported them from the coasts of Africa, American blacks are slowly emerging from the four hundred years of hell which, nonetheless, were marked by the struggles of the great "rebel slaves" and their descendants (DuBois, Malcolm X, King), and by the women in the struggle who showed an even more overwhelming tenacity, to the point that it becomes uncanny: Harriet Tubman and Angela Davis.

§ 27 Chartres Cathedral

Two poles: Chartres and Nara,[1] poles of an axis around which the Earth turns. We chance almost at random on Chartres. Chartres in the Beauce.

The two shrines are immediately evoked in order to open a discussion later on concerning the "right to difference."[2]

Few things remain in our memories or in specialized books, and nothing at all on the Beauce plain, of its first-century inhabitants or of their dwellings. Our Lady of Chartres remains. Breathtaking. In Japan, the shrines of Nara remain.

For what follows, Chartres was not chosen with great effort. Nor was Nara. I had them, so to speak, at hand, but at each place on the planet an axis crossing it ends: two poles of equal value.

The builders of cathedrals were foreigners come from the construction sites of Burgos, Cologne, Brussels: foremen, figure carvers, stonecutters, manufacturers of stained-glass windows, alchemists of enamel ...

—We're about to go stand in front of *The Tree of Jesse*[3]—those numerous foreigners were building a church that would be French, then. Muslims were maybe there for a part of it, small or great, Toledo only a few weeks away by horseback.

Hands, and minds, worked a lot. We have no record of wall posters, around 1160, asserting the value of manual labor.[4] That may be because the stonecutter—to take that example—at first hewing the stones coarse-ly, tried to copy the figure carvers a little, and his joy was great when he completed the first leaf of ivy that, along with others, would form the band encircling the nave at Amiens. No longer a stonecutter, he is a sculptor. It is not inconceivable, then, that some stoléru[5] taught him that manual labor is a servitude from which he could extricate himself through intellectual investigation. That is how he little by little invents those different methods of leverage that, lessening his pain, led him to the posters revalorizing the exhausting labor he had just had the weakness to relinquish ...

The nave at Chartres is today French and a national—worse, cultur-al—jewel. But the chapter that decided on its coming into the world was made up, like the construction team, of men from all over.

Vagabonds, probably, more or less well-organized in heterogeneous bands, rather than settled workshops, built what remains—the most beautiful thing that remains in France, especially there, and that official France brags about possessing.

Those men from all over of course did not make up the core of the Chartres population, nor did they mix with the already existing core. They will go on to work and die anywhere at all.

A country is not a fatherland [*patrie*]. It is highly unlikely that a region could be a fatherland naturally made up of men and women who, having the same values, would have greater equality with one another and would know each other better. If France, with all its regions, were a chocolate Easter egg full of little chocolate eggs, each egg would not be a fatherland.

Let us take up the old-fashioned word "affinity." Men who have the same affinities are not in the same chocolate egg. Lovers of Chartres and Nara are as numerous in Morocco, in South Africa, in Germany, in Greece, in Japan, in Holland, in all the nations of the world, even, as in France or Beauce.

The Tree of Jesse is the theme of the central panel of the royal portal. Instead of the Italian Mona Lisa, the minister, [André] Malraux, could have sent *The Tree of Jesse* to Japan for an exhibition, the sudden levitation of contemporary and ancient works of art placed into orbit around the globe would have made it possible.[6]

If extreme mobility is a sign of modernity, why not send, whole and by air, Chartres cathedral to spend almost a year in Tokyo? And not its life-sized replica in polyester, since the sky is full of so many works of art that take the plane from one country to an-other—Tutankhamen. Matisse. Van Gogh, Etruscan art, Pierre Boulez, The Apocalypse of Angers, take world tours several times a year.

To whom does *The Tree of Jesse* belong? Undoubtedly to the people of Beauce, who found it there at the foot of the cradle, and who never saw it. Just as the Turks own the Venus de Milo.

Is Chartres cathedral French, Beauce, or Turkish?

Perhaps the region should bring a little fatherland into the big one and so permit each Frenchman to have two of them—because as it is, he's the only one in the world who can't pronounce this grandiose asininity: "Every man has two fatherlands, his own and France."[7]

No longer will Pharaonic civilization, despite the recent restorations of Rameses II, despite the ridiculous royal salute accorded to two wooden crates containing his mummy cut in two,[8] be able to recognize itself in Sadat's Egypt, nor ancient provinces in the new administrative districts.
If these districts are to move us, for them to tremble or smile at us, we will have to appeal to the dead provinces.

If every man has a value equal to every other man, every corner of the earth, even the most barren, is worth every other—hence, I hope I'll be forgiven, my total detachment with regard to any particular region, but hence, too, my emotion sometimes when I am faced with what has been abandoned. To keep my interest, it had better be scrap.[9]

Without building a cathedral, every nomad—the Sahraoui[10] for instance—loves the stony corner where he has put up his tent and that he will leave. Pitching camp and breaking camp [*foutre le camp*], hope and slight heartbreak mixed together.

The fatherland is not a nation. At best, it can be a threatened nation, an ill nation, a wounded or troubled nation.

France was certainly a fatherland for many during the first weeks of the Exodus [of 1940]. For the five years that followed, it was fatherland for many fewer Frenchmen.

If danger disappears or if only its theatricality dissolves, the nation becomes again the piece of a more delicate administrative wheel.

One can still wonder if the multiplicity of media might not be more efficient for the rapid, true, smooth functioning of an increasingly complex society.

Each region already does its own things. Like the southern ones that, every morning, polish and shine their sun. To every stranger who sounds Parisian, they explain how they have formed, chiseled, polished, labored on the sun, and how before they came, there lived, in night and fog, shivering populations who died of cold and tuberculosis.

—"But our hot sun cures everything ..."

I repeat, without knowing why, that a homeland can be known as a homeland only in the misfortunes that come from elsewhere.

Obviously, each one of us is tempted to go carry misery elsewhere.

Virtues of the soil. Happiness of being at home, on one's ground.

Desire for the underground: appropriation of ground for the exploitation of those underground by the grasping foreigner.

The homeland is on the pellicular surface of the ground—thanks to its deep foundations, to its superimposed crypts, Chartres cathedral doesn't risk yielding the plain to the wheat fields.

When they intone, at their work tables, the beautiful names of French villages, poets must have a sardonic grin. This thousand-year-old country smells of the stake: Albi, Montségur, Rouen, Nantes, Paris. . . . And of decay: the hanged men of Bretagne, the drowned men of Nantes—

again!—the besieged of La Rochelle . . . So?

Where and how were the union and unity of France made, in what places? Let us not forget the little Bretons, Basques, Corsicans, Alsatians, Picards, Normans, who discovered they were French in Algiers, Tannanarive, Hanoi, Timbuktu, Conakry ...
Our zouaves and our marines were there.

They returned to the metropolis to be more equal among themselves, to have the same rights and values, able to look each other in the eye at the same level. Rights of free men, obviously.

Royal France was made by iron, by fire, in all the burnings inside France—with one exception but a considerable one—the Crusades.
Bourgeois France was made by iron, by fire, in burnings and in France Overseas.

The day before yesterday the world. Today the region. Tomorrow Europe.
It seems we have been perceiving the breathing of a being we thought less alive: the ideal sphere is inflated, stretched, and directed toward one single government. It inhales. And everything retracts, breaks up, cracks into tiny fatherlands. It exhales.
For years, we have felt that all men were alike. Today, we pretend to believe in the "right to difference" for the peoples of "over there."
Yesterday, under blinding differences, we discovered the almost ungraspable sameness of our fellow creatures; today, by administrative decree, we dissolve that sameness so that difference can above all be manifest.

In the name of this "right to difference," let us protect the spirituality of India. The wretchedness of Calcutta is nothing compared to it. And let us protect the innocence of Africa. At least may our fat-men's spirituality find itself in the death wards of Dacca[11] and our innocence in the barbed wire of Djibouti. From afar, let us admire the transparency of those who disembody themselves for us.

And Chartres inside? And *The Tree of Jesse*? And Nara in Japan? And our cultural gifts—expensive missiles with a weak impact: really it's not much when we know that, despite "that," an Arab in Paris will have no real peace except in his wretched douar,[12] his true homeland.

Each nation has its own spirit, yes; so what? Each country, in fact, has "its right to difference," so what?

And each region its own.

All the provincial conscripts, from Charles X to Poincaré, after having taken part in brutal conquests over a great part of the world, after having stretched around the earth the red sash of the French Empire, their sons and their grandsons experienced the backwash. Maybe it's up to the French Left to undertake the opposite of bourgeois republics.

We shouldn't reproach the men of yesterday with anything. Let today's men act differently. Real fidelity is often to do the opposite of those to whom one vows fidelity.

Perhaps we should expect something else of the Left besides a well-moderated arrangement of French territory, expect it, rather, to discover, to lay bare this: that "sameness" and "difference" are two words to indicate one single mode of the real.

We must not allow the "right to difference" to let a thousand men die of hunger. With or without new regions, the French can live, but not the Palestinians, Bengalis, Sahraouis, not yet. The picturesque quality of the world—of the Third World surviving in a high Middle Age—camouflages similarity and even sameness.

Cuban soldiers helping Angola,[13] that was a beautiful manifestation of the Left in the world.

If the idea of modernity has any meaning, it is because of the mobility of the age. But one could say that nostalgia is an element of man and that it is prudent to have one's country house, one's countryside, one's land, one's territory, however restricted it may be. Maybe? Do we want to leave in order to come back? Or only to know that an intangible place exists?

I'll sum up: a more or less Saxon chapter, or one more or less impregnated with Latinity and Christian myths, bathing in paganism in which Fairies and the Virgin are confused, the chapter of Chartres ordering troupes of stonecutters, vagabonds, but talented, brilliantly uses the ribbed vault, then the ogival arch, in the midst of an unsophisticated populace and pious whores whose wages are used to pay for the stained glass, on the other side of the world from it rice planters around Nara, the two peoples had much in common, their smile, laughter, tears, fatigue, and they also have the right to difference.

§ 28 Violence and Brutality

> The deep hypocrisy and the barbarity of the bourgeoisie are displayed
> with impunity before our very eyes, whether we look at the large cities
> where its domination has taken on respectable, civilized forms, or at
> the colonies where it is simply brutal.
>
> —Karl Marx, cited by Andreas Baader[1]

Journalists like to throw around words that grab our attention, but
they have little concern for the slow germination of these words in the
minds and consciences of individuals. Violence—and its indispensable
complement, nonviolence—are two examples. If we reflect on any vital
phenomenon, even in its narrowest, biological sense, we understand that
violence and life are virtually synonymous. The kernel of wheat that ger-
minates and breaks through the frozen earth, the chick's beak that cracks
open the eggshell, the impregnation of a woman, the birth of a child can
all be considered violent. And no one casts doubt on the child, the
woman, the chick, the bud, the kernel of wheat. The trial against the RAF
(Rote Armee Fraktion), the trial of its violence, is very real, but West
Germany, and with it all of Europe and America, want to fool themselves.[2] More or less obscurely, everyone knows that these two words, trial
and violence, hide a third: brutality. The brutality of the system. And a
trial against violence is brutality itself. The greater the brutality, and the
more outrageous the trial, the more violence becomes imperious and necessary. The more oppressive brutality becomes, the more will the violence
that is life be required to the point of heroism. Here is a phrase from
Andreas Baader: "Violence is an economic potential."[3]

When violence is defined or described as above, we must say that it is
brutality: the gesture or theatrical gesticulation that puts an end to freedom, for no other reason than the will to negate or to interrupt the
accomplishment of a free act.

The brutal gesture is one that halts and suppresses a free act.

With this distinction between violence and brutality, it is not simply a matter of replacing one word with another while leaving intact the accusatory function of the statement with regard to those who use violence. Rather, it is a matter of rectifying an everyday judgment and of not allowing the powers that be to make use of words as they please, as they have done and still do in relation to the word brutality, which here, in France, they replace with "unfortunate mistakes" or "setbacks."

Just as the examples of necessary violence are innumerable, so are acts of brutality, since brutality always steps in to oppose violence—by which I mean, again, an uninterrupted dynamic that is life itself. Brutality thus takes the most unexpected forms, often not immediately discernable as brutality: the architecture of public housing projects; bureaucracy; the substitution of a word—proper or familiar—by a number; the priority, in traffic, given to speed over the slow rhythm of the pedestrian; the authority of the machine over the man who serves it; the codification of laws that override custom; the numerical progression of prison sentences; the use of secrets that prevent the public from knowing what concerns it; the useless slaps and blows in police stations; the condescending speech of police addressing anyone with brown skin; the obsequious bowing for the sake of a generous tip and the mockery and crudeness if there is none; goose-stepping soldiers; the bombing of Haiphong,[4] the eighty-thousand dollar Rolls-Royce . . . Of course, no enumeration could exhaust the facts, which are like the multiple avatars through which brutality imposes itself. And all the spontaneous violence of life that is carried further by the violence of revolutionaries will be just enough to thwart organized brutality.

What we owe to Andreas Baader, Ulrike Meinhof, Holger Meins, Gudrun Ensslin, and Jan-Karl Raspe—to the RAF in general—is that they have made us understand, not only by words but by actions, both in and out of prison, that violence alone can bring an end to the brutality of men.[5] A remark is necessary here: the brutality of a volcanic eruption, of a storm, or in a more everyday form, that of an animal, calls for no judgment. The violence of a bud bursting forth—against all expectation and against every impediment—always moves us.

There is obviously one chance: namely that brutality, by its very excess, would destroy itself, or rather, not that it would change its ends—by definition it has no ends—but that it would come to wipe itself out, to annihilate itself in the long run, when faced with violence.[6] The colonization of the Third World was nothing but a series of brutal acts, very numerous and very long, with no other goal than the now rather atrophied one of serving the strategy of the colonialist countries and the wealth of companies investing in the colonies.

From this there resulted a poverty, a despair that could not help but breed a liberating violence.

But never, in all that we know of them, have the members of the RAF allowed their violence to become pure brutality, for they know that they would immediately be transformed into the enemy they are fighting.

One preoccupation is particularly remarkable in their correspondence and depositions: without worrying over anecdotes about the Kremlin, the pompous pronouncements of de Gaulle concerning some dinner with Stalin, or other details reported by the Kremlinologists that have about as much significance as the sentimental transports of the queen of England, the RAF insists on demonstrating that, from Lenin to the present, Soviet policy has never ceased to support the peoples of the Third World. However one might wish to explain it, this policy has never faltered. At times it has been, and quite often is, embarrassed by the intense complexity of feudal or tribal relations, to which may be added the interests and contradictory maneuvers of the former colonial powers and of the United States; but since 1917, despite what Western commentators tell us, and despite whatever its internal policy may be, the Soviet Union has always taken the side of the weakest and most vulnerable countries, whether through agreements between one government and another, or through votes in the UN and in international organizations.

Many people know this, that is certain. But in Europe—by which we must understand also the European world of America—and especially in West Germany, which is so virulently anti-Soviet, the RAF is the only group to say it clearly. In short, the RAF reaffirms a politically obvious fact that has been obscured in Europe.

Is this why the Red Army Faction has received so little—despite the resonance of their political arguments, smothered, it's true, by a violent action here called "terrorism" (parenthesis: another word, "terrorism," that should be applied as much and more to the brutalities of bourgeois society)—is this why they have received so little acceptance, let us say, from certain leftist tendencies?

There may be yet other reasons: the Red Army Faction seems to be the opposite of May '68, but also its continuation. Especially its continuation. From the beginning, the student uprising—but not the factory strikes—gave itself an air of insurrection that translated into skirmishes in which the two sides, the police and the protesters, attempted with more or less elegance to avoid the irreparable. The nocturnal games in the streets had more in common with dance than with combat. The demonstrations were verbose, and were open even to the police and to the provocateurs of the Right. As for the continuations of that month of May, we perceive them as a sort of lacey fringe, an angelic, spiritualist, humanist lace. The RAF was organized both with the hardness of a well-tightened bottle cap and with an impermeable structure, with a violent action that ceases neither in prison nor out, and that with great precision leads each of its members to the limits of death, to the approach of a death undergone while opposing—still violently—the brutalities of courtrooms and cells, and this even unto death itself.

Heroism is not within the reach of just any militant. We might well think that the more casual leftists, skewered by Ulrike for their "purely verbal radicalism," are frightened away by a determination with such real consequences.

In this long correspondence and in these statements, the word Gulag does not appear. The negative things that the Soviet Union has done, is supposed to have done—without being conjured away—give way to the positive things it has done and is doing. Each member of the RAF accepts, claims, demands to be—entirely, unto torture and unto death— one of the islands in this archipelago of the Western Gulag.

The entire "Statement of Ulrike for the Liberation of Andreas at the Berlin-Moabit Trial" says very clearly and explicitly that it is the very brutality of German society that has made the violence of the RAF necessary.[7] We understand this when we read the statement, particularly the passage that begins: "Guerrilla warfare, and not only here, for it was no different in Brazil . . . we are a group of comrades who have decided to act, to leave behind the state of lethargy, the purely verbal radicalism, the more and more empty discussions of strategy, we have decided to fight."[8]

Germany has become what the United States expected it to become: its easternmost defensive shield, but its most offensive one as well. In the face of this brutality perpetuated according to a logic gone mad, and forbidding or eroding an almost outlawed Communist Party, the only opposition remaining for the RAF was that of a heroic violence. Let us admit for a moment that the correspondence between Andreas, Ulrike, and their comrades grew out of and was fortified by necessities that became more and more inaccessible, more and more "inhuman"; then we have to wonder who is the cause: this inhuman Germany desired by America. And we also have to wonder whether the aggravation is not brought about by prison and isolation, by the monitoring systems—from reading them, one has the impression that the prisoners are inside a giant ear—the surveillance systems, the silence, the lights; and whether the aggravation is not deliberate—on the part of Buback and the system he works for—so that the prisoners would appear monstrous to us, so that their writings would distance us from them, so that their death, slow or brutal, would leave us indifferent; so that we would no longer think it's a question of human beings tortured by others but a monster that has been captured.[9]

If this was the goal of Buback and the system, they have lost: Holger gives us a terrifying portrait of someone who opposes the capitalist brute; Ulrike, Andreas, Gudrun, and Jan-Karl, throughout their correspondence, have succeeded in convincing and moving us.[10]

Here is a quote from Ulrike: "The cops, with their tactics of psychological warfare, are trying once again to reverse the facts that the guerrilla war had put back in their proper perspective. Namely that it is not the people who depend on the state but the state that depends on the people; that it is not the people who need the joint-stock companies of the multinationals or their factories, but that it is these capitalist bastards who need the people; that the goal of the police is not to protect the people from criminals, but to protect the order of imperialist exploiters from the people; that the people do not need justice, but justice needs the people; that we do not need the presence of American troops and bases here, but that U.S. imperialism needs us.

"Through personalization and psychologization, they project onto us what they themselves are: the clichés of the anthropology of capitalism, the reality of its masks, its judges and prosecutors, its prison guards, its fascists: some bastard who takes pleasure in his alienation, who lives only to torture, to oppress and to exploit others, whose existence is based entirely on his career and advancement, on throwing his weight around, on profiting from others; who revels in exploitation, hunger, misery, and in the *stripping bare of billions of human beings in the Third World and here.*"[11]

I underline this phrase because it reveals that the poverty of the Third World—physical, moral, intellectual poverty—is constantly present within them, that the RAF lives this poverty in its mind and body.

When they denounce the brutalities of the United States and its privileged agent West Germany, their primary concern is this subservient Germany, but at the same time and in the same movement they are also concerned with all the poverty and misery of the world. And when they write this, the members of the RAF prove not only the hidden generosity and tenderness of every revolutionary, they are also articulating a very delicate sensitivity with regard to what here, in Europe, we continue to call the dregs of society.

If Marx's analysis is correct—"Revolutionary progress makes its way when it provokes a powerful counterrevolution that closes in on itself, engendering an adversary that can only lead the insurrectionary party to evolve in its struggle toward a true revolutionary party"—then we must recognize that the RAF, at the cost of sacrifices which this time are superhuman, has decided to "make its way,"[12] with all that this implies of solitude, incomprehension, internal violence.

They are in this dangerous situation, careful to refuse the pride associated with it and aware that their thought must be rid of every residue of stupidity, so as to be sharpened more and more by an ever more precise analysis. Attentive also to the tactics the system uses against them. During the trial of August 26, 1975, Andreas stated this very succinctly: "The state is fighting with all the means at its disposal—Schmidt has said this often enough, that it's a question of putting every possible means to work—and these are precisely all the organized means of repression, lies, manipulation, technology—this has to do with the image of imperial omnipotence he tries give himself, in opposition to the historical tendency consciously articulated in our politics, in insurrection, and it is here that this politics appears to be antagonistic to society and therefore illegitimate."[13]

In reading certain statements made in the courtroom, we understand how much honesty and subtlety they have needed in order to show up the structures of Organization, to say, by way of tape recorders set up by the court, to say clearly and explicitly what they have tried to do, to describe the situation in Germany (the Germany of Brandt and Schmidt)—a Germany that America has imposed and whose bourgeoisie, so proud of the deutsche mark's successes, considers itself absolved of Nazism, thanks to its anticommunism.[14]

It is obvious, moreover, that West Germany's opposition to any Communist Party openly recognized as such is in large part responsible for the existence of the RAF, which proves in a striking fashion that social-democracy is democratic in its discourse but inquisitorial when it sees fit. And with its "clean" torture, "refined" by modern techniques, it is inquisitorial with a clear conscience and without remorse.

Germany has abolished the death penalty. But it brings death through hunger and thirst strikes and enforces isolation through the "deprecia-

tion" of the slightest sound except that of the prisoner's heart. Locked in
a vacuum, he eventually discovers in his body the sound of pulsing blood,
the sound of his lungs, that is, the sound of his organism, and thus he
comes to know that thought is produced by the body.

To say that the situation in which the imprisoned members of the RAF
have been placed is criminal, is to say nothing. Moral judgment ceases, in
the consciences of the judges themselves and in those of the population
who have been led to a state of absolute peace through the mediation of
the press, and therefore through pressure. It is to be feared that Germany
will feel itself purified when "they are all dead, and dead from their will
to death," therefore "dead because they know they are guilty," since for
Germany this is the tranquilizing significance of the hunger and thirst
strikes that may end in death.

While reading this book by Andreas and Ulrike, Gudrun and Jan-Karl,
let us remember that the German journalists have spoken up against feeding them through a tube and have decreed that the duty of the doctor is
to place food within reach of the prisoners: it is up to them to live or die.[15]

In very much the same manner, the judges let themselves off the hook
by decreeing that it is the lawyers who, because they are incapable of per-
suading their clients, are guilty of the offense—or the crime?—of failing
to assist a person in danger.[16]

But to accuse the German government, the German administration,
the German people—what does that mean? If the United States were not
physically present in Germany, if its ambition had not become so swollen,
if Europe had not, whether explicitly or otherwise, assigned to West
Germany its function as the police of the East, this thorn called the RAF
sticking in the too fat flesh of Germany would perhaps not be so sharp,
and Germany might not be so inhuman.

Or, if you like, I see here a twofold phenomenon of contempt.
Germany is seeking to create—and to a certain extent has succeeded in
creating—a terrifying, a monstrous image of the RAF. On the other hand,
and through the same movement, the rest of Europe and America, by
encouraging the intransigence of Germany in its torturous activity
against the RAF, is seeking to create—and to a certain extent has succeeded in creating—a terrifying, a monstrous image of Germany.

§ 29 Interview with Tahar Ben Jelloun

Tahar Ben Jelloun.—Jean Genet, you have carefully read the bill proposing new laws on the conditions for entry, residence, and work applicable to immigrant workers in France.[1] What are your thoughts after reading it?

Genet.—Just wait. France will decidedly leave colonial time and space much later. The gems of Bangui illustrate and illuminate this primary truth:[2] even if other colors have replaced the symbolic pink of the empire on the global map, the French still live with their superiority, except that it's buried more deeply inside them, lower down, probably in the depths of their intestines.[3] This once haughty superiority, aware that its days are numbered, is growing vicious. And it's all the more irritated now that France is full of blacks, Arabs, people of mixed race, who almost never lower their eyes anymore: their gaze is on a level with ours.

Something had to be done!

Of course, the ever greater casualness of black and brown men and women is not at the origin of this law. This casualness, however, is a sign.

T.B.J.—A sign of what?

G.—The immigrant workers are unlike Bokassa on every count, except this one: after using them, sometimes to the point of using them up, France throws them away.[4]

The Africans we call immigrant workers have never particularly wanted to work in France. They preferred Belgium, Holland, or Germany, where their rights are no more respected than here but where the salaries are higher. Now, North Africa especially—and even more in the countryside, where the men were less politicized and therefore more docile—

178

has been scoured by strange recruiting agents charged with bringing back labor power for French factories.

In 1967, I was in Madrid, at the train station, when a train full of Mauritanians was divided in two. One part was to go through Port-Bou, the other through Hendaye. Two of the recruiting agents showed them where to go, watched over them, held on to all the passports and the tickets.

At the time, all this Saharan muscle was indispensable in Saint-Nazaire and Thionville.[5]

Even after being completely done in, they will try to survive in Nouadhibou.[6]

T.B.J.—For you, a community that is forced to leave its homeland in order to sell its labor power is already excluded from life; it's a question of survival . . .

J.G.—They didn't think they were leaving their homeland for good. They were encouraged to leave for what seemed like a promotion. The hiring and the pick-up were carried out in a rather old fashioned way; except for the location, which wasn't a fairground, the whole thing had an air of livestock trading. The recruiter squeezed their muscles, looked at their teeth and gums, felt for the firmness and solidity of their hands. This was happening even just a few years ago. But the drought in the Sahel left too many dehydrated workers in the sand. And on top of that, the recession had begun . . . when the Africans realized that they had been taken for a ride, it was too late.

T.B.J.—If an English engineer came to work in France . . .

G.—Those we call "immigrant workers" are men who should not be considered only that—though this is what Stoléru does from beginning to end, in a text explaining a "new statute."[7]

Foreigners in France, yes; living abroad, yes. And each one of these men are also: an astonished tourist, someone who is momentarily exiled, illiterate in the language of the country he now finds himself in, where it is difficult to feel at ease, where he is a also an amazed witness . . . everything, in short, that a Frenchman would be beyond his own borders—in Switzerland, for example—but the displaced Africans have been designated once and for all as immigrant workers, which amounts to saying that they belong to an underclass, an essence assigned to them and which they cannot shake off, for the administration is watching. It has its training personnel, its designated spaces—Arenc . . .[8]

T.B.J.—Did you say Arenc?

G.—No, I was only asking you if the Arenc prison was demolished.

The fact that an "immigrant worker" is a human being should go without saying. But here, everyone, particularly the administration, sees what the peasants long ago saw in the words *nomads, gypsies, vagabonds*: the place for them—very temporary—is the entrance or the exit from the village, next to where the waste is dumped.

"Immigrant workers"—there is even an added layer of shame in this—and Stoléru ought to be attentive to this—for the immigrant works *with his hands*. When he invited a Malian garbage collector to the Élysée—one New Year's Day, with cameras there to capture the event—that is probably what the president wanted to show: the hands of the invited worker are rather cumbersome in the midst of a receiving room.[9] They are more suited to holding a balaclava. And there are no jackhammer operators under the chandeliers of the Élysée Palace.

T.B.J.—Is France a dream or a misunderstanding?

G.—All capitalist countries, whether neocolonialist or not, protect their national work force. None of these states, with the exception of France, has crowned itself with a halo for being a model of civilization. The African who comes to France to work, to study, to walk around, you might think that he would leave with a kind of amazement. . . . We others, as "civilizations," we know now that civilization is also this bill being proposed against the poorest people in the world.

T.B.J.—And yet it's a civilized country.

G.—No one doubts that the very highest authority has assigned to France the mission of rescuing Africa from its misery. . . . Besides, France is feminine; she has all the gentle virtues of the mother and the lover. France is a Most Benevolent Lady [*la Très-Bonne*]. We hoped (it's the least she could do!) that she would open her arms to all her old slaves.

T.B.J.—But this is an old story . . .

G.—How did it start? In Morocco it was like this: toward the end of Lyautey's rule, around 1930, the French did not have the right to buy land belonging to the tribes.[10] They got around this obstacle by turning this land into private property and paying Moroccan front men. Once the tribes were dispossessed of their traditional land, nothing remained for the men but to leave, to work elsewhere, first in the Moroccan ports, then in Paris, finally in our provinces, where, since they were used to wearing babouches, they were slowed down by the clumsy boots they had to lug around on their feet.

The same thing happened—or almost the same—in Tunisia with the signing of the Bardo Treaty, when one of the Bey's son-in-laws sold several thousand acres of land to French merchants, very cheap and "cleared" (which means purified, rid of any Arab encampments).[11]

Even earlier, a little after 1830, Marshal Bugeaud, the future duke of Isly, had begun to populate Algeria using the method everyone knows about now: French soldiers in a row on one side, facing a row of "girls" from Toulon on the other, a drum roll, and each soldier marched forward to "the one" exactly opposite him. They were married. The new couple went immediately to draw lots for the plot of land that would make them property owners.[12]

Before 1914, there were relatively few immigrant workers in France, besides the Italians of course. It was thanks to Verdun or Chemin-des-Dames that the natives had the honor of spilling French or assimilated blood. In 1944, there was Garigliano, in 1954, Dien Bien Phu . . .

T.B.J.—Do you think that racism is more prevalent in France than in other European countries?

G.—Other European countries—what a question! In France, I have always been aware of this racism which is part of its very fabric, although it is always changing. When I was young, people hated the Jews and loved the Moroccans and the Senegalese who cleaned the gutters.

The aggression of the French during the colonial conquests was intensified by an almost natural racism. Now that this aggression has come to appear ridiculous, what remains is a racism concerned with exploitation by the stupidest means possible. After "Let's use this starving labor power" comes "Let's get rid of all these darkies."

T.B.J.—Is there any hope that this bill won't pass?

G.—Without much faith in such things, one can always hope that there will be a reprieve, a divine grace that would give every French person a measure of humanity.

If such a law were voted in, and if French people were still capable of any sane behavior, they would act as some communists and some aristocrats did during the Occupation: they would provide false papers to workers in danger, they would shelter them secretly, certain priests would help them, networks would be created, functionaries would look the other way, and perhaps France would be called Denmark.[13]

§ 30 *The Brothers Karamazov*

Artistic or poetic works of art are the highest form of the human spirit, its most convincing expression: that is a commonplace that should be filed under the rubric "eternal truth." Whether they are the highest form of the human spirit, or the highest form given to the human spirit, or the highest form taken, patiently or quickly, by a lucky chance, but always boldly, it is a question of a form, and this form is far from being the limit to which a human can venture.

Let us go to Dostoyevsky, or rather to *The Brothers Karamazov*, masterpiece of the novel, a great book, a bold instigation of souls, excess, and excesses. This is how I think about it too, and add a wish to laugh in the face of the false and very real imposture that determines the destiny of this book. Dostoyevsky at last completes something that would make him supreme: a farce, a piece of buffoonery at once enormous and petty, and since it is exercised over everything that made him such a possessed novelist, it is exercised against himself, and with shrewd and childlike methods, which he uses with the stubborn bad faith of Saint Paul.

If he carried this novel inside himself for more than thirty years, it is possible that he wanted to write it seriously, that is to say, like *Crime and Punishment* or *The Idiot*, but in the course of writing, he must have smiled, perhaps first at one of his techniques, then at Dostoyevsky the novelist, and finally he must have let himself be carried away by jubilation. He was playing a good trick on himself.

Knowing little about the techniques of composing novels, I still don't know if a writer begins a book with its beginning or with its end. In the case of *The Brothers Karamazov*, I find it impossible to see if Dostoyevsky wanted to begin with the visit of the Karamazov family to the starets Zossima, but even if I had to wait for the death and stench of the starets, from that moment on, I was on the track of something.

Everyone expects a miracle: the opposite happens; instead of a corpse remaining intact, which would be the least to ask, the corpse stinks. So, with a sort of delicious relentlessness, Dostoyevsky does everything to disconcert us; we wait for Grushenka to be a bitch: at Katya Ivanovna's, Alyosha first sees a beautiful young woman, *seemingly* very good and generous, and in her enthusiasm, gratitude, and tenderness, Katerina Ivanovna kisses his hand. Shocked, Grushenka in turn brings Katerina Ivanovna's hand to her mouth, breaks out laughing, and insults her rival. Humiliated, Katerina chases Grushenka away.

When Alyosha returns to the monastery, the starets's corpse smells worse and worse; windows had to be opened. Alyosha goes out. At night, he throws himself on the ground, kisses the earth. He even claims to have experienced a visitation at that moment, and he ends up, with his monk's robe, in Grushenka's apartment.

What allows Alyosha to remain pure, we know, is his smile on all occasions when someone else in his place would be disturbed: when he is still a monk, Lisa sends him a note, and, determined to marry her, he smiles and quite seriously consents to become her husband. Later on, when the boy Kolya tells him, "in brief, Karamazov, you and I are in love with each other," Alyosha blushes a little, and agrees. Alyosha smiles, he is twenty years old. A similar amusement, at the age of sixty, makes Dostoyevsky smile: one gesture or another can be interpreted as one likes. The Prosecutor at the trial explains Dmitri Karamazov's motives, and the lawyer, just as shrewd, gives them an opposite meaning.

Every action has a meaning and an opposite meaning. For the first time, it seems to me, the psychological explanation is destroyed by another (opposite) psychological explanation. The actions or intentions that we have a habit—in books and even in daily life—of considering as wicked lead to salvation, and kindly acts and intentions provoke catastrophe. Kolya raises a dog that little Ilyusha thought he poisoned or killed with a pin. Ilyusha, having fallen ill, hopes only that when Kolya arrives and the dog returns, Kolya may finally visit Ilyusha and bring the dog: Ilyusha's joy is so great that he dies of it.

Ivan Karamazov's dilettante, sure-of-himself attitude makes Dmitri hurl words and even deeds at his father; they lead him to Siberia.

At the beginning of the trial, Ivanovna speaks warmly about Dmitri; fifteen minutes later, she reads a letter from Dmitri to the court: Dmitri is condemned.

Dostoyevsky shows hostility toward socialism, and even toward psychology.

Against socialism he is fierce (see the scenes in which Kolya, by his behavior, ridicules socialism), but once again, the seed must die: it is a socialist revolution that permits millions of Russians to read Dostoyevsky today.

As to psychology, he handles it well: unlike his other novels, where he gives only a straightforward explanation of motives, here, he will also give the opposite explanation: with the result, for the reader, that everything—characters, events, everything—means this *and* also its opposite, nothing is left but tatters. The fun begins. Both ours and the novelist's. After each chapter, we're sure: there's no truth left. And a new Dostoyevsky appears: he clowns around. He amuses himself by giving a *positive* explanation of events, and then as soon as he perceives that this explanation is true in the *novel,* he offers the opposite explanation.

Masterly humor. Game. But risky, because it destroys the *dignity* of the narrative. It's the opposite of Flaubert, who sees only *one* explanation, and the opposite of Proust, who heaps up explanations, who posits a great number of motives or interpretations, but never demonstrates that an opposite explanation is permissible.

Did I read *The Brothers Karamazov* badly? I read it as a joke. With affirmation, and worthily, Dostoyevsky destroys preconceptions about what a work of art should be with this book.

It seems to me, after this reading, that every novel or poem or painting or piece of music is an imposture if it does not destroy itself, I mean does not construct itself as a carnival duck shoot, where it is one of the heads we aim at.

They talk a lot these days about laughing at the gods. The work of art constructed on assertions alone, which are never questioned, is an imposture that hides something more important. Frans Hals must have laughed a lot with *The Women Regents* [*of the Haarlem Almshouse*] and *The Regents* [*of the Old Men's Almshouse*]. Rembrandt, too, with the sleeve of *The Jewish Bride*.[2] Mozart, composing his *Requiem* and even *Don Giovanni*. Everything was allowed them. They were free. Shakespeare, too, with *King Lear*. After having had talent and genius, they know something rarer: they know how to laugh at their genius.

And Smerdyakov?

Because there are four of them, the three brothers Karamazov. The gentle Christian Alyosha doesn't say a single word, doesn't make one gesture, to show that this worm is his brother.

I'd like to talk about Smerdyakov.

§ 31 Interview with Antoine Bourseiller

His birth certificate states: Born Dec. 19, 1910, at 10 A.M. Mother:
Gabrielle Genet. Father: unknown. Except for his books, we know
nothing about him, including the date of his death, which he assumes
to be imminent.[1]

Shadow and Light[2]

Genet.—I don't see why I should remain silent about myself, I'm still
the one who knows me best.

The most important things, what was most important to me, I put
them in my books. Not because I speak in the first person: the "I," in that
case, is nothing but a character who's been slightly magnified.

I am closer to what I wrote, really, because I wrote it in prison, and I
was convinced that I would never get out of prison.

I'll try to give you an explanation of why I liked going back to prison,
for whatever it's worth, I don't know. I have the impression that sometime
in my thirties, around thirty, thirty-five years old, I had in a sense
exhausted the erotic charm of the prisons, prisons for men, of course; and
since I always loved shadows, even as a child, I loved them perhaps to the
point of going to prison. Of course I don't mean to say that I stole in
order to go to prison; I did it so I could eat. But in the end it led me perhaps intuitively toward the shadows, toward prison.

And then, around thirty-five, thirty-six years old, I wanted to travel, I
wanted to go to the Orient, to Kathmandu, for example, long before all
of you did. But by the time I got to Istanbul I'd had enough, I was sick
of traveling. I went back to Greece, and for the first time I saw something
that for me was astonishing: shadows, yes, but mixed with light. And the
four years I spent in Greece were probably the sunniest of my life.[3] Mixed
with shadows. In this case, the shadows were, I could say, the shadows of
the steam baths, of the soldiers' movie houses, where the presence of the

soldiers really stood out. I loved Greece also because it's one of the countries—along with the countries of the Arab world—where the erotic charge is probably the most intense, and that may be why I stayed so long. In any case, I no longer had any desire to go to prison.

I loved Greece for yet another reason, which I'll tell you about. It was, it is, the only country in the world where the people were able to venerate, to honor their gods, and also not to give a damn about them. What the Greek people did in relation to Olympus, the Jews would never have dared and would still never dare to do for Yahweh, no Christian would dare to do for the Crucified, no Muslim for Allah. The Greeks were able at the same time to mock themselves and to mock their gods. That to me is astounding.

When I was a kid I grew up Catholic,[4] of course, but the god—God, that is—was mostly an image; it was the guy nailed to the cross, the girl—what's her name?—Mary, getting pregnant from a dove. None of this seemed to be very serious. God, well, he wasn't very serious; he didn't count for much in my little world as a kid between one and fifteen years old.

When I was fifteen, I think, fourteen or fifteen, I had an illness, perhaps quite serious, or not serious, a childhood illness in any case. And every day at the Public Welfare, at the hospital of the Public Welfare, every day, a nurse brought me a piece of candy, and she said to me, "The sick boy in the next room sent this to you." After a while I got better, after about two weeks. I wanted to find this guy who had sent me candy, to thank him, and I saw a boy of sixteen or seventeen who was so beautiful that everything that had existed for me up to then no longer mattered. God, the Virgin, Mary, nobody existed anymore; he was God. And do you know what his name was, this guy who was only a kid? His name was Divers.[5] Like the other one who was called Personne, in a way. And this Divers who, if he still exists, must be seventy-four or seventy-five years old, this Divers has a long line of copies who were all the lovers I had until about ten years ago. But not faded copies, on the contrary, copies that were sometimes more beautiful than the original.

So, as for God—it was after all in Greece that I knew him best. In Greece and, as I said, in the Arab countries.

Abdallah and Jean

I met Abdallah, I took him to Greece; he was a deserter.[6] He was half German, half Algerian—so half French at the same time, since his father was Algerian, and therefore French—and he had to do his military service during the Algerian War. I got him to desert, and we went to Greece, where he learned to walk the tightrope. But Aballah is so much a part of my inner life that I prefer not to speak of him in front of the camera.

Just as I prefer not to speak of Jean Decarnin, who died as a young communist, at the age of twenty-one, fighting against the Germans.[7] They gave me examples of two different but equally heroic deaths, and that, I keep it all to myself. I don't want to say any more about it.

Giacometti

Antoine Bourseiller.—Could you talk about Giacometti?

Genet.—Yes, because I still have the straw of his kitchen chair embedded in my rear end, after he made me sit there for some forty-odd days while he did my portrait.[8]

He didn't let me move or even smoke, I could only turn my head a little; but then there was such beautiful conversation on his part.

A.B.—He is one of the people you have most admired, you said?

G.—The only one.

A.B.—The only one?

G.—Yes. I could say that I am grateful to Greece because it taught me two things I didn't know: cheerfulness and incredulity. Alberto taught me to appreciate dust, to have a sensibility for things like that.

A moment ago I evoked the country where I was most able to breathe: Greece. I spoke to you of the man I most admired: Giacometti. My life is almost over. I am seventy-one years old and you're looking at what remains of all that, of my history and my geography. Nothing more. It wasn't much.[9]

Rimbaud

"O let my keel burst! Let me go to the sea!"[10]

What's surprising is that "O let my keel burst!"—the boat itself says that, the Drunken Boat, and in slang "keel" [*la quille*] means "leg." When he was seventeen, Rimbaud said: "O let my keel burst!" That is,

"O let my leg . . . " And at thirty-seven he had his leg cut off, by the sea, at Marseille. That's all I wanted to say.

There is, it seems, though I can't prove this, with every man, every man, whether a poet or not—"poet" doesn't mean much—but with every man there is, at a given moment, something like a prophetic gift with regard to himself, that he himself does not see. I'm convinced that Rimbaud meant to say, and did say, that his leg would be cut off. I'm convinced that he wanted his silence. I'm convinced—to stay within the realm of the poets—that Racine wanted his silence; I'm convinced that Shakespeare really wanted anonymity, in the end, and Homer too.

So what is it that acts through each man and that each man, at one given moment or another, can unveil, and perhaps bring into the open? I don't know. Maybe nothing.

Sacred Time

One thing is sacred for me—and I knowingly use the word sacred—time is sacred. Space doesn't matter. A space can be reduced or enlarged enormously, it has little importance. But time—I have had the impression, and still do, that a certain amount of time was given to me at birth. Given by whom? That I don't know, of course. But it seems to be given by a god. But, in any case, don't imagine a god—even if it's not a question of a dancing god—don't imagine a god who moralizes the way you do, with a shadowy face like the one you know. That's not it. It's a god who is cheerful enough to guide me and to make me win at chess, for example. And then, in the end, it's something like what I was saying to you yesterday, it's a god that I invent, as one invents rules. I refer to him, that's a given, but I invent him. That's all I can tell you. But he doesn't dance, like the one Nietzsche would like to believe in; he doesn't dance, but he amuses himself. In any case, he amuses himself with me; he does-n't leave me for a second.[11]

The most anonymous man has the same amount of time, or less time, or more time, it doesn't matter, but that time, it's sacred. Not only can I not touch it—others can touch it, that is, they can get rid of me, kill me, but I can't—but during this time, during . . . now, seventy years, it has been imperative for me to work this time. I could not leave it fallow, so to speak. I had to work it almost in a blaze, and almost day and night.

In my case, and obviously as a joke, one can say that in a way I have been preoccupied with transforming this time into a volume, into several volumes.[12] And nothing will remain of any of that, the day I die, when I am vaporized, nothing at all will remain because I will not be here anymore. So volumes, no volumes, the whole thing is a joke. Posterity—only for posterity does it have any meaning, but not for us.

The Black Panthers

I would have liked to talk to you about the Black Panthers, who were not simply a phenomenon that produced an event, at once poetic and political, in the United States. You have to imagine these poor whites who found themselves in a subway or in an elevator next to bearded men with long hair, men and women with vertical hair, horizontal beards, aggressive beards and hair like corkscrews that scratched the whites who wanted get away but couldn't.[13]

One day I was supposed to go speak in an American university called Stony Brook, about fifteen miles from New York. The university is in a forest, a nice little area; we were going by car, there were three or four cars containing the Panthers and me. I said to David Hilliard, "Come along with us," and David doesn't answer. But he finally did answer; he said, "No, there are still too many trees." Only a black American could give that answer. For him, a tree was first of all a plant with branches from which black people had been hung.[14]

What remains with me from the blacks I knew? If America interests me a little, it's because the blacks are like black characters on a white page. They are the black characters set off against the pale whites of America.[15]

The Palestinians

In a region located about eighteen miles from Amman, almost on the Jordan River, there was a battle between the Palestinian fedayeen and the Jordanians, between the troops of the Palestinian fedayeen and the Jordanian troops of King Hussein. A French film maker had asked Arafat, or one of his friends, for authorization to film the fighting, since he himself was involved in the fighting, that is, he was very close to the combat zones. But they didn't want to, the leaders of the military didn't want to. The film maker thought perhaps that they were concerned for his life and wanted to protect him. But that's not it at all; in my opinion it was for a completely different reason. The Palestinian leaders were aware of the dangers of the camera, the kind of seduction exerted by the camera on every type of narcissism, and they knew that the fighters, aware of being filmed, would fight badly. They would not fight as well; they would run the risk of preferring their narcissism to the instinct for survival.

You can see how beautiful the fedayeen are. Certainly, their revolt is gratifying to me, as is that of the Black Panthers, but I don't know whether I could have stayed so long with them if physically they had been less attractive.

It seems that militants committed to the same cause are only brains that are more or less thoughtful; their bodies and faces are elsewhere.

I'm not sure whether I could make love with a militant. I'm not sure whether I could take as my own the cause of a body or a face with no charm. And charm does not lie in beauty, but in a way of being that I have neither the time nor even the means to describe to you. But there are bodies and faces that make war with each other, that do not agree with each other, that will never accommodate each other. No one speaks of this.[16] Without being in love with them, Giacometti chose his models.

Mettray

One of the subtleties of the Mettray colony's inventors was that they knew not to put up a wall.[17] To this day there is still no wall there. When we were in Mettray, there was only—and this is much more persuasive— a hedge of laurels and a strip of flowers; carnations and pansies. It's much more difficult to escape when it's simply a question of crossing through a patch of flowers than if there's a wall for you to climb.

So in a certain way the inventors were not complete idiots either. They had invented this little piece of poetry; they terrorized us with pansies, carnations, laurels, etc.

You saw Mettray, you filmed it, you photographed it, you explored it, you saw what it is.[18] You had certain emotions. So did I.

The people who organized it, that is, the Baron Demetz and his heirs, brought in an enormous fortune.[19] So we knew about all that, it was the result of crooked deals taking place far above us, going well beyond what- ever thefts we may have tried to pull off. And we knew that the profes- sions they were teaching us were fake.[20] Mettray, which was a hard labor camp for children, changed its name several times within three years. (I was there for three years.) At first it was called the Mettray Penal Colony, then it was a "Reformatory," then a "Reform School," and then . . . I've forgotten all the names, but each one sounded nicer than the last, and we had never been condemned by any judge. We were there either for theft or for some little crime, the kinds of things kids would do, tiny things. We were let off, and handed over to the Mettray penal colony. Which didn't change the fact that it was a hard-labor camp—that's all it was!

The Judges

Apparently, it never occurred to the judges that if a kid goes to prison, he'll go back, that he'll think: well, why not? As long as prison remains unknown to him, he'll be afraid of it. When he goes back, he thinks: no big deal, I can go back there. You're a lot less afraid of prison when you've known it firsthand than when you haven't.

So what are you trying to do, or what are these upstanding people or government people trying to do when they try to "reinsert"—the word they always use—young criminals back into society?[21] They want to castrate them. Castrate them of what, of what poetry? Of the poetry that you find precisely in kids like those. If they committed thefts, large or small, or robberies, large or small, if they ran away and became vagabonds—the kind of thing you do when you're fifteen or sixteen and stay gone for three months, six months—the reason is that society didn't suit them. So isn't it a kind of insult when you try to "reinsert" them?

Now decent people go to prison, I mean young people or grown men who find themselves in a situation they weren't prepared for and that disorients them for a moment. People who steal because they're hungry, because they want a motorcycle, or things like that; they didn't want to run away from society, they wanted to be integrated into it. But the real prisoners—I almost want to quote a line from Baudelaire: "But the true voyagers are those who leave / In order to leave . . . "—the real prisoners are only those who go to prison because they like it, because they hate this society, in any case because they're bored and sick of it.[22] And these people don't commit suicide. I think that the only people who commit suicide are people who have never loved prison, and probably because you can only hate the social world as it is, as it is now.

The children we were at Mettray had already refused conventional morality, the social morality of your society, because as soon as we were in Mettray, we gladly accepted the medieval morality that says that the vassal obeys the lord, I mean a very, very clear-cut hierarchy based on force, honor—what one still calls honor—and on giving one's word, which was very important. Whereas now, on the contrary, everything depends on the written word, the signed contract, dated in the presence of the notary, the authorities, and so on.

You know that sometimes inside an ordinary egg there is another smaller one. In this colony for children between the ages of eight and twenty-one, there was a poor population of about three hundred little delinquents, and then what was called a *collège de répression* with fifteen to twenty kids, sons of rich parents, who were considered rebellious.[23] These other kids didn't have to work; they were given a military education that was supposed to turn them into officers of the navy or the Foreign Legion. The Mettray penal colony was such a rich and unique thing, with its fields, its woods, with its cemetery, its history and its legend. . . . I hardly dare to speak to you of myself, but when I was put there, the woods, the cedars, the parks, the streams, the fields, the meadows, the pond, the cemetery, it was all mine. Paradoxically, in the hell that you photographed, that you saw for yourself, I was happy. I came to know this feudal morality that rules over the prisoners in the child labor camps still existing in France.

I lost something when I wrote and when I received monetary benefits from what I had written. I definitely lost a certain freshness. What has given me a little freshness, if I've had any, is insecurity.

Writing

I will hazard an explanation: writing is the last recourse when you have betrayed. There is something else I'd like to say to you: I realized very quickly, as young as fourteen or maybe fifteen, that all I could be was a vagabond and a thief, not a good thief, but a thief all the same. I think my only success in the social world was or could have been along the lines of a ticket inspector on a bus, or a butcher's assistant, or something like that. And since this kind of success horrified me, I think that I trained myself at a very young age to have emotions that could only lead me in the direction of writing. If writing means experiencing such strong emotions or feelings that your entire life is marked out by them, if they are so strong that only their description, their evocation, or their analysis can really allow you to deal with them, then yes, it was at Mettray, and at fifteen years old, that I began to write.[24]

Writing is perhaps what remains to you when you've been driven from the realm of the given word.

§ 32 Interview with Bertrand Poirot-Delpech

Bertrand Poirot-Delpech.—France has eliminated the death penalty.[1] I would like to know what effect it had on you to learn that in France people won't have their heads cut off anymore.

Genet.—The elimination of the death penalty leaves me completely indifferent. It's a political decision. I don't give a damn about French politics, it doesn't interest me. As long as France does not engage in what has been called North-South politics, as long as it is not more concerned with immigrant workers or the former colonies, French politics doesn't interest me at all. Whether or not white men's heads get cut off or not doesn't particularly interest me. The settling of scores between judges and hoodlums, as people call them, for me this isn't very interesting.

B.P.-D.—The fact that punishments are being reduced or eliminated doesn't really interest you?

G.—In France, no, I don't give a damn.

B.P.-D.—If we found a way to create a society in which there is no punishment, you would still not be satisfied?

G.—Creating a democracy in the country that used to be called the "metropole" in relation to its colonies, is still to be creating a democracy that works against black countries, Arab countries, and others. . . . Democracy has existed for a long time in England, although most likely only among the English there. I don't know English history very well, but I believe that democracy has flourished for a long time in England, when the English colonial empire flourished, but also that it was exercised against the Indians.

B.P.-D.—You think that the economic or political luxuries of the wealthy countries always takes its toll on the backs of Third World countries?

G.—For the moment, that's all I see.

B.P.-D.—And what society satisfies you—or, well, disgusts you least?

G.—There I cannot answer you politically but rather almost religiously. Both evil and good alike are part of human nature and are expressed through individuals or societies. I cannot judge, I don't know what will have resulted from the former colonial empires. I don't know what good they will have done, I know what evil they have done. Perhaps they have also done good, but it is all so inextricably mixed together that I will never be satisfied by a political system, whatever it may be.

B.P.-D.—Are you talking about a kind of anarchism?

G.—Probably not. I have taken sides, you see, I have not remained indifferent. When I was at Mettray, I was sent to Syria, and the big man in Syria was General Gouraud, the one who had only one arm—that's what we called him, "One-Arm."[2] He bombed Damascus, and since I was learning a little Arabic, I would leave the neighborhood at exactly four o'clock and would return whenever I wanted. The kids in Damascus, the boys, took great pleasure in showing me around in the ruins that General Gouraud's cannons had left. So I already had a double image of the hero and all the crap he got away with, the disgusting bastard that Gouraud was in the end.

I suddenly felt that I was entirely on the side of the Syrians. At first it was probably a sly sort of feeling, one that would make them see me in a good light, make them like me and include me in their card games.

Playing cards was forbidden by the French government. So I would go with them to the little mosques until four or five in the morning, and I spoke ill of Gouraud so that they would see me as a friend. But gradually I came to understand that Gouraud—and what he represented—was a real son-of-a-bitch.

B.P.-D.—How is it that, instead of writing in slang or inventing a language, you entered into the language of the enemy, that is, its fine language, the language of authority and power? Didn't you end up writing in the language of Gouraud after all?

G.—I'm not so sure that Gouraud used my language when he wrote. In any case, you're right, it was necessary first of all to seduce the people you're talking about, those among whom you no doubt count yourself—the French intelligentsia.

B.P.-D.—You seduced them with a language that is often described as classical, a language you didn't really shake up or disturb. You used it in the form in which it came down to you. But first of all, who taught you to write French so correctly?

G.—Grammar.

B.P.-D.—But was there a moment in school, or at Mettray, when you were given a taste for writing well?

G.—I'm not sure it really happened there.

You're reproaching me for writing good French? First of all, what I had to say to the enemy had to be said in his language, not in a foreign language, which slang would have been. Only someone like Céline could do that. It took a learned man, a doctor to the poor, Bardamu, to dare to write in slang.[3] He was able to change the perfectly correct French of his first medical thesis into slang, with the three dots, and so on.

I was a prisoner, I couldn't do that. It was necessary for me to address the torturer precisely in his own language. The fact that this language was more or less embellished with slang takes nothing away, or almost nothing, from its syntax.

If I was seduced by language—and I was—it wasn't in school; it was around the age of fifteen, at Mettray, when someone, probably by chance, gave me Ronsard's sonnets.[4] And I was utterly dazzled. I had to make myself heard by Ronsard. Ronsard would never have tolerated slang. . . . What I had to say was so . . . , it bore witness to so much suffering, that I had to use that language and no other.

B.P.-D.—You made Ronsard into your guardian?

G.—Since this was one of the first strong emotions I had both for the French language and for poetry, it's quite natural that I would maintain a kind of fidelity to him.

B.P.-D.—There is a risk, then, in writing like Jean Genet. The torturers say, "He's not dangerous. He writes so well!" Recuperation through beauty! Could one compare the way you take hold of the language of the torturers with the way the maids take over the dresses of Madame? Or is it more natural for you? When you embrace this music and this charm of language, are you following a strategy or an instinct?

G.—I would like to say that it's a strategy, but despite everything, before going to Mettray, I went to school and I did after all learn to read and write French.[5]

B.P.-D.—Do you like to read things that were recently published?

G.—The last book I tried to read was a book by Raymond Abellio.[6] It seemed to me very badly written and quite confused.

B.P.-D.—You have said that Rimbaud "chose" silence.[7] Is this true for you as well?

G.—I don't know why Rimbaud chose silence. I said that he understood that he had to be silent. For me, it seems to me that, since all my books were written in prison, I wrote them to get out of prison.[8] Once I was out of prison, there was no longer any reason to write. My books helped me get out of jail, but what was there to say after that?

B.P.-D.—Is there not a part of you that is still in prison?

G.—No, no. What part of me?

B.P.-D.—Perhaps the memory of those you left behind there, who died there or who are still there now?

G.—No, a part of me remains more in the countries exhausted by the French, like Morocco, with its nine million people, absolutely poor, or in Mali, or elsewhere.

B.P.-D.—You never had the idea of writing so that those people would leave prison?

G.—No. I'll say again that the elimination of the death penalty leaves me completely indifferent. I'm not at all keen on the idea of young guys being put in jail, but it's between them and their judges, the governments, and so on, not between them and me.

B.P.-D.—There are a lot of us who regret this silence of yours.

G.—Oh! You'll get over it.

B.P.-D.—Let's come back to your choice of a classical language. Why?

G.—Before saying things that were so singular, so particular, I could only say them in a language familiar to the dominant class, it was necessary for those I call my "torturers" to hear me. Therefore, I had to attack them in their language. If I had written in slang they wouldn't have listened to me. There's something else, too. The French language is fixed, it was fixed in the seventeenth century, more or less. Slang is always evolving. Slang is mobile. Céline's slang is going out of style, it's already almost antiquated. People understand it only in *Journey to the End of the Night* because this book preserves a rhetoric admitted by the bourgeoisie. The books that came after that I don't know very well, but I have the impression that they plunge straight into slang and that before long they'll be unreadable.

B.P.-D.—But you're much more subversive than Céline. Céline says to the torturers, "Everything is shit." This kind of nihilism suits them just fine. Whereas what you say is, "We'll put you in the shit"; with you there is revolt, while with him there's a sort of dejection and even whining. What you say is much more intolerable to the "torturers."

G.—The real torturers, in fact, don't read me.

B.P.-D.—But they fear you; they know you're there.

G.—They don't give a damn, they don't give a damn. No, there's no use exaggerating the importance of all that.

B.P.-D.—Can you give us an example of your grammatical choice?

G.—It's simple. The first sentence of the first book I wrote goes like this: "Weidmann appeared before you in a five o'clock edition . . . "[9] The printer, the foreman, asked me to correct it by replacing "you" with "us." He said, "It's 'Weidman appeared to us,' isn't it?" I stuck to "appeared to you" because I was already marking the difference between you, to whom I'm speaking, and the I who speaks to you.

B.P.-D.—You were creating a distance?

G.—I was creating a distance but also respecting the rules, your rules.

B.P.-D.—You never established rules of your own?

G.—I believe that in the end my whole life has been against white rules.

B.P.-D.—What do you mean by white?

G.—White people. I mean that, even now—and I'm seventy-two years old!—I can't vote.[10] Even if you think it's not very important, I am not fully a French citizen.

B.P.-D.—You don't have full civil rights?

G.—No, no. There are crimes I committed that were never given full amnesty, one for theft and a two-year prison sentence, among others. And then I deserted twice.[11]

B.P.-D.—Have you added up all your sentences, how long they lasted?

G.—Yes: fourteen years.[12]

B.P.-D.—You have spoken a great deal about a hierarchy of glory that would be a hierarchy of crime. . . . What is the most poetic crime?

G.—No. I meant that two words placed together, or three or four, and two sentences, can be more poetic than a murder. If I had to choose between poetic expression through words or—if it exists—poetic expression through acts, I would choose poetic expression through words.

B.P.-D.—What words seem to you to be strongest and closest to an act?

G.—It's in their assemblage, their confrontation. There must be at least two.

B.P.-D.—Is there any happiness in writing? Did you experience a profound joy in writing?

G.—Only once.

B.P.-D.—What were you writing?

G.—*The Screens*. The rest was incredibly boring, but I had to write it to get out of prison.

B.P.-D.—What year was *The Screens*?

G.—Let's see, I think it was in 1956 or 1957. In any case I was correcting the proofs when de Gaulle came to power in 1958, I think that's it.[13]

B.P.-D.—I remember the production at the Odéon.[14] There was a row of cops protecting the theater. How did that effect you, having a play produced in a national theater defended by the police?

G.—Well, it left me with the impression that really the police are inconsequential, and the French government too.

B.P.-D.—This inconsequence must have been a pleasure for you?

G.—I had noticed it long before.

B.P.-D.—But to have them caught once again in a trap like that must have been rather enjoyable?

G.—Sure, I would have liked to start the whole thing over again with Maria Casarès at the Comédie-Française; they asked me for *The Balcony*. But I wasn't able to do it there, they didn't want Maria Casarès.[15] So she's more dangerous than I am.

B.P.-D.—*The Screens* presents death as something that, in the end, isn't very frightening or important. Is that your opinion?

G.—It's Mallarmé's opinion too: "This shallow stream . . . "[16] You know the rest. Death . . . or the passage of life to nonlife, doesn't seem very sad to me, or very dangerous for oneself, when one changes the vocabulary: the passage from life to nonlife instead of from life to its demise, suddenly it's almost consoling, isn't it?

It's the change of vocabulary that's important. To play it down. This word is often used now: "to play down the situation." I'm playing down the situation, which, if I use other words, will make a dead man of me.

B.P.-D.—A dramatic author who plays down . . . ?

G.—Exactly. If I attempted to develop a certain kind of dramaturgy, it was in order to settle accounts with society. Now it's all the same to me; the accounts have been settled.

B.P.-D.—You are free of anger and drama?

G.—Oh! I'm saying this in such a peremptory and spontaneous way that I wonder if it really is without anger or drama. You're touching on something there. I believe that I will die still with some anger directed at you.

B.P.-D.—And hatred?

G.—No, I hope not, you aren't worth it.

B.P.-D.—Who is worth your hatred?

G.—The few people whom I deeply love and who make me feel tenderness.

B.P.-D.—Has it happened, though, that you have loved a scoundrel, or not?

G.—I don't make the same distinction as Sartre between scoundrels and other kinds of people. Since I'm incapable of defining beauty, I'm absolutely incapable of defining love, of knowing . . . The man you would call a scoundrel according to your objective point of view, from my subjective point of view he ceases to be one. . . . Just think, when Hitler gave a thrashing to the French, well yes! I was glad, this thrashing made me happy. Yes, the French were cowards.

B.P.-D.—And the other things he did, the extermination camps, that was amusing too?

G.—At first, really, I didn't know about that. But what I'm talking about is France, not the German people or the Jewish people, or the communist people that Hitler massacred. It was a question of the corrective the German army gave to the French army.

B.P.-D.—And you found that amusing?

G.—Oh, intoxicating, let me tell you.

B.P.-D.—And the thrashing that Hitler took later was also a thrill?

G.—Oh! I was already quite indifferent. The French started their rotten treatment of people in Indochina and Algeria, in Madagascar, and so on. You know the history, better than I do.

B.P.-D.—But not all of the defeats, after all, were very uplifting. What about Poland, what did you think of that?

G.—Listen: did France react when around a thousand people, men, women, and children, as they say in the papers, were killed by the police under Hassan II of Morocco, in Casa?[17] When did the French ever react? I'm very familiar with Morocco, you know. The poverty there is enormous, immense, and no one says a word about it here.

B.P.-D.—In Poland, it's not only a question of poverty but of the destruction of freedoms.

G.—And you don't think freedom has been destroyed in Morocco?

B.P.-D.—But who's defending them, who is defending the Arab people? Qaddafi?

G.—Maybe you haven't noticed, but I'm not Arab and I can't speak for the Arabs, nor for Qaddafi. But I know what effect the name Qaddafi has on Americans and Europeans, of course.

B.P.-D.—In short, you're not a citizen of any place?

G.—Of course not.

B.P.-D.—If you had to define a homeland [*patrie*], what would it be? Language?

G.—Oh, no! I said that one day, partly as a joke, in *L'Humanité*; they had asked me to write a text.[18] For me, a homeland would really be three or four people. Oppressed people. I would belong to a homeland if I fought for one, but I have no desire at all to fight for the French, or for anyone else, not even for the Black Panthers. The Panthers wouldn't have wanted me to fight for them.

B.P.-D.—Fighting is often ideological or symbolic, and in that sense the artist or the writer has a place in it. Have you not felt that you were fighting with the pen?

G.—You sound like Simone de Beauvoir.

B.P.-D.—It isn't possible to fight with the pen?

G.—No. Of course I went to a few demonstrations with Sartre, with Foucault, but it was very harmless, the police were even very polite, establishing a kind of complicity with us, and we became complicit with them.[19] Surreal police.

B.P.-D.—So with writing one can get out of prison, but one can't change the world?

G.—I can't, in any case. No.

B.P.-D.—Can it change others individually? Is a reader changed by what he reads? Are there books that changed you?

G.—In the end, no. I believe—I don't have any proof—but I believe that the education that comes from books, paintings, or other things, the education that one receives, is opposed by a personal factor I don't know how to name otherwise. I'm incapable of discerning its contours, its limits, but every person takes his nourishment from everything. He isn't transformed by reading a book, looking at a painting, or hearing a piece of music; he is transformed gradually, and from all these things he makes something that suits him.

B.P.-D.—And if a "torturer" says to you that he was changed by reading Jean Genet, that this is the "nourishment" he found?

G.—If that happened, I'd ask him to show me proof.

B.P.-D.—What proof?

G.—Well, that's up to him; he's the one who would have to show it.

B.P.-D.—Through actions?

G.—I don't know; I don't think a man can be transformed by what I wrote. He can despise what I wrote or be absorbed by it. Besides, a torturer is never completely a torturer. Within you who are speaking to me now, there is a share of guilt, a guilty party. I can't clearly distinguish it, but it's because you have never really stepped over to the other side.

B.P.-D.—But look how Sartre was changed by you!

G.—No.

B.P.-D.—I think so.

G.—Oh, no!

B.P.-D.—I'm sure of it. In any case, he was changed by what he wrote about you.[20] Were you yourself changed by what he wrote?

G.—Well, I never made it all the way through what he wrote; I found it pretty boring.

B.P.-D.—True, it's very long, you have a good excuse.

G.—It's stupefying.

B.P.-D.—Not stupefying, but long. Did you ever meet Pierre Goldman?[21]

G.—Not personally.

B.P.-D.—Did you follow what happened to him?

G.—Yes, well, I mean he wrote to me from Fresne or from La Santé, I forget which. Some of his friends came to see me and he sent me a letter saying that he absolutely wanted to break with all his old friends.

B.P.-D.—And Mesrine?[22]

G.—Hats off!

B.P.-D.—What makes you say "hats off!" when you learn that someone has pulled off a job? I mean Mesrine. Is it rather the beauty of the act or its comic force, its derisive force?

G.—How old are you? Were you around for the defeat in 1940? Now that was very comic. . . . Those decorated gentlemen carrying canes, but with a sharp point on the end so they could pick up butts to smoke without having to bend over; those ladies from Auteuil or Passy who were selling newspapers, *Paris-soir* or *Le Figaro* . . . There were a lot of things like that, very uplifting.

B.P.-D.—Have there been other events besides the defeat in 1940 that have uplifted you so much?

G.—Yes, there was the extraordinary staying power of the Algerians and the North Vietnamese when they fought off the French, and the Americans, of course.

B.P.-D.—You place the defeat of the latter on the same level as the heroism of the former?

G.—No, not at all. Thanks not only to their heroism but also to their intelligence, their resourcefulness, and so many other things, the North Vietnamese were finally able to force the ambassador to Saigon to take his flag under his arm and get the hell out.[23] Doesn't that make you laugh? You said to me, perhaps somewhat spitefully, that after all the German army was also the army of the camps and the torturers; but the debacle of the French army was also that of the great military corps who condemned Dreyfus, wasn't it?

B.P.-D.—And Italian terrorism, the Red Brigades?

G.—I don't want to talk about the Red Brigades right now, but if you want, I will talk about Baader. Almost everyone in France, even on the Left, was against Baader, and the Left forgot completely that he was one of the first to protest against the shah in Berlin. Now people only want to think of him as the spoilsport of German society.

B.P.-D.—The former leftists in France seemed to have chosen nonviolence. If this weren't so, and if terrorism worked the way it does with the Red Brigades, how would you react?

G.—I already told you how old I am. I wouldn't be very effective because I can't see very well, but I would definitely be on their side.

B.P.-D.—Even if it brought with it an even more repressive state?

G.—Against whom would it be repressive? A few whites who had no difficulties imposing repression in Algeria as well as in Tunisia?

B.P.-D.—In other words, your argument would be this: too bad if the white states do to themselves what they have inflicted on others?

G.—I wouldn't say too bad, but all the better. That's the only correction I would make.

B.P.-D.—Is there a certain pleasure in evil for you? You never smile so much as when you describe a certain kind of misfortune . . .

G.—Whose misfortune? After all, it's not the misfortune of the poor that makes me smile, but that of the victors.

B.P.-D.—But you know very well that when a state grows stronger, it's the poor who raise the first glass.

G.—The French are not poor. The really poor in France are the immigrant workers. The French are not poor. They benefit from the fact that France used to be a colonial empire.

B.P.-D.—Still, there are some five million French people who earn less than three thousand francs a month; that's quite a few.

G.—No, it's not really so many, you know, out of fifty-three million.

B.P.-D.—There are no poor people in France?

G.—There are proportionately fewer poor French people than there are poor people elsewhere. Maybe not less than in West Germany or in Sweden, but less than in the United States where, in certain black ghettos, there is horrendous poverty.

B.P.-D.—You make a sharp distinction between the poverty of whites and the poverty of blacks?

G.—I'm not the one who makes the distinction.

B.P.-D.—When it's a question of whites, it doesn't seem as unjust to you, it doesn't bother you?

G.—Let's just say that up to now blacks never did anything to me.

B.P.-D.—It almost seems that if a white person is subjugated, for you that's not anything very serious?

G.—No; indeed.

B.P.-D.—Does being white make one guilty? A sort of original sin?

G.—I don't think of it as original sin; in any case not the one the Bible talks about. No, it's a sin that is completely deliberate.

B.P.-D.—You didn't want to be born white, from what I can tell?

G.—Oh, in that sense, by being born white and being against whites, I have played all the boards at once. I'm thrilled when whites are hurting and I'm protected by the power of whites, since I too have white skin and blue eyes, or green, or gray.

B.P.-D.—In sum, you're on both sides.

G.—I'm on both sides, yes.

B.P.-D.—You like being in such a situation?

G.—It's a situation that, in any case, has allowed me to introduce chaos into my own home.

B.P.-D.—There's a play called *The Blacks* that recounts all that very well.

G.—Yes, perhaps.

B.P.-D.—And the Polish, who have white skin like you, who never colonized anyone and who have been crushed flat every thirty years or so, that leaves you indifferent?

G.—They let themselves be crushed flat every thirty years. . . . I'd like to put an end to this comparison you keep bringing up by saying that in the end it's their business. They let themselves be crushed, indeed, half of them by the Soviets, the other half by Hitler. Long before that, it was the Swedish. This is all a matter of war between whites, they were almost provincial wars, local wars, almost a "button war [*la guerre des boutons*]."[24]

B.P.-D.—You wrote an article in *Le Monde* that created quite a stir.[25] You seemed to be justifying the Soviet Union on a few points. Have you changed your mind since the invasion of Afghanistan?[26]

G.—No, I haven't changed my mind.

B.P.-D.—But here you have whites crushing nonwhites.

G.—I don't really know what's happening in Afghanistan, and I have the impression that you don't really know either. You read *Le Monde*, a newspaper that, although not fascist, is right wing, after all, even though it spoke out for Mitterrand, right?

B.P.-D.—That's another debate.

G.—Okay, if you like, but anyway that's how I see it.

B.P.-D.—*Le Monde* was on its own, really, during the Algerian war . . .

G.—No, it knew very well how to use quotation marks. It knew how to use them when it had to.

B.P.-D.—Let's go back to Afghanistan. You don't think there's any oppression going on there?

G.—I really don't know anything about it.

B.P.-D.—Doesn't it seem to you that, in a place where there are tanks, there is a reason to suspect oppression?

G.—Are there as many tanks as you say?

B.P.-D.—This is what people are showing us. They're also showing us fighters in the mountains who are not the opposite of the North Vietnamese you spoke of before; but then we weren't there to verify it.

G.—You're not engaging in a real debate with me. You're not really jumping into it. You're trying to get me to jump into it, but you, you're just sitting there.

B.P.-D.—I'm not the one we're here to listen to.

G.—I'm ready to answer all your questions.

B.P.-D.—Do you think the Soviets are less in the wrong to be in Kabul than the Americans were to be in Saigon?

G.—I think that power, whatever it is, is power. But if a kid, a two- or three-year-old child was playing with a bottle of cyanide, I'd do what I could to take it away from him. I'm not really sure about this subjugation of people you've been referring to. I have no proof because all the newspapers reporting on Afghanistan are newspapers belonging to the system we live in now, which is so anti-Soviet.

B.P.-D.—If there were a direct war between the USSR and America, which side would you be on?

G.—My answer is clear: of course I would be on Russia's side.

B.P.-D.—Why?

G.—Because Russia destabilizes, it's a ferment. The United States doesn't seem to me to be a ferment anymore.

B.P.-D.—A ferment of what?

G.—I don't know yet; in any case, of disorder for you, for the Western world.

B.P.-D.—And do you think that the USSR is a ferment for its own population?

G.—I've never set foot in Russia, but I have been to the United States. I can imagine the Soviet Union after having seen the United States.

B.P.-D.—American-style freedom is in no way a ferment?

G.—I asked a similar question to Angela Davis. Obviously, she chose the Soviet Union.

B.P.-D.—Now do you really believe in a future for this disorder, for this disquiet let loose by the Soviet Union? Or is it because it's a source of fear for the bourgeoisie?

G.—Both; I always place a certain trust in disquiet and instability because they are signs of life.

B.P.-D.—Isn't this force in any way a harbinger of death?

G.—Anything can be a harbinger of death, obviously.

B.P.-D.—You believe in force—since we can't say that the USSR really practices persuasion or conviction.

G.—Yes they do, conviction too. The Western world stepped all over me, it didn't convince me.

You're talking about the dictatorship exerted by the Soviet Union. That may be. But have you thought of the dictatorship exerted by the United States, for a long time now, on us and the rest of the world? So, without the Soviet Union, what weapon would there be against the United States? Who would dare to apply the brakes to the ambition of the United States if it weren't for the 1917 revolution?

B.P.-D.—You said before that the divine or some unknown god amused you; I'd like to know what amuses you in that god?

G.—If you're talking about the God of the Jews, or of the Christians, there wouldn't be much of anything amusing about him. But it happens that I was given the catechism. The priest in the little village where I grew up—I was eight, nine years old—was a priest who had a reputation for screwing all the soldiers' wives. That's right, the women who had stayed behind in the village during the war. He wasn't taken very seriously; people laughed at him a little. The catechism was recounted in such an idiotic way that it seemed like a joke.

B.P.-D.—You sometimes speak of beauty in relation to a person, a face. What is it more generally?

G.—The beauty of a face or a body obviously has nothing to do with the beauty of a line from Racine. If a body and a face are radiant for me, they may not be so for other people.

B.P.-D.—So, to each his own notion of beauty, whether it's a face or Racine. You don't have a definition of beauty?

G.—No. But do you have one? That's what interests me.

B.P.-D.—No, it's Genet's beauty that's interesting. If someone tells you that you have a tremendous innocence in your face, does it bother you?

G.—No.

B.P.-D.—Does it flatter you?

G.—Quite a bit, yes. Since we know now that the innocent are perverse.

B.P.-D.—Is there a pleasure in having an innocent-looking face but knowing oneself to be perverse?

G.—I don't have an innocent-looking face. If you tell me I have an innocent face, then I do. If you think I don't, then I don't. But it would be much more of a pleasure for me if you told me I did and if you thought I did.

B.P.-D.—Not only do I think you do, I'd say that the Angel of Reims looks downright villainous next to you.[27]

G.—The smile on the Angel of Reims . . . You're right, he's a two-faced hypocrite.

§ 33 Four Hours in Shatila

In Shatila, in Sabra, goyim massacred goyim—what does that have
to do with us?

—Menachem Begin (in the Knesset)[1]

No one, nothing, no narrative technique can ever say what they were
like, the six months, and especially the first weeks, that the fedayeen spent
in the mountains of Jerash and Ajloun, in Jordan.[2] Others before me have
given an account of the events, laid out the chronology, described the
successes and mistakes of the PLO. The feeling in the air, the color of the
sky, the earth, and the trees, these can be told; but never the faint intoxication, the sense of gliding over the ground, the sparkle in everyone's
eyes, the openness of relations not only between the fedayeen themselves,
but also between them and their leaders.

There under the trees, everything and everyone was quivering, light-
hearted, filled with wonder at a life so new to everyone, and in these
vibrations there was something strangely still, alert, reserved, and protected, like someone praying without saying anything. Everything
belonged to everyone. Everyone was alone in himself. And yet perhaps
not. In short, both smiling and strained. The area of Jordan to which
they had withdrawn, out of a political choice, was a zone stretching in
length from the Syrian border to Salt, and bounded by the Jordan River
and the road from Jerash to Irbid. About sixty kilometers long and twenty kilometers wide, it was a mountainous region covered with holm oaks,
little Jordanian villages, and sparse crops. There under the trees and the
camouflaged tents, the fedayeen had set up camps for combat units
equipped with light and semiheavy weapons. Once the artillery was in
place—it was meant to be used mainly against possible Jordanian operations—the young soldiers looked after their weapons, taking them

apart to clean and oil them, and putting them back together with the greatest speed. There were even some who accomplished the feat of taking them apart and putting them back together blindfolded, so that they could do it at night. Each soldier developed an amorous and magical relationship to his weapon. Since the fedayeen had only just left adolescence behind, the rifle as a weapon was a sign of triumphant virility, and it brought with it the certainty of being. Aggression disappeared: they showed their teeth in a smile.[3]

The rest of the time, the Palestinians drank tea, criticized their leaders and the rich—Palestinians or otherwise—and insulted Israel, but they talked especially about the revolution, the one they were engaged in and the one they were about to undertake.

For me, if the word "Palestinians" occurs in a title, in the text of an article or a tract, it immediately evokes the fedayeen of a specific place—Jordan—at a time that can be easily dated: October, November, December 1970, January, February, March, and April 1971. It was then, and there, that I saw the Palestinian Revolution. The extraordinary evidence of what was taking place, the intensity of this happiness at being alive, is also called beauty.

Ten years passed and I heard nothing from them, except that the fedayeen were in Lebanon. The European press spoke offhandedly, even disdainfully, of the Palestinian people. Then suddenly there was West Beirut.[4]

～

A photograph has two dimensions, so does a television screen; it is impossible to walk through either. From one wall of the street to the other, arched or curved, their feet pushing on one wall and their heads leaning against the other, the blackened and swollen corpses I had to step over were all Palestinian and Lebanese. For me, as for the remaining inhabitants, moving through Shatila and Sabra was like a game of leapfrog.[5] Sometimes a dead child blocked the streets, which were so narrow, almost paper-thin, and the dead were so numerous. Their odor is no doubt familiar to old people: it didn't bother me. But there were flies everywhere. If I lifted up the handkerchief or the Arab newspaper placed over a head, I disturbed them. Infuriated by my gesture, they swarmed over the back of my hand and tried to feed off of it. The first corpse I saw was that of a fifty- or sixty-year-old man. He would have had a ring of white hair if a wound (an ax blow, it seemed to me) had not split open his skull. Part of the blackened brain was on the ground next to the head. The entire body lay in a sea of black, clotted blood. His belt was unbuckled, only one button of his pants was fastened. The feet and legs of the dead man were naked, black, purple, and blue: perhaps he had been taken by surprise at night or at dawn? Was he running away? He was lying in a small alley immediately to the right of the camp entrance across from the Kuwaiti embassy. Was the Shatila massacre carried out in hushed tones, or in complete silence? After all, the Israelis, both soldiers and officers, claim to have heard nothing, to have suspected nothing, even though they had been occupying this building since Wednesday afternoon.

Photography is unable to capture the flies, or the thick white smell of death. Nor can it tell about the little hops you have to make when walking from one corpse to the next.

If you look closely at a dead body, a strange phenomenon occurs: the absence of life in the body amounts to a total absence of the body, or to its constantly receding as you look at it. Even if you move closer, so you think, you will never touch it. This happens if you contemplate it. But if you make a gesture in its direction, stoop down next to it, move an arm or a finger, suddenly it is very present and almost friendly.

Love [*l'amour*] and death [*la mort*]: these two words are quickly associated when one of them is written down. I had to go to Shatila to see the obscenity of love and the obscenity of death. In both cases, the body has nothing left to hide: positions, contortions, gestures, signs, even silences belong to both worlds. The body of a thirty- or thirty-five-year-old man was lying on its belly. As if the entire body were nothing but a bladder in the shape of a man, it had swollen from the sun and from the chemistry of decomposition to the point of stretching the fabric on the pants which were about to burst open at the buttocks and the thighs. The only part of the face I could see was purple and black. Just above the knee, the bent thigh revealed an open wound beneath the ripped fabric. What was the origin of the wound: a bayonet, a knife, a dagger? Flies all over the wound and around it. The head larger than a watermelon—a black watermelon. I asked what his name was; he was a Muslim.

"Who is this?"

"A Palestinian," a man in his forties answered me in French. "Look at what they did."

He pulled back the blanket covering the feet and part of the legs. The calves were naked, black, and swollen. On the feet were black unlaced boots, and the ankles were tied very tightly by a strong rope—its strength was obvious—about three meters long, which I arranged so that Mrs. S. (an American) could photograph them clearly.[6] I asked the forty-year-old man if I could see the face.

"If you want, but look at it yourself."

"Will you help me turn his head?"

"No."

"Was he dragged through the streets with this rope?"

"I don't know, sir."

"Was it Haddad's people?"[7]

"I don't know, sir."

"The Israelis?"

"I don't know."

"The Katayeb?"[8]

"I don't know."

"Did you know him?"

"Yes."

"Did you see him die?"

"Yes."

"Who killed him?"

"I don't know."

He quickly walked away from the dead man and from me. He turned back to look at me and disappeared into a small side street.

Which alley do I take now? I was drawn on by fifty-year-old men, by young twenty-year-olds, by two old Arab women, and I felt like I was at the center of a compass whose every radius pointed to hundreds of dead.

I will add this here, without really knowing why I'm placing it at this point in my story: "The French have the habit of using the tired expression 'dirty work'; well, since the Israeli army ordered the Katayeb or the Haddadists to do the 'dirty work,' the Labor Party had its 'dirty work' done by the Likud, Begin, Sharon, Shamir."[9] This is a quote from R., a Palestinian journalist who was still in Beirut on Sunday, September 19.

Among them or alongside them—all the tortured victims—I cannot get this "invisible vision" out of my mind: the torturer, what was he like? Who was he? I see him and I do not see him. He is everywhere I look and the only form he will ever have is the one outlined by the grotesque poses, positions, and gestures of the dead, attended by clouds of flies in the sun.

Since the American marines, the French paratroopers, and the Italian *bersaglieri* who made up the intervention force in Lebanon left so quickly (the Italians arrived on a ship two days late but fled in Hercules airplanes!),[10] since they left a day or thirty-six hours before their official departure date, as if they were escaping, and on the eve of Bashir Gemayel's assassination—are the Palestinians really wrong to wonder whether the Americans, the French, the Italians had not been warned to get the hell out and fast, if they didn't want to appear to be mixed up in the bombing of the Katayeb headquarters?[11]

The fact is, they left very quickly and very early. Israel brags about itself and its effectiveness in combat, its preparedness for battle, its ability to take advantage of circumstances and to create circumstances to take advantage of. Let's see: the PLO leaves Beirut in triumph, on a Greek ship, with a naval escort. Bashir, hiding it as well as he can, visits Begin in Israel. The intervention of the three forces (American, French, Italian) ends on Monday. Bashir is assassinated on Tuesday. Tsahal enters West Beirut on Wednesday morning.[12] The Israeli soldiers were advancing on Beirut on the morning of Bashir's funeral, as if they were coming from the port. With binoculars, I saw them from the eighth floor of my building as they arrived in single file: a single column. I was surprised that nothing more was happening, since a good rifle with a sight could have picked them off, every one of them. Their ferocity preceded them.

And the tanks followed. Then the jeeps.

Tired out from such a long early-morning march, they stopped near the French embassy, letting the tanks go on ahead, heading straight into Hamra.[13] The soldiers sat down on the sidewalks, one every ten meters, their rifles pointed straight ahead, their backs against the wall of the embassy. With their long torsos, they looked to me like boas with two legs stretched out in front of them.

"Israel had promised the American representative, Habib, not to set foot in West Beirut and above all to respect the civilian populations of the Palestinian camps. Arafat still has the letter in which Reagan promised him the same thing. Habib is supposed to have promised Arafat that nine thousand prisoners in Israel would be released. On Thursday the massacres in Shatila and Sabra began. The 'bloodbath' that Israel claimed it was avoiding by bringing order into the camps! . . . " That's what a Lebanese writer said to me.

"It will be very easy for the Israelis to deflect all the accusations. Journalists in all the European newspapers are already hard at work proving their innocence; none of them will say that on the night of Thursday to Friday, and then from Friday to Saturday, Hebrew was spoken in Shatila." That's what another Lebanese said to me.

The Palestinian woman—for I couldn't leave Shatila without going from one corpse to another, and this game of snakes and ladders led inevitably to this marvel: Shatila and Sabra leveled, with real-estate battles raging to rebuild on this very flat cemetery—the Palestinian woman was probably old since she had gray hair. She was stretched out on her back, laid or left there on top of the rubble, the bricks, the twisted iron rods, no comfort. First, I was surprised to see a strange twist of rope and cloth that went from one wrist to the other, holding the two arms apart horizontally, as if crucified. The black and swollen face was turned toward the sky, black with flies, with teeth that looked very white to me, a face that seemed, without the slightest movement, to be grimacing or smiling or screaming a silent and uninterrupted scream. Her stockings were black wool, her dress with pink and gray flowers was slightly hitched up or too short, I don't know which, showing the upper part of the calves, black and swollen, again with delicate shades of mauve matched by a similar purple and mauve in the cheeks. Were these bruises, or were they the natural result of rotting in the sun?

"Was she beaten with a rifle butt?"

"Look, sir, look at her hands."

I hadn't noticed. The fingers on both hands were spread out like a fan and the ten fingers had been cut as if by a gardener's shears. Soldiers, laughing like children and happily singing, had probably enjoyed finding these shears, and using them.

"Look, sir."

The ends of her fingers, the top joints, with the nail, were lying in the dust. The young man who, very calmly, with no emphasis, was showing me the torture undergone by the dead, quietly placed a cloth over the face and the hands of the Palestinian woman, and a piece of cardboard over her legs. I could no longer see anything but a heap of pink and gray cloth encircled by flies.[14]

Three young men pulled me into an alley.

"Go in, sir; we'll wait for you outside."

The first room was what remained of a two-story house. The room was quite peaceful, even welcoming; an effort at happiness, perhaps even a successful effort, had been made using various leftovers, with foam rubber stuffed into a destroyed piece of wall, with what I thought at first to be three armchairs but which were in fact three car seats (maybe from a junked Mercedes), a couch with cushions covered with loud flowery material and stylized designs, a small silent radio, two unlit candelabras. Quite a peaceful room, even with the carpet of spent shells covering the floor. . . . A door slammed as though from a draft. I walked on the spent shells and pushed on the door that led into the next room, but I had to force it: the heel of a boot was preventing it from letting me through, the heel of a corpse on its back, next to two other corpses of men lying on their bellies, all of them stretched out on another carpet of empty copper shells. I nearly fell several times because of these shells.

At the other end of this room another door stood open, with no lock or latch. I stepped over the dead bodies as one crosses chasms. In this room were the corpses of four men piled on a single bed, one on top of the other, as if each had made an effort to protect the one underneath him or as if they were gripped by some erotic lust now in a state of decomposition. This pile of shields smelled strongly, but it didn't smell bad. The smell and the flies, it seemed to me, had gotten used to me. I no longer disturbed anything in these ruins and in this quiet.

"During the night from Thursday to Friday, and then from Friday to Saturday and Saturday to Sunday, no one had kept vigil with them," I thought.

And yet it seemed to me that someone had come to see these dead men before me, and after their death. The three young men were waiting for me at some distance from the house, a handkerchief over their noses.

It was then, as I was leaving the house, that I was struck by a kind of faint attack of madness that almost made me smile. I said to myself that they would never have enough boards or carpenters to make the coffins. But then, why would they need coffins? The dead men and women were all Muslims, who are sewn into a shroud. How many meters would it take to enshroud so many dead? And how many prayers. What was missing here, I realized, was the cadence of prayers.

"Come, sir, come quickly."

This is the moment to write that this sudden and very momentary madness that had me counting meters of white cloth gave my steps an almost energetic liveliness, and that it may have been caused by something a Palestinian woman, a friend of mine, had said to me the day before.

"I was waiting for someone to bring me my keys (which keys: to her car, to her house, I only remember the word *keys*), when an old man went running by. 'Where are you going?'—'To get help. I'm the gravedigger. They've bombed the cemetery. All the bones of the dead are out in the open. I need help gathering up the bones.'"

This friend, I believe, is Christian. She also said to me: "When the vacuum bomb—it's also called an implosion bomb—killed two hundred and fifty people, all we had was one box. The men dug a mass grave in the cemetery of the Orthodox church. We filled up the box and then went to empty it. We went back and forth under the bombs, digging out bodies and limbs as best we could."

For three months people have used their hands for two different functions: during the day for grasping and touching, at night for seeing. The electricity outages made this blind man's education necessary, as it did the climb, two or three times a day, up that white marble cliff, the eight-floor stairway. All the containers in the house had to be filled with water. The telephone was cut off when the Israeli soldiers, along with their Hebrew inscriptions, entered West Beirut. The roads around Beirut were also cut off. The constantly moving Merkava tanks showed us that they were watching over the entire city, though at the same time we figured that their occupants were afraid the tanks would become a fixed target.[15] They must also have feared the activity of the Murabitoun and the fedayeen who had been able to remain in parts of West Beirut.[16]

The day after the Israeli army entered the city, we were prisoners, but it seemed to me that the invaders were less feared than despised; they inspired disgust more than fright. None of the soldiers laughed or smiled. It was certainly not a time for throwing rice or flowers.[17]

After the roads were cut off and the telephone silenced, unable to communicate with the rest of the world, for the first time in my life I felt myself becoming Palestinian and hating Israel.

At the sports stadium near the highway from Beirut to Damascus, a stadium already almost destroyed by aerial bombardment, the Lebanese deliver piles of weapons, all apparently deliberately damaged, to Israeli officers.

In the apartment where I'm staying, each one of us has a radio. We listen to Radio Katayeb, Radio Murabitoun, Radio Amman, Radio Jerusalem (in French), Radio Lebanon. Everyone is probably doing the same in the other apartments.

"We are linked to Israel by many currents that bring us bombs, tanks, soldiers, fruit, vegetables; they take our soldiers, our children to Palestine . . . in a constant and ceaseless coming and going, just as we are linked to them, so they say, since Abraham—in his lineage, in his language, in our common origins . . . " (a Palestinian fedayee). "In short," he added, "they're invading us, stuffing us, choking us, and they would like to embrace us with both arms. They say they are our cousins. They're very sad to see us turning away from them. They must be furious with us and with themselves."

~

To claim that there is a beauty peculiar to revolutionaries raises a number of problems. Everyone knows—or suspects—that young children and adolescents living in traditional and strict environments have a beauty of face, body, movement, and gaze quite similar to the beauty of the fedayeen. The explanation is perhaps this: breaking with the ancient order of things, a new freedom emerges through the layers of dead skin, and the fathers and grandfathers have a hard time extinguishing the spark in their eyes, the energy pulsing in their temples, the surge of blood through their veins.

On the Palestinian bases in the spring of 1971, this beauty subtly pervaded a forest enlivened by the freedom of the fedayeen. In the camps there was yet another kind of beauty, slightly more muted, that took hold through the reign of women and children. The camps received a sort of light that came from the combat bases, and as for the women, the explanation of their radiance would require a long and complex discussion. Even more than the men, more than the fedayeen in combat, the Palestinian women appeared strong enough to maintain resistance and to accept the changes brought by a revolution. They had already disobeyed the customs: by looking men straight in the eye, by refusing to wear the veil, by leaving their hair visible and sometimes completely uncovered, by speaking with a firm voice. Even the briefest and most prosaic of their acts were the fragments of a confident movement toward a new order, unknown to them, but in which they sensed a freedom that would be, for them, like a cleansing bath, and for the men a glowing pride. They were ready to become both the wives and the mothers of heroes, as they already were for their men.

In the woods of Ajloun, the fedayeen dreamed of girls, perhaps, and it seemed that each one outlined next to him—or modeled with his gestures—a girl pressed against himself; hence this grace and strength—with an amused laughter—of the fedayeen in arms. We were not only in a pre-revolutionary dawn but in a gray zone of sensuality. A crystallizing frost gave to each gesture its own gentleness.

Constantly, and every day for a month, always in Ajloun, I saw a strong and wiry woman crouching in the cold—but crouched like the Indians of the Andes, certain black Africans, the Untouchables of Tokyo, the gypsies in a market, in a position ready for sudden departure, in case of danger—beneath the trees, in front of the guardhouse, which was a small durable structure hastily bricked together. She would wait barefoot, in her black dress trimmed with braids along the hem and along the sleeves. Her face was severe but not mean, tired but not weary. The commando leader prepared an almost empty room, then signaled to her. She entered the room. Closed the door, but did not lock it. Then she came out without saying a word and without smiling, and returned on bare feet, and very upright, to Jerash or to the camp at Baqa. I learned that in the room reserved for her in the guardhouse she would take off her two black skirts, remove all the envelopes and letters that had been sewn into them, put them in a bundle, and knock once on the door. She would give the letters to the leader, go back out, and leave without saying a word. She would return the next day.

Other older women would laugh over having nothing more for a hearth than three blackened stones, which in Jebel Hussein (Amman) they laughingly called "our house."[18] They showed me the three stones, sometimes lit with glowing coals, laughing and saying with such childlike voices, "Darna."[19] These old women belonged neither to the revolution nor to the Palestinian resistance: theirs was a cheerfulness that has ceased to hope.[20] Above them, the sun curved onward. A pointing finger or outstretched arm formed an ever thinner shadow. But on what soil? Jordanian, by virtue of an administrative and political fiction decided by France, England, Turkey, America. . . . "The cheerfulness that has ceased to hope"—the most joyful because the most hopeless. They could still see a Palestine that had ceased to exist when they were sixteen years old, but finally they had a soil to stand on. They were neither above it nor below it, but in a disquieting space where the least movement would be a wrong one. Under the bare feet of these supremely elegant octogenarians, these tragediennes, was the earth solid? This was less and less true. When they had fled Hebron and the Israeli threats, the earth seemed solid here, there was a feeling of lightness and everyone moved sensuously in the Arabic language. As time passed the earth seemed to experience this: the Palestinians were less and less bearable even as these Palestinians, these peasants, were discovering mobility, quick steps, running, the play of ideas reshuffled almost every day like cards, as well as weapons put together and taken apart, and used. Each of the women takes turns speaking. They laugh. One of them is reported to have said:

"Heroes! What a joke. I gave birth to and spanked five or six of the ones in the *jebel.*[21] I wiped their behinds. I know what they're made of and I can make more."

In the still blue sky the sun has curved onward, but it's still hot. These tragediennes remember and imagine at the same time. To be more expressive, they point their finger at the end of a sentence and stress the emphatic consonants. If a Jordanian soldier happened to pass by, he'd be delighted: in the rhythm of their words he would hear the rhythm of the Bedouin dances. Without any words at all, an Israeli soldier, if he saw these goddesses, would unload his automatic rifle into their skulls.

~

Here, in the ruins of Shatila, there is nothing left. A few silent old women hastily hiding behind a door with a white cloth nailed on it. As for the very young fedayeen, I will meet a few of them in Damascus.

If someone chooses a particular community outside of his birth—whereas to belong to this people one must be born into it—this choice is based on an irrational affinity; not that justice has no part in it, but this justice and the entire defense of this community take place because of an attraction that is sentimental, or perhaps sensitive or sensual. I am French, but I defend the Palestinians entirely, without judgment. They are in the right because I love them. But would I love them if injustice had not made them a wandering people?

In Beirut, in what is still called West Beirut, almost all the buildings have been hit. They have different ways of collapsing: like a many-layered pastry crushed by the fingers of some giant King Kong, indifferent and voracious; or at other times the three or four top floors lean deliciously in an elegant pleat, giving the building a sort of Lebanese drape. If a facade is intact, take a walk around the building and the other walls are pocked with bullet holes. If all four sides are unscathed, it's because the bomb fell from the airplane into the center and made a pit where there was once a stairwell or an elevator.

In West Beirut, after the Israelis arrived, S. told me this: "Night had fallen, it must have been around seven o'clock. Suddenly a loud metallic noise, clank, clank, clank. My sister, my brother-in-law, and me, we all ran to the balcony. It was a very dark night. And every now and then there was a flash, like lightning, less than a hundred meters away. You know that almost right across from us there's a sort of Israeli headquarters: four tanks, a house occupied by soldiers and officers, some guards. Darkness. And the clanking sound is coming closer. Flashes; a few lit torches. And then forty or fifty kids, about twelve or thirteen years old, beating in time on little metal jerrycans with rocks or hammers or something else. They were screaming, chanting loudly in time: 'La ilaha illa Allah, la Katayeb wa-la Yahoud' (There is no God but Allah; no to the Katayeb; no to the Jews)."

H. said to me: "When you came to Beirut and Damascus in 1928, Damascus was destroyed.[22] General Gouraud and his troops, the Moroccan and Tunisian infantrymen, had fired on Damascus and cleaned it out. Who did the Syrian population blame?"

Me: "The Syrians blamed the French for the massacres and the destruction in Damascus."

Him: "We blame Israel for the massacres at Shatila and Sabra. These crimes shouldn't be placed only on the shoulders of the Katayeb who took over the job for them. Israel is guilty of allowing two companies of Katayeb into the camps, of giving them orders, of encouraging them for three days and three nights, of bringing them food and drink, of lighting up the camps at night."

H. again, professor of history. He said to me: "In 1917, Abraham's coup was rewritten, or, if you like, God was already the prefiguration of Lord Balfour.[23] God—as the Jews used to say and still say—had promised a land of milk and honey to Abraham and his descendants, but this region, which did not belong to the God of the Jews (these lands were full of gods), this region was populated by the Canaanites, who also had their gods, and who fought against the troops of Joshua until they stole the famous Ark of the Covenant, without which the Jews could never have won. In 1917, England did not yet possess Palestine (that land of milk and honey), since the treaty giving it a mandate had not yet been signed."[24]

"Begin claims that he came to the country . . . "

"That's the name of a film: *Une Si Longue Absence* [*sic*; So long an absence].[25] Do you see that Pole as the heir of Solomon?"[26]

In the camps, after twenty years of exile, the Palestinians were dreaming of their Palestine, no one dared to think or say that Israel had thoroughly ravaged it, that where there had been a barley field now there was a bank, that the power plant had taken the place of the creeping vine.

"Let's replace the fence around the field?"

"We'll have to redo part of the wall next to the fig tree."

"All the pans must be rusted—we need to buy an emery cloth."

"Why don't we run an electrical line out to the barn?"

"Oh no, no more hand-embroidered dresses; you can get me a sewing machine and another one for embroidering."

The old people in the camps were miserable; perhaps they were also miserable in Palestine, but nostalgia produced magical effects there. They were in danger of remaining prisoners of the unhappy spell of the camps. It's not certain that this segment of the Palestinians would leave the camps without regret. This is the sense in which an extreme destitution becomes fixated on the past. Whoever has known such destitution also knows, along with its bitterness, an intimate, solitary, unspeakable joy. The camps in Jordan perched on rocky slopes are bare, but around their edges there is an even more desolate bareness: shanties and tents full of holes inhabited by families glowing with pride. Only a complete lack of understanding of the human heart could make one deny that men can become fond and proud of their visible wretchedness; this pride is possible because visible wretchedness is counterbalanced by a hidden glory.

The solitude of the dead in the Shatila camp was even more palpable since they were frozen in gestures and poses over which they had no control. Dead just any old way. Dead and abandoned where they lay. But around us, in the camp, all the affection, tenderness, and love lingered in search of the Palestinians who would never again answer.

What can we say to their parents who left with Arafat, trusting in the promises of Reagan, Mitterand, and Pertini, who had assured them that no one would touch the civilian population of the camps?[27] How to explain that the massacre of children, old people, and women had been allowed and that their bodies had been abandoned without a prayer? How can we tell them that we don't know where they're buried?

The massacres did not take place in silence and darkness. Lit by Israeli flares, Israeli ears listened closely to Shatila from the beginning, on Thursday evening. What festivity, what reveling happened there where death seemed to take part in the pranks of soldiers drunk on wine, drunk on hate, and drunk no doubt on the joy of pleasing the Israeli army as it listened and watched, as it encouraged and incited them. I didn't see this Israeli army listening and watching. I saw what it left behind.

To the argument: "What did Israel gain by assassinating Bashir; entering Beirut, reestablishing order, and averting the bloodbath."

What did Israel have to gain by massacring Shatila? Answer: "What did it gain by entering Lebanon? What did it gain by bombing the civilian population for two months; chasing out and destroying the Palestinians. What did it want to gain in Shatila: the destruction of the Palestinians."

It kills men, it kills the dead. It razes Shatila. It won't miss out on the real-estate speculation on the newly improved land: it's worth five million old francs per square meter in ruins. But "cleaned up," it'll go for . . . ?

I'm writing this in Beirut where, perhaps because of the close proximity of death, still covering the ground, everything is more true than in France:[28] everything seems to happen as if, wearied and overwhelmed with being an example, being untouchable, exploiting what it thinks it has become—the inquisitorial and vengeful saint—Israel had decided to let itself be judged coldly.[29]

In short, thanks to a skillful yet predictable metamorphosis, it is now what it has long been in the process of becoming: a loathsome temporal power, a colonizer in a way that no one can any longer dare to be, the Definitive Authority that it owes both to its long malediction and to its status as chosen.

Many questions remain:

If the Israelis did nothing but light up the camps, listen to it, hear the shots fired from so many shells—I stepped on tens of thousands of them—who was actually shooting? Who was risking their skin by killing? The Phalangists? The Haddadists? Who? And how many?

What happened to the weapons that left all these dead bodies behind? And where are the weapons of those who defended themselves? In the part of the camp I visited, I only saw two unused antitank weapons.

How did the murderers get into the camps? Were the Israelis at all the exits controlling Shatila? In any case, on Thursday they were already at the Akka hospital, across from one entrance to the camp.

The newspapers reported that the Israelis entered the camp of Shatila as soon as they knew about the massacres and that they stopped them right then, that is, on Saturday. But what did they do with the killers? And when the latter left, where did they go?

After the assassination of Bashir Gemayel and twenty of his associates, after the massacres, when she learned that I was back from Shatila, Madame B., a woman of the upper class in Beirut, came to see me. She walked up the eight floors of the building (no electricity); I thought of her as old, elegant but old.

I said to her: "Before the death of Bashir, before the massacres, you were right to tell me that the worst was on its way. I saw it."

"Please don't tell me what you saw in Shatila. My nerves are too sensitive, I have to stay calm so that I can bear the worst that's still to come."

She lived alone with her husband (seventy years old) and her maid in a large apartment in Ras Beirut.[30] She is very elegant, very careful about her appearance. She had period furniture, Louis XVI, I think.

"We knew that Bashir went to Israel. He was wrong. An elected head of state ought not associate with those people. I was sure something bad was going to happen to him. But I don't want to hear about it. I have to be careful to steady my nerves for the terrible blows that are still to come. Bashir should have returned that letter in which Begin calls him his 'dear friend.'"

The upper class, with its silent servants, has its own way of resisting. Madame B. and her husband "do not entirely believe in reincarnation." What will happen if they are reborn as Israelis?

The day of Bashir's burial is also the day the Israeli army enters West Beirut. The explosions draw closer to our building. Finally everyone goes down to the shelter in the basement. Ambassadors, doctors, their wives, daughters, a UN representative to Lebanon, their domestics.

"Carlos, bring me a pillow."

"Carlos, my glasses."

"Carlos, a little water."

The domestics also speak French and so are allowed into the shelter. It may be necessary to look after them, their wounds, their transportation to the hospital or the cemetery, what a mess!

It is important to know that the Palestinian camps of Shatila and Sabra consist of miles and miles of very narrow alleys—for here even the alleys are so thin, so skeletal, that sometimes two people cannot walk together unless one of them turns sideways—alleys cluttered with rubble and debris, stone blocks, bricks, dirty multicolored rags, and at night under the light of the Israeli flares that illuminated the camps, fifteen or twenty gunmen, even if well armed, could never have succeeded in carrying out this butchery. There had been gunmen, but a lot of them, and probably squads of torturers who split open skulls, slashed thighs, cut off arms, hands, and fingers, dragged the dying on a rope after binding them hand and foot, men and women who were still alive, since the blood flowed from the body for a long time, to the point that I couldn't tell who had left this stream of dried blood in the hallway of a house, from the pool at one end of the hall to the doorway where it disappeared in the dust. Was it a Palestinian? A woman? A Phalangist whose body had been cleared away?

From Paris, it is indeed possible to doubt everything, especially if you don't know anything about the layout of the camps. It is possible to let Israel claim that the journalists from Jerusalem were the first to bring news of the massacre. How did they communicate it to the Arab countries in the Arabic language? And how in English and French? And when exactly? And to think of the measures taken in the West when a suspicious death is discovered, the fingerprints, the ballistics reports, the autopsies, and the experts' second opinions! In Beirut, hardly had the massacre become known when the Lebanese army officially took charge of the camps and immediately swept away the ruins of the houses along with the remains of the bodies. Who ordered this hasty action? Yet this was after the statement had spread throughout the world that Christians and Muslims had killed each other, and after the cameras had recorded the ferocity of the carnage.

Akka hospital, which was occupied by the Israelis, across from an entrance to Shatila, is not two hundred meters from the camp, but forty. They saw nothing, heard nothing, knew nothing?

For that's exactly what Begin declared in the Knesset: "Goyim massacred goyim, what does that have to do with us?"

My description of Shatila was interrupted for a moment, but I must finish it. There were the dead bodies I saw at the end, on Sunday, around two o'clock in the afternoon, when the International Red Cross came in with its bulldozers. The stench of death was coming not from a house or a tortured victim: my body, my being, seemed to emit it. In a narrow street, underneath a jutting wall, I thought I saw a black boxer sitting on the ground, stunned from a knockout, a look of laughter on his face. No one had had the heart to close his eyelids; his bulging eyes, as though made of very white porcelain, stared at me. He looked downcast, defeated, with his arm raised, pressed against this angle of the wall. He was a Palestinian, dead for two or three days. If at first I saw him as a black boxer it was because his head was enormous, swollen, and black, like all the heads and all the bodies, whether in the sun or in the shadows of the houses. I walked near his feet. I picked up an upper dental plate from the dust and set it on what remained of a window sill. The hollow of his hand held out toward the sky, his open mouth, the opening of his beltless pants: so many hives where the flies were feeding.

I stepped over another corpse, then another. In this dust-ridden space, between the two bodies, there was at last a very living object, intact amid the carnage, a transparent pink object that might still be of some use: an artificial leg, apparently made of plastic, wearing a black shoe over a gray sock. When I looked closer it became clear that it had been brutally wrenched from the amputated leg, since the straps that usually held it to the thigh were all broken.

This artificial leg belonged to the second body. The one on which I had seen only one leg and one foot with a black shoe and a gray sock.

In the street perpendicular to the one where I saw the three bodies, there was another dead body. It didn't completely block the way, but it was lying at the entrance to the street so that I had to walk past it and turn around to see this sight: sitting on a chair surrounded by silent and relatively young men and women, a woman was sobbing—a woman in Arab dress who as far as I could tell was sixteen or sixty. She was weeping over her brother whose body almost blocked the street. I moved closer to her. I looked more carefully. She had a scarf knotted around her neck. She was weeping, mourning the death of her brother there next to her. Her face was pink—a baby's pink, more or less uniform, very soft, tender—but there were no eyelashes or eyebrows, and what I thought was pink wasn't the top layer of skin but a deeper layer edged in gray skin. Her whole face was burnt. Impossible now to say how, but I understood by whom.

With the first bodies, I made it a point to count them. Once I got to twelve or fifteen, surrounded by the smell, the sun, tripping over every piece of rubble, I couldn't do it anymore, everything was blurring together.

I have seen a lot of collapsed apartment buildings, gutted houses with eiderdown floating out, and was indifferent, but when I saw the ones in West Beirut and Shatila, I saw the horror. The dead generally become familiar to me, even friendly, but when I saw the ones in the camps I could discern nothing but the hatred and joy of those who had killed them. A barbaric celebration had unfolded there: rage, drunkenness, dances, songs, curses, laments, moans, in honor of the voyeurs laughing on the top floor of the Akka hospital.

~

In France, before the Algerian War, the Arabs were not beautiful, they seemed odd and heavy, slow-moving, with skewed, oblique faces, and then almost all at once victory made them beautiful; but already, just before it became blindingly clear, when more than half a million French soldiers were straining out their last breaths in the Aurès Mountains and throughout Algeria, a curious phenomenon became perceptible, working its way into the faces and bodies of the Arab workers: something like the approach, the presentiment of a still fragile beauty that would dazzle us when the scales finally fell from their skin and our eyes. We had to admit the obvious: they had liberated themselves politically in order to appear as they had to be seen: very beautiful. In the same way, having escaped from the refugee camps, from the morality and the order of the camps, from a morality imposed by the necessities of survival, having escaped at the same time from shame, the fedayeen were very beautiful; and since this beauty was new, or we could say novel, or naive, it was fresh, so alive that it immediately revealed its attunement with all the beauties of the world that have been freed from shame.

A lot of Algerian pimps passing through the night at Pigalle used all they had for the Algerian revolution. Virtue was to be found there too. I believe it was Hannah Arendt who distinguished between revolutions that aspire to freedom and those that aspire to virtue—and therefore to work.[31] Perhaps we ought to recognize that the end pursued—obscurely—by revolutions or liberations is the discovery or rediscovery of beauty, that is, something that is impalpable and unnamable except by this word. Or rather, no: by beauty we should understand a laughing insolence spurred by past misery, by the systems and men responsible for misery and shame, but a laughing insolence which realizes that, when shame has been left behind, the bursting forth of new life is easy.

But on this page the question should also, and above all, be the following: is a revolution a revolution if it has not removed from faces and bodies the dead skin that distorted them? I'm not talking about an academic beauty, but rather the impalpable—unnamable—joy of bodies, faces, shouts, words that are no longer dead, I mean a sensual joy so strong that it tends to drive away all eroticism.

~

Here I am again in Jordan, in Ajloun then in Irbid. I pull from my sweater what appears to be one of my white hairs and I place it on Hamza's knee as he sits next to me.[32] He takes it between his thumb and middle finger, looks at it, smiles, puts it in the pocket of his black jacket, pats it with his hand, and says:

"A hair from the beard of the Prophet is worth less than this."

He takes a slightly deeper breath and starts again:

"A hair from the beard of the Prophet is not worth more than this."

He was only twenty-two years old, his thoughts leapt with ease far above the forty-year-old Palestinians, but there were already visible signs—visible on himself, on his body, in his gestures—that linked him to his elders.

In the old days, the farmers used to blow their noses into their fingers. A flick of the wrist sent the snot into the thorn bushes. They would wipe their noses on their corduroy sleeves which, after a month, were covered with a pearly sheen. So did the fedayeen. They blew their noses the way nobleman and prelates took snuff: slightly bent over. I did the same thing, which they taught me without realizing it.

And the women? Night and day they embroidered the seven dresses (one for each day of the week) of the engagement trousseau offered by a groom, generally older and chosen by the family, a rude awakening. The young Palestinian women became very beautiful when they rebelled against their fathers and broke their needles and embroidery scissors. Into the mountains of Ajloun, Salt, or Irbid, into the forests themselves, there settled all the sensuality liberated by rebellion and by rifles, let's not forget the rifles: that was enough, everyone was more than happy. Without being aware of it—but is that true?—the fedayeen were perfecting a novel beauty: the vivacity of their gestures and their visible weariness, the quickness and brilliance of the eye, the clearer tone of voice all became allied with a swift response and with its brevity. Its precision too. They had eliminated the long sentences, the glib and learned rhetoric.

Many people died in Shatila, and my friendship for them, my affection for their rotting corpses was great also because I had known them. Blackened, swollen, rotted by the sun and by death, they remained fedayeen.

~

At around two o'clock in the afternoon on Sunday, three soldiers of the Lebanese army, rifles ready, led me to a jeep where an officer was dozing. I asked him:

"You speak French?"

"English."

His voice was dry, perhaps because I had just awakened him with a start.

He looked at my passport. He said, in French:

"You're coming from there?" (He pointed toward Shatila.)

"Yes."

"And you saw?"

"Yes."

"You're going to write about it?"

"Yes."

He handed back my passport. He signaled me to leave. The three rifles were lowered. I had spent four hours in Shatila. About forty corpses remained in my memory. All of them—and I mean all of them—had been tortured, probably amidst drunkenness, songs, rites, the smell of gunpowder and, already, rotting flesh.

No doubt I was alone, I mean the only European—with a few old Palestinian women still clutching a torn white cloth; with a few young, unarmed fedayeen—but if these five or six human beings hadn't been there and I had discovered this slaughtered city, the Palestinians lying there black and swollen, I would have gone mad. Or did I? This city that I saw crumbled and scattered on the ground, or thought I saw, that I walked through, lifted and carried by the powerful stench of death—had all that taken place?

I had only explored, and very poorly, one twentieth of Shatila and Sabra; I saw no part of Bir Hassan or Bourj al-Barajneh.[33]

～

It is not because of my inclinations that I experienced the Jordanian period as if it were a charmed adventure. Europeans and North African Arabs have spoken to me of the spell that kept them there. As I lived through this long stretch of six months, barely tinged with night for twelve or thirteen hours, I came to know the lightness of the event, the exceptional quality of the fedayeen, but I sensed how fragile the edifice was. Wherever the Palestinian army had assembled in Jordan—near the Jordan River—there were checkpoints where the fedayeen were so sure of their rights and their power that, day or night, the arrival of a visitor at one of the checkpoints was an occasion for making tea, talking amid bursts of laughter and brotherly kisses (the one they embraced was leaving at night, crossing the Jordan River to plant bombs in Palestine, and often would not be coming back). The only islands of silence were the Jordanian villages: they kept their mouths shut. All the fedayeen seemed to be slightly raised off the ground by a very light glass of wine or a little puff of hashish. What was it? Youth, unconcerned with death and in possession of Czech or Chinese arms to fire into the air. Protected by weapons that shot so high and talked so big, the fedayeen weren't afraid of anything.

Any reader who has seen a map of Palestine and Jordan knows that the terrain is not a sheet of paper. The terrain along the Jordan River is in high relief. The whole venture should have had the subtitle "A Midsummer Night's Dream," despite the hot-tempered words between the forty-year-old leaders. All that was possible because of youth, the pleasure of being there under the trees, playing with weapons, being away from women, that is, of conjuring away a difficult problem, of being the most luminous because the sharpest point of the revolution, of having the approval of the population in the camps, of being photogenic no matter what they did, and perhaps of sensing that this fairy tale with revolutionary content would soon be wrecked: the fedayeen didn't want power, they had freedom.

At the Damascus airport on the way back from Beirut I met some young fedayeen who had escaped from the Israeli hell. They were sixteen or seventeen years old: they were laughing; they were a lot like the ones in Ajloun. They will die like them. The struggle for a country can fill a very rich life, but a short one. This, we recall, is Achilles' choice in the *Iliad*.[34]

§ 34 Registration No. 1155

Beginning with Lyautey's entry into Morocco, or with the establishment in 1913 of the local bureaus, there were only two ways to describe Morocco: in terms of strategy, and then in terms of exploitation.[1] We know this from all the reports on local affairs and from the studies of the anthropologists.

There was also a way of describing the Moroccan who had been born as a soldier or a worker: they were Moroccan soldiers, Moroccan workers.

Some papers found in an old cabinet at the flea market tell us what it sufficed to know about them.

The word "skeleton" comes immediately to mind. They are indeed skeletal, these forms with their ten or twelve categories, making it impossible for us to understand that an entire world of events, both individual and collective—rebellion, mourning, revolutions, loves, killings, diseases—had taken place in these bodies now circumscribed by a Christian corporal attentive to his cold calligraphy.

Who we have been, we French, who we still probably are—these archives, all too well maintained and preserved, spit it all back in our faces.

Recto

You have before you a first document (1155) entitled "Carte d'identité de protégés français" (Identity card for residents of the French protectorate). Indeed, Morocco was a protectorate.

The document is from 1940. Some time after that, "protégé no. 1" (I'm speaking of the Sultan Muhammad ben Yussef) was arrested with his family in the middle of the night, on August 23, 1953.[2] The French exiled him first in Corsica, then in Madagascar. What was a "carte de protégé français" worth then?

Card no. 1155 concerns a Moroccan worker named Salah, born in Morocco the same year I was born in Paris, 1910.

Born presumably in 1910. There was no office of civil records.

Hence no doubt all the precautions:

Father's name.[3]

Paternal grandfather's name.

Mother's name.

Maternal grandmother's name.

Tribe.

Faction . . . Here there is introduced a delineation or a foreign—a French—way of cutting things up: What is a faction? Do factions apply only to those in our protectorates?

Faction or fracture?

There is yet another:

Region or territory?

Verso

Worker. Race: Moroccan.

The notion of race, in any case of races within the human species, would be abandoned in 1945. In 1940, then, there remained only the Moroccan race?

Name: Salah Ahmed Salah.

First Name: no first name or included in name above.

Height: 1 m 67.

Hair: black.

Skin color: brown.

The right and left thumbprints mark the signature.

But why did he sign with his thumbs a list of descriptive information no part of which he could have read if he was illiterate?

The inside of the document informs us of a vocabulary that does not concern us: *shashiyya, tarboosh, serwal, duwar, kundura,* indigenous . . . [4]

Other records were established on December 29, 1939. We were at war.

Before going off to die at Monte Cassino, the Moroccans first passed through Le Creusot, and the foundry there.[5] They couldn't read or write, they knew nothing of Germany.[6] "We" pulled one over on them.

"We" means France.

France continues as it has, with hardly any difference.

As we can see, the file and the card are pink. The same pink as the one that used to color the map of the globe, indicating the French Colonial Empire.

§ 35   Interview with Rüdiger Wischenbart
and Layla Shahid Barrada

Rüdiger Wischenbart.—Jean Genet, you came to Vienna for a demonstration relating to Sabra and Shatila and the massacres that took place a year ago. Right now the situation in the Middle East is very tense.[1] Arafat is surrounded in Tripoli. There is a danger of a large-scale conflict between the United States and Syria. What are the possible effects of such a demonstration, and of your involvement in such a situation?

Genet.—They're obviously not very great. But the fact that Austria, and Chancellor Kreisky in particular, have recognized Arafat as the representative of the PLO, and therefore of the Palestinians, this may have a significant effect.[2] It was in this capacity that I was invited here by the International Progress Organization.[3] But I am aware of the limitations of a singular intervention like my own.

R.W.—We have heard that it was more or less by chance that you were in Beirut at the time of the Sabra and Shatila massacres. How was it that you got into the camp at Shatila and what did you see there?

G.—No, I wasn't there by chance, I had been invited by the *Revue d'études palestiniennes*.[4] We left for Beirut together with Layla Shahid. If you like, I'll retrace the chronology of what happened during my stay there. We arrived in Damascus on September 11, 1982, then went by road to Beirut, on September 12. And on Monday, September 13, we visited the city. It's important for me to mention something, and to rectify General Sharon's statements that about thirty houses had been destroyed in Beirut.[5] That is not true. If he's attached to this figure thirty, I would say that there were maybe thirty houses that had not been hit, but the whole city of Beirut had been hit. If it wasn't the south facade of the house, it was the north facade or on the sides or sometimes in the middle. But all the houses of Beirut had been hit except thirty, since Mr. Sharon is so attached to this figure.

So that Monday I saw Beirut. On Tuesday, Bashir Gemayel was assassinated.[6] He was killed, and the assassination was attributed to the CIA as well as to Mossad.[7] Which one was it? I don't know any more than you do, probably. The next day, Israeli troops crossed into the Passage du Musée, passed through other parts of West Beirut, and occupied the camps at Shatila, Sabra, and Bourj al-Barajneh, among others. The reason they gave was that it was necessary to prevent a massacre. But the massacre took place. It is difficult to say that the Israelis wanted this massacre. Indeed I'm not sure of this myself. But they allowed it to happen. It was carried out, in a way, under their protection. Since they lit up the camps. They lit up the camps at Sabra, Shatila, and Bourj al-Barajneh. When you send up flairs, it's in order to do reconnaissance, it's to help the people who are on your side. The people on Israel's side were obviously the ones who committed the massacre.

R.W.—You were in the Shatila camp not long after the massacre. What did you see there?

G.—I was in the Shatila camp on Sunday, September 19, the day after the massacres. But I would like for the people listening to be aware of the topography of the place. I tried to get into the Shatila camp before that Sunday, but you know that all the entrances to Sabra, Shatila, and Bourj al-Barajneh, as well as the one across from Akka hospital, were closed by Merkava—that is Israeli—tanks. It was necessary to wait for the massacre to take place and for everyone to be dead or dying or wounded, before the Israelis went away and left the Lebanese army to occupy the camp, for reasons of sanitation—so they could bury the dead and possibly take care of those who could still be helped. That's when I was able to go in, that is, when the Israeli army was handing the camp over to the Lebanese army. There was a moment of flux between ten A.M. and a quarter after ten on Sunday, and this allowed me to go in.

R.W.—After your visit to Shatila, were you able to speak with other Palestinians, with Lebanese, or probably even with Christians who had been witnesses?

G.—Of course. I spoke using the minimal Arabic I know, the minimal English, and sometimes in French. Of course. I spoke with survivors, even with some wounded, with women who survived by hiding and who had found a way to get out of the camp and to come back Sunday morning. Of course.

R.W.—There was an investigation ordered by the Israeli parliament concerning the question of responsibility. Were your observations and your investigation at the site more or less the same as the parliamentary investigation?

G.—The goal of my visit and that of the investigation were quite different.[8] According to what I have read, and according to what people have told me, including some Israelis, the goal of the investigation was to rescue Israel's image. Fine. An image holds no interest. I'm not going to give you a certain image, one that will be erased when I go somewhere else, to Syria for example, or if I go to Germany or to South America. So I don't give a damn about the image. When the investigation was carried out by Israel, its purpose was to rescue the image. That's not why I went. The reason I went was to perceive a reality, a political and human reality. So I don't have much to say about Israel's goals in its investigation. In my opinion, its investigation was part of the massacre. I'll explain myself: There was the massacre that tarnished an image, and then there was the investigation that erased the massacre. Am I making myself clear?

R.W.—In the meantime, the situation has changed a great deal. It looks like Arafat is very close to surrendering in Tripoli. Have you had any recent contact with the PLO? What do you think about the current situation?

G.—My comrade here next to me is part of the PLO, so I've had direct and constant contact with the PLO.[9] It surprises me to hear you speak of Arafat surrendering, since that's exactly what Arafat has not done. In his prison in Tripoli—a dangerous prison, if you like—he has found a way to have forty-five hundred Palestinian prisoners released and to hand over six prisoners of war to Israel.[10] So where do you see the surrender, or the need to use the word surrender?

R.W.—What I mean is that right now Arafat is surrounded, on one side by the Syrian army, who is supporting the rebels within the PLO; and on the other side he has the sea at his back and is trying to negotiate a departure from Tripoli under the protection of the UN. It is a dire situation, after all.

G.—A dire situation, but a situation that always occurs in revolutionary movements. There is always a split within a revolution or a revolutionary movement, and the split or apparent split that has emerged, probably provoked by Syria, is not so dire for the moment. And it's Syria who is obliged to allow Arafat and the forty-five hundred fighters to leave Tripoli.

R.W.—What led you to become so intensely involved with the PLO? Before, it was really quite rare for you to take sides so concretely with a group or a political movement, with the exception of the Black Panthers in the United States and the Red Army Faction in West Germany.

G.—What led me to it was first of all my personal history, which I don't want to recount. It's of no interest to anyone. If someone wants to know more about it, they can read my books; it's not very important. But I will say one thing, which is that my earlier books—I stopped writing about thirty years ago—were part of a dream or a daydream. Having survived this dream and this daydream, and in order to obtain a sort of fullness of life, I had to enter into action. You mentioned the Black Panthers, the German Red Army Faction, and the Palestinians, if I understood correctly. Very quickly, I will answer by saying that I went immediately toward the people who asked me to intervene. The Black Panthers came to Paris and asked me to go to the United States. It was Klaus Croissant who came to ask me to intervene in support of Baader.[11] It was the Palestinians who asked me to go to Jordan ten years ago. Layla Shahid asked me to go to Beirut a year ago. Obviously, I have been drawn toward people in revolt. But this is quite naturally because I myself need to question society as a whole.

R.W.—So Genet as a rebel, as a fighter?

G.—Listen: In 1967—I don't know who was at the origin of the war, was it Nasser, was it Israel? I don't want to say for sure—but I was in England. I took the train to Paris, just like that, I took the train. The other people in my compartment were all English. I asked them, "So where are you going?" They said, "To help Israel." And all of them were Jewish. I imagine that you wouldn't stop to wonder why the English would go to help Israel when it was in danger. Why are you asking me the reason for going to help a people in danger? There were affinities between the English Jews and Israel. Between the Palestinians, the Panthers, the Red Army Faction, and myself, there are affinities. And it's natural for me to go and help them. I can't help them very much, since a seventy-three-year-old man can't do much to help a young people in revolt. Nevertheless, I help them to the extent that I can.

R.W.—What affinities are there between the PLO, the Black Panthers, the Red Army Faction, and you?

G.—What affinities were there between the English and the Israelis entering a war in 1967?

R.W.—In your text "Four Hours in Shatila," and also, of course, in your earlier books, you always speak of the beauty that is also found in what you have seen. Even the beauty that has a certain macabre and tragic place in what is happening in Lebanon. That is another reason for me to ask you why you went to Lebanon and to Palestine.

G.—I've also been inside banks. I've never seen a banker who I thought was beautiful. And I wonder whether this beauty you're speaking of—it's still a problem for me, I'm also asking myself this question—I wonder if the beauty you're speaking of, that I spoke of in this book, doesn't come from the fact that those who revolt have regained a freedom they had lost. I'm not making myself understood?

R.W.—Yes, a little.

G.—Yes . . .

R.W.—What does this beauty consist of? And this freedom?

G.—The beauty of revolutionaries is visible in a sort of casualness and even insolence in relation to the people who have humiliated them. Don't forget that you're talking to a man who has lived for seventy-three years in France, a country that had an immense colonial empire. So on a personal level I was crushed for reasons I don't need to explain to you right now, I was crushed by the concept of France. Quite naturally, I was drawn toward people in revolt who asked me to join up with them. This beauty I'm speaking of, which it's best not to insist on too much—I'm afraid it will be taken the wrong way—this beauty lies in the fact that former slaves have gotten rid of slavery, submission, and servitude and have acquired a freedom in relation to France or, for the blacks, America, or for the Palestinians, I would say the Arab world in general.

R.W.—In today's world—where politics is something that takes place between two superpowers—isn't that a vain hopefulness, with no chance, no real hope?

G.—You're asking me difficult questions that demand a lot of thought and you're not giving me time to think. I would obviously need to think about them for four or five days. You spoke of superpowers. It's true. But these superpowers leave a margin for certain groups of people to liberate themselves from sub-superpowers. When you say that this hope or this hopefulness is vain . . . a quick and almost hostile response comes to mind: what in this world is not vain? I'm asking you this question. What in the end is not vain? You're going to die, I'm going to die, they're going to die. . . . Okay . . .

R.W.—I don't have an answer.

G.—Of course not. And you'd like for me to have one in the next ten minutes?

R.W.—No. When you were in Lebanon last year, did you not sometimes feel like a spectator, even though you went there for a Palestinian journal? Since, in the strict sense, it wasn't your combat that you were bearing witness to. After all, you're not Palestinian.

G.—Well, exactly. Let me explain something. When the Palestinian leader in Paris asked me to go to Jordan—I'm going back twelve years now—the Palestinian people, whom I knew about only through French newspapers and journals, were indeed relatively unknown to me.[12] I wondered where I was going. I'll tell you about one memory I have. I was in Deraa, the small border town between Syria and Jordan. There was fighting every day between the Palestinian and the Jordanian forces. There was a house the PLO had bought or rented, I don't know which, and turned into a sort of hospital. And in this hospital they welcomed foreigners like me who came with Palestinians, who wanted to help the Palestinians however they could. And you're right to say that, at first, I was a spectator. I arrived as a spectator. Not long after I had walked into the room, someone asked me—like someone did just now—if I wanted a coffee. They made a coffee and brought it to me, and I saw two Palestinians in combat uniform, paratrooper style, with berets. They were smiling and laughing, they were speaking a guttural Arabic, they were leaning on their elbows on two wooden containers. They were laughing and I remember how they drummed with their fingers on the containers, how their fingers were sharp and dry and they hammered on the containers with a sort of self-assurance.[13] When I walked out I saw the containers—they were talking to each other while leaning on two coffins. And in fact they were waiting for two bodies, two dead Palestinians who came from somewhere else and who were brought in bags and then put into the containers. I'm telling you this because it's the first impression I had of the Palestinians, and right away, yes, almost immediately I was struck by the weight, by the truth of the Palestinians' gestures. When I had left Paris I was still under the influence of a literary Orient. Even if it was spoken of in the newspapers, it was in a literary way, they referred to . . . I won't go so far as to say *A Thousand and One Nights*, but almost. Having already seen a little of the Arab countries—already at the age of eighteen I was walking through the souks in Damascus—and indeed that was the Orient, the traditional Orient. And

I saw a people who performed gestures with a real weightiness, a real weight. There was a weight of reality, of the real. All the Arab countries gave out packs of cigarettes. No cigarette was lit or smoked negligently. A cigarette had its sense. A water bucket taken by an Arab woman to a water fountain had its sense. You saw her bucket, you saw the water, you saw the woman. In short, what I feel now, and what I felt almost that very day, is that this people was the first in the Arab world to have a rapport with itself, a modern rapport. And its revolt was modern.

R.W.—I'm always struck by this aspect that I would call unreal, when, in Europe for example, we receive news of the fighting in Palestine, in Lebanon, between Palestinians and Arabs, between Palestinians and Israelis—hearing about the victims of the fighting has almost become something we're accustomed to. And it's only when something very spectacular happens, like the massacres in Sabra and Shatila, that we realize it's a question of real dead bodies, of people who die, who suffer, who are killed. What do you think about this unreal perception that we have as mere spectators?

G.—Well, I'm not placing the emphasis on the Palestinians because of your unrealism, but I do place the emphasis on you who transform everything into something unreal because you can then take it in more easily. It's after all much easier to admit an unreal death, an unreal massacre, than a real woman who carries real letters into a real camp. You see that it is first of all you who accept the massacres and transform them into unreal massacres. It's not impossible that yesterday, when you saw Layla Shahid's photographs of the massacres, this was the first time you had seen documents that weren't produced in a studio.[14] Since all the documents transmitted by your newspapers and illustrated magazines, or all the journalists' descriptions are seen as if they had been produced in the studios. The photos you saw yesterday didn't come from Hollywood.

R.W.—When you were in Lebanon, were there ever times when the Palestinians didn't accept you?

G.—I never felt that, not with the Black Panthers nor with the Palestinians. I don't think that ever happened. I am even quite sure that they never refused my presence. The welcome the Palestinians gave me— not in the camps, but on the bases, that is, at the very edge of the Jordan River, across from Israel—this welcome was so warm that I cannot believe they would have refused me for a single moment.

Now, there are two things, maybe three, that the Palestinians—not that they hid them from me, but that they didn't tell me spontaneously: the radio wavelengths, the placement of heavy artillery, and the funds received by the Palestinians from abroad, or by King Faysal, and so on. As for the rest, nothing was concealed from me.

R.W.—Did your involvement in these matters also have a personal significance for you?

G.—Yes. First I'll tell you that Arafat himself signed a letter for me allowing me to move around on all the bases. At first he told me that he wanted to sign the letter in the name of the Fatah. I insisted, I told him no, he had to sign this letter as the president of the PLO. He hesitated a little and then finally signed the letter as the president of the PLO, so that I could go from the Fatah to the FDLP, with Georges Habache, which I did, or with others: I could really go everywhere.[15] And I'll tell you once again that on the bases it happened that I would be by myself and the Palestinians who met me didn't ask for my papers. The first thing they would say when I met a small group, the leader of a small group, they would say, "You want some tea?" And it was only after we had drunk the tea and they had offered me something to eat that they would say, "Do you have the right to circulate?" And I would show them the letter from Arafat.

R.W.—There is an image of Jean Genet, the writer, as a solitary figure. In these encounters, whether with the Black Panthers or with the Palestinians, you're looking for collective groupings, very strong groups. Is that what attracted you?

G.—Yes, yes. Because . . . Here I'll say something very brief about my personal history. I could say that I began in prison by writing five books, not six, but five. And creating always means speaking of childhood. It's always nostalgic. Mine was, in any case, as is modern writing in general. You know as well as I do, or probably better, that the first sentence of Proust's entire work begins like this: "For a long time I went to bed early." And he recounts his entire childhood which takes up fifteen hundred pages or more than two thousand pages. So when I wrote I was thirty years old, when I started writing. When I was finished with writing, I was thirty-four, thirty-five years old. But that was a dream. It was in any case a daydream, a reverie. I wrote in prison. Once I became free, I was lost. And I didn't find myself again in reality, in the real world, until I was with these two revolutionary movements, the Black Panthers and the Palestinians. And so then I submitted myself to the real world. I said: it is necessary to do this today, and you must not do what you did yesterday; in short, I was acting in relation to the real world and no longer to the grammatical world. . . . To the extent that you can oppose the real world to the world of daydreaming. Of course if you press the issue further, we know very well that dreaming also belongs to the real world. Dreams are realities. But we also know that you can act upon dreams in a way that is almost unlimited. You cannot act upon the real in an unlimited way. A different discipline is necessary, one that is no longer a grammatical discipline.

R.W.—I told you that I read your text "Four Hours in Shatila" not exclusively as a testimony, but also as a novel. By which I mean that I think this text contains the substance of a novel that could be written for example on the current situation in the Middle East. Your immediate response was: "No, no, no, it's not a novel, I really went there."

G.—I said that it's not a novel because for me the word novel refers almost immediately to daydreaming, to unreality. *Madame Bovary* is a novel. In that sense, it's not a novel. To the extent that the novel is used to define a literary genre, it's not a novel.

R.W.—But it's also the writing in this text, which recalls Genet the chronicler, the literary writer.

G.—But do you also get a sense of the world of the Palestinians?

R.W.—Of course.

G.—Good.

R.W.—If you like, one gets a sense both of the world of the Palestinians and of the figure who is describing it.

G.—Good. Then I have only one thing to say to you. Which is that Degas, who worked with images, once wrote a sonnet. He showed it to Mallarmé and Mallarmé didn't like it. And Degas said to Mallarmé, "And yet I put a lot of ideas into it." And Mallarmé answered, "A poem isn't made of ideas, it's made of words." This little story I told, I didn't tell it with ideas belonging only to me. I told it with words that are mine. But in order to speak of a reality that was not mine.

R.W.—Still I'd like to ask: for you, what exactly is this great difference between the literary witness and the witness who is a reporter, for example? Because you have insisted very emphatically that you stopped writing about thirty years ago.

G.—I won't ask you to read my books from thirty years ago, but if you want to try, you'll see that it's not the same writing. But you will also see that it's the same man who is speaking.

R.W.—In this text on Shatila, one has a sense of the Palestinian world, one sees various figures. You said that the beauty you described in this text consisted in the feeling of freedom these people have.

G.—Wait a minute. Not only that. I believe that at the beginning of our conversation I emphasized the weight, the effectiveness, the weightiness of their gestures. This is what creates this beauty. Now I'm asking you: Don't you feel that beauty is more in reality? What are painters looking for? Whether it's Rembrandt, Frans Hals, or Cézanne? Aren't they looking for the weight of a reality? Isn't that it?

And they found it. Each of the men I mentioned found it for himself. But don't you feel that the Arab world in general has no weight? That it is being held up by the force of authoritarian and even police regimes? I'm asking you.

R.W.—I've never traveled in the Arab world. I'm not directly familiar with it.

G.—Well, in their revolt the Palestinians have taken on precisely this weight—oh, I'm afraid of being very literary here—but they have taken on the weight of Cézanne's canvases. They are imposing! Each Palestinian is real. Like Cézanne's Sainte-Victoire mountain. It's real, it's there.

R.W.—Why do you say that you're afraid of being too literary?

G.—Because I'm afraid that your program, this interview, will send me back thirty years.

R.W.—Layla Shahid just asked you what the difference is for you between the books from thirty years ago and now?

G.—In those books, and in prison, I was the master of my imagination. I was master over the element on which I was working. Because it was entirely my own daydream. But now I am no longer the master of what I saw, I am obliged to say: I saw men tied up and bound, I saw a woman with her fingers cut off! I am obliged to submit myself to a real world. But still with the old words, with words that are mine.

R.W.—In your plays, especially, I have the impression that the characters have lost all dignity, all pride too. In this text on Shatila what is striking is no doubt this search for the dignity of the people you describe. Is that not also one of the profound differences?

G.—Since you've brought up the plays I wrote, can you tell me which plays you're talking about?

R.W.—I'm thinking especially of *The Balcony*.

G.—Yes, the goal of *The Balcony*—its goal was also amusement, its goal was also to fulfill a contract. You know that it was commissioned. I was given a lot of money and I was obliged to write it. But at the same time, I didn't paint the portrait of just any world, but of the Western world. If you recall the themes addressed in *The Balcony*, the main one is that of the brothel, and each dignitary or client in *The Balcony* goes there to search for his dignity, an apparent dignity, the dignity of a bishop, a general, a judge.

R.W.—And it was also the dignity of a costume.

G.—Of course.

R.W.—What you wrote about the Palestinians and also what you experience with them, isn't that a totally different kind of dignity?

G.—Completely different. It wouldn't occur to me to talk to you about Yasser Arafat's kaffiyeh.[16] I noticed a lot of things about Yasser Arafat and his kaffiyeh. You know, Arafat is bald, he has no hair. And there are fringes on a kaffiyeh. And I remember he always did this, as if the fringes were like hair. I'm talking about this with you now. But it wouldn't occur to me to write a piece on Arafat's handling of the fringes of his kaffiyeh. A bishop, or even the current pope, are entirely contained in their costumes. Arafat is not contained in his kaffiyeh. He is still elsewhere. But imagine if the pope were dressed like you or me!

R.W.—There is almost a Jean Genet–as–moralist who is revealed or who appears in this text.

G.—It doesn't bother me if you say that about me. But don't confuse a moralist with a moralizer.

R.W.—Has your literary work become for you a personal past that still weighs on you, when you work or travel or write today?

G.—I believe you're the one who asked me if I now disavowed the art-work. Or writing. Of course not. It's thanks not to the books I wrote, but to the disposition I found myself in, in which I placed myself, in which life placed me to write books, thirty years ago, it's thanks to this that a year ago I was able to write the little essay you're talking about. . . . If I hadn't done this work on myself . . . You said—and you're right—that very likely I went as a spectator. You asked me if I wasn't a spectator. Indeed, when I was young I understood very soon that every path was blocked for me. I went to school until I was thirteen, a local public school. The most I might become was an accountant or a petty func-tionary. So I was already putting myself in a position not to be an accoun-tant, not to be a writer—which I didn't know how to be—but to observe the world. Since I couldn't change the world, I observed the world. At the age of twelve or fifteen years old, I was already creating within me the observer I would be, and therefore the writer I would become. But this work I did on myself remains.

R.W.—I asked you if a revolution or even a revolt still had any sense in a world so divided between superpowers. Given what you're saying now, I'll ask my question again: isn't this revolt that is so important to you very much like a gratuitous act, an existential revolt? And here I'm thinking more of Camus than Sartre.

G.—I don't know Camus's work very well. I found the man himself very irritating. I knew him . . . very moralizing, that one was! No, I think that even if the world is divided between two great powers—you're referring to the United States and the Soviet Union—the revolt of every man is necessary. One can carry out small daily acts of revolt. As soon as you introduce just a little disorder, or to put it another way, as soon as you introduce your own singular, individual order, you're engaged in revolt.

R.W.—You've emphasized the differences between the East and the West, differences in culture and in living conditions. Doesn't this also, and at the same time, change these conceptions of revolt and revolution?

G.—You know, I'm French, at least juridically, since I have a French passport. But when I went to school, from the age of six to twelve or thirteen years old, the East, and therefore Islam, was always presented to me in French schools—and I think it was similar in Austrian schools, at least because of the Turks—Islam was always presented as a shadow cast by Christianity. Myself, little Frenchman that I was, I lived in the light. Everything that was Muslim was in shadow. And in the shadow that I cast on Islam since the Crusades. You see? So in a way I was conditioned by my very education as a Christian and a Frenchman.

R.W.—The types of revolt you spoke of were nevertheless very individual gestures. If we're talking about the Black Panthers, the Palestinians, revolutions, it seems to me that there's a big difference. That's something that also demands the submission of the individual to this order, the revolutionary order, the order of command for such and such a combat group. Does this not bother you, this apparently necessary gesture of submission?

G.—Layla Shahid is here with us. Layla asked me to write for the *Revue d'études palestiniennes*, and at first I said no. I said no because everything I knew about the Palestinians was from thirteen years before, or ten years at least, and was communicated to me through *Le Monde*—which is an unbelievably racist newspaper, although they hide it—through other newspapers, through television, so I knew nothing about the real world of the Palestinians. And then, since she insisted, I placed myself—not enormously, but in a small way, in the service of the Palestinians, I said: the simplest thing would be to go to Beirut. So I went to Beirut with Layla. I placed myself, then, at her disposal. When Layla asked me to come to Vienna to speak to you, among other things, well, I came. But no, in fact it doesn't bother me. On the contrary. I would say that in a way I feel an even greater freedom. Now that I know that to a certain extent—not very large, because I'm old—but to a certain extent I can help a movement like the Palestinians, strangely I feel all the more free.

R.W.—Why strangely?

G. (laughs)—Because I had the impression that you were somewhat academic; it was a slip of the tongue.

R.W.—Intellectual revolt in Europe in this century has in fact often been very solitary, and that's why it has often been challenged by organized movements, by revolutionary movements. I'm thinking of the disputes between the surrealists and the communists, and among French intellectuals in relation to May '68. It's a whole history, a whole tradition. Hence my question.

G.—Listen: the day the Palestinians become an institution, I will no longer be on their side. The day the Palestinians become a nation like other nations, I won't be there anymore.

R.W.—The intellectual as *franc-tireur*.

G.—Exactly.

R.W.—And your Palestinian friends know this and accept it?

G.—Ask them. Ask Layla Shahid.

R.W.—I'm asking you.

G.—I think that's where I'm going to betray them. They don't know it.

R.W.—In an interview with Hubert Fichte, you said toward the end that you always lie a little when you talk. I couldn't tell if this was entirely ironic.

G.—I'll tell you. It was partly a joke, but deep down, that's what I experience. I am true only with myself. As soon as I speak, I am betrayed by the situation. I'm betrayed by the person listening to me, quite simply because of the fact of communication. I'm betrayed by my choice of words. When I speak to myself, I'm less sensitive about myself. I don't have time—and anyway it's pointless—to tell myself a lot of nonsense, and I'm also too old to lie to myself. And it's in solitude that I accept being with the Palestinians. It's not when I say yes to Layla, yes, I'll go with you . . . it's not at moments like that. It's when I'm alone and I decide on my own. And there I think I'm not lying.

R.W.—In recent years you have been silent, you've neither published nor appeared in public. At the same time you've been concerned with very concrete political issues. Meanwhile, we've seen a return of your plays, notably *The Balcony* and *The Blacks*.

G.—*The Screens* too.

R.W.—Yes. Chéreau directed one of your plays, as did Neuenfels and Peter Stein.[17] Do you still have any interest in this?

G.—No. Really, all that seems very distant. It doesn't interest me. I was glad to have met Stein, he's an intelligent man. It's always nice to meet someone who's intelligent. I was glad to have gone to Berlin because it's a city I like a lot, especially because of the Prussian population, the people I mean, the Berliners who have so much humor, much more than in Munich for example. . . . I was glad to go to Berlin because it's part of my youth too. I lived in Berlin when I was twenty-two, twenty-three years old. I didn't live there long, but enough for me to be able to find my old walks again. All along the Spree. And I found them three months ago. I was happy . . . I like Chéreau . . . I didn't see what Neuenfels did.

R.W.—You didn't see the productions after meeting them?

G.—No. I saw Peter Stein's and Chéreau's. But when Chéreau asked me to do *The Screens*, I told him: you can have the freedom to do what you want, but don't count on me to give you advice or to tell you how I see things. That's what I said to Stein, too. It doesn't interest me anymore, I would even say that it's really irritating to hear things I've written. Still, there's *The Screens*, which is my last play, and it's from about 1966.[18] You know, it's been a long time, and I've done other things.

R.W.—I asked this question also because in these works violence, man's attitude toward violence, always plays an important role.

G.—I'm afraid you're confusing the two words—a confusion I pointed out in an article I published five or six years ago in *Le Monde* on violence and brutality—I'm afraid you're confusing violence and brutality.[19] I'm going to push you—don't be offended. I'm being brutal . . . now if I hold you back like this to prevent you from falling, I'm no doubt violent, but I'm preventing you from falling. It's not the same thing. You don't think so? If I'm brutal, just like that, on a whim or for fun, I can be brutal, but then it leads to nothing. But if I'm violent, for example when a man or a woman is raising a child, when they teach him "*A, B, C, D,*" the child whines, the child gets bored and the mother insists, "*A, B,*" she's inflicting violence, she's teaching him something when he'd rather be playing. But it's a good violence. The irritated mother can smack him at any moment, then she's brutal. I'm afraid that in your choice of words you're confusing the brutality of the Israelis, for example, and the violence of the Palestinians, which is good, at least in my eyes. They inflict violence not only on the Israelis, but also on the Arab world, the Islamic world in general and even the Western world that refuses them.

R.W.—You're probably right about this confusion of words on my part. But I want to return specifically to this difference between violence and brutality as it's represented on the stage.

G.—They are works of art, but all my plays, from *The Maids* to *The Screens*, are after all, in a certain way—at least I'd like to think so—they are after all somewhat political, in the sense that they address politics obliquely. They are not politically neutral. I was drawn to plots that were not political but that took place within a purely revolutionary movement.

R.W.—Yes. Hence the great difference, in my opinion, when a play is put on thirty years after it was written; its form has changed. The context is different. When Chéreau or Peter Stein direct one of your plays today, it becomes a very different play from the one you wrote at the time.

G.—Of course. Since you mentioned *The Screens*, when it was produced at the time, a lot of people were against it, against the play and against me, because they saw it as a direct reference to the Algerian War. And they were against it because the Algerians had found a way to gain their independence. Now I don't think that Chéreau makes any reference to the Algerian War in his production, and the text never makes any reference to it either.[20] But the play holds up because of what might be called its theatrical virtues.

R.W.—Just as I might imagine *The Balcony*, for example, as a harsh satire of present-day political life.

G.—That's possible. I didn't really have *The Balcony* in mind . . .

R.W.— . . . there's also *The Blacks* . . .

G.—You know, I saw *The Blacks* in Berlin, but it was in German.

R.W.—Are you interested in the theater as a spectator?

G.—No, no, I never go to the theater. No. I'll tell you this: all of my plays were commissioned. Jouvet commissioned *The Maids* from me.[21] I don't remember who commissioned *The Blacks*, it was a well know Belgian director.[22] At any rate, the plays were commissioned. Jouvet didn't say: you have to write me a play about maids. He simply said: I'd like to put on a play with only two actresses, since I don't have much money. So I thought of the maids, but all of the plays were commissioned from me. So this was a more indirect way for me to address political issues. Not politics as such, as it's practiced by politicians, but to address social situations that would provoke a politics.

R.W.—When you're with your Palestinian friends, do you have the impression that they also see you as Jean Genet the writer?

G.—Certainly not. They've never read my books, except maybe Layla who's read one or two of them. I don't know . . . I don't think so.

R.W.—Is that a relief?

G.—To tell the truth, I don't think about it.

R.W.—You are known for having no address. Where do you live?

G.—Yes, you know, I was invited to a palace where I had never set foot, but which I had dreamt of when I was a kid—I was twenty years old when I was here in Vienna—I always dreamed of staying in the Imperial Hotel, but I was a vagabond. Well, I've been staying here for two or three days. But after this I'll go to the little hotels. I'm thinking about going back to Morocco.

Layla Shahid.—There are certain things that were touched upon which interest me from another angle. This relation to death and to people who play with death. I'd like to ask you, Jean—when you were in Jordan, you stayed with the fedayeen a long time and with fighters who faced death on a daily basis. Did you ever sense any fear in them?

G.—Fear is something you have to see . . . fear in the sense in which I experienced it, when the hand of a cop comes down on my shoulder and I know he's going to take me to prison. Then I'm afraid. It's not the same fear. Since you asked me the question in this way, the Palestinians, the fedayeen who were leaving, who were eighteen years old and who were in the Jordan River Valley, they were afraid, from what I could understand about them, they were afraid and at the same time they wanted martyrdom, and therefore glory, even if this glory is found only by very few. I will mention not as proof, but almost as proof, the selection of a uniform. They were particularly well dressed when they left. They would leave in the evening, at night. They had leather jackets. Very tight. They had uniforms, bracelets, a whole arrangement that was somewhat ceremonious.

They knew they would probably die, but they also knew they were carrying out a ceremony that went beyond them. Is that what you were asking?

L.S.—Yes. I ask you because I myself am fascinated by this ability that fighters have to face death.

G.—We're talking about Sunni, right? Sunni fedayeen, not Shiite.

L.S.—I don't know, because I never saw them as Sunni or Shiite, nor as Christians. What I saw was their youth and their aptitude for facing death. I remember—and this is also something that fascinated me during the war in Lebanon and now in Tripoli, when I look at the faces of the fighters who are fighting—there is always a kind of smile, a light that you can see among the young people, thirty-five years old at most, who are going out to meet almost certain death.

G.—They're even calm.

L.S.—Calm and smiling. And I wondered what makes their relation to death what it is.

G.—First, it looked to me like a ceremony. In any case, they didn't undertake their descent to the Jordan, or wherever they were going, as just any ordinary moment. They went freely. And I don't think you can say the same about the black soldiers, the Senegalese or Moroccans, the Algerians and Tunisians that France used during the wars against Germany and Austria. Those guys didn't know why they were being sent into the slaughter. The blacks—and there were a lot of them buried at Verdun—didn't know where they were going. They fought, and one might well wonder why. They did not leave smiling and with the ceremonial of the fedayeen, who knew they were accomplishing a free act. This is one of the things I thought about when I met a young fedayee, eighteen years old, who was challenging the authority of Abu Hani. He challenged him. I said to him: but he's your leader. And he answered saying: But when I joined the Palestinian Liberation Army, the ALP, I did so freely, I was seventeen. And they accepted my request to join because I made it freely. I chose to go. But I didn't choose to keep my eyes closed all the time. If they took on a man who was free when he was seventeen, I should be free at eighteen to be able to present my point of view.—And that's what he was doing.

L.S.—I believe it's this freedom and this form of combativeness that the West doesn't understand. The West, and its intellectuals in particular, see the Palestinian fighters as soldiers. But for me they are not soldiers at all.

G.—No. But they are warriors.

L.S.—They are warriors, and there's a big difference between a warrior and a soldier. I felt this in particular when we were together in Beirut and we saw the Israeli soldiers passing by with their weapons on their backs, and then they sat down. We both went out to look at them. I remember their weariness and their sadness . . .

G.—Yes, they couldn't take it anymore.

L.S.—They had soldiers' faces. I felt the difference between their relation to death, the Israeli soldiers' relation to death, and that of all the fedayeen I had seen, who had a completely different expression on their faces.

G.—There were civilian Lebanese fighters who came down and were smiling and calm and who are probably all dead. We saw the Israeli soldiers coming up, they passed between the French embassy and Layla's building. They walked out ahead of the tanks. They couldn't take it anymore. It was hot, it's true, and they had their weapons, but really the road they had traveled was not that long. They came from East Beirut to West Beirut, it was four or five kilometers, and they were already exhausted. And they were afraid, it was obvious. Their tanks were moving around constantly. And not long before this, we saw groups of leftist militants, Lebanese patriots who were defending their city . . . twenty-two, twenty-three years old, dressed in civilian clothing, armed. They went out to meet them. They weren't smiling the way one smiles at a vaudeville or a comic play or film. They were calm.

L.S.—A peculiar sort of serenity . . .

G.—A serenity, yes.

L.S.—Don't you think that the expressions we saw on the faces of the Israeli soldiers showed, beyond any fatigue, a certain absence of conviction in the reasons for which they were going off to die? During the entire occupation of Beirut and long after, during the occupations of the Chouf and then of the South, I sensed that there was something new in the Israeli army, something like a feeling of the total uselessness of their death.[23] You could feel it later in different movements that took place in the army, when they were saying, We don't want to die because we don't understand why we keep dying.

G.—In this case, perhaps they had a presentiment of the uselessness of this war, since, in fact, it hasn't done any good for Israel.

R.W.—There is a point which for me is absolutely unimaginable, which is to see what it means to have such chaos in Beirut, for example,

such hell for ten years, or even for the Palestinians who for twenty, thirty, forty years have lived in camps, what that must be like. And how quite
simply one can survive it, and survive also morally.

G.—There is that, there is this conviction in revolt, but there is also the
fact that they can't take it anymore. Because I saw something else. I saw
when a French priest who supported the Palestinians—I forget his name,
but it doesn't matter; he was in the Baqa camp where there were between
sixty thousand and eighty thousand people, in Jordan, thirty or forty kilometers from Amman. The Jordanian troops learned of the existence of this
priest in the camps. And they wanted him to leave. The women said no.
He will not leave. In fact, they took him out one night on the sly, they led
him away. The women decided to revolt. . . . So the Jordanian army had
the Baqa camp surrounded—I saw three rows of tanks go into Baqa camp.
Hussein was in Paris, he wasn't in Amman. His brother, Hassan, was
regent at the time. So he called his brother to ask him what he should do,
whether he should fire on the women because they had left the camp with
their children and all their things, saying, "We're leaving, we're leaving the
camp. If you want to occupy the camp, we're leaving it. But there's only
one place for us to go: home, to Palestine." In other words, to Israel. So
there they were leaving on foot for Palestine which was fifty or sixty kilometers away. So now they're gone. But what's Prince Hassan going to do,
what's the army going to do, what's his brother going to do? His brother,
advised by Pompidou, or by someone else, or not advised at all, said, "No,
you have to let them be, you can't shoot at women, you have to withdraw
the tanks." And the Jordanian army was damn well beaten by what? And
by whom? By a group of women, by thirty thousand or forty thousand
Arab women who decided to go against the tanks. And they risked being
shot down. I'm relating this incident to you because I was a witness.[24] It
wasn't told to me, I saw it.

L.S.—When you spoke of what you saw among the Palestinians as
being modern in relation to the monotony of the current Arab world . . .

G.— . . . not only the monotony, the utter lifelessness . . .

L.S.— . . . I think in particular of the women, the Palestinian women.
And I think you were particularly sensitive to the Palestinian women in
Jordan. For my part, I was particularly sensitive to the Palestinian women
in occupied South Lebanon. Where do you think this strength comes
from on the part of the Palestinian women, in their questioning of so
many things that are part of the tradition?

G.—Well very simply because the women—and in general Arab women are slaves to Arab men—are freeing themselves from their husbands. They are freeing themselves first of all from the mustaches. Isn't that right?

L.S.—I'm asking you if you saw it.

G.—Of course. It's so obvious. The women handle submachine guns as well as the men. They want to do everything as well as the men.

L.S.—Yes. But simply handling submachine guns is sometimes seen as insufficient. Besides, Algerian women often complain that they too handled weapons, but that afterward this didn't do them much good.

G.—Well, what the Palestinian Revolution will become once it has its territory and is made into an institution, I don't know. In the camps you can already see the basis of what might become a territorial gain and an institution of the Palestinian Revolution. Already in the camps—you know this better than I do—you know that the camps are divided into villages and that the same people who lived in Palestine—now Israel—are grouped together as they were in their villages. The same affinities, the same Palestinian dialect, the same habits. But it goes further than that: already, in the Baqa camp or in the Gaza camp there are orange vendors, farther on their are mandarine orange vendors, farther on their are eggplant vendors, there are cloth vendors, and everything is being organized according to the usual way of life. I'm afraid that by becoming a set pattern, this schema will be reproduced again when Palestine has a territory. For the moment, I adhere completely to Palestine in revolt. I don't know if I will adhere—I will probably, even certainly be dead by then—but if I were alive I don't know if I could adhere to a Palestine that has been made into an institution and has become territorially satisfied. But is that important? I wonder. I think that for the Palestinians, what you were saying when you spoke of this possibility of maintaining a certain serenity despite the violence they experience, despite the living conditions, I think that the reason for this serenity lies precisely in the fact that the Palestinians, before becoming warriors—that is, before their expulsion from Palestine and the beginning of the organized military rebellion, from 1948 to about 1965—they lived as a very calm, well-behaved people, with no arms or military operations, with no PLO, no Fatah, no hijackings, without disturbing the well-being of Western citizens, without filling the pages of the press. And I think that during this period you didn't see a lot of serenity in people's faces. I think that there is an affirmation of existence in the very fact of rebelling. I saw the camps before the PLO took control of them, that is, before 1969. The majority of the camps were run by the local authorities of the country, the Jordanian army in Jordan, the Lebanese army in Lebanon, on the military and police level, and by the UNRWA on the social and economic level.[25] After the birth of the political movement and the Palestinian military, the Palestinian organizations took charge of the camps. This was called "the rebellion," "the overthrow." And there was a physical transformation of the people. First, they expelled the local armies—Jordanian, Lebanese, and so on—and they themselves became organized. And beginning at that moment, they felt that they existed. Without a national territory. But they existed nonetheless. And I think that this was, this is what is most important for them. To continue to feel that they exist. In their actions, even if their final objective is the liberation of their national territory: but the most important thing is that while they are on this road they continue to have the freedom to exist precisely in their actions. But no Palestinian has a Palestinian passport. That doesn't exist.

R.W.—In political discussions in the West about the Palestinians, it is often said that one of the key questions would be the recognition of the existence of Israel by the Palestinians, by the PLO. Is this important for you? Or is the phase involving treaties between nations already past?

G.—It is so far past that Arafat does everything he can so that forty-five hundred prisoners in the Ansar camp, and then six Israeli prisoners, will be released, and so that Israel will finally accept Arafat's conditions. Well, is that recognizing them or not recognizing them?

R.W.—Do you agree with that?

L.S.—Yes. I think that really it's a false debate. The question of recognition is a thoroughly false debate. What good does it do for the Israelis to say that they recognize the PLO, if their soldiers—who are usually reservists, and therefore people from everyday life, doctors, professors, students, shoemakers, electricians—when they were drafted into the Israeli army, and then were at the gates of Sabra and Shatila, and were watching the camp and saw—and they said so in the Kahan Report—they saw women and children right in front of them being murdered, right before their very eyes. They didn't react! They didn't even spontaneously go to help the children. Okay, they consider the men enemies because they are potential combatants. But how can it be that not a single soldier spontaneously went to protect a child, to say to the murderers who were killing them: "Stop, you can't kill a child!" Not a single one! In the best of cases, the soldiers went to find their superiors in the headquarters across from the camp . . .

G.—Very few.

L.S.—That's right, in the best of cases there may have been one or two who went to tell their officers: something's happening in the camp. And the officer answered: it's none of your business, don't bother with that. And they obeyed.

R.W.—Can you say why?

L.S.—Yes. The answer is that from 1948 to 1982, Zionist policy as a whole—which includes that of the worker's party of the current opposition as well as that of Likud in the current government—has been based on the nonrecognition of the existence of something called a Palestinian human being. When Begin says, "They're animals on two legs," it's not Begin who is saying it. It's the majority of the Israeli population, on a conscious and unconscious level. Because if they had accepted the idea that they are humans like themselves, they would have been incapable of not reacting. There would have been at least one who would have reacted. Jean was with me in the Israeli headquarters about forty meters away—there's a street between the camp and the Israeli headquarters, where there were at least five hundred Israeli officers and soldiers—it's not even forty meters away, since it's only a single street. So that all the massacres that were carried out on this side of the camp, and there were a lot, happened right before their eyes.

G.—And they lit up the camp at night.

L.S.—In the Kahan Report, a soldier told of how he threw up when a Phalangist who had taken a child up to an Israeli soldier said to him, "I'll take him to the hospital," and then he took him and slit his throat right next to them. And the soldier said, "I threw up." But throwing up is not an act.

For me, real recognition is one that comes from the individual who can no longer allow things to be done to a Palestinian human being that he would not have done to a human being who is Jewish or Christian, meaning Israeli or Western. That's when it becomes real recognition. But if recognition is limited to a treaty signed at the United Nations, it has no value. In the West people made a big deal out of the Kahan Report and the demonstrations of four hundred thousand people in Tel Aviv calling for an investigative commission after the massacres of Shatila and Sabra, now organized by the Peace organization. And at every opportunity this is brought forth as proof of Israeli democracy. In my opinion—and I agree with Jean who said this earlier—the demonstration and the report are an integral part of the massacre. It's almost the staging of a play whose content is the massacre and whose scenery is the Kahan Report and the demonstration. I'm not casting doubt on the personal motivations of each protester; what I'm saying is that once the Israeli citizen has gone out to protest, he has put himself at ease. His army, made up largely of reservists, we mustn't forget this, and therefore of citizens—no one can say, "The army, that has nothing to do with me," since everyone is potentially the army, potentially a soldier—the army perpetrated a massacre, and I, I have protested, now there's no reason to come after me, I did my duty. I demonstrated for an hour. This has given you the privilege of being called the citizen of a great democracy. Then the next day territories continue to be annexed, peasants expelled, houses destroyed, people tortured in Israeli prisons, and five thousand political detainees in Ansar are not considered prisoners of war. And you, what have you done in the meantime? Nothing. Because your conscience is at ease. Because you protested and now you're doing nothing. It's a farce, because the West believes in this false practice of democracy. And the ones who are paying the real price are the Palestinians. Because the image of Israel has been whitewashed after the Kahan Report. And because even those responsible obtained . . . Sharon himself, whose responsibility is recognized by everyone, obtained a position as minister, without portfolio, but he remained a minister. They withdrew Begin, who was the head of a terrorist organization called Irgun, under the British mandate. They replaced him with Shamir, the former head of the terrorist group. So what has really changed after the demonstrations? After the report? Absolutely nothing. They really pulled one over on us, and on the West who applauded and who went right along with the whole production, the whole comedy.

G.—In my opinion, no. The West didn't just go along; it was complicit.

L.S.—You think it was complicit?

G.—Well, yes, because we saw the French boats, the American boats, the Italian boats taking off the day before, twenty-four hours or thirty-six hours before the death of Bashir Gemayel. They left before the end of their assignment. And then Bashir was assassinated; Israel used the pretext of Bashir Gemayel's assassination to enter West Beirut when it was the French and Italian armies that had been in charge of the Passage du

Musée and the Palestinian camps. And that's where they went in, very quietly, and then the next day they perpetrated the massacres, which lasted three days.[26]

R.W.—But if you say that the West is complicit, there is also the equally troubling fact that the Arab countries, their brother countries, as they're called, did not act either, quite to the contrary.

G.—But we said that at the beginning. All the Arab regimes except the Palestinians are decrepit and upheld by police systems. They don't want to get their hands dirty. Because, obviously, they'd be trounced by the Israelis, who are also the American army.

L.S.—Yes, since every Jewish American citizen has an automatic right to Israeli citizenship and can serve at any moment in the Israeli army. And then, of course, also because Israel's arms come primarily from the United States, even those which the United States forbids, like phosphorous or antipersonnel bombs. But if the Arab regimes are as you say, there are the masses of Arabs, the Arab populations, whether they're in the bourgeoisie, among the intellectuals, or even in parties of the Left, who are now living through the end of an epoch. It's a kind of decline, a situation of total apathy because of the problems experienced by this mass of people. When you realize how bad the repression is in most Arab countries, you can understand why people cannot speak out. There are political prisoners sentenced to thirty or fifty years of prison for having expressed an opinion, peacefully, without arms. Ideas, not military operations or attempts to overthrow the state. In most Arab countries, there are people doing life sentences for crimes of opinion. So can we ask people in such a situation to protest in the streets, to publish, to go out and defend the Palestinians? I will not hide the fact that for the majority of Palestinians and Lebanese, who for three months now have resisted the most powerful army in the world, there has really been terrible disappointment, because they were not supported by any real expression of Arab public opinion. They have suffered a lot from this. But I think it's wrong to throw this image back at us when we accuse the West. Here I am in Vienna, and I see the whole anti-Semitic past of Vienna. I see the entire responsibility of Europe at the end of this century in the creation of the Jewish problem. And I say: how ironic that I, a Palestinian, coming from the Middle East, where I have never seen any problems with eastern Jewish communities, here I am explaining to the Austrians, trying to exonerate myself, to convince people that I don't hate the Jews. And the country that persecuted them, that remained silent during the entire period of Nazi Germany, this country is my accuser, my judge. The roles are reversed. Why does the West today ask Arabs for support of the Palestinians and a recognition of the Israelis? And this Europe that is responsible for their persecution, responsible for their destiny, poses as our judge. And we, we're the accused. And you, as an Austrian, don't you feel that you have some responsibility for Israel's situation and consequently for that of the Palestinians?

G.—I can ask you a simple question. It will be quick. What did the Austrians do to the Jews from 1939 to 1945?

R.W.—Well, for example, there were several hundred thousand Jews. Now there are only about ten thousand in Vienna.

G.—Okay. I don't need to be told what happened to the others, that I know. And what have the Jews done to the Austrians during the last thirty-five years?

R.W.—Nothing.

G.—And what did they do to the Palestinians?

R.W.—Fought a war.

G.—Against the Palestinians, who did nothing to the Jews, who were even completely unaware of them. There you have it. I think that's the problem.

L.S.—Yes. That's the problem, and to me the problem is evidence of a very great cowardice, because you have retreated and have made those who were weakest pay the price of the Holocaust and of the expulsion of the Jews from Europe.

G.—The weakest, and the weakest link in the Arab world, the Palestinians.

§ 36 Interview with Nigel Williams

Jean Genet.—I believe that my criminal record contains fourteen convictions for theft.[1] Which amounts to saying that I was a bad thief, since I was always getting caught.

I was in prison, I was locked up; I said yesterday that in one trial I could have been given life imprisonment.[2] I would never have gotten out of prison. So I was convinced that no one would read my book. I could say what I wanted, since there would be no readers. But it turns out that there were readers.

~

Nigel Williams.—Monsieur Genet, you were born in 1910. Is that right?

G.—Yes.

N.W.—In Paris?

G.—Yes.

N.W.—But you didn't know your parents, I believe?

G.—At the time? No. Not now either.

N.W.—Were you not raised in a family?

G.—Yes, I was, but not in my own.

N.W.—Was it difficult to live in a family that wasn't your own?

G.—You're asking me to speak of my childhood feelings. To speak of this in an adequate way, I would have to do a sort of archeology of my life, which is absolutely impossible. I can only tell you that the memory I have of it is the memory of a difficult period, indeed. But by escaping from the family I escaped from the feelings I might have had for the family and from the feeling the family might have had for me. I am therefore completely—and I was from very early on—completely detached from all family feeling. That's one of the virtues of the French Public Welfare system, which raises children quite well precisely by preventing them from becoming attached to a family. In my opinion, the family is probably the first criminal cell, and the most criminal of all.

If you like, now at my age I do see the child I was, but I see him among other children who were kids like me, and all their struggles, all their humiliations, and all their courage seem rather derisory to me, rather distant . . .[3]

∼

I had indeed stolen before, but I wasn't sent to Mettray for theft. I was sent to Mettray because I took the train without a ticket. I took the train from Meaux to Paris without a ticket. And I was sentenced to three months of prison and to the Mettray colony until the age of twenty.[4]

N.W.—Do you think that if you had paid for that train ticket, your life would have been completely changed?

G.—Listen . . . Do you believe in God?

N.W.—Sometimes.

G.—Well, ask him. Ask him if my life would have been completely changed. Me, I don't know.

∼

I think that at Mettray the relations between the older brother (who was in a position of authority) and the colonists, the other young people like me (who were bound by relations of submission), I think this was a spectacle the guards enjoyed quite a lot. You could say that the guards were the first spectators, and we, we were the actors. And they delighted in the pleasure of seeing.

N.W.—Was the discipline at Mettray very harsh?

G.—Oh! The discipline was very, very strict. I assume it was a military discipline. Does Mettray interest you?

N.W.—Very much.

G.—You see, Mettray was created in 1840, under Louis-Philippe. It was at the beginning of France's colonial voyages throughout the world. The French empire, which you have certainly heard about—France still had a navy of sailing ships, and Mettray was used to provide sailors. In the courtyard of the Mettray colony, there was a huge sailing boat, and we learned how to handle boats on land. But in any case the discipline wasn't even a military discipline, it was the discipline of sailors. For example, we slept in hammocks; all the boys my age, all those who were being punished, slept in hammocks. The language we used among ourselves was a language that came form sailors. It was sailors' slang.

~

N.W.—In your books you spoke of the love in the colony. For you, did love begin with a boy?

G.—Did you say "love [*l'amour*]"? I thought you said "death [*la mort*]"!

N.W.—Love, I want to talk about love, not death!

G.—Right, okay. What was the question?

N.W.—For you, love didn't start with the family, but with a boy, I believe . . .

G.—No! Not with *a* boy, but with two hundred! What are you talking about!

N.W.—With two hundred?

G.—Well, one at a time . . .

N.W.—But didn't you have a favorite, a special one?

G.—Oh! Favorites, special ones, you know, there were so many!

N.W.—Did you engage in a politics of homosexuality?

G.—But is there a homosexual politics? How could you think that while I was still a child—let's say that I felt my first sexual attractions around the age of thirteen or fourteen—how could you think that at such an age I could have decided to make homosexuality a political issue?

N.W.—Yes, of course, I understand. But now, in our era, it's a political question. Because you were one of the first to talk about it in . . .

G.—What are you talking about! What are you talking about! Listen, you had Oscar Wilde. . . . If we think of England alone, you had Oscar Wilde, Shakespeare, Byron, and so many others. . . . What are you talking about!

N.W.—Were you proud of that?

G.—Of Byron and Oscar Wilde? I was never proud of Byron!

~

The French refused me since they put me in prison, and at the same time I wanted nothing other than this: to be chased out of France, to escape from the oppressive French atmosphere and to know a different world. There weren't many passports, but when you finished military service they gave you a booklet that had more or less the same format as a passport. I added a photograph to it and when I presented it to the customs officers, as soon as it had two or three stamps on it, the booklet was valid![5]

N.W.—Did you start stealing because you were hungry?

G.—You could say that two things were involved together (since you like this word, "involved"): on the one hand there was hunger, real hunger, meaning a stomach demanding food, and then on the other hand there was the game. It's amusing to steal, much more amusing than answering questions for the BBC!

N.W.—But it wasn't funny when you were caught by the cops, was it?

G.—When I was caught by the cops, obviously that was . . . a fall into the abyss. It was the end of the world. When a policeman's hand . . . You see, like that . . . [He moves forward and places his hand on Nigel Williams's shoulder.] That, I knew what that meant.

N.W.—Oh! It still frightens me. When I was a kid I stole, but . . . I'm still afraid of the police.

G.—Yes, but the hand that comes from behind, that comes down on your shoulder . . .

N.W.—Not very pleasant, is it!

G.—No. But you have to pay for the pleasure you take in stealing.

N.W.—Yes.

G.—You have to pay for everything.

~

N.W.—During the period of the Occupation, were you happy with the presence of the Germans in France?

G.—Thrilled! I was thrilled! I hated France so much—and still do—so much that I was utterly thrilled that the French army had been beaten. It was beaten by the Germans, it was beaten by Hitler, I was very happy.

N.W.—Is it still like that? Are you not at all proud of being French or of writing in French?

G.—God, no! Oh, no!

~

I was telling you that I started writing my first book on pieces of paper that were supposed to be used for making paper bags. And I wrote about the first fifty pages or so of *Our Lady of the Flowers* on this paper.[6] Then I was summoned to the law courts for a hearing on my case—I forget which theft it was for—and I left the papers on the table. The shop foreman had keys, he could enter the cells at any moment, and while I was in court he went into my cell and saw the papers covered with writing. He took them and handed them over to the director of La Santé Prison— since you're confusing the two words love and death, I'll tell you that the director of La Santé was called Monsieur Amor. The papers were given to him, and the next evening when I came back to my cell, they were gone. So the beginning of my novel had disappeared. I was called to the director's office the next day and he gave me three days of confinement in my cell and three or six days of dry bread. And they just dumped my papers. Well, what did I do? When I left the cell after the three days were up, I went to the supply room and ordered a notebook, which was within my rights. I hid under the covers and tried to remember the sentences I had written, and I started over on what I had done.

～

N.W.—Let's imagine that we met the writer Jean Genet himself. Would it be the real Jean Genet that we'd meet?

G.—Is there a fake one running around? Is there a fake Genet somewhere out there in the world? Am I the real one? You're asking me if I'm the real one. Well, where is the fake one?

N.W.—Okay, I understand.

G.—Perhaps after all I am an impostor who never wrote any books. Perhaps I am a fake Jean Genet, as you say.

～

N.W.—Have you always felt like someone who is separated, set apart?

G.—Listen, you're there, I'm here, and at this moment I feel separated too. I have always felt separated, whether in the Morvan or in your house.

N.W.—But have there ever been any moments when you didn't feel separated?

G.—No.

N.W.—Never in your whole life?

G.—No.

N.W.—Even, I don't know, when you were with someone, even in love? You believe that man is always alone?

G.—Man, I don't know, I don't want to generalize. But me, yes.

N.W.—And has that caused you anxiety?

G.—Not at all. What would cause me anxiety would be if there were no distance between you and me.

N.W.—And how can one get closer to another human being?

G.—I prefer not to get closer.

N.W.—You prefer always to keep at a distance?

G.—Oh, yes.

N.W.—But why?

G.—What about you, do you prefer to keep at a distance?

N.W.—Not always, no.

G.—And why is that?

N.W.—Because I like the experience of being with someone, of being involved with someone.

G.—Well, I don't!

N.W.—It's a little bit like the game you play in your plays?

G.—The last play I wrote was written thirty years ago. You're speaking to me of something I've completely wiped from my memory: the theater.

～

I practically never went to the theater. I had seen a few plays, but not many. Not many, and they were plays by Alexandre Dumas. . . . But it wasn't really very difficult, because—as I explained to you yesterday, I think—my behavior in relation to society is oblique. It's not direct. It's also not parallel, since it intersects and crosses through society, it crosses through the world, it sees the world. It's oblique. I saw the world from an angle, and I still see it from an angle, though perhaps more directly now than twenty-five or thirty years ago. The theater, in any case the theater that I prefer, is precisely the kind that grasps the world from an angle.

You could say that what interests me is to do work that is as good as possible. (The cameraman is asking me to position myself in a certain way.) Of course, in this sense I became interested in the work, but I didn't look at it and ask: was this a new kind of work, this theater? I don't know, and it's not my place to say, but in any case, it amused me. It's a theater that, if it wasn't new, was certainly awkward. And being awkward, perhaps it had something new about it. Because it was awkward.

~

I was in the theater that was occupied by the students in May '68. It wasn't just any theater, but the one where *The Screens* had been staged.[7] If they had been real revolutionaries, they wouldn't have occupied a theater, especially not the National Theater. They would have occupied the law courts, the prisons, the radio. They would have acted as revolutionaries do, the way Lenin did. They didn't do that. So what happened? That theater is like this, right? It's more or less round, a theater in the Italian style. On the stage there were young people holding placards and giving speeches. These speeches came from the stage into the hall and then came back to the stage—there was a circular movement of revolutionary speeches that went from the stage to the hall, the hall to the stage, the stage to the hall, the hall to the stage . . . it went on and on and never went outside the theater, you see? Exactly, or more or less, the way the revolutionaries in *The Balcony* never leave the brothel.

N.W.—Did it make you laugh to see that?

G.—It neither made me laugh nor . . . I'm just saying that's how it was.

N.W.—But you weren't really for the revolutionaries?

G.—You mean the pseudorevolutionaries.

N.W.—Or for the real revolutionaries, like Lenin?

G.—I'd rather be on Lenin's side, yes.

~

I had a dream last night. I dreamed that the technicians for this film revolted. Assisting with the arrangement of the shots, the preparation of a film, they never have the right to speak. Now why is that? And I thought they would be daring enough—since we were talking yesterday about being daring—to chase me from my seat, to take my place. And yet they don't move. Can you tell me how they explain that?

N.W.—Yes. Uh . . . How they . . . ?

G.—How they explain that. Why they don't come and chase me away, and chase you away too, and then say, "What you're saying is so stupid that I really don't feel like going on with this work!" Ask them.

N.W.—Okay, sure. [He speaks to the technicians and translates Genet's question into English.]

G.—The sound man too.

N.W.—[Nigel Williams asks the sound man, Duncan Fairs, who

answers that he doesn't have much to say at the moment, that the people who work every day lose their sense of objective judgment about what they're doing and remain prisoners of their little personal world. He adds that the technicians always have something to say after the filming, but that if they spoke in front of the camera it would cost a lot of money and would be very expensive for the film production company.] Is that what interested you about your dream: disrupting the order of things. In a certain way you wanted to disrupt the order that exists in this little room?

G.—Disrupt the order of things?

N.W.—Yes.

G.—Of course, of course. It seems so stiff to me! I'm all alone here, and here in front of me there are one, two, three, four, five, six people. Obviously I want to disrupt the order, and that's why yesterday I asked you to come over here. Of course.

N.W.—Yes, it's like a police interrogation?

G.—There's that, of course. I told you—is the camera rolling? Good— I told you yesterday that you were doing the work of a cop, and you continue to do it, today too, this morning. I told you that yesterday and you've already forgotten it, because you continue to interrogate me just like the thief I was thirty years ago was interrogated by the police, by a whole police squad. And I'm on the hot seat, alone, interrogated by a bunch of people. There is a norm on one side, a norm where you are, all of you: two, three, four, five, six, seven, and also the editors of the film and the BBC, and then there's an outer margin where I am, where I am marginalized. And if I'm afraid of entering the norm? Of course I'm afraid of entering the norm, and if I'm raising my voice right now, it's because I'm in the process of entering the norm, I'm entering English homes, and obviously I don't like it very much. But I'm not angry at you who are the norm, I'm angry at myself because I agreed to come here. And I really don't like it very much at all.

N.W.—But your books are taught in the schools, right here in England.

G.—Oh! What are you talking about!

N.W.—It's true. I myself studied Genet at the university.

G.—Hmm . . .

N.W.—Do you like that?

G.—There's both a feeling of vanity . . . and at the same time it's very unpleasant. Of course, there is this double . . . , this double imperative almost. Is the camera rolling?

N.W.—Yes, it's rolling.

G.—Good. Ask me questions then, since the system says that I'm the one who's supposed to be interrogated.

~

N.W.—You're not living in France now, right?

G.—No. In Morocco.

N.W.—You have a house in Morocco?

G.—No.

N.W.—You're "hanging out" there with friends, if I can use that term?

G.—No, I live in a hotel.

N.W.—Why Morocco?

G.—Can I ask you a question? Why not Morocco? And why this question? Because you want to transform me again, you too, into a myth, because you belong to your—what's it called—BBC, huh?

N.W.—Or else perhaps because there is another reason, because you have an affinity with the country, the people, because you like the landscape . . .

G.—Oh! You know, I like all the landscapes. Even the most destitute, even England . . .

N.W.—You can live anywhere?

G.—Yes, yes, yes. Absolutely. Of course.

N.W.—It really doesn't matter.

G.—No . . .

N.W.—And what do you do with your days there?

G.—Ah! Yes . . . You want to bring up the problem of time? Well, when it comes to time, I'll answer the way Saint Augustine did: "I'm waiting for death."

Appendix 1: The Members of
the Assembly

Chicago makes me think of an animal which, oddly, is trying to climb up onto itself. Part of the city has been transfigured by the life—or the parade, in both senses of the word—of the hippies.

At about ten o'clock Saturday evening, the young people have lit a sort of bonfire in Lincoln Park. Nearby, hardly visible in the darkness, a fairly dense crowd has gathered under the trees to listen to a band of black musicians—flutes and bongos. An American Indian, carrying a furled green flag, tells us that tomorrow they'll to take it to the airport where Senator McCarthy is expected to speak.[1] The unfurled flag bears, against a green background, the painted effigy of a seventeen-year-old boy—some say an Indian, others say a black—killed two days before by the Chicago police.[2]

The cops arrive in small waves, so far with no animosity, to put out the fire and disperse the demonstrators. A word about these latter: the demonstrators are young people with a gentleness that is almost too gentle, this evening at least. If couples are lying on the grass in the park, it seems to me it is in order to have angelic exchanges. The whole thing strikes me as extremely chaste. The darkness covering the park is not the only reason all I can see are shadows embracing one another.

Some of the dispersed demonstrators have regrouped and are intoning a kind of two-syllable chant, similar to a Gregorian chant, a funeral dirge in memory of the dead boy. I can hardly describe the beauty of this plaintive lament, of the anger and the singing.

Around the park, which is covered in almost total darkness, the first thing I see is a proliferation of American cars, heavy with chrome, and beyond them the city's giant buildings, every floor lit from within, I don't know why.

Will these four days allotted to the Democrats begin with a vigil in memory of a young Indian—or black—murdered by the Chicago police?[3]

If man is or seeks to be omnipotent, I'm inclined to accept the gigantism of Chicago; but I would also like for the contrary to be accepted: a city that could fit in the hollow of one's hand.

Sunday, Midway Airport, Chicago. McCarthy's arrival. Virtually no police, and the few who check our press credentials aren't paying much attention. Opposite the press platform, which is actually the empty trailer of a parked truck, there are three other similar platforms: one is occupied by a mostly brass orchestra made up of musicians in their thirties and forties, the other by a rock group whose members are in their twenties. Between them is the one set up for McCarthy and his staff. McCarthy's plane is a few minutes late; the crowd gathering behind the press platform consists of men and women whose faces have that peculiar expression which only deep honesty and hope can give.

McCarthy finally arrives; and all at once the crowd comes alive: every man, woman, and child shouts, "We want Gene!";[4] they hold up signs, without the usual slogans, but generously decorated with flowers drawn or painted according to each one's whim, and it is this flower-crowd that McCarthy is going to address. He is extremely relaxed; he's smiling; he's about to speak, but the battery of microphones is dead. Sabotage? A smile. He walks over and tries the mikes by the thirty- or forty-year-old musicians: dead. Still smiling, he tries the mikes of the rock group in their twenties: dead! Finally, he goes back to his platform and tries his own microphones, which in the meantime have been repaired, at least to a certain extent. He smiles. He also looks very serious and declares that he will start speaking only if the men and women farthest from the platform can hear. Finally, he gives his speech, and you have all heard what he said on the television.

When he leaves the speaker's platform, you get the impression that no one is protecting him, aside from the sea of flowers painted by the men and women filled with hope.

A few hours later at McCarthy's headquarters in the Hilton Hotel, there seems once again to be virtually no police protection, or if there is, it is subtle, invisible. We are received with great courtesy.

This brings me to what in my opinion is one of the basic questions I ask myself: after eight months of campaigning, what made it possible for this little-known senator—although he bears a name that is all too well known and covered in shame—for McCarthy to inspire so much enthusiasm, in other words, what concessions did he make?[5] In what ways has his moral rectitude been undermined?

And yet the fact remains that all his speeches, all his statements, demonstrate intelligence and generosity. Is it a trick?

For a city like Chicago, where the black population is so large, I notice that very few blacks came to greet and cheer him.

The First Day: The Day of the Thighs

Their thighs are very beautiful under the blue cloth, thick and muscular. It all must be hard. This policeman is also a boxer, a wrestler. His legs are long, and perhaps on the way up to his member you'd find a furry nest of long thick kinky hair. That's all I can see, and I must say it fascinates me—that and his boots, but I can guess that his superb thighs continue up to an imposing member and a muscular torso, made firmer every day by his police training in the cops' gym. And, even higher, his arms and hands that must know how to put a black man or a thief out of commission.

In the compass of these solid thighs, I can see . . . But the thighs have moved, and I see that they are superb: America has a magnificent, divine, athletic police force, often photographed and on display in dirty books . . . but their thighs are slightly parted, ever so slightly, and in between, in the crack that goes from the knees to the oversized member, I can just make out . . . let's see, it's the whole panorama of the Democratic Convention, with its star-spangled banners, its star-spangled chatter, its star-spangled dresses, its star-spangled skimpy outfits, its star-spangled songs, its star-spangled fields, its star-spangled candidates, in short, this whole ostentatious parade, but the color has too many facets, as you have seen on your television screens.

What is not brought to you by your television is the odor. Yes, I said odor—which might after all have a certain relation to order? The Democratic Convention is being held in the immediate vicinity of a cattle yard, and I can't help wondering if the air reeks from the decomposition of Eisenhower or from the decomposition of America in its entirety.[6]

A few hours later, around midnight, I meet up with Allen Ginsberg and we go to a demonstration of hippies and students in Lincoln Park: their determination to sleep in the park is their gentle, still too gentle, but certainly very poetic reaction to the nauseating spectacle of the convention.[7] Suddenly, the police begin to charge, with their faces twisted into grimacing masks meant to terrify: and in fact everyone turns around and clears out. But I know perfectly well that these brutes use other much more terrifying methods and masks when they go to hunt down blacks in the ghettos, as they've done for the last 150 years. It's a good, healthy, and moral thing, after all, that these gentle, blond hippies are charged at by these thugs decked out with that terrifying snout that protects them from the effects of the tear gas they're spreading everywhere.

I would like to end the first day with this: the woman who opens her door to let us in while we're trying to escape from these brutes in blue is a very beautiful young black woman. Later, when the streets have finally grown calm again, she tells us we should sneak out through a back door that opens onto another street: without the police suspecting it, we did a disappearing act after hiding in a house full of magic tricks. But despite everything, those enormous thighs of policemen, who were high on LSD, rage, and patriotism, were fascinating to see.

Tomorrow: another night, another sleep-in in Lincoln Park, for this Law which is no law must be fought.

The Second Day: The Day of the Visor

In truth we are bathed in a Mallarméan blue. The second day afflicts us with the azure helmets of the Chicago police. A policeman's black leather visor intrudes between me and the world: a shiny visor in whose neat reflections I might be able to read the world, a visor no doubt polished several times a day to keep it in such fine condition. Attached to the visor is the blue cap—Chicago wants us to think that its entire police force, and in particular this policeman standing here in front of me, have come down from heaven—made of high quality sky-blue cloth. But, really, who is this blue cop in front of me? I look into his eyes and can't see anything but the blue of his cap. What is his deadpan gaze trying to say? Nothing. The Chicago police are, and are not. I shall not pass. The visor and the deadpan gaze are there. The visor so shiny that I can see myself and lose myself in it. I have to attend the next part of the allegedly

Democratic Convention, but the cop with a black visor and blue eyes is there. Beyond him, I can nevertheless make out a well-lit sign above the convention floor: there's an eye followed by CBS News, a configuration that evokes for me, both in French and in English, the word *obscene*. But who is this policeman in a blue cap with a black visor? He's so handsome I could fall into his arms. I look at his expression again: finally I can see through it; it's the look of a beautiful young girl, tender and voluptuous, hiding behind a black visor and a blue cap. She loves this celestial color: the Chicago police force is feminine and brutal. She does not want her ladies to meekly obey their husbands with their sky-blue hair, dressed in robes of many colors . . .

And where's the convention in all this? It's democratic, it babbles away, you have seen it on your screens: its purpose is to conceal a game that is both simple and complex, and which you prefer to know nothing about.

Around ten that evening, part of America broke away from the fatherland and was suspended between earth and sky. The hippies gathered in an enormous hall, as bare as the convention hall is gaudy. Here, everything is joyous, and in their enthusiasm several hippies burn their draft cards, holding them up for everyone to see: they will not be soldiers, but they may well be prisoners for five years. The hippies ask me to go up on the platform to say a few words: these young people are beautiful and very gentle. They're having an Unbirthday Party for a certain Johnson who, as far as I can tell, hasn't been born yet.[8] Allen Ginsberg has lost his voice: he chanted too long and too loud in Lincoln Park the night before.

Order, real order, is present here, I recognize it. It is the freedom offered to each person to discover and invent himself.

Around midnight, again in Lincoln Park, the clergy—it too between earth and sky to escape from America—is holding religious services. I'm struck by the charm of a different kind of poetry, but one that has its own beauty. And what about the trees in the park? At night they bear a strange fruit, clusters of young people hanging in their branches. I am as yet unfamiliar with this nocturnal variety: but that's how it is in Chicago. The clergymen invite us to sit down: they're singing hymns before a huge wooden cross. They also make jokes, using slang. "Sit or split."[9] The cross, borne by several clergymen, recedes into the night, and this imitation of the Passion is very mov——— . . . I don't have time to finish the word: enormous spotlights are turned on us, and the police are rushing toward us throwing canisters of tear gas. We have to run. Once again, it's those policemen, azure but inexorable, who are chasing us and chasing the cross. Spellman-the-cop would have had a good laugh.[10]

We take refuge in Ginsberg's hotel, on a street by the park. My eyes are burning from the tear gas: a medic pours water on them and I get soaked down to my feet. In short, the awkward and bumbling Americans first tried to burn me, then a few minutes later tried to drown me.

We go to Allen Ginsberg's room for a little while to regain some calm. And what about the convention? And democracy? The newspapers have kept you updated about them.

We leave the hotel: another azure policeman—unless it's the pretty girl in drag—holding his club the same way, exactly the same way I hold a black American's member, escorts us to our car and opens the door for us. There can be no mistake about it: we are white.

The Third Day: The Day of the Potbelly

Chicago has nourished the potbellies of its police, which are so fat that you'd think they're fed from the slaughterhouses of a city that resembles three hundred Hamburgs piled one on top of the other and consumes three million hamburgers a day. A policeman's beautiful potbelly must be seen in profile: the one that's blocking my way is a midsized potbelly (de Gaulle could qualify as a cop in Chicago). It's midsized, but well on its way to perfection. Its owner fondles and caresses it with both of his beautiful but heavy hands. Where did they all come from? Suddenly we're surrounded by a sea of police potbellies blocking our entrance into the Democratic Convention. When they finally let me in, I will understand more clearly the harmony that exists between these potbellies and the bosoms of the lady-patriots attending the Convention. There is harmony, but also rivalry: the wives of the gentlemen who govern America have arms as thick as policeman's thighs. Whole walls of potbellies. And walls of police surrounding us, shocked at our unexpected presence at the Democratic Convention, furious at our unconventional attire; they are thinking that we are thinking what they think, namely that the Democratic Convention is the Holy of Holies. The mouths atop these potbellies talk things over in a little huddle. Walky-talkies bark and screech. We all have the electronic passes needed to enter the amphitheater. The head of the police, in plain clothes and a potbelly, arrives. He checks our passes, our identification, but, clearly a man of taste and discretion, he doesn't ask for mine. He offers me his hand. I shake it. The bastard. We enter the aisles of the Convention Hall only to be relegated to the section reserved for the press. More police potbellies are there, blocking our way once again. Can we go in and sit down? Some even fatter and more robust potbellies inform us that there is no room for us inside: within the hallowed halls of the convention, segregation is being practiced against four or five white men who had the audacity to show up without a tie, a mixed group of longhairs and bald heads, with a few beards thrown in. After long negotiations, we are authorized to enter and sit down. From the fatigue that has just overwhelmed me I can deduce that what I am witnessing is a resounding lie, voluptuous for those who live off it. I hear numbers being ticked off: they're counting the votes from New Jersey and adding them to the ones from Minnesota. Never having been very good in math, I am amazed that this science is used to choose a president. Finally, victory and a great uproar. Their victory: Humphrey has been nominated. The potbellies have chosen a representative. This madness without madness, this spouting of mauve songs, gaudy but gray, this exorbitant lie of talking potbellies, you have seen and heard its pale reflections on your television screens.

I feel a pressing need to go out and grope a tree, go down on the grass, screw a goat, in short, to do what I'm used to doing.

A few hours before going to the convention, where our free and easy ways stunned the police and made them suspicious, we took part in the peace march organized by David Dellinger in Grant Park.[11] Thousands of young people were there listening peacefully to Phil Ochs who was singing, and to others who were talking; we were covered with flowers.[12] A symbolic procession set off toward the slaughterhouse. A row of blacks in front, then behind them, in rows of eight, everyone who wanted to join the demonstration. No one got very far: more potbellies charged, throwing tear gas at the young people. Trucks fill with armed soldiers moved endlessly up and down the streets of Chicago.

To the Hippies

Hippies, young people of this demonstration, you no longer belong to America, which has repudiated you in any case. Long-haired hippies, America is tearing its hair out because of you. But you, between earth and sky, you are the beginning of a new continent, an Earth of Fire rising strangely above what was once this sick country, or hollowed out beneath it: an earth of fire first and, if you like, an earth of flowers. But you must begin, here and now, another continent.

Fourth Day: The Day of the Revolver

Is it necessary to say that it's all over? With Humphrey's nomination, will Nixon be the master of the world?[13]

The Democratic Convention is closing its doors. The police, here as elsewhere, will be less brutal, if they can. And will the revolver, in turn, have its say?

The Democratic Convention made its choice, but where exactly, in what bar full of drunks, did a handful of Democrats make their decision?

Across from the Hilton Hotel, in Grant Park again, there is a sumptuous happening. The young people have climbed up on a bronze horse topped by a bronze rider. The horse's head is bowed, as if in sleep, and on his mane there are young blacks and whites holding black flags and red flags. A burning youth that, I hope, will burn all its bridges. They're listening, attentive and serious, to a presidential candidate who was not invited to the convention: Dick Gregory.[14] Gregory is inviting his friends—there are four or five thousand of them in the park—to come home with him. They won't let us march to the amphitheater, he declares, but there's no law that says you can't come to my house for a party. But first, he says, the four or five policemen who were stupid enough to get caught in the crowd of demonstrators have to be set free. With great wit and humor, Gregory explains how the demonstrators should walk: no more than two or three in a row, stay on the sidewalk, don't cross against the red. He says that the march may be long and difficult, since his house is in the black ghetto of South Chicago. He invites the two or three defeated delegates (meaning McCarthy's delegates) to lead the march, since any police whose job it is to stop it might be less brutal with them.

We move along a hedge of armed soldiers.

At last America is moving because the hippies started shaking it off their backs.

The Democratic Convention is closing its doors.

As usual, a few thoughts in no particular order:

America is a heavy island, too heavy: it would be a good thing, for

America and for the world, if it were destroyed, reduced to powder.

The danger for America is not Mao's *Thoughts*; it's the proliferation of cameras.

As far as I know, there were no scientists among the demonstrators: is it that intelligence is stupid, or is science too compliant?

The police are made of rubber: their muscles are hard rubber; the convention itself was nothing but rubber; Chicago is made of rubber that chews chewing gum; the policemen's thoughts are made of soft rubber. And Mayor Dailey is made of wet rubber . . .

As we leave the Democratic Convention, a young policeman stares at me. Our exchange of looks is already a settling of scores: he has understood that I'm the enemy, but none of the police was aware of the natural but invisible route—like the one for drugs—that led me, through an underground or celestial pathway, into the United States, after the State Department had refused to give me a visa to enter the country.[15]

Too many star-spangled banners: here, as in Switzerland, a flag in front of every house. America is Switzerland flattened by a steamroller. A lot of young blacks: will it be the delegate's hot dogs or a revolver bullet that will kill the Democrats before it's too late?

Fabulous happening. Hippies! Marvelous hippies, it is to you that I address my final appeal: children, flower children of every country, in order to fuck the old bastards who are giving you a hard time, unite, go underground if necessary to join the scorched children of Vietnam.

Appendix 2: A Salute to a Hundred Thousand Stars

Americans, are you asleep?

You don't know that mourning does not have the same meaning here and over there.[1] Here, in America, you mourn in luxury, and when one of your blond soldiers is killed, but really killed, the way they know how to kill over there—skull crushed, members scattered, sex organs stupidly torn off, butts exposed—by a Viet Cong soldier, the mother—or widow—goes to pick out long veils of crepe, a new and perhaps desired adornment, and the dead soldier's family will hang a little star in the window of their house.

The death of your child is a pretext for decorating your home. And since nothing in heaven and on earth sparkles more than stars, I imagine that you look forward to the death of many of your sons, in Vietnam.

And over there? Well, over there is over there. In the cemetery you ceaselessly and savagely dig with your bombs, there is no mourning. There is not a single family that drapes itself in crepe, and for them there are no more stars in heaven. There is not a single family that has any room left for grief, so completely have hatred and the knowledge of hatred replaced everything else in their hearts.

You, in your country with its air too pure, in your cities eternal for only a few more years, you have never seen a Viet Cong, and you think that the men your sons have gone off to hunt on some kind of safari, whose various stages of escalation show the weakness of grammatical redundancy, are people like yourselves.

(Let it be said in passing: I think you are losing the war because you are ignorant of elegant syntax.)

I hope that you won't deprive yourselves of this pride which exalts you when a soldier dies over there, for the purpose of granting you another star, it would seem.

I know, from personal experience, that the Viet Cong are not like you, but I will not tell you what the difference is. I would suggest nonetheless that you bring a Viet Cong widow into your home so that she can teach you how one remains tearless even while burning inside after one's husband has been murdered by your boys.

And speaking of your boys, aside from the fact that they've gone off on the longest safari of the century, what are they doing? They're fucking the prostitutes in Saigon, both the men and the women, they're being robbed of their dollars, and, when they're dead and still in one piece, they gladly get themselves buggered, or else, if they're captured alive, they meet with the most surprising adventures.

Ladies and Gentlemen, do you know the story of the little eight-year-old girl who captured a six-foot-two-inch paratrooper, blond of course? She made him her doll. A giant doll that opened its mouth and closed its eyes—blue eyes, of course. She made a dress for him out of the parachute, and with the bolts—your bolts! from your shot-down planes—she fashioned some earrings and necklaces for her doll: little Viet Cong girls mourn for their dead differently than you.

Let us return, for your pleasure and mine, to all those chopped off penises, those adolescent, American penises that will never get hard again: the penises, gone forever, of your blond-headed children, destined to lie scattered on distant shores.

Americans, are you asleep? Are you dreaming? May the words I write make you sleep even more deeply, may they make your dreams even sweeter, O widows, O mothers and daughters! I do not doubt that in the proud depths of your grief you will discover great stores of pleasure. What a pleasure to live with dead men hardly twenty years old!

But the Viet Cong will strike back: they are domesticating swarms of bees as cruel as they are, to kill your handsome soldiers; they are setting up the stakes of a happiness that will be with them until death: their methods are poetic, like your hippies' trips, and your bombardiers are powerless before a capacity for poetic invention that you cannot even imagine.

Instead of listening to your Texan, your Westmoreland, your Abrams, or your computers, if only you would let the Mad Women among you—your mothers and your widows—rave freely, you might discover in their raving the subtle reasoning still capable of saving you from catastrophe: but your ideas, your own ideas, are too flabby and too absorbed, with their flabbiness, in mourning.[2]

(You are losing this war because you don't listen to the singing of the hippies.)

But you will never see the Viet Cong, you will never know who they are: between them and you there is Hawaii, isn't there? There is the Pacific Ocean, so aptly named, there are your bombs and your boys. Unless . . . if the sound of the Viet Cong digging their tunnels under the barricades and barbed wire of Khe Sahn is no longer to be heard, could it be because these tunnels are about to emerge somewhere in the American countryside, not far from the Pentagon?[3]

. . . Unless the little Viet Cong girl gets tired of her doll—the six-foot-two-inch paratrooper—and sends him back in a trunk, by way of Moscow and Stockholm.

So you will never know that a family's pain, its distress, are not metamorphosed into proud veils of star-spangled crepe but rather into hatred and rage. Mourning over there involves an even greater ferocity, a new boldness, such as would shake the very foundations of your American morality.

Are you dreaming, farmers of free America?

Work well and efficiently, defoliate,[4] level all things to the ground, destroy the surface of the land and, underground, under thousands of stars, this people with high cheekbones and slanting eyes, this joyous people (for intelligence is a source of joy), will continue to live, nurtured by the hatred they bear you.

In the open air, in the free air of free America, you are working hard, and this atomic bomb that was created in your sumptuous universities— if you have any guts, won't you find it necessary to use it?

But this makes you stop and think. One doesn't repeat the experience of Nagasaki unless one wants to make it perfectly clear that one is heart and soul against the yellow race.

(Americans, you are losing this war because you invented Coca-Cola.)

And yet, as for the Bomb, you will turn to it again. Since your genius brought it to perfection, it must be used. Reflect for a moment on the sadness of unused objects. In your silos, the grain is bursting; in your nests, monstrous eggs are waiting and growing impatient. Soon they will take off and fly on their own over Vietnam, North and South Vietnam, which seem to be two but which in their hatred for you are one. So go ahead and exterminate those delicate families who know everything about America while you know nothing about them. Your Rusks,[5] your Westmorelands, your Abrams, your marines, your boys, your girls, your mothers, who are so good and furrowed, hope to destroy an underground civilization of extreme sensibility, so that they can't see those stars multiplying in your windows. And in this way, oh star-spangled land, it will always be Christmas among you, thanks to the Viet Cong who kill and to your blond children who die.

The only country where I've seen a handsome truck driver whistle at a pretty girl as he passes by is yours, and it's truly a pleasant sight to see. And the fact that your police are so handsome is something no one can fail to admire. I'm also not surprised that your plastic flowers are more beautiful than the natural flowers of any other country in the world. That God would be so deeply revered, in your churches and temples, this is something that throws me off a little, since I thought you prostrated yourselves only before your green god, the dollar. If the landscape around Camp David is so gentle, it's because President Eisenhower is full of gentleness. If, in the end, the blacks do you so little harm, it's because the harm you are guilty of here is relatively minimal. That you are human enough to set up reservations for the Indians you haven't killed, that you bury your cats and dogs, that Billy Graham hypnotizes you by reading verses from a cruel Bible, that your daughters blithely wear clothes made of cotton picked by blacks in the South, that you have built expressways so wide and long that they border on the ridiculous, that your dogs call you by your first name, that your horses recite speeches to which you respond with conviction, that your airports are really yours, that the richest man in the world is an American, that the largest opera in the world is the Met, that, finally, the image of God himself is complacently reflected in your countryside, your cities, your souls: by these and a thousand other blessed signs, I recognize that you are a great people.

(Americans, you are losing the war because the Italians are the only ones who have mastered the art of putting their hands in the pockets of their pants.)

No woman, no woman, no woman, no woman, no woman, no woman: your sons, before dying, will not know the tenderness of a woman's hand on their sweating brow, they are falling in love with Viet Cong soldiers, whose aim is sure.

No woman, think of it, except the prostitutes, male or female, in Saigon; no woman, but with the Viet Cong soldier, dry and fervent, waiting in a thicket, ready to discharge his rifle or bazooka against them, once and for all; no woman, and with nothing but a sterile and solitary masturbation in the shithouse, if they have a few minutes of respite; no woman: but perhaps you prefer it that way: aside from the gold stars, and aside from the men, perhaps you'll be able to make a few lucrative deals, and your slightly mustachioed wives, if they no longer have a son still flourishing in flesh and mind, will preserve in their heaving bosoms the image of a son whom they have made a hero, a son who will die a pitiful death, hiding as best he can in some rice paddy, in a brothel, in a river or a stream, or who will have allowed himself to become the giant doll of some eight-year-old girl worried about keeping her high cheekbones intact.

So many heaps of black cloth, so much crepe sold to give some flair to your mourning! You're convinced that God is on your side: I won't say to you that there is no God, but rather that there is not one side and then another.

Over there is over there, and no prolonged mourning: over there, they are weaving the stuff of their hatred for you, an entire people is poisoning itself in order to corrupt you: but no mourning like the kind you carry on here, no grief felt the way you feel it, no stars, no greatness of soul, no dyed hair—for the mothers and widows—no permanents and no sky-blue hair dyes.

(Americans, are you asleep, are you dreaming?)

There are yet other things you do not know: the paratrooper—the doll that has already been abandoned, even though it's still so adorable, by the little Viet Cong girl and has metamorphosed into a pretty red-headed girl with a provocative bust. She's waiting on tables in General Giap's underground mess hall.[6]

A civilization superior to yours is being worked out in the underground spaces of Vietnam. I have the impression that you're passing through life with your head screwed on backwards, you're perfectly capable of it, with your machines, your drilling techniques, your embalmed Cardinal Spellman,[7] your girls with perfect legs all from the same mold, your space shuttles, your helicopters, your Nobel prizes, your helicopters that crash, your B-52s that are shot down, your toilets constantly flushing, with all your dollars you regurgitate, your Fulbright who wishes for peace over there the better to count and subjugate his blacks over here, with your

Oppenheimer who wanted the bomb then changed his mind, with your Plexiglas buses, your infantile gadgets, your luminous roses, your Central Park devoid of the crimes that used to give it a hint of poetry at night, with what remains of Shirley Temple, with your countryside cut by tractors, your California peaches, your Don Schollanders who line up their gold medals but remain virgins, with the recklessness that makes you exploit the exploits of Bonnie and Clyde without having experienced them, with your redskins either massacred or shunted into reservations, with your . . . your . . . your . . . your . . . American culture is all that.[8]

And your scientists, and your professors, and your artists, and the whole raucous pageant of American good will: if they really want to end the Vietnam War, they should go set up camp in Hanoi. In the Pentagon, your military strategists would be in a fine mess if they found, mixed in with the Viet Cong population they're bombing, ten thousand of your scientists, the pride of your country in your opinion, and the ten thousand scientists (or a hundred thousand, since your computers make mistakes) would find themselves in a fine mess too under the rain of bombs let loose by your blond pilots. No doubt about it. But think about all the stars you'd have! And all the lavish mourning of a nation! Then your Texan would go to mass and have a one-on-one talk with God. The God of the armed forces, of course.

"We were obliged to destroy this village in order to save it." Thus spoke one of your colonels—one of your hare-brained American colonels!—who set fire to a village in South Vietnam.

Americans, Americans, if you are so set on this grandiloquent mourning, it's time you remembered this line from Rilke: "You must create chaos within yourselves so that new stars will be born."[9]

Chaos, Birth, Stars—this says everything.

But you are sleeping, perchance without dreaming, you are losing your head, and the war, at the very moment I am writing these lines on your soil, to the memory of a young Viet Cong soldier named Do-Van-Phe, murdered by a marine who was himself torn to pieces by badly aimed shots fired by an American patrol near Khe Sahn.

I'm writing these lines in New York, in room 911 (call the police by dialing 911), even though your embassies refused to give me a visa to enter your country, while your police, the most capable in the world—in Bolivia—didn't even notice that they were letting a thief and a homosexual into your midst.[10]

An afterthought: you may find some consolation in the thought that it was not the Americans who invented death, even if they invented almost everything else. And that in any case the Viet Cong, like the Americans and like all men everywhere, must die. If there has been a lot of discussion, since Nietzsche, of the death of God, we have to keep in mind that it was God who started it all by decreeing the death of man. Yes. But if that's true, and this seems to me extremely important, every man who kills makes of himself an accomplice of God or, what amounts to the same, his instrument, as the Inquisitors liked to say. On this point the Bibles on your nightstands, which you expect to show you the way, will give you the last word. But if God were really dead? Personally I have no insight into the matter, but it does appear that he's in hiding for the moment.

And if God were really dead?

Chronology

Jean Genet is born on December 19, 1910, in Paris, of an unknown father. His mother leaves him, at the age of seven months, with the Assistance Publique, or Public Welfare (a state agency that took charge of abandoned or orphaned children). Adopted by an artisan's family in the village of Alligny-en-Morvan, he is raised as a Catholic and goes to school at the local public school. A good student, he receives the Certificate of Primary Studies, but at thirteen he is withdrawn from school by his foster parents. Placed in a vocational center, he runs away after ten days: he dreams of adventures and travels. After running away several more times, and after a series of petty crimes, he has his first experience of incarceration at the age of fifteen, before being placed in juvenile detention until the age of adulthood in the Mettray penal colony.

At eighteen years old, in order to leave the colony, he enlists in the army before being conscripted. After volunteering to serve with troops in the eastern Mediterranean, he is assigned, in 1930, to a company of sappers and miners based in Damascus, where he lives for eleven months. The following year he enlists again and spends nineteen months with a colonial battalion in Morocco. After several terms of duty—a total of six years in the military—he deserts the army in 1936 and leaves France to avoid prosecution. He wanders across Europe for a year with false papers. Repeatedly arrested, imprisoned, and expelled, he travels through Italy, Yugoslavia, Czechoslovakia, Poland, Austria, Germany, and Belgium.

In July of 1937 he returns to Paris and, within the space of seven months, is faced with a dozen charges for desertion, vagrancy, falsifying documents, and especially theft.

1942–1964

In the autumn of 1942, while Genet is incarcerated in the Fresnes prison, his first poem is printed at his own expense: "The Man Condemned to Death." He is in prison also when he writes *Our Lady of the Flowers* the same year, and, the following year, *Miracle of the Rose*. He is on the verge of being sentenced to "perpetual imprisonment" when Jean Cocteau appears in court on his behalf. He is released on March 14, 1944, shortly after the "underground" publication by Paul Morihien and Robert Denoël of *Our Lady of the Flowers*.

Thanks to the publisher Marc Barbezat, Genet begins to escape from the circle of clandestine publication. In less than three years, from 1945 to 1948, he writes three novels in quick succession, *Funeral Rites, Querelle of Brest*, and *The Thief's Journal*, as well as a collection of poems, a ballet (*'Adame Miroir*) and three plays (*Deathwatch, The Maids*, and *Splendid's*). Following a petition backed by a group of writers and headed by Cocteau and Sartre, he is finally granted a definitive reprieve by the president of the republic in 1949; he will never go back to prison. That very year, Genet stops writing and falls into a six-year silence which the 1952 publication of Sartre's *Saint Genet, Actor and Martyr* only deepens. He finds a provisional solution to this crisis, however, in the theater: between 1955 and 1961, Genet writes and publishes three plays (*The Balcony, The Blacks*, and *The Screens*) which place him in the forefront of the contemporary theater. He also writes a few brief but important essays on art; one of the most significant of these is devoted to his friend Alberto Giacometti.

1964–1986

After working for several years on an immense project—a vast cycle of seven plays—Genet learns, on March 12, 1964, of the suicide of Abdallah, the young acrobat for whom he had written *Le Funambule* [The Tightrope Walker]. Deeply shaken, Genet announces to his closest friends his decision to renounce literature. Despite the interest he shows in the staging of *The Screens* in Paris in April 1966 and the publication of his *Letters to Roger Blin*, he undergoes a period of severe depression. In May 1967, not long after writing a will, he is found unconscious in his hotel room in Domodossola, a border town in Italy, after taking a massive dose of sleeping pills.

A new period begins for Genet on December 22, 1967, when he sets out on a long journey—experienced as a kind of renaissance—to East Asia, including a stay in Japan. Upon his return to France, he is overtaken by the events of May '68 and the exhilaration of the student uprising. He soon publishes his first political article, in homage to Daniel Cohn-Bendit. Three months later, invited by an American magazine to "cover" the Democratic Convention in Chicago, Genet travels for the first time to the United States and takes part in the large demonstrations of the American Left against the Vietnam War. Back in Paris, he becomes more and more interested in the problems of Algerian and Moroccan immigrants and takes an active part in numerous demonstrations in support of their cause.

The great political year of Genet's life, however, is 1970. On February 25 of that year a leader of the Black Panther Party asks for his support. Genet refuses to sign any petitions but instead proposes to wage a campaign for the Black Panthers in the United States. For two months, from March 1 to May 2, he shares their life and travels with them throughout the United States, speaking in a number of universities and to the press. On October 20, in response to the invitation of a delegate of the Palestinian Liberation Organization in Paris, he travels to Jordan to visit the Palestinian refugee camps. He plans to spend eight days there, but ends up staying for six months. In early November, in the Wahdat camp, he meets Yasser Arafat, who gives him an official pass and asks him to bear witness to the Palestinian drama.

After four different trips to the Middle East, Genet is arrested by the Jordanian authorities and is expelled from the country on November 23, 1972.

Denied a visa for the United States, forbidden to enter Jordan, Genet withdraws to France; he returns to Paris, which, despite a great deal of movement, will be his primary place of residence for the next ten years, and where his political activity continues to increase. He publishes a large number of newspaper articles, takes a side during the presidential elections of 1974, becomes associated with the Groupe d'informations sur les prisons, and attempts finally to convince a number of writers (including Jacques Derrida, Juan Goytisolo, Pierre Guyotat, Jacques Henric, and Philippe Sollers, among others) to put together a collection of writings on black American prisoners and on the Palestinians. At the same time, beginning in the early 1970s, he begins a work based on his experiences in the Palestinian camps and with the Black Panthers—a work he will repeatedly abandon and take up again and that fifteen years later will lead to the publication of *Prisoner of Love*.

During the periods when he loses hope of finishing his book, Genet busies himself with other projects: thus, from 1976 to 1978, he works to develop a film script entitled *La Nuit venue* [Nightfall], which relates a young Moroccan immigrant's first day in Paris. Just before shooting is to begin, however, Genet withdraws from the project without explanation. Three years later, the same incident occurs: Genet signs a contract to make a film telling the imaginary story of the Mettray penal colony, but after more than a year's work on the script he recoils again before the prospect of its realization.

In May 1979, Genet learns that he has throat cancer and begins a treatment which, although it weakens him considerably, enables him to live a few more years.

In September 1982 he returns to the Middle East and happens to be in Beirut on the 16th and 17th of that month, when the massacres in the Palestinian camps of Sabra and Shatila are perpetrated. A witness to the tragedy, Genet, who has not been writing for a long time, takes up his pen once more and writes the most important of his political texts, "Four Hours in Shatila."

A few months later, in July 1983, while living in Morocco, he begins to assemble, unify, and rework the notes and sketches of the book on the Palestinians and on the black Americans which he will work on continuously, and ever more urgently, in the face of a worsening illness.

He returns one last time to Jordan in July 1984 to revisit the places and people he had described in his book, which he finishes in November 1985. Genet then returns to Paris and gives the manuscript of *Prisoner of Love* to his editor.

In March 1986, after carefully correcting the first proofs, he travels to Morocco and, upon his return, takes a room in Jack's Hotel, rue Stéphane-Pichon, in Paris. He receives the second round of proofs of his book and begins to reread them. He dies during the night of April 14–15, 1986.

On April 25 he is buried, in accordance with his wishes, in the small Spanish cemetery in Larache, near Tangiers, Morocco. The cemetery is located on a cliff overlooking the sea. It is flanked on one side by a municipal prison, on the other by a *maison de rendez-vous*.

On May 26, 1986, *Prisoner of Love* appears, published by the Éditions Gallimard.

Notes

Preface

1. *L'Ennemi déclaré* is designated as volume 6 of Genet's *Oeuvres complètes*, published by Gallimard.—Trans.

"J.G. Seeks . . ."

An untitled, previously unpublished text, written in Tangiers and based on a handwritten copy annotated by the author. (For this text, as for those that follow, the reader may refer to the introductory note placed before the notes for each chapter.)

INTRODUCTORY NOTE

This collection opens with a text that does not strictly belong with the rest of the writings included here. It is in accordance with the author's wishes that it has been placed here as a prologue, without regard to chronology; in the project he sketched in 1984 for the publication of his major articles, he chose to place it at the beginning of the work (it was provisionally entitled "Page from Tangiers" in reference to the place where it had been written).

In September of 1975, steps were taken to have it published in a collection of texts in honor of William Burroughs and Brion Gysin, though Genet did not follow up on this plan. In the few lines that would have introduced Genet's text, Brion Gysin, an American painter and poet, recalled the circumstances in which it was written. This brief introduction sheds light on the status of this ambiguous text, at once comic, cruel, and serious, with its use of pastiche (notably, the style of a personals ad) which it puts to other more subtle uses:

"In Tangiers in 1970 Genet asked me what had happened to the underground English newspaper the *International Times*. When I told him that the editors were having problems with the English authorities because of the personals ads run by people searching for certain kinds of friends, he exclaimed: 'Friends? What I'm looking for is an enemy of my stature!' And he wrote the following text . . . " (Brion Gysin).

The fact that Genet wanted to publish his political articles with this text as their prologue gives more than a passing indication not only of the identity of their author, presented partly as a fictional character ("J.G. seeks . . . "), but also of the mode of reading appropriate to the different writings in this collection, whose general tone and secret note are given to us at the outset.

Sources: Interview with Laurent Boyer (Éditions
Gallimard). Archives of Gallimard.

ENDNOTES

1. The particular focus on England in this text is no doubt related to the English newspaper (the *International Times*) referred to in the conversation that inspired the piece (see the introductory note above).

Chapter 1: Interview with Madeleine Gobeil

Interview conducted in January 1964 in Paris for *Playboy* magazine. The present version follows the typed transcript approved by the author.

INTRODUCTORY NOTE

At the insistence of Simone de Beauvoir, Genet agreed in January 1964 to meet with Madeleine Gobeil, a young Canadian student hired by *Playboy* to do two interviews of prominent French personalities. After first choosing Jean-Paul Sartre and Brigitte Bardot, the magazine's editors then decided (for reasons that remain rather perplexing) that they preferred Jean Genet to the latter.

Genet agreed to participate on two conditions: the first was that the interview would not under any circumstances be published in France; the second was that he would share with his interlocutor the compensation for the piece ("We'll split it," he told her), the two thousand dollars paid by the American monthly.

The interview was recorded during five meetings in Genet's room at the Meridional Hotel, 36 boulevard Richard-Lenoir, in Paris. A photographer took a series of photographs, three of which were printed with the article.

In the brief introduction by Madeleine Gobeil, which remained unpublished, she wrote:

"Genet has no permanent address. We know only that during the past four years he has lived at times in Greece, at times in Turkey, rarely in France. He met with us in his small room with bare, yellowed walls. . . . Five books, which he takes with him everywhere he goes, lay scattered on the table: poetry by Villon, Baudelaire, Mallarmé, and Rimbaud, and Nietzsche's *The Birth of Tragedy.* Exceptionally, the recent work by Jean-Paul Sartre, *The Words,* was there on the table as well. Genet is no doubt the only living writer who does not possess a single copy of his own books. 'Why would I have my own books,' he said, 'they're written; it's finished.'"

Once complete, the interview was transcribed by Madeleine Gobeil and reviewed by Genet, who approved it. It was published a few weeks later in the April 1964 issue of *Playboy* (vol. 11, no. 4, pp. 45–53), under the title "Jean Genet: A Candid Conversation with the Brazen, Brilliant Author of *The Balcony* and *The Blacks,* Self-Proclaimed Homosexual, Coward, Thief, and Traitor."

Much abbreviated and modified according to journalistic norms, the interview was preceded by a rather long introduction that included what was then known of Genet's biography, presenting him as "the most important French writer since World War II" and "probably the greatest living playwright."

A French translation of the text published by *Playboy* appeared in the June 1981 issue of *Magazine littéraire* and since then has been frequently republished. The interview is here restored to its complete form based on the speakers' actual words.

It is worth noting that scarcely two months after this interview, in which Genet speaks with a rare openness of his preoccupations and his works in progress, there occurred one of the great ruptures that marked his life. With the death of Abdallah in March 1964, a new page would be turned: Genet abandoned literature and, a few years later, embarked on his political journey. Thus this text, which inaugurates the writer's relationship with the press and the media, also marks the end of a chapter in his biographical history.

> Sources: Interview with Madeleine Gobeil. Archives of
> Madeleine Gobeil, *Playboy,* Jean Genet / IMEC (Institut
> mémoires de l'édition contemporaine)

ENDNOTES

1. The American premier of *The Blacks* took place on May 4, 1961, at the Saint Mark's Playhouse in New York, directed by Gene Frankel. The play was remarkably successful and went through 1,408 showings (see Richard C. Webb, *Jean Genet and His Critics* [Metuchen, N.J., and London: Scarecrow Press, 1982]).

2. The film version of *The Balcony* was directed by Joseph Strick in 1962; it features Peter Falk and Shelley Winters, a screenplay by Ben Maddows, and music by Igor Stravinsky.

3. *Our Lady of the Flowers*, published in New York in 1963 by Grove Press in a (new) translation by Bernard Frechtman, had been very favorably received in the press.

4. *Saint Genet, Actor and Martyr* had just been published in New York by George Braziller in September 1963, in a translation by Bernard Frechtman.

5. These terms are taken from Genet's work: "I owned to being the coward, traitor, thief, and fairy they saw in me" (*The Thief's Journal*, trans. Bernard Frechtman [New York: Grove Press, 1965; first published in French in 1949], p. 176).

6. Genet left prison for the last time in March 1944.

7. On the basis of our current knowledge of Genet's prison record—and if we count the years spent in a penal colony—we can estimate that Genet spent between five and six years in prison.

8. Kennedy had been assassinated only a few weeks previously, on November 22, 1963.

9. The exact citation reads: "Poetry or the art of using leftovers. Of using shit and making you eat it." *Pompe funèbres* (Paris: Éditions Gallimard, 1953), coll. "L'Imaginaire," p. 190. [This passage is not in the original *Oeuvres complètes*, vol. 3, published by Gallimard in 1953, and is therefore not included in Frechtman's translation.—Trans.]

10. Published in 1961 by the Éditions L'Arbalète, *The Screens* was not produced in France until 1966, when it was directed by Roger Blin at the Théâtre de l'Odéon. It was in Germany, in fact, that the world premier took place, on May 19, 1961, at the Schlosspark Theater in Berlin, directed by Hans Lietzau. The production planned for New York, however, did not take place until 1971 (directed by Minos Volonakis at the Chelsea Theater Center).

11. The publisher Genet is referring to is Paul Morihien, Jean Cocteau's assistant; in December 1943, in collaboration with Robert Denoël, he published *Our Lady of the Flowers* in an underground edition. It was therefore among Cocteau's circle of friends that the book found its first readers.

12. This incident was related several times by Genet (notably, in the interview with Nigel Williams). But it seems rather to have occurred at the time of writing his second novel, *Miracle of the Rose*, as a letter sent to Marc Barbezat from La Santé Prison on December 2, 1943, appears to confirm. (See Jean Genet, *Lettres à Olga et Marc Barbezat* [Paris: Éditions L'Arbalète, 1988], p. 14).

13. Caryl Chessman, born in 1921, was sentenced to death for rape and armed robbery. During the twelve years he spent in prison, he mended his ways, pursued his studies, organized his defense, and published an essay on his prison experience, *Cell 2455*. Despite his popularity and the support of numerous intellectuals, his appeal was rejected and he was executed in Soledad Prison in 1960.

14. This friend was Anna Bloch. A Jew married to a German industrialist, she

fled to Brno, Czechoslovakia, around 1937, and came to Genet's aid during his wanderings through Europe after he had deserted from the army. See the letters Genet sent her in 1937–38, published under the title *Chère Madame* (Hamburg: Éditions Merlin, 1989).

15. See the interview with Hubert Fichte, where Genet tells the same story, with some variations.

16. What Genet says here is slightly inaccurate: it was not Guillaume Hanoteau, a writer and a lawyer in Maurice Garçon's firm, who brought "The Man Condemned to Death" to Cocteau, but Roland Laudenback, future editor of *La Table Ronde*. Furthermore, the publication of the booklet was not at all paid for by Cocteau, but by its author.

17. " . . . that saintliness which to me is still only the most beautiful word in human language" (*The Thief's Journal*, p. 214).

"We shall be that eternal couple, Solange, the two of us, the eternal couple of the criminal and the saint" (*The Maids*, in *"The Maids" and "Deathwatch": Two Plays*, trans. Bernard Frechtman [New York: Grove Press, 1982], p. 63).

18. François Mauriac, "Le Cas Jean Genet," *Le Figaro littéraire* (March 26, 1949).

19. On this point see "Comment jouer *Les Bonnes*," in *Oeuvres complètes*, vol. 4 (Paris: Éditions Gallimard, 1968), p. 269.

20. The Front de libération nationale (FLN), an Algerian nationalist party, was the driving force behind the struggle for Algerian independence.

21. After several victories (notably at Chimay, on June 2, 1963, where he won the grand prize), Jacques Maglia gave up automobile racing following a serious accident on the Solitude racetrack, near Stuttgart, on July 18, 1965. (Maglia was present during the interviews with Gobeil.)

22. Long considered a "red bishop," Cardinal Liénart was associated with the efforts of the worker priests whose cause he supported; he played a decisive role at the Second Vatican Council, presided over by Pope John XXIII on October 11, 1962.

23. This is the first mention of any such collaboration with the composer Pierre Boulez; the project was neither abandoned nor brought to a conclusion. Genet did leave behind some sketches of a libretto that were found after his death.

Chapter 2: Lenin's Mistresses

Article published May 30, 1968, in *Le Nouvel Observateur* (special edition, no. 185).

INTRODUCTORY NOTE

This article is, to my knowledge, Genet's first intervention in a specifically political arena. Unlike most of the texts that follow, it is a response neither to a commission nor to an urgent situation.

It is important to note that this article deals with the events of May '68, which will remain, whether in praise or disparagement, one of Genet's essential references and, perhaps, the point of departure for his political itinerary. This text also allows us to gauge Genet's initial political sympathies, which at this period seemed far removed from those of the communist party and the journal *L'Humanité*, with which he would be associated six years later.

On Genet's statements and actions during May '68, the following articles from the press can be consulted: Michel Clerc, "Quand Jean Genet vient boire à la Sorbonne le petit-lait de la Révolution" [When Jean Genet comes to the Sorbonne to lap up the milk of revolution], *Aurore* (May 31, 1968): 2; Nicole Duault, "A la Sorbonne: 'Ma supériorité sur vous, c'est que je suis inculte,' déclare Jean Genet" [At the Sorbonne: "I am superior to you because I am uncultivated," declares Jean Genet], *France-soir* (May 31, 1968): 3; Jean Lebouleux, "Genet: Non aux idoles, oui à l'homme" [Genet: No to idols, yes to man], *Combat* (May 31, 1968): 13.

ENDNOTES

1. We can surmise that the "traveler" in question is none other than Jean Genet, who was indeed in Tangiers—where he was staying after a long journey that took him to the Far East—when rumors of the student uprising brought him back to Paris.

2. Daniel Cohn-Bendit, born in 1945 in Montauban, was the principal figure of the May '68 uprising and the spokesman for the libertarian movement, known as the March 22 Movement.

3. See the article by Georges Marchais, "De faux révolutionnaires à démasquer" [Unmasking false revolutionaries], *L'Humanité* (May 3, 1968): 1–4. In this article, the author, at the time a member of the political bureau of the Communist Party, denounces "the German anarchist Cohn-Bendit."

4. An unsigned article published May 2, 1968, in *Minute* (no. 318, pp. 4–5), entitled "Il faut en finir avec le chienlit de Cohn-Bendit" [It's time to have done with Cohn-Bendit's chaos], mentioned Cohn-Bendit's Jewish origins.

5. Sartre's interview with Cohn-Bendit was published in *Le Nouvel Observateur* on May 20, 1968, with the title "L'Imagination au pouvoir" [Imagination in power].

6. Université de Paris III, located on the rue Censier in the Latin Quarter.

7. Secretary of France's most powerful labor union, the CGT (Confédération générale du travail).

8. Certain newspapers had spread the rumor that Cohn-Bendit's girlfriend was a young student at Nanterre and the daughter of the minister of Youth and Sports (see *Minute* [May 9, 1968]: 5 and 7).

9. Born in Paris in 1874, Stéphane Lauzanne was, in 1920, the chief editor of the newspaper *Le Matin*. Nadezhda Krupskaya: companion and wife of Lenin. The biographical information about Lenin seems to have come largely from Genet's reading of Jean Fréville's *Lénine à Paris*, published in April 1968 by Éditions Sociales.

10. On May 16, 1968, Cohn-Bendit took part in a televised debate for the news program on Channel 1 of the ORTF [Office de radiodiffusion-télévision française; French Office of Radio and Television, the former French broadcasting service.—Trans.].

11. Tomás Masaryk (1850–1937), founder and first president of the Czech Republic.

12. Order pronounced May 22, 1968. (Cohn-Bendit was not a French national.)

13. This was the first demonstration in which, along with the students, unions and political parties of the Left participated as well.

Chapter 3: The Shepherds of Disorder

Article published March 1, 1969, in Paris, in the journal *Pas à pas*, on the occasion of a screening of Nikos Papatakis's film *Les Pâtres du désordre* [The shepherds of disorder].

INTRODUCTORY NOTE

Written at the request of Nikos Papatakis, the original purpose of this text was to accompany the release of the film *Les Pâtres du désordre* in the United States. It was therefore in principle not meant to be published in France—which perhaps explains why it was quietly published in a small city newspaper. In any case, Genet apparently authorized the director, who was a longtime friend, to make whatever use of it he wished.

Born in Addis Ababa of a Greek family in 1918, Nikos Papatakis met Genet in Paris in 1945. The manager (from 1947 to 1954) of La Rose Rouge, the famous Saint-Germain-des-Prés literary cabaret, he was the main producer of Genet's only film, *Chant d'amour* [A song of love]. In 1963, he began to make films and directed his first, *Les Abysses*, inspired by the same true story as *The Maids* (the crime committed by the Papin sisters). The film caused a scandal and received the support of Jean-Paul Sartre, Simone de Beauvoir, Jacques Prévert, André Breton, and Jean Genet, all of whom defended it in the pages of *Le Monde*.

Genet published the following text at the time, entitled "From One End to the Other, a Tornado":

"'All the pain in the world . . . ' The well-known phrase could also be used to describe the tornado that is, from one end to the other, *Les Abysses*.

One would have to be deaf not to hear through the rumbling the miniscule but precious complaint of two girls who, despite themselves, were to be torn from their own slow degradation.

These two sisters (they are the only two in the film who matter) are seen for the first time in the midst of the flames, already bitten by the fire.

One might become indignant at the stubbornness with which Nico Papatakis worked to grasp and to develop this paroxysm for two hours. But I think we must agree to keep our eyes wide open when an acrobat executes a life-threatening move." (*Le Monde*, April 19, 1963, p. 15)

Four years after *Les Abysses*, Nikos Papatakis secretly filmed *The Shepherds of Disorder* while the military regime was in power. The film had its world premier in Paris on February 20, 1968, at Bobino.

Genet's text, which does not seem to have its own title, was published in March 1969, in the first issue of the journal *Pas à pas* (pp. vi–vii), in Paris.

> Sources: Interview with Nikos Papatakis. Archives of
> Edmund White.

ENDNOTES

1. The coup of April 21, 1967, had brought a military junta to power in Greece which abolished the Constitution and the parliamentary system.

2. Theodora, the empress of the Eastern Empire, died in 548 B.C. A dancer and a prostitute, according to Procopius, she became the mistress and then the wife of Justinian I.

3. A Greek actress whom Nikos Papatakis had just married.

Chapter 4: Yet Another Effort, Frenchman!

Article written February 24, 1970, the day after Jean Genet's testimony in the trial of Roland Castro, in Paris, and published in *L'Idiot international.*

INTRODUCTORY NOTE

At the origin of this text, as of the trial of Roland Castro, there was a social tragedy: during the night of January 5–6, 1970, five immigrant workers of African descent died of asphyxiation in a room of the residence hall called the "Foyer de solidarité franco-africaine," located at 27 rue des Postes, in Aubervilliers. With no heating or electricity, they had tried to warm themselves by lighting a fire in the lid of a garbage can, using garbage to feed the fire. Their deaths abruptly revealed the housing conditions of immigrant workers: in this small suburban housing unit there were more than sixteen people stuffed into each room, without ventilation or light, for a rent of seventy francs per person.

On January 10, the day of the funeral, while Jean-Paul Sartre spoke to the television cameras, a group of two to three hundred people occupied the offices of the CNPF (Conseil national du patronat français [National Council of French Employers]), located at 31 avenue Pierre I de Serbie; among them, Maurice Clavel, Marguerite Duras, Jean Genet, Pierre Vidal-Naquet. The leader of the action, Roland Castro, shouted slogans from the balcony and harangued the crowd.

It didn't take long for the police to intervene. The protestors occupying the CNPF were brutally ejected. Jean Genet and Maurice Clavel were clubbed and shoved into the stairway; Pierre Vidal-Naquet's face was covered with blood. . . . One hundred sixteen people—including Genet and Marguerite Duras—were taken away in police vans to the Centre Beaujon and ordered to stand at attention. They were released a few hours later, with the exception of Castro, who tried to escape through a window of the van on the way to the station.

Castro's trial took place on February 23, 1970, in Paris. Genet came to testify and to explain his presence at the offices of the CNPF.

"We were looking for the killer responsible for what happened at Aubervilliers," he shouted, "and he is right here in the dock."

At the end of the hearing, Roland Castro was sentenced to one month in prison.

Genet's article consists of two parts: the first repeats his statement in the witness stand; the second, dedicated "to Roland Castro and his comrades," is an evocation of the trial. It was published on March 1, 1970, in issue no. 4 of the journal *L'Idiot international* (p. 24).

Sources: Interviews with Roland Castro and Patrick
Prado. Archives of *L'Idiot international.*

ENDNOTES

1. This first sentence—with its fractured syntax—seems to have been added at the last minute as a kind of "headline" for the publication of the text. Genet's statement at the trial of Roland Castro begins with the next sentence.

2. For the circumstances of the tragic events, see the introductory note.

3. Roland Castro, born in Limoges in 1940. An architect and a political activist, he was one of the significant figures of May '68 and the main organizer of the VLR (Vive la révolution) movement.

4. A reference to the short work by Sade (forming a part of the longer *Philosophy in the Bedroom*): "Yet Another Effort, Frenchman, If You Would Become Republicans," written in 1795.

5. A Muslim cemetery in a southern suburb of Paris where the five Africans had been buried.

Chapter 5: "It Seems Indecent for Me to Speak of Myself . . . "

Preliminary statement for a debate organized by the Black Panther Party, March 10, 1970, at the Massachusetts Institute of Technology, in Cambridge. The text presented here is based on the manuscript.

INTRODUCTORY NOTE

Despite its brevity, the text of this speech provides a good introduction to Genet's experience with the Black Panthers. It was written about five days after the writer's clandestine entry into the country (see note 1 of "May Day Speech").

Almost immediately after arriving in New York, Genet was taken on a dizzying round of talks organized by the Black Panthers and given in large American universities, which gladly opened their doors at the very mention of his name.

The task assigned to Genet was to stir up and encourage support, on the part of students and intellectuals, for the ideas of the Black Panthers. Beginning with his first appearance at Yale, however, Genet became aware of the primary obstacle that he would encounter throughout most of his travels in the United States: the curiosity of a public interested exclusively in literary questions.

Irritated—to say the least—by the questions of large crowds who seemed to be interested only in his life and work, Genet decided to explain at the outset and, he hoped, once and for all, what he was doing there. This preliminary statement thus had a specific function—that of forestalling irrelevant questions— and in all honesty cannot be considered in isolation: for the writer, if perhaps not for us, what was most important in his statement lay in the political debate that followed it, about which we know little more than the general issue it addressed. This is no doubt the reason why this text (which Genet may have presented also at other talks) was not, to my knowledge, published anywhere in the press.

Presented March 10, 1970, this speech was Genet's third public appearance during his time with the Black Panthers. It was given before an audience of fifteen hundred people, made up of students, professors, and guests of the Massachusetts Institute of Technology, where it took place. The debate at which the text was read was led by Douglas Miranda, one of the leaders of the Black Panther Party. Genet, with the help of a translator, spoke a great deal, calling on students to struggle against racism and to give their support to Bobby Seale, chairman of the Black Panthers, who was being tried for murder. After reading the text printed here, Genet refused to answer any questions not bearing on political matters. The meeting concluded with the screening of a film about Bobby Seale.

Sources: Interviews with Marie-Anne Thomson de Pury.
The Archives of Alexandre Bouglione, Edmund White,
and Jean Genet / IMEC.

ENDNOTES

1. At the time of Genet's arrival in the United States, Bobby Seale (born in 1936), the cofounder and chairman of the Black Panther Party, was in prison. Arrested in August 1969 in California, he was first accused of inciting a riot in Chicago in August 1968; then, more seriously, of having ordered the "liquidation" of a member of his party, Alex Rackley, suspected of having provided information to the FBI, whose body had been found in New Haven. Bobby Seale was waiting to be sentenced and was in danger of receiving the death penalty. (Found innocent after a long and sensational trial, he was acquitted and released in 1971.) See Gilbert Moore, *A Special Rage* (New York: Harper and Row, 1971).

2. Genet had a tendency to consider his "theatrical period" to be more unified than it actually was. In fact, *Deathwatch* and *The Maids* (not to mention *Splendid's* or the numerous plays which have been lost or destroyed, such as *Héliogabale, Don Juan*, etc.) were written before the six-year silence he mentions here.

3. Ronald Reagan, then governor of California, had recently agreed to extradite Bobby Seale, who was about to be transferred to New Haven, Connecticut, a state in which the death penalty was in force.

4. Richard Wright (1908–60), author of *Black Boy*, is considered the greatest black American writer of his generation. The homage paid to him here should no doubt be taken in a symbolic sense, since the first French translation of a book by Richard Wright [*Les enfants de l'oncle Tom* (a translation of *Uncle Tom's Children*)], dates from 1946, two years after Genet's final release from prison.

Chapter 6: Letter to American Intellectuals

A talk given on March 18, 1970, in the Albert Jorgensen Auditorium at the University of Connecticut, and published several times in different forms and with various titles. The present version is based on a partial manuscript and on the text published at the beginning of the booklet entitled *Here and Now for Bobby Seale*.

INTRODUCTORY NOTE

We have chosen to present here a composite text including a section based on an English translation. [The passage from "Because of the very fact . . . " to the end of the text is a modified version of the unsigned translation appearing in *Here and Now for Bobby Seale*.—Trans.] This text is in fact representative of the numerous talks given by Genet in March and April 1970 in American universities in the company of the Black Panthers.

The title—which is taken directly from the manuscript and not from the various publications of the text—indicates at the outset the intended addressees of these talks (and perhaps of the majority of his writings): the writer is addressing not activists but "intellectuals" in general. And more specifically, as a reading of the text makes clear, white intellectuals. The kind of support the Panthers were asking of Genet was thus clearly defined: to serve as a mediator between them and the whites. Genet thus walks the thin line between the blacks he is accompanying, but to whom he cannot be assimilated, and the whites from whom he distances himself but whom he is addressing.

Written in New York in the small room occupied by Martin Kenner, a black militant Genet stayed with for a few days, the letter was read for the first time in the large auditorium of the University of Connecticut [at Storrs] on March 18, 1970, during a conference that had been organized entirely by the Panthers' security officers. Two people spoke: Jean Genet and David Hilliard, chief of staff of the Black Panther Party, who were meeting for the first time (see the description of this meeting in *Prisoner of Love*, trans. Barbara Bray [Hanover, N.H.: University Press of New England, Wesleyan University Press, 1989], p. 260).

The audience was largely white but included a small number of black students. Announced by flyers and posters, the conference also drew academics and intellectuals from New York. The meeting began at 8:00 P.M. and lasted about two hours. Introduced by Douglas Miranda, a leading member of the party, Genet—whose statements were translated by an interpreter—opened the discussion by reading this text.

About halfway through, however, his intervention was interrupted by a bomb threat: the police informed the Panthers that they had received several telephone calls claiming there was a bomb in the auditorium. Suspecting that the police had invented the story in order to have the event called off, Douglas Miranda informed the audience of the danger but declared that the meeting would continue and that the auditorium would not be evacuated: "If there's a bomb here," he added, "then I know I'm not afraid of death, and if the lives we have led up to now in this country have been torture, if we have lived with our backs to the wall without being able to do anything about it, maybe then our deaths would have some meaning."

He then turned the proceedings back over to Genet, who, before taking up his speech again, spoke directly to the audience which responded with applause: "Now it's understood that we've exploded. We're dead. So now we are on the other side of death."

The meeting continued without incident. At the end, Douglas Miranda asked if the audience had any questions for the speaker. Genet added that he was indeed ready to answer questions, "as long as they're asked in an intelligent way." The warning was effective: no one asked any questions. David Hilliard ended the meeting with a call to the students to organize and to demonstrate for the release of Bobby Seale.

Since this text has been published in various earlier forms, a brief overview of its publication history is provided here:

1. First publication: March 28, 1970, in *The Black Panther*, under the title "Bobby Seale, the Black Panthers and Us, White People" (vol. 4, no. 17, p. 7).

2. Printed again with extensive modifications: May 31, 1970, again in *The Black Panther*, under the title: "Here and Now for Bobby Seale" (p. 26).

3. Reprint of the preceding text with slight modifications and under the same title: June 1970 in the journal *Ramparts*, in a translation by Judy Oringer (vol. 8, no. 12, pp. 30–31).

4. Reprint of the first version, with slight modifications, and of the unaltered third version in the booklet including four essays by Jean Genet, entitled *Here and Now for Bobby Seale*, published in English, probably in the latter part of 1970, by the Black Panther Party Community News Service.

The present version of the text is based on a partial manuscript (two pages in folio) that was available for consultation. The missing section has been taken from the beginning of the booklet *Here and Now for Bobby Seale*.

> Sources: Interview with Marie-Anne Thomson de Pury
> and M. Hardy. Archives of Thierry Bodin, The Black
> Panther, Edmund White, and Jean Genet / IMEC.

ENDNOTES

1. See note 1 of the preceding chapter. On March 15, 1970, Bobby Seale had been transferred to the New Haven prison and had been charged with accessory to murder.

2. Capital of the Republic of North Vietnam, Hanoi had undergone violent bombardments by American planes since 1964.

3. The English version includes a phrase here that is not in the manuscript: "We know that their is a collusion between the police and the mafia distributing these drugs."

4. John Mitchell, famous for his slogan "law and order," was the prosecuting attorney in the trial of Bobby Seale; as attorney general under Richard Nixon, he became implicated in the Watergate scandal.

5. "Stony Brook University" refers to the State University of New York at Stony Brook.

6. The Long March is the name given to Mao Tse-Tung's retreat into northwest China in 1934, which helped him to bring peasants from many regions into the revolutionary cause. The Hundred Flowers campaign, as it is called, was carried out in 1957 against bureaucratism and dogmatism. The Cultural Revolution took place between 1965 and 1968 in reaction to "revisionism" and to the threat of a return of the bourgeoisie.

Chapter 7: May Day Speech

Speech given May 1, 1970, in New Haven, Connecticut, during a large demonstration in support of the Black Panthers. The text is based on a type-script that was corrected and annotated by Genet. It includes the appendix that was added when the speech was published by City Lights Books.

The "May Day Speech" is probably the most important statement Genet made while in the United States. Given outdoors before an enormous crowd of more than twenty-five thousand people, it was addressed to the relatively diverse group of protesters who, in response to a call put out by the Panthers, had come together for the large demonstration that took place from May 1–3, 1970; it included students, intellectuals and revolutionary activists, as well as members of various movements (messianic, hippie, yippie), who assembled on the grounds of Yale University, in New Haven, to protest the charges against Bobby Seale, incarcerated at the time in the very same city. The speakers included leaders from every current of the revolutionary Left: Jerry Rubin, Abbie Hoffman, Dave Dellinger, Ralph Abernathy, David Hilliard, and others.

Genet gave his speech on the first day of the demonstration. Because his presence in the United States was relatively illegal (see note 1), his intervention had not been previously announced to the press. (The same day, however, the *New York Times* published an article on him entitled "Genet Emerges as an Idol of the Panthers"). The author, using a microphone, read the first lines of his manuscript in French, then Elbert "Big Man" Howard, minister of information of the Black Panther Party, took over, reading an English version of the text.

This is the last of Genet's interventions in the United States. The day before, he had received a summons from the Immigration Services in Connecticut demanding that he show his identification papers and his visa. The day after the speech, May 2, Genet left the country by crossing the Canadian border.

The "May Day Speech" was published in English under this title in the summer of 1970 by City Lights Books in San Francisco, in the form of a small booklet of twenty-eight pages. The speech was published with an introduction by Allen Ginsberg and with an appendix Genet himself had written for the booklet.

In his introduction, Ginsberg describes Genet as the "most eminent prosateur of Europe and saintly thinker of France, most shy poet of XX Century." Commenting on the speech, Ginsberg adds: "The exquisite common sense of Genet's document on racism was immediately apparent—to those of us whose consciousness attended his classic language. . . . And the Panthers and their righteous cause and the grievous, mean, bitter, murderous injustice dealt them by our Government was explained again clearly once for all and established irrevocably in conscience and consciousness, in *white terms*, unmistakable, and in language that commanded a new 'delicacy of heart' as the next political dimension of White Reality."

The text, given here in its entirety, includes the additions Genet wrote by hand on the typescript. Excerpts from the speech and the appendix were published in French in the journal *Jeune Afrique*, November 10, 1970, under the title "J'accuse."

> Sources: Interviews with Marie-Anne Thomson de Pury,
> Monique Besse, and Jeannette Bredin. Archives of
> Gallimard, Edmund White, Jean Genet / IMEC.

ENDNOTES

1. The "unusual circumstances" in which Genet entered the United States are these: after the American consulate in Paris had denied him a visa, Genet arrived on March 1 in Canada, where he made the same request, once again without success. He then decided to try to enter the country through one of the least-used border stations. He went there in the company of Jacques Maglia. Taking advantage of a moment of distraction on the part of the passport agent, who, upon seeing two Frenchmen arrive, began to hum "La Marseillaise," Genet switched his own passport with that of his companion, who had just passed the checkpoint; the agent then put a second stamp on Maglia's passport and let Genet through. Genet met up with the Panthers in New York the evening of March 5.

2. The events referred to here took place on April 14, 1970, in a New Haven court, where Jean Genet, David Hilliard, and Emory Douglas (minister of culture of the Black Panther Party) attended a hearing in the trial of Bobby Seale.

At a certain moment during this hearing, Bobby Seale's lawyer, Charles Garry, handed a statement written by his client to David Hilliard, who began to read it out loud. A policeman tried to stop him. When David Hilliard and Emory Douglas resisted, they were arrested and sentenced immediately to six months in prison. Genet, despite his vigorous protest, was expelled from the courtroom; an hour later he wrote an account of the arrests for the *International News Service*, a newsletter published April 17, 1970, by the Committee to Defend the Black Panthers at Yale University. A few days later, the Panther leaders were released after making an apology to the court.

3. This other incident took place April 28, 1970, when Genet, two white lawyers for the Panthers, and Thomas Jolly, a lieutenant in the Panthers, boarded a flight from Los Angeles to New York. (When Thomas Jolly was apprehended by the federal police, his three companions decided to get off the plane and took a later flight.)

4. Spiro Agnew, vice president of the United States, led a virulent campaign against the Black Panthers. He was forced to resign in 1973 and was prosecuted for corruption.

5. This line of argumentation is partially repeated in "Interview with Michèle Manceaux." Georges Clemenceau was the director of the newspaper *L'Aurore*, in which in 1898 Zola published "J'accuse." Jean Jaurès described it as "the greatest revolutionary act of the century."

6. This appendix was not read in New Haven.

7. The Warren Commission was formed after Kennedy's assassination to clarify the circumstances of his death. Its report, published on September 27, 1964, supported the claim that Kennedy had been killed by Oswald and that the latter had acted alone.

Chapter 8: Interview with Michèle Manceaux

Interview conducted in Paris on May 10, 1970, published in *Le Nouvel Observateur* under the title "Jean Genet chez les Panthères noires" [Jean Genet among the Black Panthers].

INTRODUCTORY NOTE

It was—quite exceptionally—on Genet's own initiative that this interview was arranged. Back in Paris after two months in the United States, the writer's new task was to encourage the creation of "Committees of Solidarity with the Black Panthers" and to heighten awareness among the French Left concerning the repression to which the Black Panthers were being subjected. To this end he contacted Michèle Manceaux, a journalist and activist, and together they decided to publish an article, in the form of an interview, in a widely circulating weekly, *Le Nouvel Observateur*. The one condition imposed by Genet was that his interlocutor's questions should relate exclusively to his experience with the Black Panthers.

The interview took place on May 10, 1970, scarcely three days after Genet's arrival in Paris, in his room at the Cecil Hotel, located at 71 rue du Conservatoire. Michèle Manceaux recorded the responses in writing, then put together the text, which Genet carefully reviewed.

The interview takes up several points that Genet had addressed some ten days earlier in the "May Day Speech." Despite these few repetitions, the general content of the interview remains original and offers a first overview of Genet's experience with the Black Panthers. The article was well received, and it marked Genet's entry onto the political scene in a much more decisive way than the text published in the same magazine in May 1968 ("Lenin's Mistresses"). A significant fact in this regard: Genet received a number of requests for support from various revolutionary groups, notably in Jamaica and in Guadeloupe, but it seems he was unable to respond, intensely preoccupied as he was with the worsening situation of the American blacks during the summer, and with the Jordanian-Palestinian conflict in September.

Published on May 25, 1970, in *Le Nouvel Observateur* (no. 289, pp. 38–41), the interview was immediately translated into English by Richard Seaver and appeared the same year, in New York, in the September issue of *Evergreen Review*. It was later translated and published in England, Germany, and Italy as well.

Source: Interview with Michèle Manceaux.

ENDNOTES

1. On February 20, 1970, Connie Mathews, international representative of the Black Panthers, met Genet for the first time and asked for his support.

2. See "May Day Speech," note 1.

3. The Paris address for the "solidarity committee" was given in a note in the interview; the address was that of the Gît-le-coeur bookstore, 6 rue Gît-le-coeur, where the office of the movement Vive la révolution was located.

4. The demonstration in New Haven (where the "May Day Speech" was given) took place from May 1 to 3, 1970; the Washington demonstration was on June 19 of the same year. These two demonstrations were initiated by the Black Panther Party and brought together all the currents of the American far Left.

5. Bobby Seale had been arrested along with seven other prominent figures of the far Left (Jerry Rubin, Abbie Hoffman, Tom Hayden, David Dellinger, Rennie Davis, Lee Weiner, and John Froines), for conspiracy to incite a riot. The trial turned out to be highly animated: after Bobby Seale called the judge—who had refused to let him represent himself—a "fascist pig," the judge ordered him to be shackled and gagged during the public hearings. When the cases were dismissed for violations of due process, the other defendants—all white—were released, but the court sentenced Seale to four months in prison for contempt of court—which made it possible to keep him in jail until the beginning of his second trial for accessory to murder on April 23, 1970.

6. The president of Yale University made this statement on April 24, 1970.

7. Here Genet takes up an analogy already suggested in "May Day Speech."

8. On May 4, 1970, four students were killed during a confrontation with National Guard troops on the campus of Kent State University in Ohio. The accident provoked an antigovernment outcry in the press and had a deep impact on public opinion.

9. The ten members of the Panthers arrested on April 30 in Baltimore were released in 1971 for lack of evidence.

10. *The Black Panther*, the official mouthpiece of the party, was widely disseminated in American ghettos; Genet published several articles in it in 1970 and 1971.

11. It was at the house of screenwriter Dalton Trumbo that Genet met Jane Fonda. That evening the Panthers raised about four thousand dollars.

Chapter 9: Introduction to Soledad Brother

Introduction to a collection of George Jackson's prison letters, written in Brazil in July 1970. The present version restores the typographical layout of the text indicated in the typescript annotated by the author.

INTRODUCTORY NOTE

This preface was originally commissioned purely as an "occasional writing" which Genet agreed to do before he had even read any of George Jackson's letters; and yet, paradoxically, it can be considered as the author's major contribution to black American revolutionary movements and one of his most beautiful political writings.

This is no doubt largely due to the very nature of the text: commenting on a book of letters written in prison, Genet was almost certainly led once again to interrogate the relations between writing and confinement, poetry and revolt, art and betrayal, and to reflect on the situation at the origin of his own work. Entirely dedicated to the defense of George Jackson, this text puts into play most of Genet's major themes and thereby takes on the force and the tone of a veritable manifesto written in the name of the "complicity" (to use his term) that binds together all "works written in prison."

The importance of this preface is related also, it must be said, to the inherent quality of George Jackson's book, now a "classic" of black American literature, and one that was also a brilliant success from the moment it appeared. First published in 1970 by Coward-McCann and Bantam, more than a half a million copies were sold in the United States in the first year, and it was soon translated into a dozen languages; Genet's introduction was quoted and discussed in the international press. On April 2, 1971, *Le Monde* published some long excerpts from the preface. The work appeared in France in 1971, published by Gallimard in the series *Témoins* (before being issued in the Folio series in 1977).

It should be pointed out, finally, that the first American edition of the book, as well as the first French edition, appeared before the death of George Jackson, who was killed in San Quentin Prison on August 21, 1971.

It was after a press conference in April 1970, in San Francisco, that Genet met Fay Stender, a young lawyer who had just taken on the case of George Jackson, a twenty-eight-year-old black detainee charged with the murder of a prison guard. Struck by the beauty of the letters he was sending her, Stender had the idea of collecting those he had written in prison and publishing them before the trial. While searching for a publisher, she thought that a preface by Genet would lend credibility to her project. The writer accepted immediately; a few days later he received some of the letters and had them translated. But it was only at the end of June that he had a sufficient idea of the whole to be able to begin writing his preface. The text was written during a stay in Brazil where Genet had traveled, at the beginning of July 1970, to attend a production of *The Balcony* directed by Victor Garcia in São Paolo.

"Introduction to *Soledad Brother*" marks the first in a series of statements by Genet concerning George Jackson, most of which are included in this collection. They form a considerable whole (especially those such as "The Red and the Black" and "After the Assassination," which further develop the writer's reflections on the prison letters), and are spread over time according to the events that marked George Jackson's story. This story is partly retraced in these texts, but for the sake of clarity, a brief synopsis is offered here:

George Jackson, born September 23, 1943, grew up in the black ghettos of Chicago and Los Angeles. At the age of seventeen, he was arrested as an accessory in the theft of seventy dollars from a gas station and was given a prison sentence of one year to life; every year, a parole committee would decide, in light of his conduct, whether to release him or keep him in detention.

Jackson was never released from prison: first imprisoned in 1960, he saw his freedom deferred from year to year and ended up spending the last eleven years of his life in the California state prisons of Los Angeles, Soledad and San Quentin. During his detention, he pursued his studies; he changed from a juvenile delinquent into a political militant, struggling against racism and for the respect and rights of blacks. He became, in the words of Huey Newton, "a living legend." In 1969 he secretly joined the Black Panther Party.

On January 13, 1970, in an inner courtyard of the maximum security row—called "O Wing, Max Row"—of Soledad Prison, a violent fight broke out between white and black prisoners. A guard named Miller, a sharpshooter positioned in a watchtower, opened fire: one white was wounded, three blacks were killed.

To calm the situation, an investigation was ordered. But three days later, on January 16, the guard was acquitted. Barely a half an hour after the verdict was announced, another white guard, John Mills, was thrown over a railing on the third floor of the prison. The prison administration quickly designated three men as guilty: George Jackson, John Clutchette, and Fleeta Drumgo.

These are the three black prisoners who came to be known as the Soledad Brothers. When Genet wrote the introduction to Jackson's book, all three prisoners were awaiting trial and were in danger of receiving the death penalty.

Sources: Interviews with Mary Clemmey and Ellen Wright. Archives of Gallimard, Alexandre Bouglione.

ENDNOTES

1. George Jackson was held in Soledad State Prison from January 1969 to June 1970, at which point the "Soledad Brothers" were transferred to San Quentin. See Min S. Yee, *The Melancholy History of Soledad Prison* (New York: Harper's Magazine Press, 1973).

2. The letters are spread out over a period of six years, from June 1964 to August 9, 1970.

3. Angela Davis, the "tender experience" to whom the collection is dedicated in part, was also one of the recipients. When Genet wrote the introduction, he had not yet seen all the letters contained in the work.

4. An allusion, this time from the point of view of a white man, to a comment by David Hilliard. See "For George Jackson," p. 66 and note 1.

5. Genet uses here a recurrent image in the writings of black revolutionaries, who frequently refer to "white blue-eyed devils." This phrase from Malcolm X is also echoed in a text cited by Hervé Hamon and Patrick Rotman: "All you need is blue eyes to be American / I've been here for a century and I'm not American." See *Génération* (Paris: Le Seuil, 1988), vol. 2, p. 96.

The color blue, exclusive to the West, thus tends to carry negative connotations in Genet's late work. We might point out, to take only one example, that the (still unpublished) film script Genet was writing around 1977, *Nightfall*, was originally entitled *The Blue of the Eye*, in reference to the color of the eyes of the train conductor who mistreats a young Moroccan immigrant, the film's main character, during his first trip to Europe.

Chapter 10: Angela and Her Brothers

Article published August 31, 1970, in *Le Nouvel Observateur*.

INTRODUCTORY NOTE

This article was written after the dramatic events that took place during George Jackson's trial. On August 7, 1970, George Jackson's seventeen-year-old brother, Jonathan, entered the San Rafael courtroom where the trial was taking place. Arms at the ready, he freed two black prisoners and took five hostages— the judge, a lawyer, and three women from the jury—with the intention of exchanging them for the three Soledad Brothers. As his van took off, the police unleashed a hail of bullets: Jonathan Jackson, Judge Harold Haley, and two other blacks were killed by the gunfire.

A few days later, the investigation revealed that the weapons used by Jonathan Jackson during the abduction had been purchased by Angela Davis, a young philosophy professor whose courses at UCLA had recently been suspended. A black woman, a member of the Communist Party and of the Soledad Brothers

Defense Committee (see note 1), Davis was accused of accessory to "murder and kidnapping" and was placed on the FBI's Ten Most Wanted list. Her photo was accompanied with the description "armed and extremely dangerous," which gave the police complete license. Fearing she would be killed if she turned herself in, Angela Davis went into hiding.

Such were the circumstances in which Genet wrote this article, originally intended as an introduction to a selection of excerpts from George Jackson's prison letters to be published in a newspaper. An earlier typescript of this text gives it a different title: "The Man Who Thought He Was Judge." Published August 31, 1970, in *Le Nouvel Observateur* (no. 303, pp. 19–21) under the current title, the article was introduced by the following heading: "In the United States, Jean Genet met Angela Davis, the beautiful young woman who refuses not only white society but also the black American middle class—and who, for that reason, has become a hunted woman."

> Sources: Interview with Angela Davis. Archives of
> Gallimard, Jean Genet / IMEC.

ENDNOTES

1. In addition to Angela Davis, the members of the Soledad Brothers Defense Committee included Benjamino Bufano, Noam Chomsky, Lawrence Ferlinghetti, Jane Fonda, Jean Genet, Allen Ginsberg, Ralph Gleason, Jack Newfield, Huey Newton, Barbara McNair, Mario Savio, Fay Stender, Robert Scheer, Pete Seeger, Terry Southern, and others.

2. Malcolm X (1925–65) was without doubt the most important leading figure of the black revolutionary movement in the early 1960s. A member of the Nation of Islam, then director of the Organization of Afro-American Unity, he was assassinated in February 1965. Poet, essayist, and orator of exceptional power, he exerted a decisive influence on the political theories of the Black Panthers.

3. On October 17, 1968, at the Olympic Games in Mexico City, two black athletes, Tommy Smith and John Carlos, first and third in the two-hundred-meter race, stood on the podium before the television cameras of the entire world and, wearing black leather gloves, raised their fists as a sign of black power. The Olympic committee gave them forty-eight hours to leave the Olympic village.

4. The idea of a "black nation" (which Genet places in quotation marks here), inherited from Malcolm X, was central to the Black Panthers' political thought. Although they remained nationalists, they nonetheless gradually moved away from their separatist leanings and advocated alliances with other revolutionary movements.

5. In the previous two paragraphs, Genet is referring in part to the Ten Points of the Black Panther Party Program and Platform, presented under the title "What We Want, What We Believe."—Trans.

6. The Minutemen: an extreme right-wing group whose self-appointed "mission" was to protect the United States from any subversion or foreign invasion.

7. Angela Davis, born in 1944, was twenty-six years old; Huey Newton and Bobby Seale, born in 1942 and 1936, respectively, were therefore twenty-eight and thirty-four years old; Eldridge Cleaver, born in 1935, was thirty-five years old; David Hilliard was about twenty-nine years old.

8. William Edward B. DuBois (1868–1963) was the editor of *Crisis* magazine, published by the NAACP. An economist, historian, sociologist, and poet, he was for a long time the most important spokesman for the black cause, and at the end of his life he was a member of the Communist Party.

9. For Richard Wright, see "It Seems Indecent of Me to Speak of Myself . . . ," note 4. Frantz Fanon (1925–61), a psychiatrist and sociologist from Martinique, author of *The Wretched of the Earth* (1961), was a fundamental reference for the Black Panther Party's three main theoreticians: Seale, Newton, and Cleaver.

10. From a letter dated July 29, 1970, signed "Jesse, Jonathan, and Laure," found in Genet's personal papers.

11. Huey Newton was accused of killing a police officer in October 1967. Incarcerated shortly thereafter, he was eventually acquitted and released in August 1971.

12. A slight inaccuracy regarding the date here: David Hilliard's sentence was handed down on April 14, 1970, in the New Haven court.

13. See "Interview with Michèle Manceaux," p. 42; there Genet speaks of two students being killed, which is correct.—Trans.

14. In the earlier version of this article, a supplementary paragraph concluded the text: "An important question remains: formerly the whites were perfect masters of the definitions of words; today they are letting themselves go. The blacks, it seems, are in the process of revising the dictionary. The former masters are no longer its masters. As for Jonathan Jackson: Assassin? Murderer? Man of Justice?

"The blacks have already decided, and, with a clear determination, Angela Davis has joined the black American nation."

Chapter 11: Angela Davis Is in Your Clutches

A statement read on October 16, 1970, in Paris, in front of the television cameras of the Video Out group after the announcement of Angela Davis's arrest. The present text is based on the manuscript.

Wanted by the police, Angela Davis was arrested in a motel in New York on October 13, 1970, two months after she had disappeared.

Genet learned of the arrest in Paris just as he was preparing to leave for the Middle East. Extremely worried, he delayed his departure, called on everyone he knew to speak in defense of the young woman, and obtained from Sartre a promise to testify at her trial. But Genet feared that, in the current state of tension prevailing in the United States, Angela Davis might serve as a scapegoat and that, under the pretext of an attempted escape, the police would attempt to do away with her.

So when the writer Pierre Rezvani asked him to record a statement on Angela Davis for a television program ("L'Invité du dimanche") featuring a story about her, he accepted immediately. The primary purpose of the short text which he wrote and then read on this occasion was to send a warning to anyone who might assassinate Angela Davis, pointing out what could happen, according to him, if they did.

The recording took place on October 16, 1970, at the Cecil Hotel where Genet was staying. As a precautionary measure, so that there would be a record of the statement in case it was censored, he asked Carole and Paul Roussopoulos, directors of the group Video Out, to make their own film of the reading.

The next day, in a meeting with François-Marie Banier, who was interviewing him for *Le Monde*, Genet spoke of the difficult time he had had at the recording session:

"They asked me to redo certain passages because I was making mistakes. Of course I made mistakes, I always make mistakes. And I make more and more. First because I'm old, then because I'm upset, and what's more I'm stoned on Nembutal. I'm on drugs. I told them so. Maybe they won't show the whole thing, but I had them filmed on video while they were filming me. And if they don't include everything I said, I know what I'll do."

In the same article, he speaks of Angela Davis: "You can't help liking Angela Davis once you know her. She is in prison, the FBI says, because she bought weapons that any American can buy. The fact is, she was arrested because she is a revolutionary and a black member of the Communist Party" (*Le Monde*, October 23, 1970, p. 3).

Despite a few murmurs, Genet's statement was not censored; it was broadcast on November 8, 1970, a week later than scheduled.

> Sources: Interview with Carole and Paul Roussopoulos.
> Archives of Carole and Paul Roussopoulos, Jean Genet /
> IMEC.

ENDNOTES

1. See "May Day Speech," note 4.

2. Ronald Reagan, then governor of California, issued the order to have Angela Davis arrested.

3. Reference to the death of Judge Herold Haley during the kidnapping attempted by Jonathan Jackson (see the introductory note to "Angela and Her Brothers").

4. The manuscript includes another sentence here, taken out by Genet: " . . . and the liberated world will go on without you."

Chapter 12: For George Jackson

A speech written most likely in Jordan in March 1971, to be given during a demonstration in London in support of the Soledad Brothers. This text was used, in fact, for a manifesto to be signed by French artists and intellectuals.

INTRODUCTORY NOTE

Initially entitled "En vrac" [At random] (the title written on the manuscript), this text consists of notes and reflections that seem to be assembled in no particular order but that are in fact tightly organized around one central theme: the trial of George Jackson considered as a trial against all black people.

It was most likely written during Genet's six-month visit to the Palestinian camps. In February 1971, he agreed to participate, along with James Baldwin, in an important demonstration in support of the Soledad Brothers that was supposed to take place on April 20 of that year in Westminster Central Hall, in London, and he wrote this text in preparation for his speech. But because Genet's stay in Jordan lasted until the end of April, he gave up the idea of going to London and authorized the publication of his speech, two months later, in the form of a manifesto accompanied by a "call" in support of the black prisoners, initiated by well-known literary and artistic figures and presented to a number of French intellectuals for their signatures.

Printed on colored paper (black and red), the manifesto presents Genet's text on three pages, signed by him and entitled "For George Jackson"; the last page presents the "call for a committee in support of imprisoned black political militants." A facsimile of this page is included in the illustrations reproduced in the present edition; it includes a brief preamble and a list of the signatories. A second smaller sheet was joined to the manifesto which was to be signed and returned to the address of Paule Thévenin.

[Under the heading of a "Call for a committee in support of imprisoned black political militants," the manifesto reads:

"In view of the trial against the Soledad Brothers—George Jackson, John Clutchette, Fleeta Drumgo—, unjustly accused, like Angela Davis and Bobby Seale, by the racist judicial system of the Nixon administration,

the undersigned intellectuals, aware that "repression will not stop unless a sufficiently powerful mass movement intervenes to push back the enemy" (Angela Davis),

protest against the ceaseless repression increasingly exerted by the American government against the black movement and demand the immediate release of all its political prisoners."

It is signed by: Jean-Louis Barrault, Roland Barthes, Maurice Blanchot, Roger Blin, Antoine Casanova, Maria Casarès, Francis Cohen, Alain Cuny, Jacques Derrida, Marc Devade, Marguerite Duras, Jean Genet, Christine Glucksmann, Juan Goytisolo, Juliette Gréco, Guillevic, Pierre Guyotat, Julia Kristeva, Monique Lange, Michel Leiris, Dionys Mascolo, André Masson, Diego Masson, Michel Piccoli, Marcelin Pleynet, Madeleine Renaud, Nathalie Sarraute, Philippe Sollers, and Paule Thévenin.—Trans.]

This manifesto was sent by mail to about one hundred people in early July 1971. However, it became obsolete with the death of George Jackson on August 21, 1971.

> Sources: Interviews with Paule Thévenin, Mary
> Clemmey, and Ellen Wright. Archives of Paul Thévenin,
> Gallimard, and the Bibliothèque nationale.

ENDNOTES

1. An image frequently invoked by Genet. See in particular "Interview with Antoine Bourseiller" and *Prisoner of Love*, p. 46.

2. Army officer Lt. William Calley was convicted of murder by a court martial in 1971 for his part in the My Lai massacre three years earlier. He was sentenced to life in prison but was released three days later on the direct orders of President Richard Nixon. After three years of house arrest at Fort Benning, Georgia, he was paroled in 1974.

3. George Jackson's prison letters had already been published in the United States.

4. Julius and Ethel Rosenberg, exemplary victims of the "witch hunts" carried out in the United States, were accused of turning over atomic secrets to the Soviets. Tried and condemned to death in 1951, they were executed in 1953. Their case was seen as the culmination of an anticommunist and anti-Semitic campaign, and it provoked a number of demonstrations and petitions.

5. Name given to the twenty-one Black Panthers arrested in New York on April 2, 1969, and accused of murder, arson, and of devising a "plan for the destruction of American society." Their trial began in February 1970; the case was dismissed the following year.

6. The last words of the Comtesse de Barry, a long-time favorite of Louis XV, guillotined during the revolution in 1793.

Chapter 13: The Palestinians

Article written at the end of May 1971, in Paris, as a commentary accompanying the photographs taken in the Palestinian camps by Bruno Barbey for *Zoom* magazine (© Magnum). Reproductions of the photographs on which Genet's commentary is based are included with the illustrations in this edition and are marked with the bracketed numbers that have been added to the text. [As noted above, these illustrations have not been included in the present volume. For descriptions of the images, see below, following the introductory note.—Trans.]

INTRODUCTORY NOTE

The first important text by Genet on the Palestinians, this commentary on ten photographs was written in Paris, around the end of May 1971, at the request of Bruno Barbey, a photojournalist who had met the writer at the end of the previous year in a Palestinian refugee camp in Jordan.

Thanks to Genet's renown, this reportage, presented as a collaboration between "a photographer and a prestigious writer" who "are bearing witness to what they saw," was published in issue number 4 of *Zoom*, a glossy "image magazine," in August 1971. With a prudence that reflects the uncertainties and ambiguities of the period, the editorial specifies that "when Genet affirms that he is anti-Zionist, this must not be equated with anti-Semitic. And it is above all not the case that *Zoom* has become the instrument of a party or a militant magazine."

A brief prefatory remark, finally, warns the reader that the writer's opinion, "however well-documented . . . it may be, cannot claim to represent the editors of *Zoom* in their entirety."

As an epigraph to this text—which is as much a reflection on the Palestinians as a commentary on the images in the photographs—we may recall these few lines from *Prisoner of Love* (p. 12):

> We had to be careful not to let the ornamentation and elegance persuade us
> that the tents were happy places, just as we mustn't trust the photographs of the
> sunny camps printed on the glossy paper of deluxe magazines. A gust of wind
> blew everything away—the canvas, the zinc, the corrugated iron—and I saw the
> misery plain as day. [translation modified]

Genet wrote this commentary approximately a month after returning from the Middle East, where he had gone in October 1970, at the invitation of Mahmoud el Hamchari, a leader of the PLO (Palestinian Liberation Organization) in

Paris. Genet had met Hamchari through a couple of friends who had supported the Black Panthers and who together with Genet had followed with great emotion the tragic events of September 1970 ("Black September"): the Jordanian army's attacks on the Palestinian camps.

Although a cease-fire agreement had been signed on September 27, there was still sporadic fighting when Genet arrived in Amman, around October 25. This fratricidal war, in the background of all the texts Genet wrote during his first visit to Jordan, set two previously allied forces against each other: the Palestinian fighters (the fedayeen), who had only recently become organized, and the Jordanian army, whose authority was being threatened by the expansion and autonomy of the Palestinian groups and who were defending, above all, the throne of King Hussein and the integrity of the nation's power.

In this complex situation, Genet took the side of the fedayeen, whom the Jordanian army was decimating, and pointed to the three other "enemies" of the Palestinian people, in order of increasing importance: the Arab regimes who officially support the Palestinian cause but hesitate to intervene; Israel, "the immediate enemy" who benefits from the situation and has made known its readiness to assist King Hussein; finally, America, who simultaneously supports the Jordanian king, the Arab regimes, and Israel, and which Genet elevates to the status of "the absolute enemy." It was no doubt through this latter point that Genet made the link with his other political engagements against the Vietnam War and in favor of the Black Panthers.

If certain signs of the times are apparent in this text, which is still tinged by the messianism of the period's revolutionary movements ("A new man will perhaps emerge . . . "), and which relies on a historical knowledge still too recent to be shaken, an attentive reader will notice that most of the themes and scenes of *Prisoner of Love* are sketched out here (some references are indicated in the notes). Aside from its inherent interest, this commentary provides a remarkable document on the genesis of the author's final work.

> Sources: Interviews with Bruno Barbey, Marie-Claude el
> Hamchari, and Nabila Nashashibi. Archives of *Zoom*,
> Jean Genet / IMEC.

[Translator's note: For purposes of reference, I have included the following brief descriptions of the photographs in question. The numbers below correspond to the bracketed numbers inserted into the text by the French editor:

1. A young man with a shaved head and a scowling, defiant expression sits on a military-type vehicle with Arabic writing on it, a band of bullets draped around his shoulders and a large automatic rifle sticking up from between his legs.

2. A group of six men and boys, some of them holding their noses, lean over a horrifically charred body splayed on its back on the ground.

3. A group of mourners stands by a corpse shrouded in a white sheet and lying on the ground.

4. Seven or eight fighters crawl on their backs beneath a layer of barbed wire in a dusty field, while a man in fatigues and a beret appears to fire a rifle at the ground between them.

5. A group of fighters, wearing ski masks or kaffiyehs, walks in single file through a wide open and desolate landscape of mud, snow, puddles and tire tracks.

6. A young man wearing a ski mask showing only his eyes reclines on his elbow, apparently in a tent, a cigarette in one hand, lightly touching an apple with the other; a large automatic weapon extends from his crotch across the entire length of the image.

7. A group of fighters, weapons lying by, sits in relaxed poses in front of a tent.

8. A sloping muddy hill with dozens of makeshift tents and shanties, no people in sight except for a lone woman in the foreground apparently about to enter her tent.

9. A woman sits before a tent with her family (most likely), her hand raised and her eyes closed in a dramatic gesture of mourning.

10. Young children (eight to ten years old?) stand in line, two by two, all dressed in combat fatigues, with small rifles slung over their shoulders.]

ENDNOTES

1. Theodor Herzl, Viennese journalist (1860–1904), author of *The Jewish State: An Attempt at a Modern Solution to the Jewish Question* (1896), is generally considered the founder of Zionism. He organized the First Zionist Congress in Basel in 1897. For a long time he remained undecided as to the exact location of the future Jewish state, and he received several offers for possible "interim solutions," notably one from England in which Uganda was proposed as a refuge for the victims of anti-Semitism.

2. Genet's note: In his books and reports, Herzl will always maintain, in perfect good faith, that Palestine was uninhabited. It is a common phenomenon among colonialists not to see the colonized: one is then only massacring phantoms, that is, no one at all. The French have done much the same thing in their colonies: in a single day they can kill five hundred blacks—but what does that matter?

3. *Fedayee*, plural, *fedayeen*: literally, "those who sacrifice themselves." Beginning in 1955, this is the name used by the first Palestinian fighters.

4. Because several Palestinian refugee camps—particularly Jebel Hussein and Wahdat—were situated in the city of Amman or in its immediate vicinity, the

fighting that took place during the ten days of Black September spread through the streets of the capital. The destruction of one part of the city was all the greater since, to remove the fedayeen, the Jordanian army used tanks, machine guns, rockets, and phosphorous bombs.

5. The status of this apparent citation is uncertain. The typescript of the first version of the text does not place the sentence in quotation marks. A passage in *Prisoner of Love* (p. 23) attributes it to a figure named Doctor Mahjoub:

> "That man [King Hussein] is a monster," Mahjoub told me. That evening he'd seemed the hungriest of us all. "He's the first head of state since Nero to set fire to his own capital."

What national pride I still possessed allowed me to reply:

> "Excuse me, Dr. Mahjoub—we did just as well as Nero long before Hussein. A hundred years ago Adolphe Thiers asked the Prussian army to shell Paris and the commune from Versailles. He did the job even more thoroughly than Hussein. And he was just as small."

6. Genet uses the expression *semaine sanglante* (bloody week), which in French history designates the week in May 1871 when the communards were violently suppressed by the French forces under Thiers.—Trans.

7. See *Prisoner of Love* (p. 144) for another version of this paragraph.

8. Elie Cohen was an Israeli spy placed in a high-level position within the Syrian administration. He turned over to Israel secret information on the defense of Golan before being arrested and hung in Damascus in 1965.

9. The month was left blank in the typed version as well as in the published text. See *Prisoner of Love* (p. 109) for a very different evocation of the same scene.

10. Genet's note: In Arabic, *militia* is pronounced "malishia."

11. The Jordanian offensive was still underway on this date, primarily in the hills of Jerash and Ajloun, the last areas still held by the Palestinians.

12. A scene also evoked in *Prisoner of Love* (pp. 3–4 and 126).

13. The Battle of Karameh, a Jordanian border town, took place on March 21, 1968; it culminated in the successful resistance of a Jordanian-Palestinian alliance against an Israeli attack.

14. This scene is taken up again in *Prisoner of Love* (pp. 36–39).

15. A well-known march composed in 1871 by Robert Planquette (1848–1903).—Trans.

16. Golda Meir was Israeli prime minister from 1969 to 1974.

17. See the development of this scene in *Prisoner of Love* (pp. 23–25).

18. The first official recognition of the Zionist project, the Balfour Declaration was published November 2, 1917, by the British government; it specifies that "His Majesty's government views with favor the establishment in Palestine of a national home for the Jewish people." Its "ambiguity," indicated

by Genet, consisted in its claim to guarantee the civil and religious rights of non-Jews in Palestine, but without mentioning their political rights.

19. The Irgun: an extreme right-wing Zionist organization, founded in 1935, which advocated the illegal immigration of Jews to Palestine, opposed the British government, and took an active part in terrorist acts carried out against the Arab population. It was dissolved in September 1948, soon after the creation of the State of Israel.

20. Genet's note: The plural of *sherif:* descendants of a so-called prophet; the Hashemites, for example.

21. The Central Committee of the PLO, which provided cohesion for the activities of the various groups, was still new, having been created only in June 1970. This committee was responsible for negotiating the cease-fire of Black September.

22. Genet's note: Run by the UN, the UNRWA deals specifically with the problem of refugees. [UNRWA stands for United Nations Relief and Works Agency.—Trans.]

23. The seven hundredth anniversary of the death of Louis IX was celebrated in 1970.

Chapter 14: The Red and the Black

Article written in Paris in August 1971, just before the beginning of George Jackson's murder trial. It was partially translated and published in *The Black Panther.* The present text is based on the typescript, edited and annotated by the author.

INTRODUCTORY NOTE

Written in August 1971, this article had a specific objective: to clear George Jackson of the charge of murder, for which he was to be tried on August 23.

It attempts to do this by way of an audacious interpretation of Jackson's book *Soledad Brother,* for which Genet had written an introduction a year earlier. Together with that preface and the text entitled "After the Assassination," the present article forms something of a triptych that as a whole represents one of the major phases of Genet's political writings.

As soon as he had finished it, Genet sent a first version of this text to David Hilliard, his main contact in the Black Panthers; Hilliard had it published in *The Black Panther* (September 11, 1971), under the title "The Black and the Red."

In view of an eventual French publication (which Jackson's death rendered moot), Genet made several changes to his text, inserting two paragraphs (in parentheses) containing circumstantial information, and expanding on several points in the margins of the typescript. It is this version, part of which has never been published, that we present here. We have nevertheless chosen to place the two paragraphs of factual information in a note, so as not to encumber the text.

> Sources: Interview with Mary Clemmey. Archives of
> Alexandre Bouglione, *The Black Panther*, Jean Genet /
> IMEC.

ENDNOTES

1. On Jackson's book, see the introductory note to "Introduction to *Soledad Brother*."

2. Genet placed the following paragraph at the beginning of the second version of this text to remind readers of some of the facts: "On January 13, 1970, a guard named Miller—a sharpshooter—shot and missed a white prisoner but killed three blacks in the courtyard of the 'adjustment center' (which means solitary confinement) in Soledad Prison. Three days later, in another section of the same prison, after the radio had announced that Miller was not found guilty of murder, the body of another guard, John Mills, was found, apparently after falling from the third floor: a fractured skull. A half an hour later, he was dead."

3. "Pigs" is in English in the original.

4. On the typescript Genet, no doubt hastily, changed the first "it" of this sentence to "if it." We note this correction here, but keep the original phrasing.

5. Richard Magee was one of the three blacks on trial who were freed by Jonathan Jackson. At the end of this paragraph, Genet again added a few lines of factual information (which a marginal note suggests to "cut"): "I will briefly recall the facts: in June 1970, Jonathan Jackson, fully armed, entered the San Rafael courtroom. His goal was to take a judge hostage and exchange his freedom for that of several black prisoners. He succeeded, but the police machine-gunned the van with the judge inside, killing the judge, Jonathan Jackson, and two other blacks. The only one to make it through unharmed was Magee."

6. Nat Turner (1800–1831) led a violent slave rebellion in Southampton, Virginia, in 1831. Harriet Tubman (1820–1913) played a major role in a slave rebellion movement during the Civil War. She had organized a network of "conductors" (the Underground Railroad) to help blacks escape from the Southern plantations and to join up with the Union army. Frederick Douglass (1817–95), a former slave, became one of the greatest black orators and was the most well-known supporter of abolition and equal treatment under the Constitution.

Chapter 15: After the Assassination

Unpublished text, written at the end of August 1971, in Paris, as a follow-up to the previous article. It was originally written for a collection that never appeared. The text presented here is that of a typescript corrected by the author.

On August 21, 1971, George Jackson was killed in San Quentin Prison, in circumstances that to this day remain obscure. According to the official police version, which was contradicted by the subsequent investigation, George Jackson tried to take advantage of the disorder caused by a riot that had broken out in the high-security section of the prison by attempting to escape, revolver in hand. He was allegedly shot after threatening a guard.

The fact that an attempted escape would have been unlikely seems evident from the fact that Jackson's trial was to begin two days later, a trial for which he had actively prepared—and at the end of which, in fact, he was pronounced innocent of the crime committed on January 13, 1970, as were his two comrades.

Although previously unpublished, this text, written for a collection of essays on the Soledad Brothers and black political prisoners, provides an indispensable complement to Genet's writings on George Jackson. It can be regarded as a continuation of the preceding article, from which it should not be dissociated.

Source: Archives of Alexandre Bouglione.

ENDNOTES

1. "Recently" is a reference to the previous article, written before the death of George Jackson.

2. Ronald Reagan was the governor of California at the time of Jackson's death.

3. See the use of the same phrase (but in the reverse order) applied to the Palestinian fighters in "Four Hours in Shatila": "this beauty was new, or we could say novel, or naive."

4. Fay Stender was George Jackson's lawyer.

5. George Jackson corresponded for several years with Huey Newton, the cofounder of the Black Panther Party, which he joined in 1970.

Chapter 16: America Is Afraid

Article written in Paris at the end of August 1971 and published in *Le Nouvel Observateur*.

INTRODUCTORY NOTE

Published on August 30, 1971, in *Le Nouvel Observateur* (no. 355, p. 33)—nine days after George Jackson's death—this article expresses, more vividly and succinctly than the previous text, Genet's immediate reaction to this event.

While it is first of all an act of protest and an accusation, this text is also an homage addressed to George Jackson, the "compatriot"—a word rarely used by Genet—of those who have "read, loved, and admired his book."

It is worth noting also that this is the last article sent directly by Genet to the editors at *Le Nouvel Observateur*, and that it was also published in English in *The Black Panther* (vol. 7, no. 2) on September 4, 1971.

ENDNOTES

1. *Corvée de bois*, or "timber duty": a pretext used for taking prisoners outside the camp in order to eliminate them during a supposed escape attempt. (The expression was used during the Algerian War.) OAS was the acronym for the Organisation de l'armée secrète, an illegal military organization formed in 1961 to oppose de Gaulle's policy on Algeria by every means possible, including torture.

2. A state prison in California. ["It killed eight black students in Georgia": Genet is no doubt referring again to the two students killed in Jackson, Mississippi, in 1970. See "Interview with Michèle Manceaux," p. 42, and "Angela and Her Brothers," p. 56 and note 13.—Trans.]

Chapter 17: Preface to L'Assassinat de George Jackson

Preface to the booklet published on November 10, 1971, by the Groupe d'informations sur les prisons (GIP) (Gallimard).

INTRODUCTORY NOTE

With the exception of a brief interview published in December 1971 in the Spanish journal *Libre*, this is to my knowledge the last text by Genet on George Jackson and the Soledad Brothers. The fate of the black writer for whose book he had written a preface was thus, for a period of eighteen months, one of Genet's most constant preoccupations: without ever being able to meet Jackson (the United States systematically denied him a visa), Genet intervened on his behalf, in the press, on the radio, and in public demonstrations, at least fifteen times between July 1970 and December 1971.

Written during the month of September 1971—a reference in the text would seem to indicate the 22nd of that month—this preface is the only contribution Genet ever made to the GIP. (Another text addressing the general question of prisons remained unpublished.)

Created in January 1971 by Michel Foucault and Daniel Defert, the GIP published a booklet entitled *Intolérable* which gave accounts of various investigations into prison life. In the spring of 1971, the members of the group decided to devote one of their publications to prisoners in black American revolutionary movements, and they wanted to meet with Genet, who was in continual contact with the Black Panthers and had the most accurate information about them. Genet drew their attention to the case of George Jackson and attended several of their meetings as an invited guest.

Published on November 10, 1971, by Éditions Gallimard, the essential aim of the booklet was to show that George Jackson's death was neither an accident nor a police blunder but a "political assassination." Together with the preface, signed by its author, it included two interviews with Jackson and three texts written collectively, in the name of the GIP, by Catherine von Bülow—who introduced Genet to the group—Daniel Defert, and Michel Foucault.

It is worth pointing out that the preparation of this booklet was the occasion for Genet's encounter with Foucault, who was himself greatly preoccupied with the question of the prison. Both of them came to politics rather late in their careers, but with firm conviction; their paths frequently crossed during the period between 1970 and 1972, and they found themselves side by side at a number of demonstrations in support of immigrant workers. Later their relations would become infrequent to the point of nonexistent, primarily because of significant political differences, not the least of which was Genet's association with the Communist Party.

> Sources: Interviews with Catherine von Bülow and
> Daniel Defert. Archives of Gallimard.

ENDNOTES

1. On September 13, 1971, police stormed Attica Prison (in New York state) to put down an uprising of black prisoners who had taken their guards hostage. Thirty black prisoners and ten white guards were killed.

2. Genet is playing on the French term for sharpshooter, *tireur d'élite*, literally "elite shooter."—Trans.

3. All quotes are from *Soledad Brother: The Prison Letters of George Jackson* (New York: Bantam Books, 1970). Page numbers, which Genet did not include but which I have added, are given in square brackets.—Trans.

4. Genet's interpolation.—Trans.

5. American politicians and military men implicated in the Vietnam War or in the repression of black revolutionary movements.

6. The sentence in brackets is not in the text of Jackson's letter (as published in the 1970 edition). I have translated it from Genet's French.—Trans.

7. Beginning with this sentence, and ending with " . . . racism, nationalism, religions," Genet quotes a long passage from one of Jackson's letters in its entire-

ty, except for four sentences that I have indicated in the notes.—Trans.

8. The following sentence was omitted from Genet's quotation: "Think of how the people of the lower classes weigh themselves against the men who rule."—Trans.

9. The following was omitted from Genet's quotation: "Look how long Hershey ran Selective Service. Blacks embrace capitalism, the most unnatural and outstanding example of man against himself that history can offer."—Trans.

10. The following was omitted from Genet's quotation: "Fat Rat Daley has ordered all looters shot."—Trans.

11. This sentence is not in Jackson's published letter.—Trans.

12. The editors of the original booklet added the following note identifying Bill Cosby:

> Black actor and comedian who played a secret agent working with another white agent in a television series. It is usually the white who wins the day, and it is always the white who wins the heart of the white woman at the end of the episode. [The following sentence was omitted from Genet's quotation: "*I Spy* was certainly programmed to a child's mentality."—Trans.]

13. Collaborator or traitor; the word comes from the name of Major Vidkun Quisling (1887–1945), a Norwegian army officer and diplomat who collaborated with the German occupying force in Norway.—Trans.

14. George Jackson's book ends by quoting these words of his brother.—Trans.

15. An indirect reference to the work by François Jacob, *La Logique du vivant*, published in January 1971 by the Éditions Gallimard (English trans.: *The Logic of Life*, trans. Betty E. Spillman [Princeton, N.J.: Princeton University Press, 1993]).

16. George Jackson was working on a second book when he was killed. It was never completed. It was published in 1972 by Random House under the title *Blood in My Eye*.

Chapter 18: Meeting the Guarani

Article published June 2, 1972, in *Le Démocrate vernonnais*, on the occasion of a performance in Vernon by the musical group the Guarani.

INTRODUCTORY NOTE

This text, which comments on a song-and-dance performance by the South American group the Guarani, arose from circumstances that remain unknown. It was published on June 2, 1972, under the heading "performance," in a local newspaper, *Le Démocrate vernonnais*, announcing an appearance of the musical troupe on June 7 in Vernon, a small town in the Eure department of France.

If the article's venue is unusual, its theme is perhaps less so: there are several references in Genet's work to the Indians of the Andes (for example, in "Four Hours in Shatila"). In any case, it testifies to the fact that, in the midst of a period of intense political activity, Genet did not set up any absolute divisions between his different areas of reflection. This text has an obvious place among the author's writings on the theater and, more specifically, on Eastern and Far Eastern forms of representation. (See "Lettre à Jean-Jacques Pauvert," in *Fragments et autres textes* [Paris: Éditions Gallimard 1990].)

Sources: Archives of Gallimard, *Le Démocrate vernonnais.*

ENDNOTES

1. The Guarani (or Toupi) are an indigenous people of South America (Brazil, Paraguay, Argentina) who live primarily from hunting and fishing. Colonized but protected in the seventeenth and eighteenth centuries by the Jesuits of Paraguay, their culture saw a remarkable but brief development. They were decimated after the Spanish conquest by a series of dictatorships and bloody wars.

2. The official language of Paraguay, where the Guarani Indians live today, is Spanish, but their own language remains very much in use.

Chapter 19: On Two or Three Books No One Has Ever Talked About

Text read by the author on May 2, 1974, for a radio program on *France-Culture.* The present text is based on the typescript and includes the appendix published the next day in *L'Humanité.*

INTRODUCTORY NOTE

After a long absence, partly for visits to the Middle East, Genet returned in force to the French political scene in May 1974. The next four texts, written during the same month, form a whole and are all linked to the presidential campaign under way in France at the time. Three of them were written at the suggestion of certain leaders in the Socialist Party to whom Genet had offered his support (see the next introductory note). The first of these texts is the only one not written in response to an external request but rather on Genet's own initiative.

The question of the presidential elections is not addressed directly: significantly, it is introduced by way of a text whose dominant theme relates to the conditions faced by immigrants in France; this theme runs quietly throughout the four articles and the last one ends with a reference to it.

As its title indicates, the present text is concerned with "two or three books" written by North African authors (with the exception of Jean Pélégri, a French writer born in Algeria). In different ways and with different approaches, their books all deal with the problems of immigration.

In April 1974, after meeting with Tahar Ben Jelloun, Genet was irritated with what he saw as the concerted silence of "a certain press," and of French intellectuals in general, with respect to these books, and he decided to give them his personal support. Through the intermediary of friends who knew of his desire to make a public intervention, he was invited to participate, on May 2, 1974, in the program *Réflexion faite*, broadcast by France-Culture, during which he read the text presented here.

Along with the charge directed against intellectuals guilty of silence, it is remarkable to note that Sartre is taken to task here for the first time, by name and with particular virulence. The polemic can no doubt be explained by certain political differences, especially in terms of the Israeli-Palestinian question (though this is still somewhat veiled here). But this polemic is so insistent (Sartre is mentioned no less than four times) as to make one wonder whether something more complicated not is being played out. Without entering into this debate, we can at least point out that, in a curious paradox, Genet's political adventure, which likely would not have taken the same trajectory without Sartre's example, will have ended up being undertaken against him.

Although it appears at first to be a literary commentary—all the books mentioned, aside from the autobiographical document by Ahmed, are novels—the text moves quickly into political issues. The editors at *L'Humanité* saw this very clearly: the day after the broadcast they published excerpts from Genet's text, together with an appendix written specifically for the newspaper, under the title "Jean Genet et la condition des émigrés" (May 3, 1974, p. 12).

This first collaboration with the newspaper *L'Humanité*, which will long remain Genet's preferred venue, marks a turning point in the writer's itinerary. Aside from the interlude of May '68, up to this point Genet's political interventions—in public at least—had dealt with social problems outside France (the Black Panthers, black American prisoners) or with international conflicts (Vietnam, Palestine). Beginning in 1974, a new phase begins to take shape, inaugurated by these four texts, in which we see Genet moving more and more toward the Communist Party and, as a consequence, inscribing himself within more identifiable political boundaries.

But it will be noticed that this participation in more narrowly French debates remains exceptional; and even though Genet was never more directly involved with the internal affairs of France than here, an attentive reading of these texts reveals that his preoccupations went well beyond the French context: what Genet sets in opposition to the representative of the parties of the Right is less the socialist candidate than "the misery of the immigrant workers," of the "formerly colonized," of the "Arabs," of "blacks," and of the entire "Third World."

> Sources: Interview with Tahar Ben Jelloun. Archives of
> Paule Thévenin.

ENDNOTES

1. The authors and books cited in this text are the following:

Tahar Ben Jelloun (born 1944 in Morocco), author of *Harrounda* (Paris: Denoël, Les Lettres nouvelles series, 1973)

Ahmed, *Une Vie d'Algérien: Est-ce que ça fait un livre que les gens vont lire?* [Life of an Algerian: Will people read a book about this?] (Paris: Le Seuil, 1973)

Nabile Farès (born 1941 in Morocco), *Le Champ des oliviers* [The olive grove] (Paris: Le Seuil, 1972)

Mohammed Khaïr-Eddine (born 1941 in Morocco) is mentioned only in passing. His most recent work to appear at the time was *Le Déterreur* [The exhumer] (Paris: Le Seuil, 1973)

Jean Pélégri (born 1920 in Algeria), *Le Cheval dans la ville* [The city horse] (Paris: Éditions Gallimard, 1972)

2. *Une Vie d'Algérien*, the autobiography of an immigrant worker, was written under the pseudonym Ahmed by an author whose identity was not revealed.

3. Fanon's essay *Les Damnés de la terre* was published by the Éditions Maspero in 1961, with a preface by Sartre that became as famous as it was controversial. [English translation: *The Wretched of the Earth*, trans. Constance Farrington (New York: Grove Press, 1966).—Trans.]

4. "Dirty hands": *Les Mains sales* is the title of Sartre's well-known play.—Trans.

5. "Disbanded" preserves the repetition of the vocable but not the joke: *débandé* also means having lost an erection.—Trans.

6. This appendix was introduced in *L'Humanité* with these few lines by Genet: "The text written for the radio, and read on the air, ends here; the regulations of the ORTF [Office de radiodiffusion-télévision française, the former French broadcasting service] prohibited me from speaking of the electoral campaign. Here is the continuation written for *L'Humanité*."

7. The Common Program was a program agreed upon by the Socialist and Communist Parties in 1972; its purpose was to bridge the gap between the two and to create unity among the parties of the Left.

8. Charles Maurras (1868–1952), a monarchist, pro-Catholic atheist and anti-Semite, founded the extreme right-wing group Action Française and edited the influential newspaper published under the same name.

9. Occident and Ordre nouveau were extreme right-wing groups that dissolved in 1968 and 1973.

10. "One of the most generous of all French intellectuals" is Sartre, who had called for a boycott of the elections.

Chapter 20: When "the Worst Is Always Certain"

Unpublished article, written around May 7, 1974, between the first and second rounds of the presidential election and, like the previous and the two subsequent articles, intended for publication in *L'Humanité*. The text is based on the typescript.

INTRODUCTORY NOTE

When the results of the first round of the presidential elections were announced on May 5, Genet decided to do all he could to support the candidate of the Leftist Coalition, François Mitterrand. Mitterrand had received 44 percent of the vote, and for the first time in many years, victory seemed possible for the Left. Genet went to the Socialist Party's offices in the Montparnasse Tower and, finding Régis Debray, Roland Dumas, and Michel Rocard, asked them what he could do to help. He was willing to work in the offices or carry out any other useful tasks. Slightly taken aback, the campaign managers suggested rather that he write articles in the press in favor of their candidate.

In all likelihood, the text presented here was written just after the first round of the elections—around May 6 or 7—and after the meeting just mentioned. For reasons that remain unknown, it was not published. Written for *L'Humanité*, it seems never to have reached the editors of the newspaper, where no trace or even recollection of it is to be found. It might have been withdrawn by Genet at the last minute, arrived after the deadline, or quite simply been misplaced.

Typewritten and, like the other texts of this period, preserved by Paule Thévenin, the text appears in a finished form and seems to have been carefully reread. Although unpublished, it cannot be separated from the group of writings presented here, to which it is obviously related.

Moreover, this text is of great interest in terms of Genet's political stance, which it explicates with great clarity. It is perhaps even the most specifically political of the author's writings in that it is addressed, with remarkable precision, to those who are most susceptible to being moved by its arguments: the voters of the far Left.

Addressing himself not to his political adversaries but—an extremely rare occurrence—to those who were apparently on the same side as himself, Genet was trying to rally support for the Socialist candidate from voters who were tempted to abstain. In doing so, he emphasized what separated him from the dominant positions of the far Left—including some which he himself at times defended.

While the present arguments are at times contradicted by other arguments made in other circumstances, the critique formulated here of anarchism, American radicalism, abstentionism, and, more generally, political extremism, is well worth bearing in mind.

> Sources: Interviews with Paule Thévenin and René
> Andrieu. Archives of Paule Thévenin.

ENDNOTES

1. Reference to the subtitle of *The Satin Slipper*, by Paul Claudel: *The Worst Is Not Always Certain.*

2. See Genet's "coverage" of the Democratic Convention in Chicago, "The Members of the Assembly," Appendix 1 in this book.

3. Genet met Allen Ginsberg several times in the United States and in France.

4. Beginning in 1973, the Black Panther movement changed its orientation and moved in a more constitutional direction, making efforts, for example, to supervise municipal elections in black neighborhoods. The Young Lords were a group of young Puerto Rican revolutionaries formed in the late 1950s. Around 1972 it began to lose momentum. The Weathermen were an extreme Left underground group made up of university students. Very active in 1970 and 1971, its members carried out a number of bombings that targeted banks, police stations, military bases . . . They took their name from a Bob Dylan song.

5. The term of office for the French president is seven years, but presidents are very often reelected for a second term.—Trans.

6. The vote for the far Left in the first round had been weak: Alain Krivine received 0.3 percent while Arlette Laguiller, in a surprise result, received 2.3 percent of the votes.

7. Arlette Laguiller, spokesperson for Lutte ouvrière (Workers' Struggle) (see the preceding note).

8. The "anti-riot law," voted in on April 30, 1970, was meant to discourage political demonstrations by assigning responsibility for any damage done during the demonstration to its organizers, who would thus be considered lawbreakers.

9. Political figures of various right-wing tendencies.

10. Jacques Chaban-Delmas had just been defeated in the first round of the elections, in which he ran against Valéry Giscard d'Estaing.

11. The primary target of this remark is Jean-Paul Sartre.

Chapter 21: Dying Under Giscard d'Estaing

Article written May 11, 1974, in Paris, the day following the televised debate between presidential candidates Giscard d'Estaing and Mitterrand; published in *L'Humanité*.

INTRODUCTORY NOTE

A crucial moment in the electoral campaign of 1974, the debate discussed by Genet in this article was broadcast live on the evening of May 10. It took place between the two rounds of the presidential elections and brought face to face the two remaining candidates, Valéry Giscard d'Estaing and François Mitterrand.

The latter had presented himself from the start, on the basis of a "common program," as the one candidate able to represent the two large groups of the Left: the Socialist Party, of which he was the secretary general, and the Communist Party, to whom a great deal of participation in the new government had been promised if he were to win.

On the Right the divisions had been more evident, and two candidates had squared off during the first round: Jacques Chaban-Delmas, prime minister, supported by the Gaullist Party, and Valéry Giscard d'Estaing, minister of Economy and Finances and director of the Independent Republican Party, whose nonconformist style, verbal ease, and relative youthfulness (he was forty-eight years old in 1974) would exert a decisive attraction on a wide range of voters. In fact, he had beaten his rival on May 5 by a very wide margin (33 percent to 15 percent), even though the latter was the favorite and was politically more powerful.

Despite his sudden rise in popularity with the public, Giscard d'Estaing's victory was far from certain, and the race between him and Mitterrand, whose chances seemed good, proved to be very close.

This was the context in which the televised debate between the two candidates took place. Genet watched the debate in the lounge of his small hotel near the Gare de Lyon. He took notes, bought all the papers the next day, and wrote the article the same day. After being typed and then handed over to René Andrieu, editor-in-chief of *L'Humanité*, it was published on May 13 exactly as Genet had given it to him (including the section titles).

It will be noticed that the Socialist candidate is almost completely absent from Genet's commentary, while the claims and the "vocabulary" of Giscard d'Estaing are closely scrutinized. This is no doubt because the political purpose of this article is not so much to discuss the program or the arguments of the candidate of the Right as to discredit the most powerful aspect of his attraction: his image.

Sources: Interviews with Paule Thévenin and René
Andrieu. Archives of Paule Thévenin.

ENDNOTES

1. See the introductory note for the circumstances of the televised debate.

2. Genet gives here a brief recapitulation of Kennedy's political "failures": the deployment of forces for a possible attack on Castro's Cuba in the Bay of Pigs (April 20, 1961); the engagement in the Vietnam War (1961); the assassination of the president of South Vietnam, Ngô Dinh Diêm, during the U.S.-supported coup (November 2, 1963); the "new frontier" project touted at the beginning of his presidency, and promising important political and social advancements as well as space exploration; and so on.

3. When Genet wrote this article, the Watergate scandal was at its height: Nixon, implicated in the affair, would soon resign (August 8, 1974).

4. That is, the day after the election results would be decided.

5. Giscard d'Estaing had said to Mitterrand, "You don't have a monopoly of the heart." This quote, like the others in the article, was taken from the televised debate.

6. See "America Is Afraid," note 1.

7. Pierre Pellissier (head of the editorial staff of *Le Figaro*) had edited the report on the debate published in *Le Figaro* on May 11, 1974, appearing under the title "Giscard d'Estaing et Mitterrand face à face: Deux conceptions" [Giscard d'Estaing and Mitterrand face to face: Two approaches]. The article had indeed replaced the word "tool" with "instrument."

8. In French the phrase reads, "Je compte tenir compte . . . ," and thus repeats the word exactly.—Trans.

9. Élysée Palace: the principle residence of the French president.—Trans.

10. Dassault: a major French aviation company.—Trans.

11. Despite Giscard d'Estaing's victory in 1974, it was nevertheless "under Mitterrand," elected president in 1981, that Genet died, in April 1986.

Chapter 22: And Why Not a Fool in Suspenders?

Article published May 25, 1974, in *L'Humanité*, after Giscard d'Estaing's victory in the presidential elections.

INTRODUCTORY NOTE

This text, the last article in the series, differs from the preceding three on one important point: it was written *after* the election results, and Valéry Giscard d'Estaing's victory (with 50.81 percent of the votes), had been announced on May 19, 1974.

Published May 25 in *L'Humanité*, six days after the defeat of the Left, the article seems superfluous. Lacking any precise political goal, it testifies to Genet's interest in the theatrical aspects of the electoral campaign, after quite clearly getting caught up in it himself; for an entire month he had been an avid spectator, and, as an expert dramaturge, he analyses it according to the laws of the spectacle.

The importance of this text, which is rather a free commentary than a political intervention, thus goes well beyond the circumstances in which it took shape, and can be placed within the context of a reflection (begun long before) on the fables of history, the tricks of representation, and the relations between theater and power, order and revolution—a reflection that is developed, at once differently and in the same sense, in *The Balcony* and *Prisoner of Love*.

We might add that in Valéry Giscard d'Estaing, the incontestable protagonist of these writings, it seems that Genet found not merely a political opponent, but an intimate and privileged adversary, a figure that was the precise obverse of his own: the well-turned product of a class, a lineage, a family, and a fortune, the perfect prototype of "Western man" as he imagined him.

ENDNOTES

1. During his campaign, Valéry Giscard d'Estaing had visited Montceau-les-Mines, near Le Creusot, in the fief of the Baron Schneider, his wife's great-grand-father. On May 12, 1974, he gave an important speech there, attended largely by factory workers, addressing social issues (he promised to raise the minimum wage and to allocate more money to social programs). [*The Extinction of Pauperism*, an economic work published in 1846 by Louis Napoleon Bonaparte (Napoleon III), emperor of France from 1852 to 1870.—Trans.]

2. A lineage attributed by public rumor to Giscard d'Estaing's wife; it has not been verified. Jules Guesde (1845–1922), an important figure in the history of French socialism, was the founder, with Paul Lafargue, of the first worker's party and of the first Marxist newspaper, *L'Égalité*.

3. Through his mother's side—the Bardoux—Giscard d'Estaing would indeed be a direct descendant of Louis XV, but through a bastard filiation.

4. Augustin, the younger brother of Maximilien.—Trans.

5. The three-day July revolution of 1830.—Trans.

6. "Le Bien-Aimé," or "the Beloved," is the nickname of Louis XV.

7. The first piece of legislation signed by President Giscard d'Estaing upon entering office.

8. On May 27, 1974, Giscard d'Estaing led a procession, on foot, up the Champs-Élysées (toward the Place de l'Étoile and the Arc de Triomphe) to celebrate the formation of the new government.

9. Alexandre Sanguinetti, politician of the Gaullist party, campaigned in support of Giscard d'Estaing during the election.

10. During the previous year, Giscard d'Estaing had appeared on television several times in shirt sleeves or in a sweater; this was a "first" in France for a cabinet member still in office.

11. Michel Poniatowski, independent republican representative and Giscard d'Estaing's "right-hand man." After the election of 1974 he became minister of the interior, a central position in the government.

12. The Roman emperor Heliogabalus (218–22) was the subject of one of Genet's very first plays, probably written in 1943; the manuscript has not yet been found. (See Albert Dichy and Pascal Fouché, *Jean Genet: Essai de chronologie, 1910–1944* [Paris: Bibliothèque de Littérature Française, 1988], pp. 201, 207).

Chapter 23: The Women of Jebel Hussein

Article published July 1, 1974, in *Le Monde diplomatique.*

INTRODUCTORY NOTE

"The Women of Jebel Hussein" possesses all the virtues of what in painting is called a sketch. With extreme concision and with a force proper to such concision, this text evokes the memory of two encounters in the Palestinian camps of Jordan which marked Genet so deeply that nearly all of his writing on the Palestinians bears their traces. The implications of these memories will be fully elaborated in *Prisoner of Love.*

This text is made up of two brief stories: the first, given the place of honor since it provides the article with its name, reports a conversation with four Palestinian women in the camp of Jebel Hussein in Amman. Included also in "Four Hours in Shatila" and developed in *Prisoner of Love* (pp. 282–86), this little scene very likely took place at the end of 1970, shortly after the events of Black September and the Jordanian army's attack on the Palestinian camps.

The second story (beginning with the phrase, "One day I said to a Palestinian woman . . . ") relates the encounter with Hamza and his mother, an episode we might be tempted to call the central sequence of *Prisoner of Love*, if the structure of the book did not dissolve the very idea of a center. This memory, which will haunt Genet for fifteen years, is most vividly evoked on pages 161–64. While the location of the event is clearly situated in the texts—in the camp at Irbid in northern Jordan—its date remains uncertain: Genet points both to the year 1970 (pp. 70 and 172) and to the month of October 1971 (p. 156). The military situation described in the narrative, however, would indicate that the episode took place a little before the end of Genet's visit to the Middle East, toward the middle of March. (The camp at Irbid was taken over by the Jordanian forces on March 26, 1971.)

Dedicated to the female figures who have such an important place in Genet's writing on the Palestinians, this homage not only expresses personal sentiments, it also attests to a social phenomenon which historians have pointed out as well.

Speaking of "the revolution in the camps," Xavier Baron thus notes that "Palestinian women played an essential role. They raised their children with memories of Palestine while the men left to find work in the Gulf or went off to fight. They also participated in the Palestinian movement by joining the militias and engaging in political activities. This allowed them to break free from the traditional environment in which they were often confined to domestic work." (See *Les Palestiniens* [Paris: Éditions Le Sycomore, 1984], p. 318.)

Finally, it is worth pointing out that this text was published together with an important article by Tahar Ben Jelloun, entitled "Jean Genet avec les Palestiniens" in *Le Monde diplomatique* in July 1974 [reprinted in *Genet à Chatila*, ed. Jérôme Hankins (Arles: Éditions Solin, 1972), pp. 75–83]. This article cited a number of statements by Genet, concerning, for example, his attachment to the Palestinian people ("It was completely natural for me to go not only toward the most disadvantaged, but toward those who crystallized to the highest degree the hatred of the West"); his discovery of the Arab world ("All the news I read about the Palestinians came from the Western press. For a long time the Arab world was presented as the shadow cast by the Christian world; but from the moment I arrived in Jordan I saw that the Palestinians did not resemble the image that had been presented in France. I suddenly found myself in the position of a blind man who has just regained his sight. The Arab world that became familiar to me when I arrived appeared much closer than what was written"); on his mistrust of the thought espoused by the Left ("To the extent that it perpetuates a Judeo-Christian type of reasoning and morality, I don't feel capable of identifying with it; it's more idealistic than political, more enervated than reasonable. As for Sartre, I realized a long time ago that his political thought is a pseudothought. If you ask me, what has been called Sartrian thought doesn't really exist. His political stances are only the hasty judgments of an intellectual who is too frightened to confront anything but his own phantoms"); on the power of the fedayee's image ("Even if its effectiveness may not be immediate, it remains an active revolutionary force"); on the persistence of European anti-Semitism, which has been "enriched" by a new racism directed against the Arabs; and so on.

Although, according to Tahar Ben Jelloun, it was totally inspired by Genet and was largely dictated by him, we cannot include this article here since many of its statements are cited only indirectly; it therefore does not belong to the conventional genre of the interview. A consultation of the article is nonetheless highly recommended.

Source: Interview with Tahar Ben Jelloun.

ENDNOTES

1. Jebel Hussein, Palestinian camp located on a hill in Amman. It was almost completely destroyed during the attack by King Hussein's soldiers, who scorched it with napalm.

2. Although Jordan was fighting together with other Arab countries in the war against Israel, King Hussein had ordered an assault against the Palestinian forces on his territory.

3. The expression "refugee camp," widely used for many years, would gradually disappear from the Palestinians' vocabulary (see Baron, *Les Palestiniens*, p. 319) after 1967.

4. Fatah (a word constructed by reversing the Arabic initials of the Palestine Liberation Movement): the name of the most independent and the most active of the Palestinian military organizations. Clandestine until April 1968, the Fatah is led by Yasser Arafat.

Al-Saika: Palestinian military organization with Syrian allegiances, formed in 1967.

5. The initial "H." designates here the figure who, under the name of Hamza, will become one of the most important to appear in *Prisoner of Love*. We may point out, however, that, according to information we have gathered, the name of the person who served as a "model" for this figure was not Hamza but another name beginning with the same letter.

During the month of Ramadan, practicing Muslims are required to fast between sunrise and sundown; this is why H.'s mother does not share the meal.

Chapter 24: Interview with Hubert Fichte

Interview conducted December 19, 20 and 21, 1975, in Paris for the German newspaper *Die Zeit*. The present text is based on the typed transcript corrected by the author and published in facsimile by the Éditions Qumran.

INTRODUCTORY NOTE

In 1975, the political activity that had dominated Genet's life since around May 1968 began to subside. Forbidden to enter Jordan, he also saw the dissolution of the Black Panther movement in the United States and the slow settling of the great wave of protest that had risen in France a decade earlier. Genet set to work, attempting to give form to the mass of notes, stories and memories he had written down, during his travels of the previous five years, on loose sheets of paper, hotel stationery or in the children's school notebooks he often used. A "great revolutionary and romantic song" was announced in the press (*Playboy*, French edition, no. 24, November 1975, p. 14).

However, in September, after looking over his first attempts to put the text in order, Genet was discouraged by what he saw and became convinced that he had not yet found the form or the key to the work he envisioned; he suspended work on the project for the time being and renounced all publication.

Cut off from his literary project, disengaged from the grip of political activity, Genet found himself doubly idle. It was just then that Hubert Fichte, a German novelist and journalist who wanted to conduct a long interview with him for the German newspaper *Die Zeit,* managed to make contact with Genet after five months of fruitless efforts. Thanks to the friendships he had established at the Éditions Gallimard, where his latest novel, *Puberty,* was due to appear, Hubert Fichte arranged an interview with Genet for the purpose of proposing and explaining his project. The first meeting took place on December 18, 1975, in the office of Laurent Boyer, Genet's contact at Gallimard. Despite his reluctance, the writer was quickly convinced by Fichte's arguments and perhaps even more by his enthusiasm; in accepting, he also indicated to Fichte the general topics he wanted to discuss.

The interview took place over the course of three meetings, on December 19, 20 and 21, in Hubert Fichte's room at the Hôtel Scandinavia, at 21, rue de Tournon. Several photographs of Genet were taken by Leonore Mau, who accompanied Fichte; these were used to illustrate the various publications of this text (and in particular the first full edition published by Qumran.).

Genet found in Fichte a true interlocutor, and whether it was because of Fichte's personality (the forty year old Hubert Fichte was both an established novelist and a noted anthropologist specializing in religions of African origin found in the Americas), his own momentary availability, or the distance that now separated him from his recent political experiences, rarely did Genet ever express himself so freely as he does here. Nowhere else—with the exception of *Prisoner of Love*—does Genet display the variety of his interests and the breadth of his knowledge, in fields as varied as architecture, music, anthropology and history. Genet pauses here to take his bearings; he evokes his childhood; he addresses the problem of homosexuality, as well as the complex relation between eroticism and politics.

After the interview was recorded, Hubert Fichte took the tapes back to Hamburg. On January 23, 1976, he sent the typed French transcript, together with a German translation, to Laurent Boyer, who sent them on to Genet. Genet carefully reread the text and made some minor changes: he added a few relatively brief interpolations and eliminated parts of certain sentences, but mostly he corrected linguistic errors and awkward expressions, while also preserving the oral quality of the text.

On February 13, 1976, excerpts from the interview appeared in the German daily *Die Zeit* (no. 8, pp. 35–7) under the title "Ich erlaube mir die Revolte" ("I allow myself to revolt"). A subtitle was added: "A Scandalous Poet—Interview with Jean Genet." Some biographical information was included with the article stating that while Genet is "probably one of the greatest poets of the century," he is "certainly the most scandalous."

The interview attracted a great deal of attention and was soon published a number of times, often on Fichte's own initiative, both in large newspapers and in homosexual magazines (Richard Webb, in *Jean Genet and his Critics*, mentions the publication of excerpts that same year in Hamburg in *Him* and *Applaus*.)

Excerpts from the interview were soon translated and published outside Germany: in London in April 1977, in issue 37 of *New Review*, in the United States in 1978, in issue 35 of *Gay Sunshine*, in Spain in February 1982, in *Chimera*, and elsewhere.

Genet had authorized Fichte to use the interview as he wished, under two conditions: the text was to be published neither in French nor as a separate volume. However, in the first months of 1981 a work consisting of a facsimile of the typescript in both languages, including Genet's corrections (for the French) and those of Fichte (for the German translation), appeared in Frankfurt, put out by the Éditions Qumran (in the "Portrait" series). It bore no other title than the names of the authors: Fichte, Genet.

Infuriated by the publication, Genet nevertheless decided not to take any legal action against the small publishing house.

A few months later, the entire interview was published for the first time in France by Jean-Pierre Dauphin and Pascal Fouché in *Magazine littéraire* (no. 174, June 1981), and was reprinted several times. It was also published as a separate volume in Italy in March 1987 (Ubulibri, Milan).

> Sources: Interviews with Laurent Boyer and Friedrich
> Fleming. Archives of Gallimard, Qumran.

ENDNOTES

1. A first meeting between Hubert Fichte and Genet had taken place the day before, on December 18, at the Éditions Gallimard. Although their conversation was not recorded, Genet refers back to it several times throughout the interview.

2. A number of unions and parties of the left organized a coordinated demonstration on December 18 to protest "the antisocial and repressive politics of power." The same day there was also a march by the "Comité national pour la libération des soldats et militaires emprisonnés" (National committee for the liberation of imprisoned soldiers and servicemen), supported by all the organizations of the far left. (See *Le Monde*, December 19, 1975, p. 1.) [The acronyms mentioned by Genet designate the three major French unions: CGT, Confédération générale du travail (General confederation of labor); CFDT, Con-

fédération française démocratique du travail (French democratic confederation of labor); CGC, Confédération générale des cadres (General confederation of management).—Trans.]

3. See "Interview with Michèle Manceaux," note 5.

4. The principal architect of Versailles was in fact the nephew of François Mansart, Hardouin-Mansart (1646–1708), who took over the construction in 1678 and finished it in 1695.

5. Oscar Niemeyer, born in Rio de Janeiro in 1907, a disciple of Le Corbusier, was, with Lucio Costa, the main architect of Brasilia, built between 1957 and 1960. Already during its first year, the new city was surrounded by a vast shanty town, the "Bandeirante"; inhabited by the families of workers engaged in the construction of the city, it grew as the city itself grew.

6. The Dominican chapel at Vence (called the Chapel of the Rosary) was completed in 1951. It is considered one of Matisse's most successful works and was constructed entirely under his supervision, from the architectural design to the making of the furniture and the conception of the liturgical vestments.

7. Genet is referring to his visit to Japan in November 1969.

8. *Iliad*, 3.525; Richmond Lattimore translation (University of Chicago Press, 1951).—Trans.

9. A painting by Goya (1792).

10. It was shortly after this reading that Genet wrote the text "The Brothers Karamazov" (see p. 182 {or refer to as chapter: see chapter 30 of this volume}).

11. On July 31, 1962, the Hamburg court rejected a demand presented by the public prosecutor's office to seize and ban the German translation of *Our Lady of the Flowers* for "obscenity and outrage to public morals." This decision led to a revision of the censorship laws and is a landmark in the history of erotic and homosexual literature in Germany. (See Helmut Boysen, "Genet acquitté," in *L'Express*, no. 586, September 6, 1962, p. 21.)

12. The northeastern border of France shared with Belgium, Luxembourg and Germany.—Trans.

13. He had been summoned by the Immigration and Naturalization Services to justify his entry into the United States without a visa.

14. See "May Day Speech," note 2.

15. "The Head of Hair," poem XXIII of *The Flowers of Evil.*

16. Genet is referring to the two *Discours concernant le jugement de Louis XVI* (Discourses Concerning the Judgment of Louis XVI), delivered to the National Convention, the first on November 13, 1790, the second on December 27, 1793.

17. This is a general interpretation of the second discourse of Saint-Just, not a citation.

18. Louis Aragon, "Avez-vous giflé un mort?" ("Did You Slap a Dead Man?"), in *Un Cadavre* (A Corpse), a tract from 1924, p. 4.

19. Sartre traveled to the Soviet Union in 1954.

20. "Fatherland or death."

21. This is the first line of the sonnet "The Tomb of Edgar Poe."

22. Genet went to the Odéon with Roger Blin on May 15, 1968, the day of the "taking" of the theater. See also "Interview with Nigel Williams," p. 263.

23. See "And Why Not a Fool in Suspenders," note 8.

24. After examining the F.B.I. archives, Edmund White was able to state without any doubt that Genet's presence among the Black Panthers had been noted from the day of his arrival in the United States.

25. George Wallace, a right-wing politician, ran several times for president of the United States.

26. Salvador Allende, elected president of Chile in 1970, installed a socialist government before being killed in September 1973 during the military takeover led by General Pinochet.

27. I.T.T.: International Telephone and Telegraph, an American company set up in Chile and implicated in the putsch.

28. In September 1971, Buffet and Bontemps, who were being held at the Clairveaux prison, took a police sergeant and a nurse hostage, then later cut their throats. Despite a campaign against the death penalty led by a number of intellectuals, they were executed on November 28, 1972.

29. See *The Thief's Journal* for a similar story.

30. On this question, see the reflection developed in the text "The Red and the Black."

31. This is probably a veiled reference to the suicide of Abdallah (see the preface), for which Genet may have felt at least partially responsible. [Abdallah Bentaga, a young Algerian acrobat, was Genet's companion for a number of years in the late 50s and early 60s. Genet personally trained him to be a high-wire artist and wrote for him the short text entitled "Le Funambule" ("The Tightrope Walker"). Apparently distraught at being replaced in Genet's affections by another young companion, Abdallah committed suicide in March 1964.—Trans.]

32. The Panathenaea was an important Athenian festival, in honor of Athena.

33. *Funeral Rites* and *Querelle* were also written after Genet left prison for the last time.

34. Genet's *Oeuvres complètes*, in fact, began to appear in 1951.

35. In the margin of the transcript, Fichte wrote the word "sait" (know) above "suis" (am), which renders the sentence more coherent. [I have incorporated this change into the text. The original typed version gives: "We'd have to talk about what I am not."—Trans.]

36. Potlatch (an ethnological term referring to practices of Indians of the Pacific Northwest): a ceremony involving the ostentatious destruction of goods.

37. A reference to the main character of Genet's novel *Querelle*.

38. Pasolini had recently been murdered, on November 1, 1976, in a suburb of Rome by a seventeen-year-old apprentice baker.

39. See a first version of this story in the "Interview with Madeleine Gobeil," and in note 14 of that text.

40. It is highly unlikely that up to 1939 Genet had read nothing but pulp novels: one need only consult his letters from 1937 to Anne Bloch, his "German friend" in Czechoslovakia (published in Hamburg by Merlin Verlag under the title *Chère Madame*.) Behind this coy gesture of the autodidact there is no doubt something deeper: a refusal to be allied with the official culture.

41. Genet was placed in the Mettray Penal Colony from September 1926 to March 1929.

42. A drug for sleep that Genet took almost every day beginning in the mid-1950s.

43. Bernard Huguenin, financial director of the Éditions Gallimard.

44. Genet had a long stopover in Karachi in early 1968 while on his first trip to Japan.

45. Mohammed El Katrani, whom Genet met in September 1974 in Tangier, remained close to Genet until his death. (A note in the unpublished film script, *La Nuit venue* [Nightfall], written in 1976 and 1977, mentions that the script was based "on an original idea of M. El Katrani.")

46. Rosa Luxemburg, Marxist thinker and revolutionary who was arrested and executed during "Red Week" in Berlin on January 15, 1919.

47. Lindbergh landed in Paris on May 21, 1927.

48. In order to leave the Mettray colony, Genet enlisted in the army and volunteered to serve with the troops in the eastern Mediterranean. Placed with a company of sappers and miners, he was stationed in Damascus from February to December 1930; at the time he was nineteen years old.

49. This is the one time that Genet, thanks to a curious slip (not corrected when he reread the text), pronounces the name of General Goudot, for whom he had worked as a secretary for three months in Morocco, in the summer of 1931.

General Gouraud, frequently mentioned by Genet though he never served under him, was High Commissioner in Syria from 1919 to 1923 and remained a legendary figure in the region for a long time after. It was under the command of General Gamelin that Damascus was bombed at the end of 1925 during the insurrection of the Jebel Druses, four years or so before Genet went there. (See Albert Dichy and Pascal Fouché, *Jean Genet, essai de chronologie* [Bibliothèque de Littérature Française, 1988], pp. 131–141.)

50. After taking power, Castro took very repressive measures against homosexuality.

51. In July 1970, Huey Newton, co-founder of the Black Panther Party, published an important article in *The Black Panther* on questions concerning homosexuality and feminism as these relate to revolution. This article may have been inspired by the letter from Genet to Bobby Seale mentioned here.

52. Cocteau testified on Genet's behalf, on July 19, 1943, at a trial in which Genet was in danger of receiving a life sentence; this testimony was decisive. In it Cocteau claimed that Genet was "the greatest writer of the age." (See Albert Dichy and Pascal Fouché, *Jean Genet, essai de chronologie*, pp. 211–17.)

53. Satiric French poet of the thirteenth century known for his biting social commentary.—Trans.

54. Genet was working on sketches of what would become *Prisoner of Love*. At the time the title of the work—a title that had obsessed Genet since the 1950s but that he ended up never using—was "Death." (On the form this work was to take, see Massin, *Continuo*, B.L.F.C./I.M.E.C., 1988, pp. 27–8).

Chapter 25: Near Ajloun

Notes taken between October 1970 and April 1971, during Jean Genet's visit to the Palestinian bases at Ajloun, Jordan, and contributed in 1977, with a new appendix, to a collection of writings in memory of Wael Zuaiter, a leading member of the PLO, assassinated in Rome. The text presented here is based on the typescript corrected by the author.

INTRODUCTORY NOTE

Passing through Rome in April 1972, Genet visited Alberto Moravia and was introduced to Wael Zuaiter, a representative of the PLO in Italy, a very open and learned man with whom Genet quickly became friends. He saw him again during a second visit to Rome at the beginning of September and was planning to take a long trip with him to the Middle East. One month later, however, on October 16, Wael Zuaiter was killed outside his apartment building, most likely by the Israeli secret service.

In 1977, when Zuaiter's former companion, Janet Venn-Brown, began to collect testimonials and essays dedicated to the memory of the Palestinian militant, she approached Genet, who agreed to participate in the homage on the condition that it not take a personalized form but rather be extended "to all the fedayeen"—as the opening dedication of the piece explicitly states. Thus he offered her a text that speaks of the Palestinians more generally, consisting of "notes" taken during his first visit to Jordan (from October 1970 to April 1971), linked together and brought up to date by a final commentary that was written for the occasion. (I have chosen to insert the article into this collection according to the date of this commentary, 1977, which modifies the temporal structure and the perspective for a reading of the text as a whole.)

Entitled *Per un Palestinese: Dediche a più voci a Waël Zouaiter*, the work was published in 1979 in Milan by the Gabriele Mazzotta publishing house, with a preface by Yasser Arafat. Aside from Genet, the contributors included Rafael Alberti, Bruno Cagli, Matta, Alberto Moravia, Elio Petri, Maxime Rodinson, Georges Saidah, Fadwa Tukan, and others.

In 1984, an English translation was also published, edited by Janet Venn-Brown, under the title *For a Palestinian*, by Kegan Paul International, London, Boston, Melbourne, and Henley.

The text presented here is based on a typescript lightly corrected by the author. Genet no doubt wished to preserve the character of these notes as such. In any case, they should be seen for what they are: a rough document, a series of impressions, observations, and reflections hastily written down, a writer's notebook. But therein also lies their interest: these hasty notes with their often hazardous syntax allow us to observe, as though on the sly but in a more vivid way, the movement of Genet's writing and the unexpected turns of his thought.

In the margin near the title, the typescript gives a date, "October 1970," which ought not to be taken in a restrictive sense: it no doubt designates the general period of Genet's first visit. (Genet did not arrive in Amman until sometime around October 25 and was not on the bases at Ajloun until about one month later.)

With the exception of the note describing the Bedouin dances that took place at the camp at Baqa, the text focuses on the combat bases located on the hills of Ajloun, a small town in the north overlooking the Jordan River; from there the commando groups set out for Israel, and it was to this area that the fedayeen had withdrawn after the Jordanian offensive. Once again, it is against the background of the deadly confrontations of September 1970, between the Bedouin units of King Hussein's army and the Palestinian fighters, that the scenes described here are set; these pages thus reflect Genet's concerns in the early 1970s (the question of Arab identity, of secular nationalism, of the relations between God and the revolution, etc.).

Let us point out finally what this text shows us first of all: in the Palestinian camps, on the bases, along the roads, Genet was taking notes. This is a supplementary proof—if one were needed—that the separation between writing and politics, which Genet himself sometimes invoked, is a fiction, or more precisely that this fiction was necessary for him to be able to return to writing from a new angle. Among the fedayeen, Genet is both an old writer who has stopped writing, and a new author reinventing his function. This is perhaps what made it possible for him to declare matter-of-factly in *Prisoner of Love*, a few years after publishing these notes, "I never made any notes at the time, along the roads or tracks or on the bases" (p. 40), or, "I had neither pencil nor paper and didn't write anything down," and to conclude from this that he was "an impostor" (p. 117)—knowing, no doubt, that the supreme imposture is writing itself.

> Sources: Interview with Janet Venn-Brown and Marie-Claude el Hamchari. Archives of Rufaida Mikdadi, Jean Genet / IMEC.

ENDNOTES

1. Genet's dedication repeats and inverts the phrase used in the title of the work in which the text appeared: "For a Palestinian." See the introductory note.

2. In the Quran, the archangel Gabriel reveals to Muhammad his vocation as a prophet by communicating to him the words of the Book which are themselves communicated by God. According to historical accounts, the first transcriptions were made on dried bones.

3. Ahmed Shukeiri, the first president of the executive committee of the PLO (from 1964 to 1967) was "one of the most controversial and thunderous speakers of the Arab world" (Baron, *Les Palestiniens*, p. 84).

4. The Palestinian hospital at Jebel Achrafieh, in Amman, overflowing with the wounded during the massacres of September 1970, was transformed into an infirmary where the surgeons operated day and night. It was taken over by the Jordanian forces on September 25.

5. Genet uses quotation marks in a peculiar way here to introduce into his text a story reported in the third person.

6. Abu Omar (the *nom de guerre* of Hanna Mikhail), a Palestinian militant whom Genet met in Paris in the spring of 1970 and who became one of Genet's closest friends when he visited the camps. He disappeared around 1976 on a boat off the coast of Beirut. He is also one of the main figures in *Prisoner of Love* (see Edward Said, "On Jean Genet's Late Works," *Grand Street*, no. 36 [1990]: 26–42).

7. Ataturk is the name (meaning "Father of the Turks") given to Mustafa Kemal (1881–1938), the founder and first president of the Turkish Republic. He initiated a series of authoritarian reforms aimed at secularizing the country (suspension of religious orders, adoption of Latin characters in place of Arabic characters, Western clothes, and so on).

8. The kaffiyeh is the headdress of the Bedouins, consisting of a piece of cloth folded into a triangle and held down by a string.

9. Ferraj, a figure in *Prisoner of Love*. Genet writes that he was "the fedayee leader whom I liked talking to best when I first arrived in Ajloun" (p. 191). Hamza, on the other hand, should no doubt be distinguished from the character of the same name whom Genet met somewhat later in the camp at Irbid and who occupies an important place in his last book.

10. *Prisoner of Love* contains two separate descriptions of this scene (see pp. 66–69 and 126–27).

11. On April 4, 1971, the fedayeen evacuated Amman: about five thousand fighters took refuge in the wooded hills between Jerash and Ajloun.

12. On the distinction between the "bases" and the "camps," see pages 87 and 88 of *Prisoner of Love*, and "Four Hours in Shatila."

Chapter 26: The Tenacity of American Blacks

Article published on April 16, 1977, in *L'Humanité*.

INTRODUCTORY NOTE

On the occasion of Angela Davis's arrival in Paris and her participation in a meeting in support of the Wilmington Ten (ten black prisoners in North Carolina condemned to heavy prison sentences for "incitement to riot") on April 6, 1977, at La Mutualité, Genet wrote his last article on American blacks. It was published on April 16, 1977, on the front page of *L'Humanité*.

Written seven years after the author had gone to the United States to work with the Black Panthers, this text presents an update of the situation of the black revolutionary movements and, even more, of his relation to them. It testifies, most importantly, to his growing sympathy with the political views of Angela Davis, at the time still a member of the Communist Party, and to the distance he had taken from the Black Panther Party, of which he speaks with attachment but in the past tense. He ironically evokes one of the prominent figures of the party, Eldridge Cleaver, who had begun to promote a brand of jeans before being struck by a mystic revelation.

The largest part of the article, however, is devoted to Angela Davis, as Genet draws attention away from himself by allowing her to speak within his text, such that the piece eventually takes the form of an interview with the militant revolutionary. (Two years earlier, Genet had conducted an interview with Angela Davis, published in *L'Unité* on May 23, 1975.)

Dedicated to American blacks, as its title indicates, the text is also dedicated more specifically to black women: it begins with the name of Rosa Parks, pioneer of the great protest movements that led to civil rights victories for blacks, and ends with the names of two other important female figures, Harriet Tubman and Angela Davis.

Sources: Interviews with Angela Davis, Charles Silvestre, and Yolande du Luart.

ENDNOTES

1. This incident, a legendary event in the United States, historically marks the beginning of the black revolutionary movements. Indeed, it was in the wake of Rosa Parks's arrest on December 4, 1955, for refusing to give up her seat to a white, that the young preacher Martin Luther King organized the boycott of Montgomery, Alabama, buses. This act initiated the large-scale nonviolent demonstrations which came to an end with the assassination of King in 1968. (See Claude Fohlen, *Les Noirs aux Etats-Unis* [Paris: Presses Universitaires de France, 1983], pp. 110–12.)

2. See "Angela and Her Brothers," note 3.

3. In English in the original.

4. After several years of exile in Algeria and a tumultuous break with the founders of the Black Panther Party, Eldridge Cleaver had moved back to France, where he became a "star among the who's who of Paris." Back in the United States in 1975, he converted to a militant evangelism before getting involved in the sect led by Reverend Moon. More recently, in 1986, he ran for senator as a Republican (see Nicole Bernheim, "Que sont les activistes devenus?" *Les Temps modernes*, no. 485 [December 1986]: 69–83).

5. While living in Paris, Cleaver had allowed his name to be used for a brand of jeans.

6. Massai was the *nom de guerre* of Raymond Hewitt, minister of education of the Black Panther Party.

7. LeRoi Jones, poet, playwright, and essayist, born in 1934, had first gained recognition as an avant-garde writer preoccupied with aestheticism, before becoming a champion of blackness and a militant for black nationalism. In 1964, he changed his name to Amiri Baraka.

8. The black pastor Ruben Ben Chavis, vice president of the Alliance movement founded by Angela Davis, had been arrested in 1974 and sentenced, along with his nine comrades, to forty years in prison for "incitement to riot."

9. The television program on Bobby Seale is given an extended commentary in *Prisoner of Love* (pp. 215–18).

10. Andrew Young, the first black representative in the UN.

11. Over the years, the Ku Klux Klan had lost its importance, but it became prominent again during the 1960s in opposition to the liberal Left and the peace movement. In 1975, the promise of full equality and civil rights for blacks provoked a strong upsurge in the movement; its membership almost doubled. (See Sophie Body-Gendron, Laura Maslow-Armand, and Danièle Stewart, *Les Noirs Américains aujourd'hui* [Paris : Armand Colin, 1984]).

12. The National Alliance Against Racism and Political Repression, an organization founded by Angela Davis in 1972, grouping together 125 multiracial organizations.

13. A phrase frequently quoted by Genet (see *Prisoner of Love*, p. 46, and "For George Jackson").

Chapter 27: Chartres Cathedral

Article published June 30, 1977, in *L'Humanité*. The text presented here follows the typographical layout of the original manuscript. The text of this chapter was translated by Charlotte Mandell.

INTRODUCTORY NOTE

On June 30, 1977, this text on the Chartres Cathedral was the first in a successful series of daily features published in the cultural pages of *L'Humanité*. Entitled "Lire le pays" [Reading the country], it presented "writings on the countryside, biographical narratives linked with a particular place, a poem on a city, tales based on tourist sites," as Charles Silvestre wrote in his brief introduction to the series,

Thus, throughout the summer, each day a writer was asked to evoke a city, a region, a place to which he or she had an attachment. One hundred and ten authors—including Roland Barthes, Roger Caillois, Milan Kundera, Louis Guilloux, Gabriel García Márquez, Françoise Sagan, Georges Simenon, Michel Tournier, and others—responded favorably to the proposal.

Two months earlier, Charles Silvestre had met Jean Genet when the latter came to turn in his latest article to the newspaper's editors, and Silvestre had the idea of asking Genet to write the first text of the series. It was quite audacious to ask Genet, whose origins he was aware of, what the "country" meant to him; amused by the theme, however, the writer accepted the proposal. He promised to have the article by the agreed upon date, and he disappeared. He did not reappear at the newspaper until the day before the piece was to be published, at a moment when the editors had despaired of seeing him in time. "I wrote something, but I'm not really sure about it," he said to Charles Silvestre, who later recounted that "there was only one thing left to do: reread the printed text. So that evening he came back, took the proofs, went over them line by line and made only one correction. The typographer had spontaneously replaced a small *s* with a capital in the name of Stoléru. In fact, that's all he came back for, to make sure the minister's small *s* stayed small . . . " ("Pour un petit 's'," *L'Humanité*, April 16, 1986, p. 16.)

Chartres Cathedral had been long admired by the author (the title *Our Lady of the Flowers* already made it possible to see the book, in a way, as a small Romanesque cathedral); but more than the cathedral, the article's object was a reflection on the notions of the "country" and the "fatherland" or "homeland" [*la patrie*]. If only because of the great importance placed on these terms in Genet's work, this article can be considered a major text and ought to be read all the more carefully in that its apparent simplicity conceals a complex reflection shot through with irony.

Not long after writing it, Genet said to Bertrand Poirot-Delpech that he had written the text "partly as a joke" (see page 201). This aspect of the text has often escaped notice. Thus Jacques Henric, taking the regional tribute literally, wrote: "Here's the old convict, the reprobate, the accursed writer banned by the 'national community,' who has suddenly become the bard of the Fatherland, slipping into Pétainiste ideology like any old Marchais or Chirac. [. . .] Barrès or Péguy could not have done better." (See "Monsieur Jean Genet, nouveau patriote" in *Libération*, September 21, 1977, p. 14.)

Less straightforward than it appears, Genet's text in fact sets itself against the theme imposed on it and works to undo the notion of "fatherland." Traversed by an undercurrent of related issues (immigrant workers, foreigners, Palestinians, West Africans, the Third World, etc.) and by references to the most current events (the campaign asserting the value of manual labor, promoted by posters that covered the walls of the capital in 1977), all of which are linked together and to the central theme, it offers much more than a historical evocation; it presents a high speed reading of History—reread from a political angle.

The original title of the first draft makes this even clearer: "Micro-Treatise on a Mini-Politics." Here are a few fragments that were not included in the final version (held in the Jean Genet archive at the IMEC) and in which Genet first formulates his definition of the fatherland:

"The true fatherland, every fatherland, is a wound. Not long ago, the French fatherland was both sparse and unified during the Occupation. Today the Palestinian fatherland exists because it is bruised and wounded.

If every fatherland had to be made up of men and women who know each other more or less by name, it could only comprise a limited number—which everyone can count and know. Some complicated calculations give the number three thousand four hundred twenty-seven men and women. Perhaps fewer, never more.

To know each other. By what measure?

We can imagine a fatherland consisting of the following: eight Moroccans, seven Japanese, eleven Germans, fifteen Cubans, a few French, a single Beauceron [someone from Beauce, the region around Chartres—trans.], etc."

Genet's article (appearing on p. 2 of the newspaper) was illustrated with three photographs of Chartres. It was introduced by a general presentation of the author by Jean-Pierre Léonardini, recalling his essential works and his more recent pieces in the newspaper's columns in support of the Palestinians and American blacks. We have followed the fragmented layout in the manuscript, in which each paragraph is clearly separated from the others by a line.

> Sources: Interview with Charles Silvestre. Archives of
> Charles Silvestre, Alexandre Bouglione, Jean
> Genet/I.M.E.C.

ENDNOTES

1. Nara, the ancient imperial city of Japan, where Japanese Buddhism began to develop in the sixth and seventh centuries. Considered the birthplace of Japanese civilization, the city has a large number of Buddhist temples and shrines.

2. The "right to difference": a slogan used during a government campaign in 1977 that sought to revalorize manual labor.

3. *The Tree of Jesse:* stained glass window from the twelfth century, located on the western facade of the cathedral, representing the genealogical tree of Christ (going back to Jesse, father of David).

4. The government campaign referred to in note 2 was carried out primarily with publicly displayed posters.

5. In 1977, Lionel Stoléru was state secretary in charge of a revalorization of manual labor, in the cabinet of Raymond Barre. (On the reasons for the small letter at the beginning of his name, see the introductory note above.)

6. It was at the initiative of André Malraux, minister of culture under General de Gaulle, that the first great international expositions took place.

7. A saying attributed to Benjamin Franklin.

8. A large exhibition devoted to ancient Egypt had recently been held at the Louvre.

9. "Scrap" translates *rebut.* What figures here in the published text and the author's manuscript is the word *rebus* (without an accent [the word is normally written *rébus* in French—Trans.]). We have preferred to give the word that seemed to be required by the meaning of the sentence—although a rebus would have precisely the sense of playing against this meaning.

10. Sahraoui: a supporter of independence for the western Sahara, a territory divided between Morocco and Mauritania and currently integrated into Morocco. Supported by Algeria, the Polisario Liberation Front had proclaimed the Sahraoui Republic, on February 28, 1976, and had organized an armed opposition.

11. Dacca (since 1983 officially spelled Dhaka), capital of Bangladesh, which is one of the poorest countries in the world.

12. *Douar* (an Arabic word from the Maghreb): a group of tents set up in a circle.

13. In March 1975, the Cuban army (supported by the Soviet Union) intervened in the violent civil war that was beginning in Angola.

Chapter 28: Violence and Brutality

Preface to a collection of writings (*Textes des prisonniers de la "Fraction Armée
Rouge" et dernières lettres d'Ulrike Meinhof* [Paris: Éditions Maspéro, 1978]) by
members of the German Red Army Faction, published as an article in *Le Monde*
on September 2, 1977. See the introductory note and the excerpts from newspaper articles included there.

INTRODUCTORY NOTE

Of all of Genet's political writings, "Violence and Brutality" is probably the
most famous, and the only one that really sparked a controversy and stirred public opinion. In the days following its prepublication on the front page of *Le
Monde*, it provoked an avalanche of letters from readers as well as public
"responses" from intellectuals, causing schisms among the newspaper's editors
and even disrupting the peace between the German press and the French newspapers, who were accused of "anti-Germanism" (see the excerpts from newspaper articles below). There was such an outcry that the director of *Le Monde*,
Jacques Fauvet, had to publish a statement, signed (exceptionally) with his initials, reminding readers that the article had appeared under the rubric "Points
de vue" [points of view], open to the free expression of opinions, and that "reg-
ular contributors" of the newspaper had expressed, on the very same page, diver-
gent opinions on the same question (see *Le Monde*, September 14, 1977, p. 6).

To understand why the article caused such a stir, three elements of the circumstances should be considered:

The first is that in this text Genet was touching on the highly sensitive question of urban terrorism, which, during the three previous years, had sent deep
shock waves through the public and caused much consternation within intellectual circles. Between 1974 (when it was possible for Sartre to visit the leader of
the Red Army Faction, Andreas Baader, in prison without causing much of a
reaction) and 1977, the political landscape had gradually changed. Even if the
repressive methods used by the German government were considered unacceptable, no political party and no well-known personality had ventured to justify the
actions of a group referred to at the time as the "Baader gang" (in order to cast
them as criminals). The defense of terrorism, as well as the praise of the Soviet
Union that accompanies it here, was thus totally anachronistic in 1977. And since
even his communist friends had themselves avoided entering the debate, Genet
found himself alone on a hazardous excursion into this heavily mined territory.

Paradoxically—although in reality this was an effect of his isolation—Genet benefited on this occasion from an exceptional venue. Refused by *L'Humanité* (see below), where its career would have been more discreet, the article had been offered to *Le Monde*; because of its author's notoriety, it was published there, slightly abridged, on the front page, and this played a determining role in the repercussions it had. Three months later, in December 1977, the text was published again by the Éditions Maspero, as the preface to a collection of writings by members of the Red Army Faction; this time it was met with infinitely fewer commentaries.

But the main cause of the uproar probably lies outside the article itself: barely three days after its publication, the president of the German Employers Federation, Hanns-Martin Schleyer, was kidnapped in Cologne, following an attack that left three people dead. In return for his release the kidnappers demanded the release of fourteen members of the Baader group who were then in prison. Excerpts from Genet's article were published on September 12 in the widely circulating magazine *Der Spiegel* (no. 38, p. 138), and it is not difficult to imagine that, in the state of extreme tension prevailing in Germany at the time, this article seemed inopportune—especially since the German magazine did not clearly indicate that it had been written before the recent events. The dramatic unfolding of the situation throughout the month of October (the spectacular hijacking of an airplane, eventually brought under control by the police; the collective suicide of the three leaders of the group; the assassination of Hanns-Martin Schleyer) ended up isolating Genet even further. The end of this episode marked the beginning of a two-year period of silence.

It appears that initially Genet had not deliberately sought a scandal. About a year before publishing the article, he had met Klaus Croissant, one of the lawyers for the Baader group, with whom he remained in contact. He considered writing a text describing the conditions in which the members of the group were being held, but he was unable to have any direct contact with them. Klaus Croissant then asked him to write the preface to the collection of texts by them that would soon be published.

The preface was written during the summer of 1977, at a time when the fate of the Red Army Faction prisoners seemed utterly hopeless: held for months in complete isolation, exhausted by long hunger strikes that were no longer having any impact on the public, they had just been sentenced to life in prison.

To give the text a wider audience, it was suggested to Genet that he publish it in a newspaper before its appearance in the book. He first went to the offices of *L'Humanité*, where he had published most of his articles of the previous three years, and spoke with René Andrieu, the chief editor. Andrieu expressed his agreement with the basic gist of the article, but said that if it were published in *L'Humanité*, it could give credibility to the rumors alleging a connection between international terrorism and the Communist Party, and thus that its effect would be the opposite of what was expected. Genet readily accepted the argument and took his article to a newspaper that could not be suspected of such ulterior political motives, *Le Monde*; after some hesitation and despite several unfavorable opinions among the editors, Jacques Fauvet agreed to publish it.

Genet's interest in the Red Army Faction was less clear and less effective than his interest in American blacks or the Palestinians; it was based on certain "affinities," to use his expression. The first is bound up in the fact that the Baader group emerged during the ferment of the widespread protests against the Vietnam War. Their actions were directed not only at the German state, but also at the United States, the great enemy in Genet's view. In addition to these common adversaries, there was also a set of common sympathies (for example, Baader had formed close relations in the early 1970s with Palestinian organizations, although these relations turned out to be based on a number of misunderstandings). Still more specifically, many of the members of the Red Army Faction had been in prison for many years, which raised the question of prison detention that had always preoccupied Genet.

Finally, more than any other movement, the Baader group faced unanimous opposition. The disapproval of its members was so intense that it was also directed at their defenders (suspected of complicity, their lawyers had been barred from the trial, from which the accused themselves were absent). More than their political thought, it was the terrorists' status as "indefensible" that inspired Genet to defend them.

> Sources: Interviews with René Andrieu, Jacques Fauvet, Catherine von Bülow, Paule Thévenin. Archives of *Le Monde*.

ENDNOTES

1. For reasons relating to the size of the book, not all of the texts that were to be printed in the collection were included, and some of them therefore remain unpublished. This quotation from Marx is thus not found in any of Andreas Baader's public statements.

2. It was an intellectual as well as a legal trial: the verdict of the latter had been handed down on April 28, 1977, in Stuttgart, sentencing Andreas Baader, Gudrun Ensslin, and Jan-Karl Raspe, the main leaders of the Red Army Faction, to life in prison.

3. This phrase attributed to Andreas Baader is in fact a quotation from Marx's *Capital*, cited in a coauthored "Statement of Andreas, Gudrun, Jan, and Ulrike" pronounced at the Stammheim trial. Its occurrence on page 142 of the book contains a minor variant. This difference, and the small errors of attribu-

tion occurring here and there, suggest that Genet had an imprecise knowledge of the texts in the collection, many of which were translated orally for him.

4. Haiphong, port town in Vietnam, created by the French in 1880 and devastated by American bombing between 1967 and 1973.

5. Genet is referring to the five authors—arrested in 1972—of the *Textes des prisonniers de la "Fraction Armée Rouge."* Two of them were already dead when Genet's article was published: Ulrike Meinhof (born in 1934, died by hanging in her cell in 1976) and Holger Meins (born in 1941, died of starvation after a long hunger strike in the Wittlich prison in 1974). As for the three other members, Andreas Baader (born in 1943), Gudrun Ensslin (born in 1940), and Jan-Karl Raspe (born in 1944), they would die soon after, on October 17, 1977, in the Stammheim prison. According to the official version, which has been disputed, it was a collective suicide.

6. It will be noticed that the "self-destruction of power" by means of its own excess—a theory shared by a number of far-Left movements and one expressed by Andreas Baader—receives harsh criticism in an earlier text whose title is explicit in this regard: "When 'the Worst Is Always Certain.'"

7. Statement of September 13, 1974, reproduced on pages 33 to 46 of the *Textes des prisonniers de la "Fraction Armée Rouge"*.

8. Genet's version of this passage is also different from the one found in the book cited in the previous note (p. 36).

9. Siegfried Buback, federal prosecutor. Considered responsible for the prison conditions that caused the deaths of several members of the RAF, he was killed on April 8, 1977, by a commando claiming to act in the name of "Ulrike Meinhof."

10. Holger Meins (see note 5), whose final letter, written five days before his death by starvation, is included among the texts published in the collection.

11. This excerpt from Ulrike Meinhof's statement of September 13, 1974, is found (in a somewhat different form) on page 42 of the book.

12. A quotation from Marx found in Ulrike Meinhof's statement of September 13, 1974 (page 44 of the French text).

13. Statement by Andreas Baader at the Stammheim trial, on page 91 of the anthology.

14. Helmut Schmidt had succeeded Willy Brandt as chancellor of the Federal Republic of Germany in 1974.

15. There was much debate in Germany after Gudrun Ensslin had been force-fed. On April 28, 1977, an Amnesty International committee had sent a telegram to the German government recalling the obligations of international law in this regard.

16. Suspected of being complicit with their clients, the lawyers who were working for the members of the RAF were arrested on several occasions.

EXCERPTS FROM NEWSPAPER ARTICLES

Presented here, in the order of their publication, are some excerpts from articles that appeared in September 1977 in French newspapers in response or in reference to "Violence and Brutality." (For letters from readers, see the section entitled "Correspondance" in *Le Monde* of September 8, 10, and 17, 1977. We should remark that the first echo of Genet's text occurred in the *New York Times* on September 7, in a short article on page 3, by Jonathan Kandell, who notes that "most European intellectuals on the left have condemned terrorism . . . with the notable exception of the novelist Jean Genet.")

Jacques Ellul, "La Violence, c'est la violence" [Violence is violence], *Le Monde*, September 8, 1977, p. 3:

It is difficult to let Jean Genet's article "Violence and Brutality" (in the September 2 *Le Monde*) pass without offering a few complementary reflections. I will not discuss his praise of "the Baader gang." . . . But I will make two points:

1. The distinction between violence and brutality: quite remarkably, here Jean Genet takes up the old classic bourgeois discourse on the subject, simply reversing it . . .

Now, these distinctions, on both sides, are purely distinctions of form, and they depend simply on the "value" that one privileges: order or revolution. . . . There is no "good violence," in either case, except in relation to this value. And we find once again the pinnacle of bourgeois discourse: "The end justifies the means." Alas! Jean Genet's entire article can be reduced to these five words! . . .

2. The second observation relates to the author's praise of the USSR. It is truly a marvel to see the several million victims of Stalinism qualified as "anecdotes about the Kremlin and other details reported by the Kremlinologists"! The supreme value of the USSR, despite a few unfortunate mistakes, is, according to Jean Genet, always to have taken the side of the peoples of the Third World, the colonized, "the weakest and most vulnerable countries."

Two remarks with respect to this claim: Jean Genet ought to reread Lenin more thoroughly; there he would learn that taking the side of conquered and colonized peoples is in no way meant to defend them, rather it is a strategic operation against imperialism. . . . And it is possible to cite a number of examples from the last thirty years in which the USSR took sides against independence movements of African or Asian peoples!

Second remark: Jean Genet entirely forgets that the USSR is the last colonial power in the world. . . . So before getting carried away by Holy Russia (sorry USSR) and justifying the actions of the "Baader gang" in reference to it, Jean Genet would do well to analyze his own arguments more closely.

V. V. Stanciu, "La Victime et le tyran" [The victim and the tyrant], *Le Monde*, September 10, 1977, p. 3:

> What troubled me about Jean Genet's article is not the justification of the assassinations committed by Baader's RAF, for I believe in the unlimited freedom of thought, even if it is aberrant. What shocks me is the lack of logic and of a sense of justice.
>
> Indeed, Jean Genet wrote this sentence: "The greater the brutality, and the more outrageous the trial, the more violence becomes imperious and necessary."
>
> What is true for the partisans of Baader ought to be true for the representatives of the German authorities. The greater the brutality of the former, the more imperious and necessary does the violence of the latter become.
>
> Legitimate self-defense, this sacred institution that places life above all principles, cannot be the privilege of antisocial criminals. . . .
>
> I agree with Jean Genet on one single point: when he claims that "the greater the brutality . . . , the more violence becomes imperious and necessary." For there is a hierarchy of horror.

Maurice Duverger, "Le Fascisme rouge" [Red fascism], *Le Monde*, September 11–12, 1977, pp. 1 and 3:

> The extremists of revolution have a pure soul and noble intentions. They deserve to be understood and explained, as Heinrich Böll, Jean Genet, and others have done. They deserve respect, these sons and daughters of the bourgeoisie who could lead a peaceful, even privileged existence, and who have chosen to be chased and hunted, waiting to be killed or imprisoned. They have a right to expect our denunciation of the scandalous prison regime imposed on them in the Federal Republic. But they do not deserve any efforts on our part to justify and excuse their actions.
>
> These actions lead to fascism . . .
>
> In the pluralist democracies, terrorists do not make up an avant-garde tied to the masses whom they can mobilize behind them. They are a handful of marginal figures who have no chance of being joined by a people, the overwhelming majority of whom rejects them. Their isolation grows along with their violence. They are perfectly aware of this. Their object is not to provoke an immediate revolution. They want to give rise to it indirectly, at the end of a long evolution, the first phase of which is the overturning of the liberal regime following the mechanism described very well in the text cited by Jean Genet: "Revolutionary progress makes its way through the creation of a powerful and unified counterrevolution." . . .
>
> Once fascism has been reestablished, how long would it take to make it disappear? . . . How long, how many generations, how much accumulated suffer-

ing would it take for the strategy of the ultraleftists to come to term, supposing it ever did?

Whoever accepts plunging a society into such a long and terrible servitude, under the pretext of freedom, is not only an objective accomplice of fascism. He becomes a fascist himself through such contempt for men.

Bernard Brigouleix, "La Presse allemande accuse d' 'antigermanisme' plusieurs journaux français dont *Le Monde*" [The German press accuses several French newspapers, including *Le Monde*, of "Anti-Germanism"], *Le Monde*, September 14, 1977, p. 6:

> The West-German press continues to be troubled by the reactions of French newspapers in general, and of *Le Monde* in particular, after the attack in Cologne. Several commentators claim that Paris is witnessing a veritable explosion of anti-Germanism.
>
> The weekly *Der Spiegel*, which is very influential in administrative circles, has published a translation of long excerpts from the "Point of View" by Jean Genet appearing in *Le Monde* of September 2, in which the author of *The Screens*, three days before the abduction of M. Schleyer and the murder of his entourage, justified the West German terrorists' recourse to violence by referring to the violence of the Federal State.
>
> This text, which few Germans had known about before then—despite several attacks in the West German press (*Le Monde* of September 13)—has given rise to harsh indignation in the Federal Republic, where people find it difficult to understand that it is simply a matter of a personal opinion formulated by a personality external to the newspaper.
>
> *Der Spiegel* follows the article with a commentary by Dieter Wild in the form of an address to *Le Monde*, in which we read: "We could make a long list of the precious things we envy you French, such as the Great Revolution and the great Jean Genet, for example. We are simply dying to include within the ranks of German literature this angel of infamy, but, for us, he is the prototype of the destroyer of the nation. Jean Genet must be defended: 'Never,' he writes three days before the attack in Cologne, 'have the members of the Red Army Faction let their force become pure brutality.' Unheard of? Well, the same author also lavished praise on Hitler, next to whom the Red Army Faction is obviously not so brutal."

Pierre de Boisdeffre, "Réponse à Jean Genet: Comment faire face à la violence?" [Response to Jean Genet: How to deal with violence?], *Le Monde*, September 17, 1977, pp. 1 and 8:

> The first reflex upon reading Jean Genet's article is to shrug one's shoulders. Indeed, a good dose of generalization is necessary to bring together, in a single

accusation, the HLM and the goose-step, the condescending speech of police and the bombing of Haiphong, the Rolls-Royce and bureaucracy. . . . [It is true] that, in certain cases—which are after all extreme cases—"the spontaneous violence of life that is carried further by revolutionaries" can and even must be opposed to "organized brutality." Indeed, we must admit it: there is nothing more legitimate than fighting tyranny! But when we are then told that "what we owe to Andreas Baader, to Ulrike Meinhof . . . to the Red Army Faction in general, is that they have made us understand, not only by words but by their actions . . . that violence alone is capable of bringing the brutality of men to an end," suddenly we understand that it is a question of something completely different.

It is a question of justifying the crimes of the RAF carried out on German soil and of positing an opposition between the very well-organized violence of these "desperados" and the "brutality" of a self-satisfied and hierarchized society. A few days later, the abduction of M. Schleyer and the assassination of his four bodyguards by the Red Army Faction gave to M. Genet's statements a meaning that was all too clear.

Coming from Jean Genet, this text is not surprising. Having observed for almost thirty years the infatuation with which the first—superb—writings from the author of *Our Lady of the Flowers* were greeted by the Parisian intelligentsia—from Jean Cocteau to Jean-Paul Sartre—I have wondered whether his intention was not to demoralize, in the radical sense of the word, the conscience of the West. The author of *The Screens* seems close to succeeding in this! . . . I continued reading, and I found in this shock-article a number of the features that long ago marked the poetic and passionate narratives of the early Genet: a taste for violence, even a defense of crime, if these emanate from an outlaw; a sort of generalized inversion that leads to baptizing Evil as Good and to sanctioning Evil ("I will steal in order to be a thief"). . . .

The universality of justice is what ought to be opposed to the universality of terror. We are still far from this goal. It is here that nonviolence calls upon us. Perhaps tomorrow it will give us the response that neither Céline, nor the generals, nor Genet have yet been able to give us.

Jacques Henric, "Monsieur Jean Genet, nouveau patriote" [Monsieur Jean Genet, a new patriot], *Libération*, September 21, 1977, p. 14:

Jean Genet, then. His life on the move, his intense and scandalous work, these we know. For postwar generations like my own, he was the new *poète maudit*, a Villon, a Rimbaud . . . almost a myth. But also a solitary and not a concerted protest, and yet one that was terribly effective against the literary nullity of the period. . . .

What consternation and sadness to read of late the few rare articles written by this same Jean Genet! . . .

Using the pretext of an ostensibly provocative justification—in the end quite politically irresponsible—of the violence practiced the Red Army Faction and of the monstrous repression exerted by the Federal Republic against its members, the author of *Miracle of the Rose* launches into a frenetic defense of the Soviet state and its foreign policy. The "Baader gang" and Brezhnev, all part of the same struggle! . . .

But that's not all: then we come to what must be called the most odious part of the article. Still referring to the USSR, Genet writes: "Despite whatever internal policies it *may have* (my emphasis) . . . , or the negative things it *may have* done . . . " Let us admire these conditionals. Solzhenitsyn, Plyushch, Bukovsky . . . and all you who have been imprisoned and subjected to the psychiatrists, the persecuted Jews, the national minorities that were crushed, the deviants who were persecuted, the millions who died in the Gulag—you are not within the order of the real. For Jean Genet you are at most a hypothesis. . . . How can we express outrage today at the doubts that certain people have dared to put forth about the reality of the Nazi concentration camps and not be just as scandalized by the ignoble conditionals that swarm through M. Jean Genet's language?

What has happened? Is it the desire to be original whatever the cost, to be solitary to the bitter end, that has driven Jean Genet to end in the guise of a Stalinist intellectual? . . . Is he driven by a kind of suicidal impulse? Or is it that the hand that wrote *The Song of the Prisoner Condemned to Death* [*sic*] is no longer quite the same as the one that traces out these words today? . . . Or could it be that sex has become strangely taboo in his texts and that this is simply the way in which the sexual symptom has of inscribing itself, despite everything, into what he writes! . . .

A strange correspondence between biographies. Today Aragon is silent on the subject of politics. Russia and the French Communist Party have found themselves a new incense bearer. That's right, the author of *Our Lady of the Flowers* and *The Thief's Journal.* Who's talking about the progress of man and History?

Tahar Ben Jelloun, "Pour Jean Genet" [For Jean Genet], *Le Monde*, September 24, 1977, p. 2:

JEAN GENET is a scandalous man. How could the society that excluded him from the beginning forgive him his lucidity today? . . .

The brutal reactions that followed his reflections on violence and brutality are easily explained. When a French intellectual speaks, there is often a class, a party, a group, a religion behind him. There are risks, but they are moderate.

Jean Genet is a man who stands alone. . . .

A recluse, alone in a society that has cursed him, Jean Genet has his own attachments. Elsewhere. In other territories that are often far away, often inhabited by distress. For Genet is a fraternal man. He recognizes his companions; he knows where they are, he moves in their direction, wherever they might be: in the shanties of North Africa, in the ghettos of America, in the occupied territories, in Palestine, in Japan, in Europe. . . .

That is what people will not forgive. They will not forgive him for placing himself concretely, physically, alongside the disinherited, alongside peoples who have been denuded and dispossessed. He himself is an outcast, a body carried to the shore by an evil wind. He has not been forgiven for standing alongside the Zengakuren in Japan, the Black Panthers, the Palestinians, the expatriated.

How could he be forgiven today, when he defends a group of people who have followed their convictions to their ultimate consequences, who are absolute in their lucidity and their desperation?

See also the articles published the following month: Jean Dauga, "Le Monde de Jean Genet" [The world of Jean Genet], *La Revue universelle*, no. 36 (October 1977): 80–82; Jean-François Josselin, "Pas de purgatoire pour Jean Genet" [No purgatory for Jean Genet], *Le Nouvel Observateur*, November 21, 1977, p. 89; and Jacques Henric, "Merci Jean Genet, vous au moins vous dites vrai" [Thank you Jean Genet, you at least are speaking the truth], *Art Press International* (December 1977): 2.

Chapter 29: Interview with Tahar Ben Jelloun

Interview conducted in Paris at the beginning of November 1979 for *Le Monde*.

INTRODUCTORY NOTE

Was Genet more affected than he appeared to be by the numerous protests in response to the publication of "Violence and Brutality"? Two years went by before his name appeared in the press again, this time in order to speak of a problem that was of particular importance to him: immigration.

Genet certainly had other concerns during this time: he had begun work on a film script for *La Nuit venue* [Nightfall] (the story of a young Moroccan immigrant discovering life in France), which he abandoned in 1978; but he was especially preoccupied with the throat cancer diagnosed in May 1979, for which he was undergoing chemotherapy treatment that left him exhausted. He was still recovering when the threat of a vote in the Senate—concerning new legislation that would facilitate processes of selection and expulsion for immigrant workers—drove him to intervene despite the state of his health.

At first he planned to write an article, but after a few false starts, he agreed, in a conversation with Tahar Ben Jelloun, that an interview would require less effort and would be more animated. This would be the form taken by most of Genet's last public interventions.

The interview took place during the first days of November 1979. This was just before the Senate was scheduled (on November 7) to discuss the proposed laws that would create a National Bureau of Immigration with the power to legislate the conditions for entry, residence, and work applicable to foreigners in French territory.

Genet's arguments, in fact, present neither a direct protest against these laws nor a discussion of their details. Rather, they denounce the spirit presiding over their conception and attempt to fundamentally rethink the ways in which France is historically bound to immigrant workers from former colonies. Once again, the question of immigration is placed against the background of colonialism, of which Genet has not only a precise knowledge but also a direct experience (he was a soldier in Morocco for eighteen months, from 1931 to 1933), and which is no doubt the touchstone of his political thought, the angle from which he approaches all the situations that came to interest him, whether the Palestinians or the black revolutionary movements.

Hoping to give the text its widest possible audience, Genet sent it to *Le Monde*, where it encountered a few difficulties at first. Still smarting from their last experience, and divided with respect to the writer's political positions, the editors were reluctant; once again, it was thanks to the intervention of the newspaper's director, Jacques Fauvet, that the interview was published, although a few days late and in a slightly abridged form, on November 11, in *Le Monde du dimanche* (p. iv). It bears the simple title "An Interview with Jean Genet" (the title of this text has often been confused with the subtitle of the column under which it appeared in the newspaper, "Immigrants") and is introduced by a brief editorial remark: "Jean Genet is indifferent on the subject of his books or plays. If he learns that immigrant workers are in danger, he reacts."

When the interview appeared, the debate in the Senate had already taken place, but this did not make it any less timely. Supported by the parties of the Right, the bill had been postponed, paradoxically, at the request of the minister Christian Bonnet—the very man who, in 1966, demanded that the Parliament deny funds to the Théâtre de l'Odéon where *The Screens* was playing—who judged the terms presented by his political allies to be too lax.

An English translation of the article was published on April 6, 1980, in the *Guardian Weekly*, no. 15, p. 13, under the title "Genet on Immigrants."

> Sources: Interviews with Tahar Ben Jelloun and Jacques Fauvet.

ENDNOTES

1. For more information on this bill, see the introductory note.
2. A reference to the very recent "diamond affair," in which the Central

African emperor, Bokassa, was said to have given diamonds to president Valéry Giscard d'Estaing—a rumor to which Giscard d'Estaing and his administration responded with a vigorous denial.

3. Concerning pink as the symbolic color of the French empire in the colonial period, see the text "Registration No. 1155," Chapter 34 in this book.

4. After having maintained close relations with Emperor Bokassa, the French government took credit for his ouster during the coup of September 21, 1979.

5. Before the recession of 1977, which affected the naval yards of Saint-Nazaire and the iron and steel industry of Thionville, a large number of immigrants worked in these two cities.

6. Nouadhibou, port and industrial town of Mauritania, located on the Cape Blanc peninsula.

7. The bill that occasioned this interview was presented to the Senate by Lionel Stoléru, state secretary responsible for matters concerning manual laborers and immigrants.

8. Arenc, a detention center near Marseille, where immigrants with an uncertain status were kept waiting while their situation was clarified.

9. On January 1, 1977, President Valéry Giscard d'Estaing invited a group of garbage collectors to have breakfast with him in his residence at the Élysée Palace.

10. Louis Hubert Lyautey (1854–1934), colonial administrator and marshal of France, was resident-general of Morocco beginning in 1912. See "Registration No. 1155," note 1.

11. The Bardo Treaty was signed in 1881; it inaugurated the era of the "French protectorate" in Tunisia.

12. It was in fact in 1840 that Marshal Bugeaud, appointed governor-general of Algeria, organized the colonization of the country. Between 1841 and 1850, 115,000 acres of land were distributed as a concession to French settlers.

13. A reference to the actions of the Danish who, during World War II, put up a passive but persistent opposition to the laws dictated by the German occupation army, especially those bearing on persons of Jewish origin.

Chapter 30: The Brothers Karamazov

Text written at an undetermined date (between 1975 and 1980), given to the Éditions Gallimard in 1981 and published in *La Nouvelle Revue Française* in October 1986. The present publication is based on the manuscript. The text of this chapter was translated by Charlotte Mandell.

It is still difficult to determine with any precision when this text was written, though it was sometime after Genet had read Dostoyevsky during a stay in Apulia, around 1975. This reading is mentioned by the author in his interview with Hubert Fichte (p. 123): "I can tell you that it took me two months to read *The Brothers Karamazov*. I was in bed. I was in Italy, I would read one page, and then . . . I'd have to think for two hours, then start again, it's enormous, and it's exhausting."

It was not until 1981 that Genet gave the manuscript to Laurent Boyer at Gallimard, "so that Georges Lambrichs can publish them in the N.R.F." Later, when he saw the typed text, he changed his mind, saying it had been a joke . . . But several years later, while he was writing *Prisoner of Love*, he took back a copy of the article, which he planned to publish simultaneously. He made no changes in the text.

This piece, published in the months following Genet's death and the appearance of his book, is therefore indeed a finished text; somewhat marginal with respect to his public interventions, it occupies a place apart in this collection. If we have decided to include it here, this is because it demonstrates what *Prisoner of Love* makes fully manifest: the development in Genet's work of a poetics that provides a counterpoint, and, more profoundly, a constant accompaniment, to his political reflections.

The text must no doubt be seen as an homage to Dostoyevsky. Cited with hardly any explanation in several interviews, the Russian novelist indeed appears as Genet's major literary reference—just as Giacometti is for sculpture, Rembrandt for painting, and Mozart, perhaps, for music.

But while this text certainly offers a precise and original reading of *The Brothers Karamazov*, it also opens onto larger issues: it sketches a veritable theory of the novel and—if we consider the final references to music, painting and the theater—of the work of art in general. In this sense, we can read these pages, held in reserve by the author, as the outline of a sort of *ars poetica* informing his last works.

The spacing of the paragraphs presented here follows that of the manuscript. The latter bears no title; we have used the one given on the typescript which the author had in his possession. This text was published for the first time under the slightly different title, "Une Lecture des *Frères Karamazov*" ["A Reading of *The Brothers Karamazov*"], in the October 1986 issue of *La Nouvelle Revue Française* (no. 405, pp. 69–72).

Sources: Interview with Laurent Boyer. Archives of Gallimard, Alexandre Bouglione.

ENDNOTES

1. See "Le Secret de Rembrandt," in *Oeuvres complètes*, vol. 5, p. 37: " . . . the sleeve in *The Jewish Bride* is an abstract painting." This painting from 1666 is also called *Isaac and Rebecca*.

Chapter 31: Interview with Antoine Bourseiller

Interview filmed in the summer of 1981, in Delphi and at the Moulin de la Guéville, in Rambouillet, and distributed as a videocassette in the series *Témoins* [Witnesses]. The present version was edited on the basis of a transcript of the soundtrack and the author's working notes. We have followed the sequential order of the film, which Genet edited.

INTRODUCTORY NOTE

Produced by Danièle Delorme, creator of the video series *Témoins*, and filmed by Antoine Bourseiller, the film from which this interview was transcribed can almost be considered a work by Genet, so significant was the role he played in its realization. From the choice of locations, to that of the long static shot that frames his image, to the nature of the themes discussed, to the ordering of the various segments, Genet in effect made decisions concerning practically every detail of this film. Even his responses to Antoine Bourseiller's questions—only three of these questions remain on the soundtrack—were premeditated, removed from the vagaries of improvisation and, for the most part, written out beforehand. Prior to the shooting, Genet wrote out a large number of notes—to which we have had access, thanks to the generosity of their present owner—which reveal both the value that Genet attached to this project and the preparatory work and reflection that preceded it. The majority of his statements on screen were already formulated there, in various versions, sometimes identically, sometimes in very different forms, but these statements always respect the oral character and the specific language of conversation.

Without losing any of its apparent spontaneity, the interview achieves, thanks to this elaboration, not only a rare density of expression, but also a sort of serenity: Genet speaks as though to himself, draws up the balance sheet of his existence, unfolds his "history" and his "geography," without deviating from the essential and without being drawn into the game of provocation which the presence of a more directly engaged interlocutor often inspired in him.

The paradox is that when Genet first accepted the idea of this film—in which he is omnipresent—it was on the condition that he not appear in it: "I will not be visible and I will not speak," he had declared to Danièle Delorme, once she had managed to soften his initial refusal, "but I do want to envisage a kind of cinematic poem based on some of my writings" (quoted in *Lire*).

In order to create this *cinematic poem*, the producer turned to director Antoine Bourseiller, who had staged *The Balcony* twice before and had remained in contact with the writer. For several weeks, they shot sequences that were meant to evoke the atmosphere of the novels, but it soon became clear that if Genet himself did not speak, the images would remained unanchored.

Reluctantly, then, he agreed to speak in front of the camera, despite the throat cancer that made it difficult for him to do so. "I will respond," he said to his collaborators, "to one question only: why am I not in prison?"

A first interview was filmed in early summer 1981 in Delphi, where Genet had wanted to go. It was complemented by a second session, filmed a little later, at the Moulin de la Guéville, Danièle Delorme's family house near Rambouillet.

Assembling the various elements (interviews, scenes evoking the novels, supplementary documents . . .), Antoine Bourseiller quickly put together the "rushes," which he projected for Genet to give him an overall idea of the film. It was then that Genet, not recognizing himself in the images he saw, decided to take over the editing of the film. He rented a room at the Bijou Hotel in Billancourt, near the studios, where he went to work each day: he focused the film on the interviews (from which he removed certain segments, notably on Ronsard, Abdallah, and the theme of the rose), eliminating almost all of the scenes of poetic evocation. Of these there remained only a small reportage on Mettray, another on the kouros in the Louvre, some excerpts from a documentary on Alberto Giacometti, and a few of Bruno Barbey's photographs of the Palestinian camps. Over these images, which were inserted between each interview segment, excerpts (chosen by Genet) from *Miracle of the Rose*, *The Thief's Journal*, *Le Funambule* [The Tightrope Walker], and "L'Atelier d'Alberto Giacometti" [The Studio of Alberto Giacometti] were read by Gérard Desarthes, J. Q. Chatelain, and Roger Blin.

When the editing was finished, the film was no more than fifty-two minutes long. Shot in 16mm and transferred to video, it inaugurated the series of writers' and artists' portraits comprising the *Témoins* collection. On the occasion of its first appearance in the fall of 1982, several newspapers published excerpts from the interview (notably the *Nouvel Observateur*, in its edition of October 20, 1982, under the title *Genet de vive voix*. It was broadcast on France 3, the coproducer of the film, the day after the writer's death.

> Sources: Interviews with Antoine Bourseiller and Danièle Delorme. Jean Genet / IMEC and a private collection.

We have placed in the endnotes (marked at points in the text where their content most closely corresponds) the most important passages of Genet's working notes as these relate to what he says in the interview. Here are a few such excerpts which appear to be independent and which, for the most part, discuss the film itself:

And how not to speak of narcissism? When I have an interlocutor and no curious witness [illegible word], I soon try to convince him, therefore to vanquish him, whatever the benefit may be for me.

In front of the camera, who is the witness who will transmit my image into the distance and to the many people there? [Several illegible words.] I would like to be praised for my sobriety or my grandiloquence: in any case, I will have been acting.

It used to be that the rough quality of static shots forced our intelligence to work almost as hard as the director's.

It's also necessary to add a point about the cinema, where my curiosity is never satisfied: in the image there is a palm tree, for example, but what's behind this palm tree? The image shows a palm tree, but what is it meant to hide? The image shows what it shows, but what does it hide? Since I have an imaginary world of my own, like everyone, a palm tree, there on the screen, obliges me to see only it and to cut short my imaginary world, which means what? Perhaps a gesture of revolt?

We have to hurry in choosing and deciding on the shots we'll keep, otherwise we'll get used to them just as one gets used to ugliness and to prison.

You are no doubt more of a positivist than I am, and what I am calling a god, you call the consciousness of good and evil. But here as elsewhere, the rules do not exist beforehand, neither in this interrogated consciousness, nor on the Tables of the Law: the rules must be invented each time. They are more aesthetic than moral, and it is through insecurity that one discovers them—or invents them. The rules that guide me and that I invent go against the rule, I mean against the law.

ENDNOTES

1. This text was projected in a static shot at the beginning of the film and was followed by the handwritten signature of Jean Genet. We might note the slight error in the time of birth (Genet was born at 7:45 P.M.), and the omission of the first given name of his mother, Camille.

2. The intertitles have been taken from Genet's working notes and are used only to indicate the separate segments of the film.

3. Genet lived in Greece between 1957 and 1960, during the time when he was writing *The Screens*. He was around fifty years old at the time (and not "thirty-five").

Excerpt from the working notes:

When I spoke of the mixture of shadows and light in Greece, I was of course not thinking of the light from the sun, and not even of the milky steam of the Turkish baths. Evoking ancient Greece (which is still present), I was thinking not only of Dionysos in opposition to the shining brilliance and the harmony of Apollo, but of something even more distant than they: the Python snake who had her sanctuary at Delphi, and who never stopped rotting there, stinking up Dionysos, Apollo, the Turkish *wali*, King Constantine, the colonels, and the suns that followed them.

Shadow and sun also mixed here: in the kores, dressed in folds down to their toes, the naked kouros, made of a marble as smooth as the thighs of Platini.

Shadow mixed with light—well, you know more about all this than I do: the Mycenaean cycles, Clytemnestra, the Theban cycles, but you know about all that.

4. In the village of Alligny-en-Morvan, where he had been placed by Public Welfare, Genet took catechism classes and celebrated his First Communion.

5. "Divers" is also the name of a character in *Miracle of the Rose.*

6. Genet met Abdallah around 1955 (see the preface to this volume), and in 1957 encouraged him to desert the army and to leave France.

7. Jean Decarnin (1923–44), dedicatee and hero of *Funeral Rites.*

8. See "L'Atelier d'Alberto Giacometti" (The Studio of Albert Giacometti) in volume 5 of Genet's *Oeuvres complètes* (Paris: Éditions Gallimard, 1979). The portraits of Genet are in the Musée d'Art Moderne in the Centre Pompidou, in Paris, and in the Tate Gallery in London.

9. In fact, Genet was seventy years old at the time.

10. "The Drunken Boat," trans. Louis Varèse (New York: New Directions, 1945), p. 101.—Trans.

11. Excerpt from the working notes: "I said to you, two days ago, that God had no place in my life. The truth is perhaps different: although I don't believe in God, I act all the time as if I were being acted upon by him, and as if he were keeping an eye on me at every moment, day and night."

12. Excerpt from the working notes: "To say that I have really worked [this time] well for seventy years, I'm not so sure, but I haven't had a moment's respite.

"The result is certainly not very beautiful, but everything that I am, and at this moment here in front of you too, everything is in progress, under construction."

13. This passage is taken up again in *Prisoner of Love,* p. 218.

14. Genet frequently quotes this phrase of David Hilliard. See *Prisoner of Love,* p. 46, and above, "For George Jackson," and elsewhere.

15. See *Prisoner of Love,* pp. 213, 218.

16. Excerpts from the working notes: "Groups of young men, no women

around, dreams of victory and of vengful acts, sheer revenge, the presence among us of arms, ammunition, grenade belts. . . . How, in such a place, could there not have been a sensuality, an erotic power. Every place we went was a dark little corner. Even in the day, night was everywhere.

"I know that no one ever speaks of the sensual repulsion or desire, the physical attraction or disgust experienced in a community of ideas. People hide it. It exists.

"The Palestinians were radiant. The Panthers too. And the inmates at Mettray."

17. See *Miracle of the Rose*, trans. Bernard Frechtman (New York: Grove Press, 1966), p. 133.

Excerpt from the working notes: "So what happened? I spent part of my youth in a reformatory, in prison, in the army, four years in Greece, in Arab countries—was it only chance that drove me to the places where I would be happy because of the absence of women, or was I guided there by a pressure coming from me?"

18. The director of the present *institut médico-professionel* refused to give Genet the authorization to film on the site. The crew therefore had to do a clandestine shoot (see Michel Cressole, "Jean Genet toujours," *Libération*, September 12, 1982).

19. Georges-Auguste Demetz (who was not a baron), together with the Vicomte de Courteille, founded Mettray in 1840. Genet's assertion that Demetz and his heirs "brought in an enormous fortune" has not been verified.

Excerpt from the working notes:

> If my four years in Greece were sunny, the years at Mettray were nocturnal. But one should not misunderstand: the crime of the Baron de Metz [*sic*] and of his successors remains just as great. In order best to exploit their 550 acres, they had children from eight to twenty-one years old who began work before sunrise, that is, they began when it was still dark and worked until it was dark again. That is also why my life here was nocturnal, since the day was given over to work in the fields. The life that I had to undergo there, and that of all the other inmates from 1840 up to now, was a slave's life. Our torture took place on a daily basis, but no life is so crushed that it does not have the force to let some little happiness grow between the cracks. And this life cultivated in the cracks was all the more cherished in that it was hidden from our torturers. I'm calling torturers not only the magistrates but also those in charge of the labor camps for children: Mettray, Aniane, Saint-Maurice, Belle-Isle; certain labor camps have disappeared, others still make up this archipelago, elsewhere called the Gulag, that is maintained and hidden in the French countryside.

20. During his first year, Genet was put to work in a brush factory at Mettray.

21. Excerpt from working notes:

Already they talked a lot about reinsertion: but into what world? Into what society? With what morality? By stealing, we had wanted in some obscure way to escape from this morality.

In reform school, in jail, in the army, we accepted, no doubt because we wanted it, a feudal morality involving honor, giving one's word, the vassal's respect for the lord, but then we were supposed to agree to the morality that puts everything in writing, in a contract that is duly signed, initialed, and recorded by the authorities.

22. Excerpt from the working notes: "Today, now that my life is over, I can say more forcefully that I loved prison. Being there is like being between the legs of a woman, or perhaps in her belly. And the inside is full of a very subtle life that includes everything from the spider's web stretched in the corner of the cell, all the way to solitary confinement. Or the escape attempts, or escape itself, which also make up the life of the prisoner? That, or writing."

23. The *collège de répression* was already closed when Genet entered into detention at Mettray.

24. Excerpt from the working notes: "It's here that I read Ronsard and Nerval. It's here that I learned theft and not work, the salutary theft that led me to prison and, in the end, a little farther."

Chapter 32: Interview with Bertrand Poirot-Delpech

Interview filmed on January 25, 1982, at the Moulin de la Guéville, in Rambouillet. It follows the preceding interview, of which it was meant to be the second part. It was separated from the earlier interview on the insistence of Genet, who authorized it to be published only after his death.

The present version is based on the one edited by Bertrand Poirot-Delpech in *Le Monde*, and has been supplemented by the transcript of the video recording.

INTRODUCTORY NOTE

When the preceding interview was finished, Genet remained unsatisfied. He felt that he had given an image of himself that was too tame and that he had not spoken enough on political subjects. For her part, Danièle Delorme believed that Genet had cut too much out of the film that she had wanted to produce. She therefore suggested, as a supplement, another interview that would allow him to address questions that had not been discussed the first time.

Despite his fatigue and his precarious health, Genet agreed. On January 25, 1982, another interview was recorded and filmed at the Moulin de la Guéville, this time with Bertrand Poirot-Delpech, whom the producer had asked to conduct the interview.

While the richness of the interview is obvious—here, for once, Genet is asked about his relationship to language—its specific interest lies perhaps in another more hidden factor related to the personalities of the two interlocutors. Much like a play, the interview, with its often tense confrontations, displays Genet's complex relationship to society and, more specifically, to the intellectual community.

Poirot-Delpech was in fact hardly a stranger to Genet. They had crossed paths on several occasions, notably on the steps of the Odéon theater during the 1966 production of *The Screens*, which the drama critics of *Le Monde* had vigorously defended. But if the interviewer's role as a critic did not especially inspire Genet with sympathy, his position at *Le Monde* provoked outright mistrust: not that he really believed the newspaper was, as he says, "right wing," but because it was precisely the organ of the Left intellectuals among whom, above all, Genet did not want to be included. Last but not least, Poirot-Delpech had just been elected to the Académie française.

A critic, a contributor to *Le Monde*, a member of the Académie—such an interlocutor could only be seen by Genet as a representative of the established order, asking him to account for himself, or as a delegate of the caste that threatened him all the more by wishing him well, and which he refers to in the first lines of the interview as "the French intelligentsia."

Poirot-Delpech had no illusions about this situation; he described Genet's attitude in the interview's brief introduction, entitled "Il fallait que j'écrive la langue tortionnaire" [It was necessary for me to write in the language of the torturers] (published in *Le Monde Aujourd'hui*, a supplement to *Le Monde*, April 20, 1986, pp. vii to ix): "Squat and thickset in his eternal leather jacket, the poet of *Deathwatch*, and the playwright of *The Maids* furrows his brow. He's not the kind of man who would regret having come, but he will not let it be said that he makes any deals with Order. The dark look he shoots at me with his blue eyes is the one he must have turned on his judges long ago. When he addresses me formally with 'vous,' there's no need to look around, it is society as a whole that he loathes in me, and me in it. I am the torturer whose language he has stolen in order to escape from the wretched, infernal law. There is hatred in his voice, softened by great tenderness, but hatred all the same."

It is clear, then, that the words exchanged in this interview are intensified by a properly "dramatic" aspect and a tension which are much less apparent in the transcribed text. This tension slightly alters the writer's behavior; more even than elsewhere, he multiplies the provocations, rigidifies his positions, and stresses everything that will distinguish him from his interlocutor; but for these very reasons, this tension betrays the great ambiguity and difficulty of Genet's literary situation.

After the interview was completed, the writer did not want to include it with the first film, as had been planned, and he asked the producer not to make it public until after his death.

Consequently, the videocassette, entitled *Dernières paroles de Jean Genet* [Last words of Jean Genet], was not distributed in the *Témoins* series until May 1986, just as *Prisoner of Love* was appearing with the Éditions Gallimard.

After the video was edited and its length reduced, the linear order of the interview was changed a great deal, and many of the exchanges were omitted. While taking account of this version, we have relied essentially on the transcript of the original soundtrack made by Bertrand Poirot-Delpech.

We include here two passages that were not transcribed but that appeared in the filmed interview; the mixed order of the edited version makes it impossible to place them accurately:

—Can you tell us about what happened at the law courts on June 16, 1940?

—I had just "served"—since I'm obliged to use your language—eight months in prison for theft, and on June 16, 1940, I went to the law courts, to appear before the appellate court, which, as it turned out, was empty. I suppose that the next day, or the day after, it was transferred to Bordeaux, in any case it wasn't there when I went. I was standing next to the police station when I saw a French officer getting undressed, taking off his clothes, his uniform, and slipping into civilian's clothes in order to camouflage himself.

—In the end, the interrogation you've put me through is ending in conversation. Well I'd like to ask you: what, after all, is the meaning of this film? I have exposed myself before your eyes, your ears. And nothing's coming from any of it.

> Sources: Interviews with Bertrand Poirot-Delpech and
> Danièle Delorme.

ENDNOTES

1. The abolition of the death penalty had been declared a few months earlier, on September 18, 1981, after the Socialist Party had taken control of the government.

2. No doubt Genet means, "When I left Mettray." Genet's voluntary enlistment was the only way to leave Mettray before the age of twenty-one, and that is how he ended up in the army. On General Gouraud, see the "Interview with Hubert Fichte," note 49.

3. Genet is deliberately confusing Céline with Bardamu, the main character in *Journey to the End of the Night.*

4. See the "Interview with Antoine Bourseiller," note 24: the name of Nerval is mentioned there alongside that of Ronsard.

5. Genet attended the local grade school in Alligny-en-Morvan and received a certificate of primary studies (see the Chronology).

6. Genet may be referring to a book by Raymond Abellio that had appeared a few weeks earlier with the Éditions Gallimard in 1981: *Approches de la nouvelle gnose.*

7. A reference to the preceding interview.

8. A generalization frequently made by Genet; only his first poems, *Our Lady of the Flowers,* and *Miracle of the Rose* were written in prison.

9. The first sentence of *Our Lady of the Flowers* [Bernard Frechtman's translation].

10. See note 9 of the preceding interview. Genet is again adding a year to his age; he had just turned seventy-one.

11. The "pardon" Genet was given in 1949 was in fact not equivalent to an amnesty: it only suspended the application of the sentence without annulling it. As for the two desertions Genet is referring to, only one of these has been documented (see the Chronology).

12. An unlikely number—unless he is referring to an overall period beginning in adolescence up to the time of his last sentence. The sum of seven years, given in "Interview with Madeleine Gobeil," seems more likely.

13. *The Screens,* probably begun toward the end of 1955, was not completed until 1960 (see *La Bataille des Paravents,* ed. Lynda Belliey Peskine and Albert Dichy [Paris: IMEC, 1991]).

14. Premiering on April 16, 1966, at the Odéon-Théâtre de France, *The Screens* provoked such violent reactions that the theater had to call in the police to maintain order for nearly two weeks.

15. When the Comédie-Française commissioned Genet to write *The Balcony,* he agreed under two conditions: Roger Blin would be the director and the role of Irma would be played by Maria Casarès. But when she was unable to sign the year-long contract demanded by the theater, the project fell through.

16. "Un peu profond ruisseau colomnié la mort" [A shallow stream, and slandered, death]: the last line of the sonnet "Tombeau de Paul Verlaine," trans. Hubert Creekmore, in Stéphane Mallarmé, *Selected Poetry and Prose,* ed. Mary Ann Caws (New York: New Directions, 1992).

17. In June 1981, in Casablanca, during riots provoked by the rising prices of food and basic necessities, security forces repeatedly opened fire on protesters, killing a large number of people.

18. A reference to the article "Chartres Cathedral," Chapter 27 in this book.

19. These were, for the most part, demonstrations and protests against the conditions faced by immigrants in France. Most of them took place around 1971–72.

20. A reference to *Saint Genet, Actor and Martyr.*

21. After emerging as one of the important student figures of May '68, Pierre Goldman (1944–79) was engaged in various revolutionary activities before moving into a more general kind of criminal activity. Arrested in 1970 and charged

with murder and theft, he was detained for several years in Fresnes before being declared innocent. He wrote an autobiographical narrative entitled *Souvenirs obscurs d'un Juif polonais né en France* [Obscure memories of a Polish Jew born in France] (Paris: Le Seuil, 1975). He wrote a letter to Genet on January 15, 1973, which is held in the Genet archive at IMEC.

22. Long considered "public enemy number 1," Jacques Mesrine, the perpetrator of various crimes (hostage-taking, hold-up, murder) and the author of a book (*L'Instinct de mort*), became famous because of his repeated prison escapes. After a lengthy pursuit, he was killed by police in November 1979.

23. On April 29, 1975, as the communists occupied the city, the American ambassador, Graham Martin, boarded a helicopter with the embassy's flag and left Saigon for good.

24. A reference to the well-known book by Louis Pergaud (1912) and to the film by Yves Robert (1962) which recount a "war" between children.

25. See the article "Violence and Brutality," Chapter 28 in this book.

26. The invasion of Afghanistan began in December 1979.

27. The "Smiling Angel" is one of the figures in the statuary of the Reims Cathedral.

Chapter 33: Four Hours in Shatila

Article written in September and October 1982 in Beirut and Paris for the *Revue d'études palestiniennes*. Indications concerning the manuscript of the text are included in the notes.

INTRODUCTORY NOTE

If "Four Hours in Shatila" can be considered the most significant political and literary text of this collection, this is perhaps because it escapes from both the literary and the political domains. Indeed, Genet puts to work all the resources of his art with a skill and assurance that prefigure the great arabesques of *Prisoner of Love*—but it is no less clear that the article is a true "reportage" on the massacres at Shatila, laid out with the precision and rigor of an official accusation.

But in truth this text eludes its own determinations. It stands alone, unclassifiable among the author's writings, and is marked by an experience that is so naked and raw that it separates the text from every genre. Thus it is important not to forget, as we locate the historical and circumstantial framework in which this text came to be written, that the testimony it offers can be reduced neither to history nor to circumstances.

In August 1982, after a ten-year absence, Genet decided to return to the Middle East in the company of Layla Shahid, who was traveling to Beirut. His physical health was at its lowest point. Greatly weakened by the cobalt treatment he was receiving for his cancer, he was extremely depressed: he spoke of having lost the desire to write; except for a few interviews, he had published nothing since 1977, and had given up on most of his projects—including the libretto he had sketched for Boulez and the film about Mettray (*Le Langage du muraille* [The language of the wall]), for which he had written a long script. He had also lost hope in ever completing the long book on the Palestinians that he had been working on for years.

His friend Layla Shahid, an editor of the *Revue d'études palestiniennes* who would later become one of the "ardent heroines" of *Prisoner of Love* (p. 228), expressed concerns about his fatigue; he responded that it was time for him to return to the Palestinians.

Without realizing it, Genet was arriving in Beirut (on September 12, 1982) at a crucial moment in the Lebanese war. The situation appeared to be calm. At the end of a three-month attack—the Israeli army was just outside the city—the Palestinian fighters, who had taken refuge in the western sections of Beirut, had agreed to leave the city; under the protection of a multinational intervention force (American, French, and Italian), most of them had just left for Tunisia, Algeria, or Yemen. The Palestinian camps had been disarmed, and since the election of August 23, the Lebanese Republic had a new president, Bashir Gemayel.

But the day after Genet's arrival, events began to gather momentum. On September 13, looking on from the balcony of Layla Shahid's apartment where he was staying, Genet watched the departure of the intervention force. Hardly were the ships out to sea when, on September 14, the president—who was also the leader of the Christian Right parties—was attacked and assassinated in his party offices. On September 15, at dawn, the Israeli army, in violation of all previously accepted agreements, entered the Lebanese capital in order to "maintain order" and to hunt down the last of the Palestinian fighters thought to have remained in the city. On the evening of the same day, the Israeli army surrounded the Palestinian camps of Sabra and Shatila on the edge of Beirut and set up its headquarters in an eight-story building two hundred meters from the entrances to the camps.

On September 16, armed squads wearing the uniforms of various Lebanese Christian militias made their way into the camps, with the support of the Israeli forces, and proceeded to "cleanse them of terrorists." Agitated by the death of their "leader," Bashir Gemayel, and most likely drunk, they rampaged for two days and three nights, carrying out a massacre that spared neither children, women, nor the elderly (the number of victims was anywhere from fifteen hundred to five thousand); the Israeli soldiers, watching over the camps from the tall building in which they were stationed nearby, did nothing to intervene and sounded no alarm.

On September 17, when a Norwegian nurse working in Shatila visited Layla Shahid's apartment, Genet learned that something was happening in the camps, to which access had been barred. The next day, he went to the camps but ran into the Israeli tanks blocking the entrances. Not until Sunday, September 19, around ten in the morning, did Genet finally manage to enter the camp of Shatila by pretending to be a journalist. The Lebanese army had taken control of the situation, and its bulldozers were hastily digging mass graves, but the corpses had not yet been buried. Genet spent four hours alone, under a blistering sun, winding his way through the camp's narrow streets. Once back in the apartment where he was staying, he locked himself in his room for twenty-four hours: when he emerged, he made it known that he wanted to leave as soon as possible. On September 22, he took a flight from Damascus, and during the month of October in Paris he wrote the article that would appear on January 1, 1983, in the *Revue d'études palestiniennes* (no. 6).

Perhaps the month spent writing the article created a distance that allowed Genet—perhaps as a way to subdue the violence of the events he was retracing—to place them within the framework of his memories of the Palestinians and to construct the text in terms of the relations between two periods: his first stay in Jordan (1970–71) and his most recent trip (1982). In this way, by playing two different moments off each other, by bringing two different layers of memory into contact, he inflects the reportage with a temporal structure not unlike that of his novels. It is not surprising, then, to learn that it was the composition of this text that represented for Genet the beginning of a return to the "act of writing" (see *Prisoner of Love*, pp. 337–38, 373).

Written on twenty-eight separate sheets of paper, the manuscript of "Four Hours in Shatila" presents an earlier version of the text that Genet reread and corrected in proofs. It reveals a hesitation regarding the article's title: above the chosen title, Genet crossed out another one that had been considered first: "Four Hours Alone in Shatila and Sabra." The numbering of the pages indicates a different order for the text: the first two pages were added last (the article thus began: "A photograph has two dimensions . . . "), as were the last two pages, which are not numbered (the text ended with the sentences: "Many people died in Shatila, and my friendship, my affection for their rotting corpses was great also because I had known them. Blackened, swollen, rotted by the sun, they remained fedayeen"). This initial ending is confirmed by the first typescript, which shows Genet's signature at that point.

Beyond these indications concerning the structure of the text, the manuscript includes variants that are mostly very minor, and a few brief additions and cuts. Three longer passages, totaling about twenty lines, were removed however from the published version with Genet's assent. We provide them here in a note indicated in the place where they occurred in the text. One had to do with the head of the main Christian party of Lebanon, Pierre Gemayel, the former "leader" of the Phalangists; the other two develop a reflection on the Jewish people, written (as the page where they occur indicates) in Beirut, that is, "in the heat of the moment"; Genet agreed to withdraw them from the definitive version of the article.

> Sources: Interviews with Layla Shahid and Elias Sanbar.
> Archives of Paule Thévenin and of the *Revue d'études palestiniennes.*

ENDNOTES

1. Statement by Menachem Begin, head of the Israeli government, on September 22, 1982, in the Knesset (Parliament) in Jerusalem. The exact quote is as follows: "Goyim killed goyim, and here they are accusing us . . . " (See J.-F. Legrain, "La Guerre israelo-palestinienne," in the *Revue d'études palestiniennes*, no. 6 [Winter 1973]: 197).

2. This passage is referring to Genet's visit to the Palestinian camps in Jordan from October 1970 to April 1971.

3. See the somewhat different version of this passage in *Prisoner of Love* (pp. 222–23).

4. The western part of Beirut, where the fedayeen had withdrawn, was attacked and bombed by the Israeli army from June to August 1982.

5. Sabra and Shatila, Palestinian refugee camps built in 1949 on the outer edge of West Beirut. At the beginning of the 1980s, these two medium-sized camps had a population of about thirty-five thousand.

6. "Mrs. S." was an American journalist who had gone into the camp at the same time as Genet.

7. A dissident officer of the Lebanese army and leader of a Christian militia (the "Haddadists") trained and financed by the Israeli army.

8. Katayeb, the main party (also called the "Phalangist" Party) of the Christian Maronite Right and far Right in Lebanon, was founded by Pierre Gemayel in 1936.

9. Likud: the Israeli political party in power in 1982, made up of Right and far Right elements. Its political opposition is the Labor Party. Begin, Sharon, Shamir: members of Likud. In 1982 they were, respectively, prime minister, defense minister, and minister of foreign affairs.

10. American transport aircraft.

11. Bashir Gemayel was the son of Pierre Gemayel, founder of the Katayeb and former leader of the Christian militias. Elected president on August 23, 1982, with the support of the Israeli government, he had just been assassinated.

12. Tsahal: the Israeli army.

13. Hamra, the main commercial thoroughfare of Beirut.

14. This scene is evoked again in *Prisoner of Love* (p. 35).

15. Merkava: the tanks of the Israeli army.

16. The Murabitoun were an organization of the "independent Nasserite" (and pro-Palestinian) left.

17. The following paragraph was eliminated in the published version: "Bashir's father, Pierre Gemayel, appeared on Lebanese television, his thin face with dark sunken eyes and very thin lips. A single expression: naked cruelty."

18. See "The Women of Jebel Hussein," Chapter 23 in this book.

19. "Our house," in Arabic.

20. This passage is taken up again in *Prisoner of Love* (pp. 284–85).

21. The word means "mountain" in Arabic.

22. Genet went to Damascus in 1930.

23. See "The Palestinians," note 18.

24. Mandate signed on April 25, 1920, and approved by the Council of the League of Nations in 1922.

25. *Une Aussi Longue Absence*, a film by Henri Colpi, screenplay by Marguerite Duras (1960).

26. Menachem Begin, born in Brest Litovsk, was part Polish.

27. The presidents of the three countries (United States, France, and Italy) who made up the international intervention force.

28. Genet seems to have written down some notes in Beirut between September 19 and 22.

29. The following is the entire passage that occurs at this point, two fragments of which were removed in the final version of the text:

> The Jewish people, far from being the most unfortunate on earth—the Indians of the Andes have gone deeper into misery and abandonment—as it would have us believe from the genocide, whereas in America, Jews rich and poor had reserves of sperm for procreation, for the continuation of the "chosen" people, in short, thanks to a skillful yet predictable metamorphosis, it is now what it has long been in the process of becoming: a loathsome temporal power, a colonizer in a way that no one can any longer dare to be, the Definitive Authority that it owes both to its long malediction and to its status as chosen.
>
> It is taking this loathsome power so far that one may wonder whether, at yet another point in its history, by bringing unanimous condemnation on itself, it does not want to regain its destiny as a wandering, humbled people whose power remains underground. It has now shown itself too much in the terrible light of the massacres it no longer undergoes but inflicts, and it wants to regain the shadows of the past to become once again—supposing it ever was—the "salt of the earth."
>
> But then what a way to behave!
>
> Could it be that the Soviet Union and the Arab countries, however spineless

they may be, by refusing to intervene in this war would therefore have allowed Israel finally to appear before the world and in broad daylight as a madman among nations?

30. Area north of Beirut.

31. The distinction Genet is referring to here is found primarily in two works by Hannah Arendt: *On Revolution* and *The Human Condition.*

32. Hamza will become an important figure in *Prisoner of Love.*

33. Bir Hassan and Bourj al-Barajneh, two Palestinian camps, not far from Shatila, where massacres had also taken place.

34. See *Prisoner of Love* for the "ancient debate" between Achilles and Homer: "Which is better, a quick death or to sing forever?" (p. 126).

Chapter 34: Registration No. 1155

Text written for the catalogue of the exhibition "La Rupture," which opened on March 1, 1983, at the Centre d'action culturelle de Montbéliard. It is a commentary on the identity papers of an immigrant worker.

INTRODUCTORY NOTE

In March 1983, the painter Antoine du Bary organized an exhibition based on a collection of old identity papers for immigrant workers from around 1940 that had been found in a filing cabinet at the Porte de Clignancourt flea market. The exhibition was called "La Rupture," and its primary theme was immigration. After opening at the Centre d'Action Culturelle de Montbéliard, the exhibition then traveled throughout France.

A bilingual catalogue (Arabic-French) was printed for the occasion to accompany the exhibition. In addition to the illustrations, it included a dozen or so texts on the question of immigration. Genet's contribution appeared first in the catalogue, just after the preface by the organizer of the exhibition. There were also pieces by Tahar Ben Jelloun, Slimane Zeghidour, Serge Moscovici, Martine Charlot, Abdellatif Laabi, and others.

In 1982 Genet had accepted Antoine du Bary's invitation to participate in the writing of the catalogue. He asked to see the papers and examined them carefully before choosing one of them, which he decided to write on for a reason that might seem somewhat random: the Moroccan worker it described was born in 1910, the same year as Genet.

Genet's text takes the form of a descriptive commentary, emphasizing once again the historical link between the question of immigration and that of colonialism. In this sense it was written in conformity with the visual form of the exhibition, where visitors would be able to see the document in question on display. In addition, a reproduction of this same document, with its distinctive pink color, appeared on the cover of the catalogue.

Published by the Centre d'Action Culturelle du Creusot, this 132-page catalogue was printed on March 1, 1983.

> Sources: Interview with Antoine du Bary. Jean Genet /
> IMEC.

ENDNOTES

1. The arrival in Morocco of Lyautey, the first resident-general of France, marks the beginning of the period of the "French protectorate," which came to an end only when the country gained independence in March 1956. The identity papers are from this period.

2. Placed in power by the French, the sultan of Morocco grew more and more sympathetic to the nationalist movement and eventually, in 1952, he spoke officially in support of his country's will to independence. These statements resulted in his arrest and deportation. When Morocco gained independence, he returned, took power and, under the name of Muhammad V, became the king of Morocco in 1956.

3. This is an enumeration of the categories listed on the inside pages of the *carnet individuel* ("individual file"), attached to the identity card.

4. Terms of Arab or eastern origin indicating types of habitation or clothing.

5. Monte Cassino, Italy, which underwent assaults from Allied troops from January to May 1944. Many lives were lost.

6. See the "Interview with Tahar Ben Jelloun": " . . . Germany, where their rights are no more respected than here but where the salaries are higher."

Chapter 35: Interview with Rüdiger Wischenbart and Layla Shahid Barrada

Interview recorded on December 6–7, 1983, in Vienna, with the participation of Layla Shahid Barrada, for Austrian Radio and the German daily *Die Zeit*. Based on the complete transcript of the interview published in the *Revue d'études palestiniennes*.

INTRODUCTORY NOTE

This interview is a continuation of the article "Four Hours in Shatila," to which it adds a number of clarifications and further developments. It took place in Vienna where Genet had gone in early December 1983, in the company of Layla Shahid, who had asked him to attend a demonstration concerning the massacres at Sabra and Shatila arranged by the International Progress Organization, a nongovernmental organization affiliated with the UN.

Hesitating at first to make the trip—he had already declined to participate in a conference in Oslo on the same question—Genet did not want to speak in public or meet with journalists. Hardly had he arrived, however, when he was harassed by the latter and finally agreed to answer a few questions, on the condition that they relate to the Palestinian problem. This condition was largely disregarded by his interlocutors, and Genet, unhappy at having been trapped and unsatisfied with his own answers, wanted to bring the experiment to a hasty conclusion; however, Rüdiger Wischenbart, a young journalist working for Austrian radio, managed to gain his confidence. After a first meeting, Genet felt that he had been able to express himself less superficially than before and agreed to allow the journalist to continue the interview the next day. Feeling more at ease, he spoke more freely of his preoccupations, explaining on a personal level his "affinities" with the revolutionary movements with which he had associated and commenting on the relation between his literary work and his various political engagements; the result is no doubt his best interview on political subjects.

A few days later, having returned to Rabat where he was living, Genet received a copy of the transcript which he reread, correcting—as he usually did—problems with the language or imprecise formulations. To Layla Shahid, however, he spoke of his dissatisfaction with oral expression, reaffirming that writing alone was capable of translating his thoughts more exactly.

Parts of the interview were broadcast at the end of December 1983 on Austrian radio, and an excerpt was published for the first time on March 23, 1984, in the German daily *Die Zeit* (no. 13, pp. 44–45), and again on October 16, 1984, in *Libération*; it was published in its entirety in the *Revue d'études palestiniennes*, no. 21 (Fall 1986): 3–25, under the title "Une Rencontre avec Jean Genet."

> Sources: Interviews with Layla Shahid and Rüdiger
> Wischenbart. Archives of the *Revue d'études*
> *palestiniennes.*

ENDNOTES

1. At the time of the interview, the situation was indeed crucial for the PLO, whose future as the sole representative of the Palestinians was in jeopardy, as was its autonomy in relation to the Arab governments. Having sought refuge in Tripoli, in northern Lebanon, Arafat was facing significant divisions among the Palestinian organizations. His troops were being attacked both on the ground by the Syrian army, in an effort to take control of the PLO, and from the sea by the Israeli navy, which was trying to prevent him from fleeing. After a long resistance, Arafat managed to find a way out of the impasse and was able to establish a renewed legitimacy for his authority.

2. After a meeting between Bruno Kreisky, Willy Brandt, and Arafat in Vienna in 1979, the PLO was officially recognized by the Socialist International.

3. See the introductory note above.

4. The trip to Beirut in 1982 seems rather to have been undertaken on Genet's own initiative.

5. West Beirut had been the target of violent bombings during the three months before Genet's arrival.

6. See the introductory note to the preceding chapter.

7. Mossad, the Israeli secret service.

8. On September 28, 1982, the Israeli government set up a commission consisting of three judges, directed by Yitzhak Kahan, to investigate the massacres. Its report, called the Kahan Report, was released on February 8, 1983; it established the moral responsibility of the Israeli government and focused on General Sharon in particular. Forced to resign, he nevertheless managed to remain in the government as a minister without portfolio.

9. Genet is referring to Layla Shahid.

10. On November 24, when he seemed to be in a difficult position, Arafat was able to negotiate the exchange of forty-five hundred Palestinian and Arab prisoners for six Israeli prisoners. The success of this negotiation was seen as a political victory.

11. Andreas Baader's lawyer (see the introductory note to "Violence and Brutality").

12. Genet went to Jordan, in October 1970, at the invitation of Mahmoud el Hamchari (see the introductory note for "The Palestinians").

13. See the evocation of this scene in *Prisoner of Love* (p. 54).

14. The demonstration in Vienna took place in conjunction with an exhibit of photographs, some of which were taken by Layla Shahid in Shatila.

15. FDLP (Democratic Front for the Liberation of Palestine): acronym for the different organizations grouped together under the PLO.

16. A passage in *Prisoner of Love* does, however, speak of Arafat's "kaffiyeh" (p. 121).

17. *The Screens* was directed by Patrice Chéreau on May 31, 1983, at the Théâtre des Amandiers in Nanterre. *The Balcony* was directed by Hans Neuenfels at the Schlosspark Schiller Theater in Berlin on March 19, 1983. *The Blacks* was directed by Peter Stein in July 1983 at the Schaubühne in Berlin.

18. This is the year of Roger Blin's production of the play at the Odéon-Théâtre de France. The original edition of *The Screens* was published by L'Arbalète in February 1961.

19. See the article "Violence and Brutality," Chapter 28 in this book.

20. Indeed, the word "Algeria" does not appear in the play.

21. This claim is debatable: the play had most likely already been written

when Genet met Jouvet in 1946. He nevertheless adapted it to the requirements specified by the director.

22. Genet is referring to the director Raymond Rouleau, who in 1955 commissioned from Genet a play that would feature black actors.

23. Chouf is a region of Lebanon occupied by the Israeli army in 1982.

24. This incident is often evoked by Genet, notably in the first pages of *Prisoner of Love* (p. 4).

25. UNRWA: United Nations Relief and Works Agency. Run by the UN, this organization deals with the problem of refugees.

26. See the introductory note to "Four Hours in Shatila."

Chapter 36: Interview with Nigel Williams

Interview filmed in London in the summer of 1985 for BBC2. The present version is based on a transcript of the film soundtrack.

INTRODUCTORY NOTE

On November 12, 1985, at 10 P.M., a fifty-eight-minute program was broadcast in England on BBC2, entitled "Saint Genet." It consisted of a long interview with the writer, intercut with documents and film segments (from *A Song of Love, The Balcony, The Maids*, etc.).

Conducted in early summer 1985, less than a year before Genet's death, this filmed interview would be his last. It was obtained with relative ease by the English television station, for ten thousand pounds sterling, paid in cash in advance, and was filmed in London over two days in the apartment of the young writer Nigel Williams, who conducted the interview. Williams had recently translated *Deathwatch* for a London production staged earlier that year.

As was his custom (the year before he had also given another interview on German television), Genet displays a mastery of the rules of the genre, which he plays with in an ironic and authoritative way, bringing his interlocutor and even the technical crew into the discussion. More than any other, this film reflects Genet's constant preoccupation with interrogating, challenging, and sometimes endangering the mode of expression he is using.

This very lively interview nonetheless took place at a time when Genet's health had begun to deteriorate considerably. In remission for a while after intense chemotherapy, the cancer he had suffered from since 1979 had returned, leaving him with little hope to live much longer. However, he was about to finish writing *Prisoner of Love*, and would send the completed manuscript to Éditions Gallimard in October. Unlike in his previous interviews, in which Genet considered his work to be "in progress" (see "Interview with Antoine

Bourseiller," note 12), here, in responding to Nigel Williams's questions, he knows that his last work has taken shape, and it is without any apparent sadness that, at the end of the program, he can say, "I'm waiting for death."

Sources: Interview with Nigel Williams. Archives of
Edmund White, Jean Genet / IMEC.

ENDNOTES

1. This is the approximate number of Genet's convictions that have so far been documented (see *Jean Genet: Essai de chronologie*).

2. Trial of July 19, 1943: Genet was liable to receive life imprisonment for "repeated theft" if the sentence handed down was for more than three months and one day. It was for three months.

3. At the end of this sentence, Genet adds (without it being very clear what he is referring to): " . . . and yet not like that."

4. Genet was sent to the Mettray colony after having run away a number of times, but, in particular, for "vagrancy and infraction of railway regulations," for which he was arrested in July 1926 on the Paris-Meaux train.

5. See *The Thief's Journal*, p. 115.

6. For another version of this story, see the "Interview with Madeleine Gobeil," p. 2 and note 12.

7. Odéon-Théâtre de France.

Appendix 1: The Members of the Assembly

Article written for *Esquire* magazine at the end of August 1968, after the Democratic Convention in Chicago. The original manuscript appears to have been destoryed. [Genet's texts for the two appendices included here were never published in French. As the editor of the French edition explains, since no French versions are extant, he chose to include there translations into French of Richard Seaver's English translations, published in 1968. However, the editors of the present volume did not acquire the rights to republish these English translations; the texts presented here, then, are translations of those printed in the French edition of *L'Ennemi déclaré*.—Trans.]

INTRODUCTORY NOTE

Written in the United States, in August and September 1968, this article and the following one—"A Salute to a Thousand Stars"—have, in part, a common history. The origin of the present article dates back to the end of March 1968, when the editor of *Esquire*, Harold Hayes, arrived in Paris. Encouraged by the success a few years earlier of an article by Norman Mailer on the Democratic Convention, he had decided to ask a number of well-known writers to "cover" the next convention, to be held in Chicago in August, where the Democratic presidential candidate would be chosen. William Burroughs and Terry Southern had already agreed, and he hoped also to persuade Samuel Beckett, Jean Genet, and Eugene Ionesco.

Beckett showed no interest, but Hayes managed to contact Genet, who was passing through Paris on his way to Morocco. Their first meeting took place at the beginning of April in Genet's hotel room, when the writer immediately told his guest that he would be more than happy for *Esquire* to publish an article by him on . . . the Vietnam War. The embarrassed Hayes explained what he wanted from Genet, who was unenthusiastic about the proposed project but finally agreed, on the condition that the magazine also publish a piece by him on the Vietnam War. But he made it clear to his interlocutor the nature of his feelings for America and Americans, and asked him if he would be able to express himself freely. The director of *Esquire* courteously assured him that as a rule the magazine allowed the authors it publishes to present their point of view with no constraints. With this, a deal was made.

(When Ionesco was asked to participate, he declined: he had other obligations; in addition, the presence of Genet, whose point of view he considered very destructive, did not seem to thrill him.)

One problem remained, however, regarding this first trip to the United States: a visa. Despite all his support, Genet was barred from entering the United States, as the American consulate informed him in November 1965 (see note 10 of Appendix 2). He therefore decided to experiment with a method which he later used whenever he wanted to go to the United States: he went first to Canada, then secretly crossed the border.

The Democratic Convention that took place in Chicago from August 25 to 28 was particularly lively during this election year: the current president, Lyndon Johnson, plagued by opposition to his "escalation" policy in the Vietnam War, had in fact announced on March 31 that he was withdrawing from the race. Another dramatic turn of events: the Democratic favorite, Robert Kennedy, had just been assassinated on June 6. The goal of the convention was therefore to provide the party with a new candidate capable of facing the formidable Republican candidate, Richard Nixon.

Two Democratic candidates were still in the running: Eugene McCarthy, a left-leaning member of the party whose stance against the Vietnam War made him attractive to young voters, intellectuals, hippy groups (then at their height), and racial and social minorities; and Hubert H. Humphrey, a traditional politician who followed the party line and who attracted and reassured the more conservative Democrats. To Genet's disappointment, it was the latter who won the nomination.

Genet arrived in Chicago on the evening of Saturday, August 24, and joined the team of *Esquire* "reporters" (they all had press passes): Burroughs and Southern, accompanied by a reputed American journalist, John Sack. At the time the city was a ferment of activity. In conjunction with the convention, an enormous demonstration had formed in support of Senator McCarthy and, even more, in protest of the Vietnam War. Large numbers of police officers were deployed to maintain order throughout the city.

Genet and his companions did not forego the demonstrations, and on August 27 they were invited up onto a platform to speak. According to accounts that appeared in the press the next day, when Genet spoke he first asked his listeners to excuse his slow speech, which was caused by the powerful dose of depressants he had taken to help him forget he was in the United States. Then, taking up a metaphor used by Burroughs, who had compared the Chicago police to "mad dogs," he added:

> I find it perfectly natural that dogs wanted to bite and even to eat hippies, students, and journalists, and it does not displease me that white Americans find themselves threatened by these dogs who for the past 150 years have done the same thing, with even greater brutality, to the blacks.
>
> It is, therefore, good that American dogs are trying to devour American whites. Let me make myself very clear: I will always be on the side of the whites bitten by dogs. But people should realize that the dogs have finally reached the point where the dogs are also capable of attacking the president of General Motors, who is vulnerable at last.
>
> Hippies, you have responded to the clownlike convention, by your demonstrations in the park, charged with poetry.

(From Anthony Lukas, "Johnson Mocked as a 'Freak' at 'Unbirthday Party,'" *New York Times*, August 28, 1968, p. 31.)

Genet's article presents a sort of "reportage" on his four days in Chicago. A translation by Richard Seaver was published in November 1968 in a special issue of *Esquire* (vol. 70, no. 5, pp. 86–89) on the Democratic Convention, which included an important editorial by Harold Hayes.

Sources: Interview with Richard Seaver. Archives of
Esquire, Edmund White.

ENDNOTES

1. Candidate for the Democratic nomination to be decided on August 27, 1968 (see the introductory note).

2. During a demonstration two days earlier, a young Indian—whose identi-

ty was only revealed after the convention—was killed during a clash with police. (The cover of the November issue of *Esquire* shows Genet, Burroughs, Southern, and Sack standing in a semicircle around the body of an actor playing dead.)

3. The convention was held from August 25 to 28, 1968.

4. In English in the original.

5. A reference to Joseph McCarthy, Republican senator who, from 1947 to 1954, led the "witch hunt" for presumed communist sympathizers.

6. Dwight Eisenhower was president from 1953 to 1961; he died in 1969, after a long illness.

7. Allen Ginsberg had been invited to cover the convention for *Eye* magazine. He stayed in a different hotel but spent the four days with Genet (who developed a great affection for him) and Burroughs.

8. Lyndon Johnson, born August 27, 1908, was celebrating his sixtieth birthday that day in the Chicago Coliseum.

9. In English in original.

10. Cardinal Spellman (1889–1967) was archbishop of New York and for many years a leading figure in the Roman Catholic Church. Using his considerable influence, he had advocated American involvement in the Vietnam War.

11. David Dellinger was one of the organizers of the demonstrations and the spokesman for the National Mobilization to End the War in Vietnam.

12. Phil Ochs: folk singer and pacifist who wrote the song "I Ain't Marching Anymore."

13. Nixon defeated Hubert Humphrey by a narrow margin in the presidential election of November 5, 1968.

14. Dick Gregory: a popular black comedian and political activist. He ran for president in 1968.

15. See the introductory note and note 10 of the following appendix.

Appendix 2: A Salute to a Hundred Thousand Stars

Article written in September 1968, in New York, and published in translation in *Evergreen Review*. The original manuscript was destroyed. [See note to Appendix 1 above.—Trans.]

INTRODUCTORY NOTE

After the Democratic convention, Genet left Chicago for New York where he gave the editors at *Esquire* the article on the Democratic Convention that he had been asked to write (see the preceding appendix and the introductory note). During the next few days he wrote the article on the Vietnam War, which, as had been promised, was to be published in the same magazine and which he considered much more important.

What happened next was predictable: at the beginning of September 1968, Genet submitted "A Salute to a Hundred Thousand Stars" to Harold Hayes, the magazine's editor; horrified at the text, he informed Genet that publishing such an article in *Esquire* would be impossible. Genet grew indignant, shouted at the top of his lungs, and flew into a rage that was hardly placated when he learned that the magazine did not intend to pay him for the article. According to Richard Seaver, who translated the text at the time, Genet entered the editorial offices in a fury and tore the manuscripts of his articles to shreds. (A few sheets that had been spared, however, were given to the French organization, Mouvement pour la Paix au Vietnam.)

The translation of the article having escaped destruction, Richard Seaver then offered to print it in the journal he edited, which was published by Grove Press, Genet's publisher in the United States. Genet, who wanted nothing more than to leave the United States as soon as possible, agreed to the publication. The text appeared in the December 1968 issue of *Evergreen Review* (vol. 12, no. 61, pp. 51–53, 87–88).

To have a better overview of this text, it is important, therefore, to keep in mind that it was written for a fashionable magazine with a large circulation appealing to readers who belonged, for the most part, to the upper classes of American society—which may partly explain the aggressivity and the crude humor it displays at times. In fact, it would seem that Genet wanted to take advantage of the unexpected venue to bring off a strategic "coup" in the personal war that pitted him against America, that is, the West. A coup whose force was certainly diminished by its publication in *Evergreen Review*, an avant-garde journal with a well-informed readership that was unmoved by the most extreme provocation, as long as it came from a "great writer."

It is also important to recall the historical context in which the article was written. After a short-lived truce, the American bombing of South Vietnam resumed with even greater intensity on August 11, 1968. In the space of two years, almost two million metric tons of bombs had been poured onto the country and the deployment of American troops had gone from 75,000 in 1965 to 530,000 in 1968. The confrontation between the two Vietnamese states had reached a high point, the North (capital Hanoi) being closely allied with the USSR and China, while the South (capital Saigon) was supported by the United States. Despite some recent successes, such as the Tet offensive, a Communist victory was not yet in sight. In the United States, and throughout the West, the demonstrations against the war had become more massive than ever; and in newspapers and journals, writers, artists, and intellectuals expressed their opposition to American policy with a virulence to which we have since become unaccustomed. The article by Jean Genet, although it did not go unnoticed, provoked neither criticism nor commentary.

Sources: Interview with Richard Seaver. Archives of
Evergreen Review, Gallimard, and Edmund White.

ENDNOTES

1. "Over there": in Vietnam. It will be noticed that throughout the essay Genet uses the term "Viet Cong," with its clear political resonance (meaning "Vietnamese Communist"), to refer to the North Vietnamese.

2. President Lyndon Johnson was a native of Texas. Westmoreland: U.S. Army general, commander of American troops in Vietnam (1964–68), then army chief of staff (1968–72). Abrams: U.S. Army general, deputy-commander of U.S. forces in Vietnam under Westmoreland, then commander in 1968. Mad Women: expression used at the time for women who publicly expressed their pain over the loss or disappearance of a son, husband, or brother.

3. Khe Sahn: a border village, and the site of confrontations between American soldiers and North Vietnamese troops.

4. American planes had spread defoliating agents over the Vietnamese countryside in order to destroy the vegetation and displace the rural populations into the cities.

5. Dean Rusk was secretary of state under Presidents Kennedy and Johnson.

6. Vo Nguyen Giap, Vietnamese general who defeated the French troops at Dien Bien Phu in 1954, then organized the People's Army of Vietnam and the fight against South Vietnamese troops and their American allies. He had recently led the Tet offensive against South Vietnam (in January 1968).

7. See note 10 of the previous appendix.

8. James William Fulbright, democratic senator and patron of the arts who had opposed the Vietnam War. Julius Robert Oppenheimer, American physicist, directed the creation of the first atomic bomb. In 1954 he asked to be relieved of his duties. Shirley Temple, who had become famous as a child actress, began a political career in the Republican Party in the 1960s. Don Schollander, a champion swimmer, won Olympic medals in 1964 and 1968. The highly successful film by Arthur Penn on the adventures of Bonnie Parker and Clyde Barrow was released in 1967.

9. An apparently unliteral citation, perhaps from Genet's recent reading (in 1966) of the *Letters to a Young Poet*.

10. In November 1965, Jean Genet was refused a visitor's visa by the U.S. State Department because, according to a letter from William Kane, chief of the Visa Office's Domestic Services Division, "information became available to the Embassy which rendered Mr. Genet ineligible to receive a visa under Section

212(a)(9) and (28) of the Immigration and Nationality Act. Paragraph (9) of the cited section of the law renders ineligible to receive visas and excludable from admission into the United States aliens who have been convicted of or admitted having committed a crime involving moral turpitude. Paragraph (28) precludes the issuance of visas to persons who are or were members of or affiliated with a proscribed organization. Mr. Genet may also be ineligible under the recent amendment of Section 212(a)(4) of the Act as a sexual deviate, subject to medical examination." (Editor's note added to the article in *Evergreen Review*.)

MERIDIAN

Crossing Aesthetics

Jean Genet, *The Declared Enemy*

Shosana Felman, *Writing and Madness: (Literature/Philosophy/ Psychoanalysis)*

Jean Genet, *Fragments of the Artwork*

Shoshana Felman, *The Scandal of the Speaking Body: Don Juan with J. L. Austin, or Seduction in Two Languages*

Peter Szondi, *Celan Studies*

Neil Hertz, *George Eliot's Pulse*

Maurice Blanchot, *The Book to Come*

Susannah Young-ah Gottlieb, *Regions of Sorrow: Anxiety and Messianism in Hannah Arendt and W. H. Auden*

Jacques Derrida, *Without Alibi*, edited by Peggy Kamuf

Cornelius Castoriadis, *On Plato's 'Statesman'*

Jacques Derrida, *Who's Afraid of Philosophy? Right to Philosophy 1*

Peter Szondi, *An Essay on the Tragic*

Peter Fenves, *Arresting Language: From Leibniz to Benjamin*

Jill Robbins, ed., *Is It Righteous to Be? Interviews with Emmanuel Levinas*

Louis Marin, *Of Representation*

Daniel Payot, *The Architect and the Philosopher*

J. Hillis Miller, *Speech Acts in Literature*